Newly Created Children of God

Newly Created Children of God

Adoption and New Creation in the Theology of Paul

Hyung-tae Kim

FOREWORD BY
John M.G. Barclay

☙PICKWICK *Publications* · Eugene, Oregon

NEWLY CREATED CHILDREN OF GOD
Adoption and New Creation in the Theology of Paul

Copyright © 2025 Hyung-tae Kim. All rights reserved. Except for brief quotations in critical publications or reviews, no part of this book may be reproduced in any manner without prior written permission from the publisher. Write: Permissions, Wipf and Stock Publishers, 199 W. 8th Ave., Suite 3, Eugene, OR 97401.

Pickwick Publications
An Imprint of Wipf and Stock Publishers
199 W. 8th Ave., Suite 3
Eugene, OR 97401

www.wipfandstock.com

PAPERBACK ISBN: 979-8-3852-1981-0
HARDCOVER ISBN: 979-8-3852-1982-7
EBOOK ISBN: 979-8-3852-1983-4

Cataloguing-in-Publication data:

Names: Kim, Hyung-tae [author]. | Barclay, John M. G. [foreword writer].

Title: Newly created children of God : adoption and new creation in the theology of Paul / by Hyung-tae Kim ; foreword by John M. G. Barclay.

Description: Eugene, OR: Pickwick Publications, 2025 | Includes bibliographical references and index.

Identifiers: ISBN 979-8-3852-1981-0 (paperback) | ISBN 979-8-3852-1982-7 (hardcover) | ISBN 979-8-3852-1983-4 (ebook)

Subjects: LCSH: Adoption (Theology)—Biblical teaching. | Bible.—Epistles of Paul—Criticism, interpretation, etc. | God—Fatherhood—Biblical teaching. | Regeneration (Theology). | Creation. | Kinship in the Bible.

Classification: BS2655.M47 K56 2025 (paperback) | BS2655.M47 (ebook)

VERSION NUMBER 10/01/25

Abstract

THE MAIN THESIS OF the present study is that Paul's use of υἱοθεσία (Rom 8:15, 23; 9:4; Gal 4:5) can be best explained by the concept of new creation understood within the Jewish context. In other words, Paul uses the metaphor of "adoption" within the frame of the new creation in Christ, and this affects both the form and content of the adoption metaphor. The concept of new creation in υἱοθεσία in Rom 8:15 and Rom 8:23 is closely related to the themes of "Spirit" and "resurrection" based on their allusions to Gen 2:7 (via allusions to Ezek 36–37) and Gen 3:16–19 respectively. In Rom 9, Paul uses the adoption metaphor to describe God's election of Israel not according to any of their qualifications but according to God's calling and mercy. This indicates that the gift of υἱοθεσία has to be confirmed and fulfilled in Christ in the context of new creation. Similarly, Paul's use of υἱοθεσία in Gal 4:5 has a connection with the new creation (καινὴ κτίσις) in Gal 6:15, in terms of a new identity in Christ regardless of ethnicity, social status, and gender (cf. Gal 3:28). Not only Gal 3:28's famous allusion to Gen 1:27 but also the Adamic narrative framework in Gal 4:1-7, which I will argue in this book, strengthen the new creation context of Paul's use of the adoption metaphor in Gal 4. In order to demonstrate the close relationship between Paul's adoption metaphor and the concept of new creation, I will investigate the concept of new creation in Second Temple Jewish writings and in Paul (Part I of this thesis: chapters 2 4) and analyze Paul's use of υἱοθεσία in light of new creation (part II of this thesis: chapters 5–7).

Although there has been a great deal of research on Paul's use of υἱοθεσία and the concept of new creation in Paul, no study has paid attention to the close relationship between them and what this relationship means for the shape of Pauline theology. For example, recent studies of ethnicity in Paul—the so-called "radical new perspective on Paul" or "Paul within Judaism"—often appeal to the Abrahamic sonship or the divine sonship in Romans and Galatians, but the sense of new creation—in terms of discontinuity, incongruity, and divine intervention in Christ—is virtually absent in their arguments. In the present study I will attempt not only to demonstrate the close relationship between Paul's use of υἱοθεσία and the new creation motif but also to show how this relationship helps us to gain a better understanding of Pauline theology through a dialogue with the "Paul within Judaism" school of scholars.

Contents

Foreword by John M. G. Barclay | xiii
Acknowledgments | xvii
Abbreviations | xix

Chapter 1: Introduction | 1
   1. Υἱοθεσία and the concept of new creation in Paul   1
   2. Recent studies on Paul's adoption metaphor   6
      (1) *The Son of God in the Roman World* (Michael Peppard 2011)   6
      (2) *Paul's "Spirit of Adoption" in Its Roman Imperial Context* (Robert Brian Lewis 2016)   7
      (3) *Adoption in Galatians and Romans* (Erin Heim 2017)   9
      (4) Conclusion of the survey of recent studies on Paul's adoption metaphor   11
   3. Literature review on the concept of new creation in Paul   12
      (1) *Neue Schöpfung* (Ulrich Mell 1989)   13
      (2) *Constructing the World* (Edward Adams 2000)   14
      (3) *New Creation in Paul's Letters and Thought* (Moyer V. Hubbard 2004)   16
      (4) *The Spirit and Creation in Paul* (John W. Yates 2008)   18
      (5) *New Creation in Paul's Letters* (T. Ryan Jackson 2010)   20
      (6) *As It Was in the Beginning* (Mark D. Owens 2015)   22
      (7) Conclusions from the literature review and a new proposal   23
   4. Conversation with the "Paul within Judaism" *Schule*   25
   5. Conclusions and overview of chapters   26

Part I: The Concept of New Creation

Chapter 2: The Concept of New Creation in the Parabiblical Texts | 31

1. Introduction   31
2. The *Urzeit-Endzeit* correlation   32
3. The concept of new creation in the book of Jubilees   33
    (1) Jub. 1:29   34
    (2) Jub. 4:26   36
    (3) Jub. 19:15-30; Jub. 23:22-31   39
4. The concept of new creation in 1 Enoch   41
    (1) The concept of new creation in the Book of the Luminaries   41
    (2) The concept of new creation in the Book of the Watchers   42
    (3) The concept of new creation in the Book of Parables   44
    (4) The concept of new creation the Book of Dream Visions   46
    (5) The concept of new creation in 1 En. 91–108   47
5. The concept of new creation in the Apocalypse of Moses   49
    (1) The corruption of Adam in the *Urzeit*   49
    (2) The hope for new creation in the *Endzeit*   51
6. The concept of new creation in Liber Antiquitatum Biblicarum   54
    (1) The influence of Adamic sin and the *Urzeit-Endzeit* framework   55
    (2) Adam and Israel   57
    (3) Israel's divine sonship and new creation   59
    (4) The new womb and the new creation in LAB 60:3   61
7. The concept of new creation in 4 Ezra and 2 Baruch   64
    (1) The concept of new creation in 4 Ezra   64
    (2) The concept of new creation in 2 Baruch   67
8. Conclusion   69

Chapter 3: The Concept of New Creation in Qumran Literature | 71

1. Introduction   71
2. The concept of new creation in the Hodayot   72
    (1) 1QH^a V:24-37   73
    (2) 1QH^a XI:20-26   78
    (3) 1QH^a XIX:12-17   83

3. The concept of new creation in the Community Rule   85
    (1) 1QS IV:20-26   86
    (2) 1QS XI:5-9   89
4. The concept of new creation in 4QInstruction (Mûsār Lĕ Mēbîn)   92
    (1) 4Q416 1:10-17   93
    (2) 4Q417 1:16-18   95
    (3) 4Q418 81:1-5   96
    (4) 4Q423   98
5. Conclusion   100

Chapter 4: The Concept of New Creation in Paul | 101

1. Introduction   101
2. The concept of new creation in 2 Cor 5:17   102
    (1) The narrative of Gen 1–3 in 2 Corinthians   102
    (2) Exegesis of 2 Cor 5:14-17   105
3. The concept of new creation in Gal 6:15   113
    (1) The parallelism between 6:14-16 and 3:27-29   113
    (2) Exegesis of Gal 6:14-16   116
4. The concept of new creation in Paul and in Second Temple Judaism   125
    (1) Similarities   126
    (2) Differences   127
5. Conclusion   128

Part II. Paul's Use of Υἱοθεσία in Light of New Creation

Chapter 5: Paul's Use of Υἱοθεσία in Romans 8 in Light of New Creation | 131

1. Introduction   131
2. Paul's use of υἱοθεσία in Rom 8:14-17 in light of new creation   132
    (1) The echoes of Ezek 36–37 in Rom 8:1-11   132
    (2) Ezek 36–37 and the new creation   135
    (3) The parallelism between God's people and the sons of God   136
    (4) Exegesis of Rom 8:14-17   138

3. Paul's use of υἱοθεσία in Rom 8:19-23 in light of new creation   147
   (1) Rom 1:18-25 and the influence of the Adamic sin   148
   (2) The eschatological hope for new creation in Rom 8:18-23   150
   (3) Exegesis of Rom 8:19-23   151
   (4) Christ's divine sonship and believers' υἱοθεσία   163
4. Conclusion   164

Chapter 6: Paul's Use of Υἱοθεσία in Romans 9 in Light of New Creation | 166

1. Introduction   166
2. Why does Paul use the term υἱοθεσία rather than the general language of sonship?   167
   (1) Israel's privileges in Rom 9:4-5 and Christ   167
   (2) Paul's radical reinterpretation of Israel's divine sonship   169
   (3) Υἱοθεσία as God's merciful act of election   171
   (4) Paul's reinterpretation of Hosea in Rom 9:25-26   174
   (5) Υἱοθεσία and God's new creation of his people from Jews and gentiles   176
3. Israel still needs the gift of υἱοθεσία   181
   (1) The connection between υἱοθεσία in Rom 9:4 and an event in Israel's history   183
   (2) Υἱοθεσία as Israel's gift and redemption in Christ   185
   (3) Israel's future salvation and the new creation motif   187
4. Conclusion   192

Chapter 7: Paul's Use of Υἱοθεσία in Galatians 4 in Light of New Creation | 194

1. Introduction   194
2. The theme of new creation as a hermeneutical key to Galatians   195
3. Exegesis of Gal 4:1-7   198
   (1) Paul's analogy in vv. 1-2: A Greco-Roman legal principle?   198
   (2) The echoes of Gen 1:28-29 in Gal 4:1 and κύριος πάντων   200
   (3) An interpretation of τὰ στοιχεῖα τοῦ κόσμου   203
   (4) Who are the "we" and "you" in Gal 4:1-7?   206
   (5) Paul's allusion to Gen 3:15 in Gal 4:4   209
   (6) Christ as the last Adam who recovers Adam's lost authority   212

(7) Adoption and new creation   216

(8) The echoes of Ezek 36:26-27 and Jer 31:33-34 in v. 6 and new creation   219

4. Conversation with "Paul within Judaism"   221

(1) The meaning of the descendants of Abraham: literal or metaphorical?   221

(2) The role of the Spirit in adoption as the sons of God   223

(3) The beneficiaries of the gift of adoption in Gal 4:5   227

5. Conclusion   231

Chapter 8: Conclusions | 232

1. The meaning of new creation in Second Temple Jewish literature and in Paul   232

2. The close relationship between the adoption metaphor and new creation   234

(1) The form of Paul's adoption metaphor as new creation   235

(2) The content of Paul's adoption metaphor as new creation   237

3. Conversation with Paul within Judaism   239

(1) Paul—apostle to the nations (pagans): an issue of audience   239

(2) Emphasis on law observance and ethnicity   240

(3) The "two-way solution"   241

Bibliography | 243
Author Index | 259
Scripture and Ancient Sources Index | 263

Foreword

IN RECENT DECADES, THERE have been several explorations of Paul's language of "adoption" (*huiothesia*) as his theological application of a Greco-Roman legal custom. But it is striking that Paul uses this term in relation to Israel (Rom 9:4), and this makes one wonder: what would be the resonances of this term, or of the concepts it evokes, within the Jewish tradition? In this fine monograph, Dr. Hyung-tae Kim explores this question by canvassing a broad range of Jewish sources from the Second Temple period and by careful attention to the key Pauline texts. The result is fresh and significant for all studies of Pauline theology.

Dr. Kim's most original contribution is to unearth the connection between "adoption" and "new creation." This connection, he argues, is clear in Galatians (where adoption language in Gal 3–4 is linked to "new creation" in Gal 6) and in Rom 8 (where "adoption" is part of the liberation of the cosmos in the coming new world, with multiple echoes of Gen 1–3). The connection between these two themes is extremely important, as it concerns the deep structure of Paul's theology. New creation, covenant, Israel, Christ, the inclusion of the gentiles, and the Spirit: all are bound up with these two Pauline themes. If adoption and new creation are mutually interpretive, they illumine together the shape of Pauline theology. In particular, if adoption is an act of new creation, salvation takes the form of a radical new beginning, not a supplement to what went before.

One of the key arguments of this book is that we should understand "new creation" as evoking not just prophetic promises but also, and especially, the Genesis narrative of creation (on an *Urzeit-Endzeit* scheme), as demonstrated here in detailed analysis of an impressive range of Second Temple texts. The scriptural story has, one may say, several moments of "beginning": aside from creation itself, Noah, Abraham, the exodus, the Davidic monarchy, and the return from exile are all stories of the beginning of something importantly new. Each of these echoes, in different ways, the story of creation, so that each is itself a kind of "creation." Even Israel's covenant, with its associated "sonship," is a repeated act of creation, not a guaranteed, "natural" process of human continuity. Tracing the theme (not only the specific vocabulary) of "new creation" across these Jewish texts indicates that "new creation" has a particular set of connotations in the Jewish tradition: it is radically dependent on the action of God; it is intrinsically universal in scope; it is an act of newness or change; and it is performed without regard to prior conditions (in technical terms, *ex nihilo*). As Dr. Kim here shows by studying the key Pauline texts, Paul inherits and sharpens these notions.

Why does this matter? If the action of God in Christ, and the "adoption" that is integral to salvation, are manifestations of "new creation," certain models of salvation are required, and certain others ruled out. In recent years, under the loosely defined label of "Paul within Judaism," it has become common to treat Paul's soteriology as a kind of Judaism-by-extension: Christ enables the addition of gentiles to the people of God, but the Jewish people and the solid continuity of covenant and Torah are left without change. The model here, one might say, is of a gentile extension to a Jewish house: the original building is given an added wing, thanks to Christ, but otherwise continues unaltered, in its own non-christological shape. Gentiles are added into the Abrahamic people, but Israel itself needs no substantial change. In his conversation with this scholarly trend, Dr. Kim offers, in effect, a very different model: as a "new creation," the whole building is fundamentally redesigned around the Christ-event, for Jews as well as Gentiles. Even the foundations are re-laid christologically, while incorporating much from the earlier ground-plan, because the divine act is comprehensive in scope, new for everyone, and given (as a form of "adoption"), not simply inherited.

Dr. Kim's case is nowhere clearer or stronger than in his exegesis of Gal 4:1-7, which he rightly uses to question components in the recent image of "Paul within Judaism." Here he finds echoes of the creation story (in 4:1-2, as in the context, 3:27-28), and here he notes how the theme of "Abraham's seed" is incorporated within the notion of adoption as children of God. Even if Jews have a special prehistory, they need adoption as much as do Gentiles if they are to receive the sonship-defining Spirit of the Son. If Christ was "born under the law to redeem those under the law" (4:4-5), Israel's Messiah does not merely add gentiles to the Abrahamic stock, but enacts a redemption (from slavery) that is needed by all. Here it is clear that adoption is a new making—or, in the terms of an interlinked passage, a "new creation" (Gal 6:15). Other interpreters of Galatians have found the same theme at the end of Gal 4, where Abraham's children in the Sarah-derived covenant are children of promise, not of flesh. From there it is a short step to Rom 9, where God's "calling" (a term linked closely to creation) is of both gentiles and Jews, called into being as "sons of the living God" (Rom 9:24-26).

By his close attention to the Pauline letters, and equally close exegesis of the relevant passages in other Second Temple texts, Hyung-tae Kim offers an exemplary analysis of a key topic and a significant contribution to contemporary debate. It was a privilege to co-supervise his doctoral work at Durham University and I am delighted that it is now available to a wide audience in this published form.

John M.G. Barclay

Lightfoot Professor of Divinity
Durham University, England

Acknowledgments

Paul's adoption metaphor is one of my favorite biblical metaphors. I became a Christian when I was a high school student. It felt awkward for me to call God Father at first, but at some point, I found myself naturally doing so. Through Rom 8:15 and Gal 4:6, I realized that the Holy Spirit in me made this possible. Also, Paul's adoption metaphor is very important in understanding Paul's theology as a whole, not only because it occurs in the most important texts in Paul's epistles (Rom 8:15, 23; 9:4; Gal 4:5) but also because it relates to recent debates in Pauline scholarship such as "apocalyptic Paul," "Paul within Judaism," "justification," etc. This personal reason, and the significance of this topic naturally led me to choose Paul's adoption metaphor as the subject of my thesis.

I would like to express my sincere gratitude to my two supervisors, Professor John Barclay and Dr. Jan Dochhorn, who have guided me to complete the thesis on which this book is based. I can never forget Professor Barclay's inspiring reply to my research proposal on this topic (an interpretation of Paul's adoption metaphor in light of new creation). He confirmed the importance of this study in a long email and made the suggestion to engage in conversation with the scholars of "Paul within Judaism" in relation to this topic. As each chapter progressed, he always provided continuous encouragement and insightful feedback, leading this project to a successful completion. I have never met a scholar with such an extensive knowledge of the Second Temple Jewish texts and ancient languages as Dr. Dochhorn. During the first year of my doctoral program, when Professor Barclay was on his sabbatical, Dr. Dochhorn taught me as my primary supervisor, and his love for the Apocalypse of Moses, in particular, deeply affects my interpretation of Rom 8. Moreover, from him, I have learned a lot of knowledge and skills for interpreting Second Temple Jewish literature. Both of my supervisors are my mentors and heroes.

During the eight years of studying abroad, I owe many people a debt of love. First of all, I thank my mother. My mother always devoted herself to me even in the midst of poor living conditions, and has provided me with bright energy that made me overcome any difficulties. And I thank my mother-in-law. My mother-in-law understood me, who suddenly entered a seminary quitting a good job as a software engineer, without expressing any displeasure, and she has supported my family in every way. Without these two mothers, this thesis would never have appeared in the world.

Also, I would like to express my gratitude to the families of Seoul Yeongdong Church and Durham Korean Church who supported me and my family while I was writing the thesis. Their support has been a great help both spiritually and materially. In the future, I would like to continue to study the Bible using an academic methodology, and eventually produce results that help the church.

Finally, I dedicate this thesis to my beloved wife Hyeon-mi Ryu. During the eight years of studying abroad, she devoted everything to me while raising three young children. To me, she is the most beautiful woman in the world and the wisest woman in the world. Also, thanks to our lovely children, Juan, Jubon, and Jia. They have provided endless joy and energy to us as a couple, growing up bright and healthy while living abroad. Thus, this thesis is the product of the hard work and effort of all of our family.

> "For from him and through him and to him are all things. To him be the glory forever. Amen" (Rom 11:36).

Abbreviations

All abbreviations of primary and secondary sources follow the forms indicated in *The SBL Handbook of Style, Second Edition* (Atlanta: SBL Press, 2014).

Chapter 1: **Introduction**

1. Υἱοθεσία and the concept of new creation in Paul

MANY SCHOLARS HAVE DISCUSSED the origin and background of Paul's adoption metaphor (Gal 4:5; Rom 8:15, 23; Rom 9:4; cf. Eph 1:5). Some have denied that υἱοθεσία originated from the Jewish tradition, since adoption, strictly speaking, was not practised in ancient Israel, and since the word does not occur in the Septuagint or in other Jewish literature from the Second Temple period.[1] Others, however, have argued that the Jewish background is the key to understanding Paul's adoption metaphor, over and against any Greco-Roman influence.[2] The most influential among these are Brendan Byrne and James Scott.[3]

Some features of Greek and Roman adoptions provide a proper context for Paul's use of υἱοθεσία. For example, the context of liberation from the power of sin fits well with the shift of *patria potestas* in the Roman legal act of *adoptio*. However, Paul's use of υἱοθεσία cannot be fully understood in light of the Greco-Roman context alone. First, Greek and Roman adoptions were normally performed between the upper classes of society, and their main purpose, the perpetuation of the family line,[4]

---

1. E.g., Hester, *Paul's Concept of Inheritance*, 58; Lyall, *Slaves, Citizens, Sons*, 95–97; Fitzmyer, *Romans*, 500; Dunn, *Romans 1–8*, 452; Burke, *Adopted into God's Family*, 70–71; Peppard, *Son of God*, 135–40; Longenecker, *Epistle to the Romans*, 703–4.

2. E.g., Jewett, *Romans*, 498; Keesmaat, *Paul and His Story*, 65. Moo and Cranfield have a nuanced discussion of the matter: Despite the lack of comparable legal practice in Jewish sources, the concept of divine sonship is deeply rooted in the Old Testament and Judaism. See Moo, *Galatians*, 268; Moo, *Epistle to the Romans*, 501; Cranfield, *Epistle to the Romans*, 397–98.

3. Byrne, *Sons of God*; Scott, *Adoption as Sons of God*; cf. Byrne, *Romans*, 250.

4. Isae. 7.30; Cic. *Dom*. 35; Lindsay, *Adoption in the Roman World*, 103.

does not fit with its use as a soteriological metaphor for sinners. The focus in Greek and Roman adoptions is largely on the needs of the adopter rather than the adoptee.[5] Second, the Greco-Roman context of Paul's adoption metaphor cannot explain the eschatological aspect between the "now" and the "not yet" in Paul's adoption metaphor (i.e., Rom 8:15; 8:23), although it could have this dual meaning in Jewish eschatology. Lastly, Paul expresses υἱοθεσία as a covenantal privilege of Israel (Rom 9:4), which does not have any connection with Greco-Roman adoption. These deficiencies can be remedied by consideration of the Jewish context of Paul's adoption metaphor.

Byrne and Scott helpfully explain the Jewish background of υἱοθεσία. Interpreting υἱοθεσία as adoptive *sonship* rather than adoption,[6] Byrne traces the usage of "Son(s) of God" in Jewish literature. He recognizes three categories of divine sonship: (1) divine beings or angelic beings, (2) the Israelites, and (3) the king.[7] He regards the second type (the Israelites) as the most important usage and argues that the meaning of sonship in the Old Testament is "the unique privilege of Israel as the people chosen and created by Yahweh" within the covenantal relationship.[8] He then investigates the language of divine sonship in the intertestamental literature and concludes that Paul's use of υἱοθεσία eschatologizes the concept of divine sonship to extend this privilege to gentiles.[9]

In contrast to Byrne, Scott argues that υἱοθεσία in the Hellenistic period should be interpreted as "adoption as son," not merely "sonship."[10] In order to address the fact that υἱοθεσία does not occur in the Septuagint and other Jewish literature, he claims that it is necessary to distinguish between the meaning of a term and its background in any particular context. That is, "although the term υἱοθεσία does not occur in any Jewish source of the period, the concept of it can be well represented by other

---

5. Lindsay, *Adoption in the Roman World*, 59.

6. By doing so, Byrne emphasizes the *status* of sonship rather than the legal *act* of adoption (Byrne, *Sons of God*, 1).

7. Byrne, *Sons of God*, 9.

8. Byrne, *Sons of God*, 16.

9. Byrne, *Sons of God*, 216.

10. Scott, *Adoption as Sons of God*, 55; Scott focuses on six word-groups that are part of the same semantic domain as υἱοθεσία, and he examines each of these word-groups in systematic detail, using computer-based lexical resources. This lexical survey enables him to conclude that in the Hellenistic period the term always denoted "adoption as son," never "sonship" (Scott, *Adoption as Sons of God*, 13–55).

terms and formulae."[11] Refuting Donner's argument that the Old Testament contains no cases of "genuine adoption,"[12] Scott claims that several examples of adoption do occur in the Old Testament (Exod 2:10; Esth 2:7, 15; Gen 48:5–6).[13] For Scott, however, the most important tradition of adoption in the Old Testament is 2 Sam 7:14a, "I will be a father to him, and he shall be a son to me," which he calls an "adoption formula." Scott argues that 2 Sam 7 uses the covenant formula in v. 24 to contextualize the adoption formula in v. 14 in order to highlight the interrelationship between the king and the people of God.[14]

Byrne and Scott demonstrate the covenantal and eschatological dimensions of υἱοθεσία when it describes Israel's privilege as God's chosen nation. Where they come up short, however, is that they fail to notice the reason Paul uses υἱοθεσία rather than υἱός. Paul uses the adoption metaphor instead of the language of general sonship in the following senses: (1) the lexical meaning of υἱοθεσία, "adoption as sons" or "the status of sonship arising out of adoption," indicates a *transition* of status, from a slave to a son;[15] (2) Paul uses the adoption metaphor to emphasize God's merciful act of election in spite of Israel's disqualification (to borrow Barclay's words, Paul highlights the "incongruity" of God's gift). Another significant point that Byrne and Scott overlook is the role of the Holy Spirit in Paul's use of υἱοθεσία. As Mawhinney stresses, "in all four NT instances in which *huiothesia* is used with regard to Christian sonship, the Holy Spirit is also mentioned."[16] Paul calls the Holy Spirit πνεῦμα υἱοθεσίας (Rom 8:15) and says that the Holy Spirit makes us cry out "αββα ὁ πατήρ" (Rom 8:15, Gal 4:6). Lastly, Byrne and Scott do not pay sufficient attention to the importance of the resurrection in Paul's use of υἱοθεσία. Paul identifies υἱοθεσία with "the redemption of our body" which indicates the future resurrection of believers (Rom 8:23). Moreover, a spirit of adoption (πνεῦμα υἱοθεσίας) in Rom 8:15 probably

---

11. Scott, *Adoption as Sons of God*, 61.
12. Donner, "Adoption oder Legitimation?," 87–119.
13. Scott, *Adoption as Sons of God*, 68–75.
14. Scott, *Adoption as Sons of God*, 100.
15. υἱοθεσία is a compound word of υἱός and θέσις "placing" (BDAG, s.v. "υἱοθεσία," 1024). The lexica and most of the commentators agree that υἱοθεσία means "adoption as sons." See Barclay, *Obeying the Truth*, 96n50; Martyn, *Galatians*, 390; Bruce, *Epistle of Paul*, 197–98.
16. Mawhinney, "Baptism, Servanthood, and Sonship," 45; cf. Rom 8:14–15, 23; Gal 4:4–6; Eph 1:3–14.

refers to the Spirit through which "the one who raised Jesus from the dead" will give life to believers' mortal bodies (Rom 8:11).

I contend that the deficiencies mentioned above can be overcome in light of the concept of new creation. In other words, Paul's use of υἱοθεσία *is best explained in terms of the concept of new creation. Paul uses the metaphor of "adoption" within the frame of the new creation in Christ, and this affects both the form and the content of the adoption metaphor.*

Here, "the concept of new creation" is *not* limited to the phrase καινὴ κτίσις. Rather, the *concept* of new creation can be explained in terms of *form* and *content*. In terms of form, the concept of new creation basically refers to *God's* creative activity to redeem humanity and all creation from the plight deeply influenced by Adamic sin. Thus, it often relates to the *Urzeit-Endzeit* schema, but it has strong elements of discontinuity, even involving a radical transition from death to life; it is a form of *creatio ex nihilo*, not a natural form of progression or a development within the frame of human possibility.

In terms of content, the concept of new creation echoes the narrative in Genesis 1–3 and encompasses various relevant themes such as cosmic renewal, building of a new eschatological temple/Eden, restoration of Adamic glory, outpouring of the Spirit and resurrection. Thus, it is about humanity and the whole creation, and concerns the restoration or fulfillment of Adamic destiny; it is thus not particular to any one ethnicity, but incorporates both Jews and gentiles.

My main thesis can be supported on the following grounds. First, the theme of "the corruption and redemption of creation" and many allusions to Gen 3:16–19 in Rom 8:19–23 suggest that Paul uses υἱοθεσία (8:23) in the context of the new creation.

Second, the concept of new creation can explain the close relationship between υἱοθεσία and the language of the Spirit and resurrection. For example, Ezek 36–37, which Paul's adoption passages (Rom 8:14–17 and Gal 4:4–7) allude to, describes Israel's restoration with the language of the Spirit and resurrection in the context of the new creation.[17]

---

17. As many scholars argue, Ezek 37:1–14 has strong links to the creation account of Gen 2. See Zimmerli et al., *Ezekiel*, 261–65; Allen, *Ezekiel*, 185; Kutsko, *Between Heaven and Earth*, 133; Levenson, *Resurrection and the Restoration of Israel*, 159; Yates, *Spirit and Creation in Paul*, 31–35. This is seen most clearly in the prominence of the "breath of life" tradition: The process of the revivification of the dead is very similar to the process of the creation of man in two stages (man is formed but becomes a living being only after God breathes life into him). The verb, נפח (to blow: Ezek 37:9), is the same as that found in Gen 2:7. Also, just prior to this passage, God promises that

Third, Paul's use of υἱοθεσία in Gal 4:5 also has a connection with the new creation in Gal 6:15, in terms of the eschatological inclusion of gentiles: "For neither circumcision counts for anything, nor uncircumcision, but a *new creation*." The only thing that matters in the new era inaugurated by God's sending of his Son and the Spirit (Gal 4:4–6) is that Jew and gentile alike should be a new creation in Christ, a new sort of humanity who receive adoption as God's children. Also, the use of "Spirit" and "hearts" in Gal 4:4–6, which many scholars recognize as an echo of Ezek 36:26–27 and Jer 31:33–34,[18] can be read in the context of the new creation.[19] This new creation inaugurates a new community of "the sons of God" that can disregard distinctions between Jew and Greek, slave and free, and male and female (Gal 3:26–29).[20]

Finally, the new creation explains well the meaning of "transition" and "incongruity" in υἱοθεσία because: (1) the new creation implies a strong *discontinuity* with the old era; (2) the new creation presupposes the *corruption* of Adam or Israel's *unfaithfulness* to God. As we shall see, this well explains why Paul uses υἱοθεσία in Rom 9:4 instead of the language of natural sonship. The citation of Hosea in Rom 9:25–26 also indicates this discontinuity and incongruity in the sense that God creates a "people/sons of the living God" from those who were "not my people."[21]

To substantiate the proposed argument, we need to investigate Second Temple Jewish texts together with the relevant Old Testament texts with the aim of identifying the connections between the concept of new creation and the relevant themes (e.g., the Spirit, resurrection, Adamic glory, etc.) as they shed light on Paul's use of υἱοθεσία. Previous studies can provide useful foundations for this project not only in identifying the connection between the concept of new creation and the relevant themes but also in finding out the meaning of new creation in Second Temple Jewish writings and Paul's letters. Thus, we should examine previous studies on the concept of new creation to obtain some useful insights to organize

---

the land will be cultivated, coming to resemble the garden of Eden in its fruitfulness (36:34–35). In this sense, Ezek 37:1–14 can be read in terms of the new creation motif.

18. E.g., Martyn, *Galatians*, 391–92; de Boer, *Galatians*, 265; Moo, *Galatians*, 269; Gorman, "Apocalyptic New Covenant," 325–26.

19. Many scholars interpret Ezek 36:26–27 and Jer 31:33–34 as a new creation in terms of the renewal of Israel's hardened heart (e.g., Kutsko, *Between Heaven and Earth*, 132; Yates, *Spirit and Creation in Paul*, 31–35; Hubbard, *New Creation*, 17–25).

20. Barclay, *Paul and the Gift*, 567; Wright also argues that in Gal 3:27–29 the "new creation" means in practice a "new family," a "new people." See Wright, *Paul Debate*, 5.

21. Cf. Barclay, *Paul and the Gift*, 534–35.

our investigation of the concept of new creation in Second Temple Jewish literature and Paul. However, we should first examine some recent studies on Paul's adoption metaphor that have been published since the two remarkable contributions of Byrne and Scott.

2. Recent studies on Paul's adoption metaphor

(1) *The Son of God in the Roman World* (Michael Peppard 2011)[22]

After Byrne and Scott, who rightly pointed out the importance of the Jewish context of Paul's use of υἱοθεσία, Michael Peppard and Robert B. Lewis call attention to its Greco-Roman context again, particularly a Roman imperial context.

In his monograph, *The Son of God in the Roman World*, Peppard argues that although the most relevant context of the divine sonship metaphor in the New Testament and other early Christian literature is the Roman sociopolitical environment of the first and second centuries, most scholars have improperly interpreted the divine sonship metaphor using conceptions from "elite theological debates of later centuries," particularly the debate at the Council of Nicaea.[23] Peppard investigates the practice of adoption, particularly among imperial families, and concludes that adoption was a crucial practice for "imperial succession, of transmitting power from father to son" for those who did not have eligible natural sons. As the title of chapter 3 "Begotten or Made" indicates, according to Peppard, there was no difference between a natural heir and an adoptive heir in terms of their power and privilege.[24] For example, Augustus, who was an adoptive son of both Julius Caesar and Jupiter, became not only "the father of the Roman people" but also "the son of God" who "incarnated (or even displaced) Jupiter's traditional fatherly role."[25]

Peppard, then, provocatively interprets Mark's description of Jesus's baptism (Mark 1:9–11) as a divine adoption in light of the perspective of Roman adoption and imperial ideology.[26] For Peppard, even in Mark's Christology, divine sonship by adoption has an essentially equal status with that of natural sonship. Thus, he claims that this is not the

---

22. Peppard, *Son of God*.
23. Peppard, *Son of God*, 3.
24. Peppard, *Son of God*, 50–85.
25. Peppard, *Son of God*, 61–62.
26. Peppard, *Son of God*, 86–131.

low Christology of typical adoptionism but "as high as humanly possible" since "adoption was the most effective method of portraying his [Jesus'] divine sonship."[27]

Building on Scott's interpretation of Christ's firstborn sonship in Rom 8:29 (cf. Rom 1:4) as adoption, Peppard argues that "Paul is not trying to separate the divine sonship of Christ from the divine sonship of Christians," but "draws them together as closely as he can,"[28] just as John's Gospel, the *Shepherd of Hermas*, and the second-century church fathers (Clement of Alexandria and Irenaeus) do.[29] Thus, according to Peppard, in the first two centuries the adoption metaphor could be used to symbolize both Christ and Christians in connection with the Roman adoption practice. After the Nicaean era, however, this mixed usage of divine sonship by adoption became separate: "Jesus is God's begotten son by nature; you [Christians] are all God's adopted children by grace."[30]

Peppard's interpretation of the adoption metaphor in light of the Roman imperial context is fresh and stimulating, but his main focus is on Markan Christology and the reception of divine sonship before and after the Nicaean era, not the Pauline adoption metaphor.[31]

(2) Paul's "Spirit of Adoption" in Its Roman Imperial Context (Robert Brian Lewis 2016)[32]

Building on Peppard's study, Lewis attempts to interpret the phrase "Spirit of adoption" in Rom 8:15 and its immediate paragraph (vv. 12–17) against the Roman imperial context.[33] In other words, Lewis claims that the first-century Roman imperial context—for example, Octavian became Julius Caesar's son through adoption—best explains Paul's use

---

27. Peppard, *Son of God*, 131.
28. Peppard, *Son of God*, 139.
29. Peppard, *Son of God*, 140–60.
30. Peppard, *Son of God*, 171.
31. Peppard deals with Paul's use of adoptive divine sonship only in six pages (Peppard, *Son of God*, 135–40).
32. Lewis, *Paul's "Spirit of Adoption."*
33. Lewis himself admits that Peppard's work "lays a foundation" for his interpretation of Rom 8, although Peppard does not investigate the connection between the notions of Spirit and adoption (Lewis, *Paul's "Spirit of Adoption,"* 28).

of the phrase "Spirit of adoption" which highlights the full and equal inclusion of the gentiles among God's people.[34]

Peppard's argument that the Spirit-sonship connection (Mark 1:9–11; cf. Rom 1:4; 8:9–30) can be understood by "reference to the Roman concepts of the *genius* and *numen*, especially as they were combined in the emperor"[35] seems to inspire Lewis to interpret the "Spirit of adoption" in light of the Roman imperial context. Lewis claims that the Emperor's *genius* (the personal guardian spirit) and *numen* (divine power) form a Latin counterpart to Paul's use of "spirit" in Rom 8:15,[36] and that "every person in Rome was acquainted with the 'spirit of adoption' that had come upon Octavian at his official adoption" in which "Octavian had received the spirit of Julius, Julius Caesar's *genius*."[37] At Octavian's adoption, the family spirit of Julius Caesar was transferred to the care of Augustus, and then the *genius* of Augustus became a representation of the entire Empire, the *genius populi Romani*. However, according to Lewis, it is the Spirit of Christ, not the *genius Augusti*, that protects the gentile believers. In Rom 8:15, for the gentile believers, a "change in divinities" has occurred.[38] In this sense, Lewis's interpretation of the "Spirit of adoption" resonates with so-called "anti-imperial Paul," which argues that Paul's letters contain a "hidden" critique of Rome and imperial ideology.

Although Lewis succeeds in extending Peppard's main thesis to the interpretation of the Spirit of adoption in Rom 8:15, his study raises many unresolved questions. First of all, Lewis diminishes a Jewish context of Paul's use of υἱοθεσία since it has "been unable to demonstrate why Paul joins the term 'Spirit' with 'adoption.'"[39] The new creation motif in Ezek 36–37, however, can provide a probable Jewish context for the "Spirit of adoption" in Rom 8:15, as we shall see in our exegesis of Rom 8 (chapter 5, section 1). Moreover, as seen above, the connection between the adoption metaphor and the Spirit is also found in Gal 4:4–6 (cf. Eph 1:3–14), where the audience does not have an immediate relationship with Rome. This indicates that the Roman imperial context is not the best explanation for the phrase "Spirit of adoption" in Rom 8:15.

---

34. Lewis, Paul's "Spirit of Adoption," 1–2.
35. Peppard, Son of God, 113–15.
36. Lewis, Paul's "Spirit of Adoption," 58.
37. Lewis, Paul's "Spirit of Adoption," 191.
38. Lewis, Paul's "Spirit of Adoption," 183.
39. Lewis, Paul's "Spirit of Adoption," 183.

Second, Lewis's argument that *genius* and *numen* are terms that form a Latin counterpart to the way Paul uses the one term "spirit" is intriguing, but there is no direct evidence for this connection. In other words, although Lewis presents some examples in which *genius* and *numen* connote a guardian spirit or force in household worship, he gives no *lexical* evidence to show that the Latin terms *genius/numen* can be translated as the Greek term πνεῦμα. The Latin equivalent of πνεῦμα in the Vulgate is *spiritus*, not *genius* or *numen*.

Lastly, one of the most fundamental questions concerning Lewis's arguments would be: "Why should we read Paul in the Roman imperial context?" Paul's probable familiarity with the Roman imperial context[40] does not provide a *legitimate* reason that we should read Paul in the Roman imperial context. Lewis seems to follow the argument of "anti-imperial Paul" school, but there is still an ongoing debate on its legitimacy.[41] According to Barclay, "From Paul's perspective, the Roman empire never was and never would be a significant actor in the drama of history."[42]

(3) *Adoption in Galatians and Romans* (Erin Heim 2017)[43]

In her monograph *Adoption in Galatians and Romans*, Erin Heim contributes to the study of Paul's adoption metaphor mainly in two aspects. First, in terms of methodology, Heim uses contemporary metaphor theories and cognitive linguistics for analyzing Paul's adoption metaphor,[44] attending to the way υἱοθεσία likely influenced the perception and emotion of Paul's audience, and to its social function as solidifying the common bonds of community members as brothers and sisters.[45] Second,

---

40. When Lewis presents his methodological considerations, he seems to regard the "familiarity of Paul and Paul's Roman audience with the imperial context" as an important reason to justify his study. See Lewis, *Paul's "Spirit of Adoption*,*"* 5–10.

41. For recent debates on this issue, refer to chs. 18 and 19 in Barclay, *Pauline Churches*.

42. Barclay, *Pauline Churches*, 386.

43. Heim, *Adoption in Galatians and Romans*.

44. Heim relies on Soskice's metaphor theory and recognizes that "metaphors have two elements—tenor and vehicle—that cooperate to create the metaphor's meaning." See Heim, *Adoption in Galatians and Romans*, 43.

45. Strictly speaking, she is not the first person who applies contemporary metaphor theories to interpreting Paul's use of υἱοθεσία. For example, Trevor Burke uses Lakoff and Johnson's metaphor theory, although Heim criticizes Burke's methodology

while previous studies on Paul's adoption metaphor usually concern investigations into the background of υἱοθεσία, which can have a potential pitfall that makes various meanings and contexts of υἱοθεσία univocal, Heim attempts to show that "the four Pauline υἱοθεσία metaphors function much like the bands of color which occur when white light is passed through a prism."[46] In other words, Heim prudently examines the individual contribution of each υἱοθεσία metaphor and highlights its distinctive meanings and implications.

With this methodology and aim, Heim exegetes the occurrences of υἱοθεσία in Galatians and Romans respectively. First, Heim interprets the adoption metaphor in Gal 4:5 as highlighting the inclusion of the gentiles in the community of faith by God's adoption rather than by law observance. According to her, it also emphasizes the vertical dimension of υἱοθεσία by focusing the audience's attention on the Triune God's actions (initiated by the Father, accomplished by the mission of the Son, and attested by the Spirit).[47] Second, Heim argues that unlike in Gal 4:1–7, the two υἱοθεσία metaphors in Rom 8 draw attention to "the acute existential and eschatological tension" which accompanies believers' experience of the Spirit, describing the more horizontal dimension of υἱοθεσία by highlighting the common bonds of community members who share the present suffering together.[48] Lastly, Heim claims that although the predominant model in play for the adoption metaphors in Gal 4 and in Rom 8 is Greco-Roman adoption, in Rom 9:4 Paul uses the Jewish sonship tradition as a model for υἱοθεσία.[49] Thus, in light of the Jewish divine sonship tradition, she interprets Paul's adoption metaphor in Rom 9:4 as "Paul's own familial description of God's covenant relationship with Israel,"[50] which is distinct from other occurrences of υἱοθεσία in Gal 4 and Rom 8, where they refer to believers' new identity in Christ.

Heim's new approach for reading Paul's adoption metaphors in light of modern metaphor theories provides a new milestone for the study of Paul's use of υἱοθεσία, but it also raises some questions.

---

as "problematic." See Burke, *Adopted into God's Family*, 32–35; Heim, *Adoption in Galatians and Romans*, 16–17.

46. Heim, *Adoption in Galatians and Romans*, 19.
47. Heim, *Adoption in Galatians and Romans*, 179–83, 326.
48. Heim, *Adoption in Galatians and Romans*, 248–50.
49. Heim, *Adoption in Galatians and Romans*, 324.
50. Heim, *Adoption in Galatians and Romans*, 320.

First, although her approach is fresh, the results of her exegesis based on the new methodology seem not very new. Thus, sometimes, it is difficult to determine whether her conclusions are drawn by her new methodology or simply by a traditional exegesis. In other words, questions arise as to how much her new methodology contributes to a fresh interpretation of Paul's adoption metaphor.

Second, it is questionable as to how important it is to find out the different meanings and contexts of each υἱοθεσία metaphor in Paul's letters rather than to recognize consistency or commonality in Paul's use of υἱοθεσία. As Heim herself admits, there are a number of similarities in Paul's adoption metaphors in Romans and Galatians.[51] Moreover, her argument about the differences between Romans and Galatians is questionable. For example, in her concluding summary, Heim points out the difference in Paul's use of υἱοθεσία in Rom 8 and Gal 4 by saying that "unlike the υἱοθεσία metaphor in Galatians 4:5, the two metaphors in Romans 8 contain a much stronger emphasis on the horizontal dimensions of community membership."[52] Given the context of Gal 4:5, however, the horizontal dimensions of community membership is one of the most important themes that υἱοθεσία in Gal 4:5 implies.[53] Moreover, we can regard the υἱοθεσία metaphor in Rom 8:15 almost as a restatement of Paul's use of υἱοθεσία in Gal 4:5 since it occurs not only with the common phrase "Abba! Father" but also with themes of the Spirit and inheritance as in Gal 4:5. Lastly, Paul's use of υἱοθεσία in 8:23 and 9:4 cannot be considered separately from the υἱοθεσία metaphor in Rom 8:15, since Paul's discussion continues from Rom 8 to Rom 9 through the common theme of υἱοθεσία.

(4) Conclusion of the survey of recent studies on Paul's adoption metaphor

After the important contributions of Byrne and Scott, there have been several monographs on the υἱοθεσία metaphor. Peppard and Lewis dealt with this topic in connection with the Roman imperial context, while Heim attempted a new approach to interpret Paul's adoption metaphor

---

51. Heim, *Adoption in Galatians and Romans*, 327–29.
52. Heim, *Adoption in Galatians and Romans*, 324.
53. As we shall see later (ch. 7, section 3), Gal 4:1–7 has many links with the immediately preceding paragraph 3:23–29, and in particular, υἱοθεσία in Gal 4:5 can be connected to Paul's horizontal emphasis in Gal 3:28.

in light of modern metaphor theories and cognitive linguistics. All these works, however, do not recognize the crucial relationship between Paul's use of υἱοθεσία and the new creation motif. In addition to this, the present study has significance in that it reconfirms the importance of the Jewish background of Paul's use of υἱοθεσία and its consistent meaning in Romans and Galatians. We turn now to an examination of previous studies concerning Paul's new creation motif.

3. Literature review on the concept of new creation in Paul

The studies on Paul's concept of new creation have focused on whether this term is mainly anthropological or cosmological.[54] Although there are a few exceptions,[55] the traditional understanding of καινὴ κτίσις in Paul was an anthropological one, as the English translation "new creature" (e.g., KJV) suggests.[56] However, since R. H. Strachan published his commentary on 2 Corinthians in 1935,[57] where he translated καινὴ κτίσις as "new creation" rather than "new creature" in light of Jewish apocalypticism, the cosmological reading of Paul's concept of new creation has come to have its voice against the anthropological reading. In particular, as Käsemann's "apocalyptic" reading of Paul took a more dominant position over Bultmann's anthropological reading of Paul, the

---

54. Some scholars claim that καινὴ κτίσις in Paul refers to "community" or "church" to overcome a limitation of the individual anthropological reading of Paul's new creation motif. For example, Wolfgang Kraus maintains that καινὴ κτίσις in the *Hauptbriefe* (Gal 6:15; 2 Cor 5:17) should be interpreted as a "Gemeindewirklichkeit" by understanding it as an eschatological realization of Isa 66:18–23 inaugurated by Christ's death and resurrection. See Kraus, *Volk Gottes*, 247–51; cf. 255–61. This ecclesiological understanding of new creation, in a broad sense, can be included in the anthropological reading.

55. As Jackson well observes, there are a few voices in early Christian literature who recognize a cosmological aspect of the concept of new creation in Paul (e.g., Gregory of Nyssa, Athanasius, and Chrysostom). See Jackson, *New Creation*, 7–9.

56. Most early Christian writers support an anthropological reading of καινὴ κτίσις in Paul (e.g., Clement, Tertullian, Jerome, Augustine, etc.). Moreover, both Luther and Calvin translated and interpreted καινὴ κτίσις as "new creature" in their commentaries. Particularly, Luther's translation of Gal 6:15—"Denn in Christo Jesu gilt weder Beschneidung noch unbeschnitten sein etwas, sondern eine neue Kreatur"—in the Luther Bible had made the anthropological reading of Gal 6:15 the standard interpretation of German scholars until the early 20th centuries.

57. Strachan, *Second Epistle*.

soterio-cosmological interpretation of Paul's new creation motif has become more and more influential in Pauline scholarship.[58]

In what follows, I will review recent important monographs on the concept of new creation in Paul's letters, focusing on the debate over its anthropological and cosmological dimensions.

(1) *Neue Schöpfung* (Ulrich Mell 1989)[59]

In *Neue Schöpfung*, Mell follows Stuhlmacher's idea that Paul's concept of new creation has been developed originally from Isaiah, proceeding through Jewish apocalyptic literature, Qumran literature, and Hellenistic Judaism.[60] Thus, in the first two-thirds of the volume, Mell painstakingly investigates the development of the new creation concept in the Old Testament (Isa 40–66), Qumran literature, Jewish apocalyptic literature, rabbinic literature, and Hellenistic Jewish literature, and he concludes that the pre-Pauline term καινὴ κτίσις is a common catchphrase in early Jewish eschatology, which refers to God's initiative in salvific action at the eschaton. In this sense, Mell regards the concept of new creation in early Judaism not as "anthropological" but as "cosmological."[61]

After his investigation of the concept of new creation in the early Jewish traditions, Mell analyzes the concept of καινὴ κτίσις in Gal 6:15 and 2 Cor 5:17. Mell claims that Paul distances his use of καινὴ κτίσις in Gal 6:15 from the end-time use of new creation in early Judaism by focusing on the present eschatological aspect of new creation. Also, according to Mell, καινὴ κτίσις in Gal 6:15 refers to a "cosmic transformation of the world," not to an "ontological transformation of a man,"[62]

---

58. Martyn and de Boer's apocalyptic interpretations of the new creation in their commentaries on Galatians are good examples of this tendency.

59. Mell, *Neue Schöpfung*.

60. Stuhlmacher summarizes his argument on the origin of Paul's concept of new creation in the conclusion of his famous article "Erwägungen zum ontologischen Charakter der καινὴ κτίσις bei Paulus": "Damit können wir unseren religionsgeschichtlichen Überblick beenden: Die Vorstellung von der Neuschöpfung ist auf Grund deutero und tritojesajanischer Tradition von der Apokalyptik zunächst in kosmologischer, dann auch in anthropologischer Hinsicht ausgearbeitet worden. Von dort her wandert sie ins hellenistische Judentum und Rabbinat, schließlich zur Gnosis. Bei dieser Wanderung wird das Motiv durch Interpretation abgewandelt. Der kosmisch-heilsgeschichtliche Horizont verblaßt, der Begriff καινὴ κτίσις verengt sich zur anthropologischen Chiffre." See Stuhlmacher, "Erwägungen zum ontologischen Charakter," 20.

61. Mell, *Neue Schöpfung*, 257.

62. Mell, *Neue Schöpfung*, 324.

since the "crucified world" appears as a counterpart to "new creation" (Gal 6:14–15).[63] Mell, however, does not totally exclude an anthropological and individual aspect of new creation. In his analysis of καινὴ κτίσις in 2 Cor 5:14–17, Mell notes the Adam-Christ antithesis and interprets Christ as an eschatological *Urmensch* in whom the people of God can participate in salvation. In this context, Mell understands "new creation" in 2 Cor 5:17 as "Grundfigur theologischer Anthropologie."[64]

Mell's study contributed hugely to a better understanding of the Pauline concept of new creation in two points. First, his study, which seems to be deeply influenced by Ernst Käsemann's apocalyptic reading of Paul, successfully called attention to the cosmological aspect of Paul's concept of new creation, while the anthropological understanding of the phrase καινὴ κτίσις had been a dominant view before Mell's monograph. Second, Mell's meticulous investigation of the concept of new creation in early Jewish traditions provides useful resources to trace Paul's concept of new creation in comparison with the new creation motif in early Judaism. In this sense, Mell's work laid the foundation for subsequent research.

However, Mell's painstaking analysis of the early Jewish traditions may be, ironically, a flaw of his study since "its irrelevance to the elucidation of Galatians 6:15 and 2 Corinthians 5:17 is underlined by the meagreness of Mell's conclusions."[65] For example, in spite of his conclusion on the new creation motif in 2 Cor 5:17 that it concerns the Adam-Christ antithesis, Mell's investigation of the new creation motif in early Judaism hardly deals with Adam motif, which is closely related to the new creation motif, as we shall see later.

(2) *Constructing the World* (Edward Adams 2000)[66]

Although the main focus of Adams's *Constructing the World* does not lie in καινὴ κτίσις in Paul's letters, this monograph is relevant to the present study in that it reveals the cosmological meaning of the terms κόσμος and κτίσις in the *Hauptbriefe*. The thesis of this monograph is that Paul's usage of the terms κόσμος and κτίσις reflects the original social-historical situations which the recipients of Paul's letters are confronting. For example,

---

63. Mell, *Neue Schöpfung*, 391.
64. Mell, *Neue Schöpfung*, 393–97.
65. Murphy-O'Connor, "Pauline Studies," 150.
66. Adams, *Constructing the World*.

according to Adams, in 1 Corinthians Paul uses κόσμος in a *negative* and *critical* sense "to stress the social and ideological distinction between the Christian community and the larger society and culture,"[67] while in Romans Paul uses κόσμος and κτίσις in a largely *positive* sense "to develop an understanding of the world as God's good and well-ordered creation," reflecting Paul's intention to pursue social harmony in the Roman Christian community's difficult situation in the years between the edict of Claudius and the persecution of Nero.[68]

In the analysis of κόσμος and κτίσις in Galatians and 2 Corinthians, Adams focuses on Paul's use of καινὴ κτίσις. While he recognizes the continuing debate as to the meaning of καινὴ κτίσις in the *Hauptbriefe*, whether it has an anthropological reference or a cosmological one, he basically agrees with Mell's argument that Paul uses this technical term in the context of Jewish apocalypticism referring to the new or transformed creation expected to follow the destruction or renewal of the world.[69] Similarly, contrary to Bultmann's anthropological understanding of Paul's use of κόσμος, Adams argues that Paul uses this term in a cosmological sense in accordance with the spatio-temporal dualism of Jewish apocalypticism.[70] Although Adams's understanding of καινὴ κτίσις in Paul is mainly cosmological, referring to the new eschatological world, he does not neglect its anthropological and ecclesiological meanings. Thus, he agrees with the argument that Paul's focus in Gal 6:14–16 is on the believing community. In this sense, he argues that "Paul is not saying that the community of Christ *is* the new creation, but he suggests that the church *belongs* to the new creation (they are *of* the new world, so to speak, though they are not yet *in* it)" (emphasis original).[71] In a similar fashion, Adams argues that although Paul uses καινὴ κτίσις in 2 Cor 5:17 with reference to the new or renewed created order, Paul's statement here embraces the individual and the community.[72]

Adams's study contributed significantly to our understanding of Paul's epistolary usages of κόσμος and κτίσις in relation to the original social-historical situations in the *Hauptbriefe*. The meaning of the phrase καινὴ κτίσις in Paul, however, plays a minor role in his research. Moreover,

---

67. Adams, *Constructing the World*, 239.
68. Adams, *Constructing the World*, 239–40.
69. Adams, *Constructing the World*, 226–27.
70. Adams, *Constructing the World*, 240–42.
71. Adams, *Constructing the World*, 227–28.
72. Adams, *Constructing the World*, 234–35.

although he concludes that Paul uses the term "new creation" in the context of Jewish apocalypticism, Adams mainly deals with the linguistic background of the terms κόσμος and κτίσις in Greek and Hellenistic philosophy without investigation of Paul's deep influence from Jewish apocalyptic literature. Regarding the Jewish apocalyptic background of καινὴ κτίσις in Paul, Adams seems to depend heavily on Mell's research.[73]

(3) *New Creation in Paul's Letters and Thought* (Moyer V. Hubbard 2004)

Hubbard's contribution to the understanding of the new creation in Paul is to remind us of the significance of its anthropological aspect. He criticizes Mell's conclusion that καινὴ κτίσις in Paul is a cosmological concept deeply influenced by Jewish apocalyptic tradition, since Mell derived this conclusion from his highly selective analysis of the Jewish Scriptures (i.e., the Isaianic oracles) and Second Temple Jewish literature. In other words, according to Hubbard, although there are other Old Testament texts and Second Temple Jewish writings which support the anthropological characteristics of the concept of new creation, Mell made his conclusion ignoring these anthropological new-creation texts. Hubbard's other criticism on Mell's methodology is that Mell concentrates on secondary sources (i.e., Old Testament texts and Second Temple Jewish writings), "leaving much of the primary source material (Paul's letters) untouched."[74]

Although Hubbard criticizes Mell's history-of-traditions approach, his own exegesis of Pauline texts also proceeds by the investigation of the Jewish Scriptures and Second Temple Jewish literature as the scriptural antecedents for Paul's new creation motif. Among Old Testament texts, however, Hubbard puts more emphasis on Jeremiah and Ezekiel, where the theme of the new covenant signifies an inward renewal of the heart in an anthropological sense, rather than the Isaianic oracles.

Criticizing Mell's methodology on Second Temple Jewish literature as "a superficial examination of isolated texts," Hubbard selects only two works of Second Temple Judaism and attempts to understand these works as a whole in order to compare Paul's new-creation motif with them. The two works of Second Temple Jewish literature are Jubilees and Joseph and Aseneth. Hubbard argues that Joseph and Aseneth provides a "far more fruitful comparison" to Paul's concept of new creation than does Jubilees.

---

73. Adams, *Constructing the World*, 226.
74. Hubbard, *New Creation*, 6–7.

He connects Joseph and Aseneth's use of cosmic imagery, which signifies transformation and new birth in conversion, to the Pauline motif of new creation. Joseph and Aseneth concerns, he argues, the problem of how a pagan can convert and be included in the people of God. Hubbard's understanding of the "plight" in Joseph and Aseneth is related to the depravity of the human heart; the "solution" is the proselyte's new creation (i.e., conversion) by the Spirit of God. He claims that on the other hand, although the concept of new creation in Jubilees and throughout Jewish apocalypses have both anthropological and cosmological aspects, the cosmological dimension receives more emphasis. Here the human "plight" is not an internal problem of the human mind but an external oppressive power, such as evil angelic beings and foreign countries.

As Hubbard's emphasis on "internal transformation" in his investigation of the Jewish Scriptures and Second Temple Jewish writings suggests, his reading of καινὴ κτίσις in 1 Cor 5:17 and Gal 6:15 is an anthropological one. After his exegesis of 2 Cor 5:14–17, he concludes that the καινὴ κτίσις in 2 Cor 5:17 is "an anthropological motif relating to the new situation of the individual 'in Christ'"[75] inaugurated by conversion or internal transformation. Here he highlights the antithesis between κατὰ σάρκα (v. 16) and καινὴ κτίσις (v. 17) and argues that it should be added to the long list of internal-external antitheses in 2 Cor 2–7 (e.g., 3:1–3, 6; 4:6–7, 7–12, 16, 18; 5:7, 12).[76] Similarly, in his exegesis of Gal 6:15, he focuses on the internal-external contrast between the outward state of circumcision or uncircumcision and the new creation as the inner transformation by the work of the Spirit.[77] Thus, he summarizes his exegesis of καινὴ κτίσις in 2 Cor 5:17 and Gal 6:15 with this sentence: "Paul's new creation expresses a reality *intra nos* not a reality *extra nos*, and functions as an alternative formulation of his central Spirit affirmation—the Spirit creates life."[78]

Although Hubbard's coherent interpretation of καινὴ κτίσις in Paul sheds light on an anthropological aspect of the concept of new creation, it raises serious methodological questions. First of all, although he criticizes Mell's history-of-traditions approach and argues that it is methodologically better first to engage with Paul's own texts and then to find its parallels in contemporary literature, he himself follows the conventional

---

75. Hubbard, *New Creation*, 187.
76. Hubbard, *New Creation*, 152, 185.
77. Hubbard, *New Creation*, 227.
78. Hubbard, *New Creation*, 232.

format which treats relevant secondary sources first. Moreover, Hubbard is not free from his criticism of Mell's "prejudicial selectivity," since his own criterion for the choice of source materials is questionable. How can he legitimize his preference of the theme of the transformation of the human mind in Jeremiah and Ezekiel over the more explicit theme of new creation in the Isaianic texts? Why does he select Joseph and Aseneth as the closest analogy to Paul's new creation, putting aside important Jewish apocalypses such as 1 Enoch and 2 Baruch? Why does he not deal with the important theme of new creation in Rom 8:19–22? The answers to those questions are probably related to his presupposition that Paul's concept of new creation is an anthropological one.

(4) *The Spirit and Creation in Paul* (John W. Yates 2008)

This monograph is important for the present study since Yates connects Paul's description of the Spirit as "life-giving" to the Spirit's role as the divine agent who brings about new creation. In other words, Yates not only points out that the Spirit's life-giving characteristic is important for Paul's concept of new creation but also rightly notes that new creation is closely related to transition from death to life or resurrection.[79]

Explaining the relationship between Gal 6:14 and Gal 6:15, Yates argues that the new creation in Gal 6:15 signifies three resurrections: those of Christ, the cosmos, and Paul.[80] For Yates, the phrase "new creation" is almost a synonym of resurrection and has christological, cosmological, and anthropological aspects: christologically, new creation is inaugurated by Christ's resurrection; cosmologically, new creation refers to the future renewal of all creation; anthropologically, new creation refers to believers' present and future resurrection. Also, pneumatologically, the spirit functions as the divine agent who brings about all three resurrections, namely new creation.

Before analyzing Paul's description of the life-giving work of the spirit, Yates looks for a possible background to this theme in Judaism,

---

79. Morales's *The Spirit and the Restoration of Israel* is another important work which focuses on the relationship between the theme of the Spirit and Paul's concept of new creation. Morales argues that the role of the Spirit in Galatians can be interpreted in terms of the new exodus and the new creation motifs. To demonstrate this, he notes that the outpouring of the Spirit is a sign of the eschatological restoration of Israel in the Old Testament and Second Temple writings. See Morales, *Spirit and the Restoration of Israel*, 13–75.

80. Yates, *Spirit and Creation in Paul*, 121.

particularly focusing on Gen 2:7 and Ezek 36–37. He argues that the tradition of the "breath of life" in Gen 2:7 was developed in a number of Jewish texts, most notably Ezek 36–37, in various ways. For example, while the Dead Sea Scrolls (e.g., 4Q504, 4Q385, 4Q521, 4Q272, 4Q418) associate the creative work of the spirit with the future renewal of creation, Joseph and Aseneth focuses on individual renewal by the spirit. Yates devotes special attention to the Hodayot where we can find the traditions from both Gen 2:7 and Ezek 36–37. He argues that the community described in the Hodayot experiences the beginning of a return to "all the glory of Adam" by means of an "inaugurated new creation" by the gift of the eschatological spirit of Ezek 36–37.[81]

Although there are no occurrences of the spirit in 2 Cor 5:17 and Gal 6:15, Yates argues that the life-giving work of the spirit is the background of Paul's statement about καινὴ κτίσις in both texts. According to Yates, in 2 Cor 5:17, given Paul's famous κατὰ σάρκα/κατὰ πνεῦμα antithesis and Paul's contrast between κατὰ σάρκα (v. 16) as the old and καινὴ κτίσις (v. 17) as the new, we can find some kind of identification between κατὰ πνεῦμα and καινὴ κτίσις. Moreover, since the death/life contrast of vv. 14–15 may echo the death/life contrast of 3:6 where the spirit is the giver of new life, Yates argues that Paul's emphasis in 2 Cor 5:17 is on a "new identity brought about by the creative work of the life-giving spirit."[82] Similarly, Yates argues that given the central role of the spirit in the logic of Paul's argument in Gal 5–6 and the three crucifixions (Christ, cosmos, and Paul) in v. 14, the life-giving work of the spirit is implicit in the phrase "new creation" in Gal 6:15.

The bulk of Yates's analysis of the Pauline passages is devoted to Rom 8. He describes the life, dramatically contrasted by death in Rom 8, as "the life of the new creation" inaugurated by the resurrection of Christ. Also, he rightly strikes a balance not only between current and future aspects of new creation but also between its anthropological and cosmological aspects by saying that this new creation is "experienced now in part through the indwelling of the life-giving spirit, and to be fully experienced in the final renewal of the cosmos brought about by the spirit himself at the resurrection of the dead."[83]

The Spirit and Creation in Paul contributes to our understanding of Paul's concept of new creation in the following aspects. First, Yates

81. Yates, *Spirit and Creation in Paul*, 82, 174.
82. Yates, *Spirit and Creation in Paul*, 119.
83. Yates, *Spirit and Creation in Paul*, 155.

rightly points out the connection between the life-giving work of the Spirit and Paul's concept of new creation. Second, Yates's argument that the new creation implies three resurrections provides a balanced understanding of Paul's concept of new creation in terms of Christology, cosmology, and anthropology. Third, he well demonstrates that the tradition of the "breath of life" in Gen 2:7 is the most important background for Paul's statements about the Spirit as giving life. This indicates that the creation narrative in Genesis can be another important background for Paul's concept of new creation.

(5) *New Creation in Paul's Letters* (T. Ryan Jackson 2010)

At first glance, Jackson's argument seems to be a balanced synthesis of anthropological (Hubbard) and cosmological (Mell and Adams) aspects of Paul's concept of new creation, as he maintains in his thesis statement: "The apostle Paul's conception of new creation will reveal that his idea is an expression of his eschatologically infused soteriology which involves the individual, the community and the cosmos and which is inaugurated in the death and resurrection of Christ."[84] However, his selection of the Isaianic texts and Jubilees as proper backgrounds for Paul's concept of new creation,[85] excluding other important materials (e.g., Jeremiah, Ezekiel, and parabiblical texts which contain the theme of new creation), shows that his position is closer to Mell's and Adams's cosmological reading of new creation than Hubbard's anthropological reading.

A new approach of Jackson's investigation of the theme of new creation in secondary sources is that he observes Roman imperial ideology as another important background of Paul's concept of new creation. Jackson argues that Roman imperial ideology was ubiquitous in the first century and had a cosmological flavor in terms of a renewal of creation. For example, he claims that Roman imperial ideology employed the term

---

84. Jackson, *New Creation*, 6.

85. Jackson justifies his selection of the Isaianic texts excluding Jeremiah and Ezekiel on the basis of its particular importance for Paul and its role as "the *Ursprung* for many streams of tradition which may have influenced Paul" (Jackson, *New Creation*, 17–18). However, his claim that Paul's conception of the new creation has both anthropological and cosmological dimensions would be strengthened by dealing with "new covenant" and "new spirit" in Jeremiah and Ezekiel. Likewise, his exclusive choice of Jubilees among many other Second Temple Jewish writings is questionable, although he argues for its special importance since it is "the only extant literature outside the Pauline corpus in which the phrase 'new creation' occurs twice" (Jackson, *New Creation*, 39).

εὐαγγέλιον in the context of an eschatological shift to a new age and a new world order. Thus, according to Jackson, Paul uses the concept of new creation in contrast with the propaganda of the imperial gospels. Although this sort of argument that Paul places the gospel of Christ in direction opposition to the Roman imperial ideology is a focus of recent scholarly interest, as seen above, it is still controversial and suffers from lack of evidence. Moreover, even if there is a parallel between the Roman imperial ideology and Paul's concept of new creation, this parallel seems to make little contribution to his central thesis.

In his analysis of the new creation in Gal 6:15, Jackson argues that it should be understood in a cosmological sense in light of Jewish apocalyptic literature and should not be restricted to the private experience of the individual.[86] At the same time, Jackson maintains, Paul makes an innovative modification of Jewish apocalyptic eschatology by moving the focal point of God's redemption of his people and the universe *from the future to the present* which has been inaugurated by the Christ-event. Also, he claims that this christological eschatology in the new creation in Gal 6:15 has cosmological, anthropological, and ecclesiological senses in a *mutually inclusive* way.[87] Similarly, Jackson finds Isaianic influence in the new creation in 2 Cor 5:17 and argues that Paul understands the new creation in Christ as a fulfillment of Isaianic prophecies where the salvation of people is intermingled with the restoration of the cosmos.[88]

Jackson's inclusion of Rom 8:18–25 in his analysis of the theme of new creation in Paul is appropriate. Although the phrase καινὴ κτίσις does not occur in Romans, Rom 1 and Rom 8 are the only two places where the term κτίσις appears in Paul's undisputed letters. Particularly, Rom 8:19–22 not only has four occurrences of κτίσις but also is one of the most important Pauline texts to reveal the relationship between humanity and creation in God's redemptive act. Thus, Rom 8:18–25 strengthens his argument that Paul's concept of new creation has both anthropological and cosmological aspects.

Jackson's main thesis that Paul's conception of new creation is eschatologically infused soteriology which has both anthropological and cosmological dimensions seems well-balanced and mostly correct. However, not only his unbalanced selection of the Old Testament texts and

---

86. Jackson, *New Creation*, 113.
87. Jackson, *New Creation*, 114.
88. Jackson, *New Creation*, 147–48.

Second Temple Jewish writings but also his unnecessary and brief survey of the Roman imperial ideology in relation to Paul's new creation theology seem insufficient for demonstrating his main thesis.

(6) *As It Was in the Beginning* (Mark D. Owens 2015)[89]

Owens's definition of new creation in the Pauline tradition is similar to Jackson's balanced definition:

> a pithy summary (resulting from an intertextual reading of Scripture) of the redemptive-historical significance of Christ's death and resurrection that encompasses the anthropological, cosmological, and ecclesiological scope of divine restoration within the conceptual framework of an *Urzeit-Endzeit* typology.[90]

His understanding of Paul's concept of new creation, however, is unique in that he highlights the framework of an "*Urzeit-Endzeit* typology" as the title of this monograph implies.[91] Also, this monograph's primary goal is "to explore the degree of continuity and discontinuity between the portraits of new creation in the *Hauptbriefe* and the letter to the Ephesians."[92] Thus, he includes Eph 1–2 in his exegesis for revealing the meaning of new creation in the Pauline tradition and concludes that there is a strong degree of continuity between the concept of new creation in the *Hauptbriefe* and Ephesians.[93]

In Owens's investigation of the background of the Pauline tradition's concept of new creation, he deals with various texts in Isaiah, Jeremiah, Ezekiel, 1 Enoch, and Jubilees, but he primarily focuses on the analysis of Isaiah (Isa 40:1–11, 43:16–21, 52:7–12, 57:14–21, 65:17–25, 66:18–24) because of the allusions to Isaianic tradition in 2 Cor 5:17b and Eph 2:13, 17. Also, during this investigation, he recognizes the presence of an *Urzeit-Endzeit* typological scheme (e.g., Isa 65–66; Ezek 47:1–12; 1 En. 25:3–6; 90:37–38; Jub. 1:29; 23:22–32).

---

89. Owens, *As It Was*.

90. Owens, *As It Was*, 176.

91. In addition to that, Owens argues that he develops Jackson's account of new creation in Paul's letters by: (1) highlighting the importance of new creation's ecclesiological aspects; (2) clarifying how Paul's concept of new creation is derived from an "intertextual reading of Scripture"; and (3) connecting the temple imagery in 2 Cor 6:16 to Paul's concept of new creation (Owens, *As It Was*, 178n12).

92. Owens, *As It Was*, 171.

93. Owens, *As It Was*, 177.

Examining the new creation in Galatians and 2 Corinthians, Owens argues that Paul understands new creation in cosmological, anthropological, and ecclesiological terms in contrast to Hubbard, Mell, and Kraus's dichotomous understanding of Paul's concept of new creation, although Gal 6:15 and 2 Cor 5:17 emphasize different aspects of new creation.[94] In particular, Owens makes a strong case for linking 2 Cor 5:14–17 with an *Urzeit-Endzeit* typology by appeal to the implied Adam Christology in vv. 14–15 and by adding 2 Cor 6:1–18 to a broad reading of καινὴ κτίσις, where the "temple of the living God" in v. 16 provides additional proof for an *Urzeit-Endzeit* typology.[95]

As It Was in the Beginning contributes to our understanding of Paul's concept of new creation by expanding the discussion to the Pauline tradition in Ephesians in recognition of the presence of an *Urzeit-Endzeit* typology in Paul's concept of new creation. Owens's understanding of new creation seems to refer to the "restoration" to an original, pristine state in God's first creation in Genesis. Paul's description of the eschatological new creation in Rom 8 and 1 Cor 15, however, seems to have other dimensions distinct from the original creation in terms of immortality and glory (Rom 8:18–23; 1 Cor 15:40–54; cf. Gal 3:28). Additionally, although Owens notes the significance of the *Urzeit-Endzeit* framework in Paul's conception of new creation, he does not deal with other relevant texts in relation to the relationship between the new creation motif and the *Urzeit-Endzeit* typology not only in Second Temple Jewish literature (e.g., 4 Ezra 14:32–35; 2 Bar. 51:1–3; 54:15, 21) but also in Paul's texts themselves (e.g., 1 Cor 15:40–54; Rom 8:18–23).

(7) Conclusions from the literature review and a new proposal

As we have seen above, many scholars have contributed to our understanding of Paul's concept of new creation. Their discussions, however, still leave unresolved questions. Firstly, the discussions have stayed around the debate concerning whether καινὴ κτίσις is mainly cosmological or anthropological rather than focusing on its meaning itself. In other words, all the focus has been on the *referent* of this phrase (what it refers to: the world,

---

94. Owens argues that while Paul highlights the cosmological aspect of new creation in Gal 6:14–16, in 2 Cor 5:14–17, anthropology receives the greatest emphasis (Owens, *As It Was*, 120). For Kraus's ecclesiological understanding of new creation, see n54 in this chapter.

95. Owens, *As It Was*, 95–97, 117–18.

the individual, or the church?) but there has been little discussion of its *meaning*: in what sense "new" and in what sense "creation"?

Secondly, methodologically we can find a general tendency that scholars' presuppositions influence their selections of secondary literature in the Old Testament texts and Second Temple Jewish writings. For example, while scholars who prefer an anthropological reading of καινὴ κτίσις usually select the Ezekiel tradition (particularly, Ezek 36–37) or the Jeremianic tradition (particularly, the Book of Consolation) as background texts for Paul's concept of new creation, the cosmological reading of new creation favors the Isaianic tradition as it continues in Jewish apocalyptic literature. This tendency raises many questions regarding its legitimacy.

Thirdly, in relation to the second point, it is striking that there have been only few studies which deal with the creation story and the Adamic narrative in Genesis (Gen 1–3) as a background for Paul's concept of new creation. As Yates's study shows, the Adamic narrative had a deep influence on the theme of new creation in Ezek 36–37. Moreover, we can find many allusions to the Adamic narrative not only in the Isaianic tradition but also in Paul's own texts in relation to the new creation motif (e.g., 1 Cor 15; Rom 8; 2 Cor 3).

For these reasons, in "Part I" of the present study, where I investigate the traces of the concept of new creation in Second Temple Jewish literature, I will focus on the creation narrative and the Adamic tradition in early Judaism in relation to the theme of new creation. In other words, moving away from fixation on the rare occurrences of the exact phrase (which is why most scholars hastily rush to Isaiah), I will ask more deeply about what is meant and how this relates to creation itself by returning to Genesis and the creation of the cosmos and of humanity within it. Since the narrative in Gen 1–3 influenced both the Ezekiel/Jeremianic tradition and the Isaianic tradition, this approach will be a good alternative to avoid the false dichotomy between the anthropological and the cosmological readings of new creation. Moreover, as we shall see later, since the influence of the Adamic narrative also appears in the Pauline adoption passages (i.e., Rom 8 and Gal 4), this approach is effective in order to reveal the close relationship between the concept of new creation and υἱοθεσία.

At the same time, I will attempt to discover the meaning of new creation itself rather than just to determine whether this motif is cosmological or anthropological. This means that I will try to understand the meaning of new creation in Second Temple Jewish writings in comparison with the creation story in Genesis. In particular, I will try to determine the meaning of "new." Does it refer to the "restoration" of the original created order or "replacement" of it? What is the meaning of "new" in terms of continuity and discontinuity with the creation story in Genesis? These will be important research questions for my investigation of the concept of the new creation in Second Temple Jewish literature.

4. Conversation with the "Paul within Judaism" *Schule*

As seen above, there has been a great deal of research on Paul's use of υἱοθεσία and the new creation motif, but no study has paid attention to the close relationship between them. What, then, does this relationship mean for the overall shape of Pauline theology and the current state of Pauline studies? One important possibility is to set the present study in conversation with recent studies of "ethnicity in Paul" (e.g., Caroline Johnson Hodge's *If Sons then Heirs*,[96] Matt Thiessen's *Paul and the Gentile Problem*,[97] Paula Fredriksen's *Paul: The Pagans' Apostles*,[98] etc.) since they often appeal to the Abrahamic sonship or the divine sonship in Romans and Galatians, but the sense of new creation—in terms of discontinuity, incongruity, and divine intervention—is completely missed in their arguments as we shall see later (chapter 6, section 2; chapter 7, section 4).

Discussions of "ethnicity in Paul" have been primarily conducted by scholars belonging to the "Paul within Judaism" *Schule* as they call themselves.[99] Magnus Zetterholm presents the two most fundamental assumptions underlying the "Paul within Judaism" school: (1) Paul's continuing Jewish identity; (2) Paul's focus on non-Jews.[100] Regarding the first assumption, the emphasis on Paul's Jewish identity leads to their emphasis on law observance and Jewish ethnicity. The second assumption concerns an issue of Paul's audience in his letters. Very intriguingly, these two assumptions are closely related to their interpretation of Paul's

---

96. Hodge, *If Sons, Then Heirs*.
97. Thiessen, *Paul and the Gentile Problem*.
98. Fredriksen, *Paul*.
99. For a basic explanation of this group, see Nanos, "Introduction." This group is also called the "Radical New Perspective on Paul," the term coined by Zetterholm. He also uses a similar expression "beyond the New Perspective." See Zetterholm, *Approaches to Paul*, 161.
100. Zetterholm, "Paul within Judaism," 176.

adoption metaphor. As we shall see later (chapter 7, section 4), some of the Paul within Judaism *Schule* maintain that υἱοθεσία was a means for gentile believers to acquire Jewish ethnicity. Moreover, concerning the issue of audience, most of the Paul within Judaism scholars claim that υἱοθεσία Gal 4 and Rom 8 is *only* for gentile believers since Israelites already have the privilege of υἱοθεσία (cf. Rom 9:4).[101]

In this context, some of the "Paul within Judaism" school go one step further and maintain that according to Paul, Israel does not need redemption in Christ. For example, John Gager claims that "Paul never speaks of Israel's ultimate redemption as a conversion to Christ. In line with this, an increasing number of readers have spoken of two ways or paths to salvation—through Christ for gentiles, through the law for Israel."[102] This is the so-called *Sonderweg* interpretation or the "two-covenant" model of salvation.[103]

The close connection between Paul's use of υἱοθεσία and the new creation motif, however, raises questions about the "Paul within Judaism" school's interpretation of υἱοθεσία. Is υἱοθεσία really a means for gentile believers to acquire Jewish ethnicity as sons of Abraham in a literal sense as well as sons of God? Is Paul's adoption metaphor really *only* for gentile believers? Further, are there two different paths to salvation for Jews and gentiles respectively? What, then, is the relationship between Paul's adoption metaphor and redemption in Christ? In the present study, I will attempt to answer all these questions through my exegesis of Paul's use of υἱοθεσία in light of the new creation motif.

5. Conclusions and overview of chapters

In the above discussion, I have highlighted the close relationship between Paul's adoption metaphor and the concept of new creation, and through the literature review on both themes, I have shown that there has been little research on the important relationship between the two themes.

---

101. E.g., Fredriksen, Gaston, Stowers, Thiessen, Nanos, et al. See n5 in ch. 6.

102. Gager, *Reinventing Paul*, 59. Gaston and Stowers also support this "two-way solution." See Gaston, *Paul and the Torah*, 23; Stowers, *Rereading of Romans*, 237.

103. The *Sonderweg* interpretation means that Israel has a *special* path to salvation apart from Christ. Most recently, Boccaccini claims that in Paul's soteriology, there are in fact *three* paths to salvation: for Jews, adherence to Torah; for gentiles, good works according to conscience and natural law; for all sinners, forgiveness through faith in Jesus Christ. But it seems a variant of the *Sonderweg* approach. See Boccaccini, *Paul's Three Paths*.

Paul's use of υἱοθεσία, however, can best be explained in terms of both the form and the content of the concept of new creation. Also, I have pointed out that significant implications of this study can be explored in conversation with the Paul within Judaism *Schule*.

Thus, we can summarize the questions to be answered through this study as follows: (1) What is the meaning of the concept of new creation in Second Temple Jewish texts, and how does it relate to Paul's concept of new creation? (2) How does the concept of new creation influence the interpretation of Paul's adoption metaphor? (3) When we interpret Paul's adoption metaphor in light of the new creation motif, how can we respond to the main arguments of the Paul within Judaism *Schule* regarding the issues of Jewish ethnicity and Paul's audience?

In order to find answers to these questions, I divide this study into two parts: the first part (chapters 2–4) examines the meaning of the concept of new creation in early Jewish literature (including 2 Cor 5:17 and Gal 6:15); in the second part (chapters 5–7), I will interpret Paul's adoption metaphor in light of the new creation motif.

In the first part, I will pay attention to two main points in particular. First, I will focus on how the Genesis narrative (or Adam motif) affects the concept of new creation in Second Temple literature and in Paul. Second, while previous studies have focused too narrowly on the Old Testament and Second Temple Jewish texts that use the precise phrase "new creation," I will look at the larger frame, and how the *Endzeit* as new creation might relate to the *Urzeit* of creation. With these points in mind, we will investigate the meaning of the new creation concept in parabiblical texts including Jewish apocalyptic literature (chapter 2), and then we will look at the new creation concept in Qumran literature (chapter 3). In chapter 4, we will clarify the meaning of καινὴ κτίσις in 2 Cor 5:17 and Gal 6:15, by comparing it with the concept of new creation in Second Temple literature and summarizing the continuities and discontinuities between them.

In the second part, I will analyze Paul's use of υἱοθεσία in light of the concept of new creation. This work proceeds through an exegesis of Paul's adoption passages, and with the results of this exegesis, I will engage in dialogue with the "Paul within Judaism" *Schule*. In the exegesis of Rom 8, I will interpret Paul's adoption metaphors in 8:15 and 8:23 in the context of new creation based on their allusions to Gen 2:7 (via allusions to Ezek 36–37) and Gen 3:16–19 respectively (chapter 5). In the exegesis of the adoption metaphor in Rom 9:4, I will demonstrate that Paul not only uses υἱοθεσία as a keyword to open the overall argument of Rom 9–11, but also uses it to emphasize the incongruity of grace in God's election and calling (chapter 6). In other words, the υἱοθεσία in Rom 9:4 does not refer to a permanent possession of Israel, as the Paul within Judaism scholars assert, but it is a gift from God and will be fulfilled through the redemption in Christ in the context of the new creation. Finally, in chapter 7, through the exegesis of Gal 4:1–7, I will substantiate that υἱοθεσία in Gal 4:5 has a close connection with καινὴ κτίσις in Gal 6:15 in terms of a new identity in Christ regardless of ethnicity, social status, and gender (cf. Gal 3:28). Also, I will demonstrate that the allusion to Gen 1:27 in Gal 3:28 and the Adamic narrative frame in Gal 4:1–7 support the new creation context of υἱοθεσία in Gal 4:5.

Part I: **The Concept of New Creation**

Chapter 2: The Concept of New Creation in the Parabiblical Texts

1. Introduction

ALTHOUGH THE ACTUAL OCCURRENCES of the phrase "new creation" are rare in the Old Testament pseudepigrapha (1 En. 72:1; Jub. 1:29; 4:26; 5:12; 2 Bar. 44:12), the conception of new creation is very important since it is a crucial concept to express the eschatological hope of the Second Temple period which characterizes Jewish apocalyptic literature. Many scholars have recognized that this theme has a connection with the theme of a "new heaven and new earth" in Isa 65–66. Most of them, however, have failed to realize that at a deeper level, the theme of new creation is rooted in the narrative of Gen 1–3. As seen above, in particular, Pauline scholars (Ulrich Mell, Moyer Hubbard, Ryan Jackson) who study Paul's concept of new creation (Gal 6:15; 2 Cor 5:17), have traced its origin from Isa 65–66, Ezek 36–37, and Jer 31, but not from Gen 1–3.

In this chapter, I will demonstrate two important points in relation to the concept of new creation in the parabiblical texts: First, it is inseparable from the creation account (and the Adamic narrative) in Gen 1–3 and refers to the eschatological renewal of the whole cosmos within an *Urzeit-Endzeit* framework; second, the language of divine sonship often appears together with the theme of new creation in the parabiblical texts. To achieve this goal, I have selected six parabiblical texts: Jubilees, 1 Enoch, the Apocalypse of Moses, Liber Antiquitatum Biblicarum, 4 Ezra, and 2 Baruch. These texts are particularly important for the present study since they not only have the theme of new creation but also describe the account of God's creation and Adam in Gen 1–3 in the context of new creation.¹ Before turning to the texts, I will define what the *Urzeit-Endziet* correlation is, since it provides a crucial framework for understanding the concept of new creation in the parabiblical texts.

2. The *Urzeit-Endzeit* correlation

In his landmark book *Schöpfung und Chaos in Urzeit und Endzeit*, Hermann Gunkel quotes the Epistle of Barnabas 6:13, Ἰδού ποιῶ τὰ ἔσχατα ὡς τὰ πρῶτα ("Behold, I make the last things like the first"), to show how the Babylonian *Chaoskampf* myth shaped both the protological narrative in Gen 1 and the eschatological narrative in Rev 12.² Thus, the *Urzeit-Endzeit* correlation refers to the framework that "in der Endzeit wird sich wiederholen, was in der Urzeit gewesen ist."³ Gunkel also depicts this framework with another expression: "der neuen Schopfung wird ein neues Chaos vorhergehen."⁴

The *Urzeit-Endzeit* correlation does not always refer to the framework that *Urzeit* is identical to *Endzeit* in the Jewish literature. As Brevard Childs rightly points out, "In deutero- and trito-Isaiah, the eschatological aspects entail not only the renewal of the primordial aspects but also 'new things' which were hidden and unknown before."⁵ Similarly, Nils Dahl's study on the correlation between the first and the last things shows that it does not simply relate to a repetition of the first things, but also relates to (1) "a restitution of creation, which has been laid under a curse"; (2) "a transformation of the first one" stressing "the superiority of the new creation"; (3) "a reservation of some of the first things for the end of the

---

1. For this reason, I exclude Joseph and Aseneth from our investigation of the concept of new creation in parabiblical texts. Joseph and Aseneth does not allude to the Adamic narrative in Gen 2–3 although it has a few allusions to the creation account (Jos. Asen. 8:9; 12:1–2). Its distinctive characteristics in genre and provenance (a Hellenistic romance written in the Egyptian diaspora) are another reason for the exclusion. However, even in Joseph and Aseneth, we can find a close relationship between the concept of new creation and the theme of divine sonship. The concept of new creation in Joseph and Aseneth concerns Aseneth's conversion (8:9; 15:5), and after her conversion, Aseneth receives the designation "daughter of the Most High" as a bride of Joseph the "firstborn son of God" (21:4–5). This probably indicates gentiles' inclusion in the covenant people of Israel in the context of new creation.

2. Gunkel, *Schöpfung und Chaos*, 369.

3. Gunkel, *Schöpfung und Chaos*, 370.

4. Gunkel, *Schöpfung und Chaos*, 370.

5. Childs, *Myth and Reality*, 77–80.

world"; (4) "the final establishment and perfection of the first one" with "the elimination of the powers of darkness."[6]

In sum, the *Urzeit-Endzeit* eschatology refers to the conception that the eschaton should restore the goodness of the beginning in the context of an apocalyptic hope of new creation. It is not merely a repetition of the beginning but rather a new transformation of creation or a perfection of the first creation. This eschatological hope for new creation appears with various types of *Urzeit-Endzeit* framework in Second Temple literature, such as flood imagery in the context of eschatological hope (e.g., 1 En. 10:16–11:2; 1 En. 93:4), restoration of Eden and the eschatological temple (e.g., Jub. 4:26; 1 En. 24:2–4), restoration of the glory of Adam (e.g., 1QS 4:20–23; 1QH^a 4:26f), and transformation of humankind or of the cosmos (1 En. 90:37–38; 2 Bar. 73:1–74:1).

3. The concept of new creation in the book of Jubilees

Together with 1 Enoch, Jubilees is one of the most significant parabiblical texts written in the Second Temple period. It is a particularly important text for the present study since it is the only ancient Jewish text where the phrase "new creation" occurs three times (Jub. 1:29; 4:26; 5:12).[7] Along with Jub. 1:29 and Jub. 4:26, Jub. 19:15–30 and Jub. 23:22–31 are also crucial texts for the present study because of the use of the theme of divine sonship in the context of new creation (Jub. 19:15–30) and its eschatological importance within the *Urzeit-Endzeit* framework (Jub. 23:22–31), although they do not use the term "new creation." In what follows, we will investigate the concept of new creation in each text and demonstrate that (1) it occurs in the framework of the *Urzeit-Endzeit* correlation; (2) it particularly relates to the establishment of the

---

6. Dahl, "Christ, Creation, and the Church," 425–30.

7. Hubbard and Jackson mention that in Jubilees, the phrase "new creation" appears twice (1:29; 4:26), but we should include 5:12 since it uses the same term ፍጥረት፡ ሐዳስ (Hubbard, *New Creation*, 36; Jackson, *New Creation*, 39). Their omission of 5:12, however, seems to be due to the fact that most scholars translate ፍጥረት፡ ሐዳስ in 5:12 as "new creature" or "new nature" rather than "new creation." In Jub. 5:12, the new creation refers to God's action to make all his works anew and righteous creation so that they might not sin forever. Thus, although most scholars translate ፍጥረት፡ ሐዳስ in Jub. 5:12 as "new nature" (Charles, VanderKam, Wintermute), this phrase fits well with the eschatological concept of new creation in the context of final judgment in connection with "the purification of sins" of all creation. I will deal with this theme in my exegesis of Jub. 4:26 below.

eschatological Temple on Mount Zion; (3) it has a close connection to the divine sonship of God's people.

(1) Jub. 1:29

The first chapter of Jubilees plays a role as a significant introduction to the whole book, and particularly its final verse announces an impending new creation which involves not only a renewal of the whole cosmos but also the establishment of the eschatological Temple:

> The Angel of the Presence, who was going along in front of the Israelite camp, took the tablets (that told) of the divisions of the years from the time that the law and the testimony were created—for the weeks of their jubilees, year by year in their full number, and their jubilees from [the time of the first creation until] the time of the new creation (ፍጥረት፡ ሐዳስ) when the heavens, the earth, and all their creatures will be renewed like the powers of the sky and like all the creatures of the earth, until the time when the temple of the Lord will be created in Jerusalem on Mount Zion. All the luminaries will be renewed for (the purpose of) healing, health, and blessing for all the elect ones of Israel and so that it may remain this way from that time throughout all the days of the earth. (Jub. 1:29)[8]

Here, we can find a clear *Urzeit-Endzeit* eschatology apparent in the phrase "from [the time of the first creation until] the time of the new creation."[9] This *Urzeit-Endzeit* correlation already appeared three times

---

8. This text is from VanderKam's translation (VanderKam, *Jubilees*, 132). Parentheses "()" in the text means that "words or letters within parentheses are supplied for the sake of the English translation." Brackets "[]" means that "something appears to be missing from the text." See VanderKam, *Commentary on the Book of Jubilees*, xxx. In this chapter, I will use VanderKam's translation when I quote a text from Jubilees.

9. The restoration of the text in brackets was first suggested by Michael Stone who argued that the omission was caused by haplography (Stone, "Apocryphal Notes," 125–26). 4Q217 (4QpapJub^b?) and 4Q225 (4QpsJub^a) provide very interesting parallels to this phrase. In 4Q217 II:1–3, l. 1 seems to have not only the Hebrew title of Jubilees ("the divisions of the times": מחלקות העתים) but also the combination of the law and the testimony ("for the law and for [the testimony . . .]": [. . . לתורה ול]תעודה) which also appears in Jub. 1:29. Then ll. 2–3 reads "for all the y[ears of] eternity, from the crea[tion . . .] ([. . . הברי]אה מן) and all[that is] created until the day" (וכל [הנ]ברא עד היום). Similarly, 4Q225 I:7 has the phrase "the creation until the [new] creation" ([. . . הבריאה עד יום הבריאה [החדשה) which is very similar to the expression "from [the time of the first creation until] the time of the new creation" in Jub. 1:29. These two parallels support Stone's suggestion. For further discussion, refer to the textual notes in VanderKam, *Jubilees*, 136, and Attridge et al., *Qumran Cave*, 27, 143.

in this chapter: (1) "what (had happened) beforehand as well as what was to come" (1:4); (2) "what is first and what is last and what is to come during all the divisions of the times that are for the law and for the testimony and for the weeks of their jubilees until eternity—until the time when I descend and live with them throughout all the ages of eternity" (1:26); (3) (starting) from the beginning of the creation until the time when "my temple is built among them throughout the ages of eternity" (1:27). Thus, it is clear that the author of Jubilees uses the concept of new creation in Jub. 1:29, where God will renew all creation, in connection with God's first creation in Gen 1–2.

We should note that here the time of new creation parallels "the time when the temple of the Lord will be created in Jerusalem on Mount Zion." This parallelism is also found in the preceding verse where "the time when my temple is built among them [Israel]" correlates with the beginning of the creation (Jub. 1:27). This implies that the garden of Eden parallels Mount Zion within the protology-eschatology correlation, as we shall see in my analysis of Jub. 4:26. As many scholars point out, the themes of the cosmic renewal and the building of a new temple in Jerusalem in this text allude to the theme of new heavens and a new earth as well as the creation of the new Jerusalem in Isa 65–66.[10] The *Urzeit-Endzeit* correlation, however, leads us to recognize that this text also relates to God's creation narrative in Gen 1–2 at a deeper level, where God created all the luminaries, the earth, and all the creatures in the earth and planted the garden of Eden and placed Adam in it.

Another important point regarding the concept of new creation in this text is that we can find a close relationship between the theme of Israel's divine sonship and the concept of new creation in Jub. 1:28:

> The Lord will appear in the sight of all, and all will know that *I am the God of Israel, the Father of all Jacob's children*, and King on Mount Zion for the ages of eternity. Then Zion and Jerusalem will be holy (emphasis added).

In the time of new creation when God rebuilds his temple in Jerusalem on Mount Zion, God will also proclaim that He is the God of Israel and the Father of all Jacob's children. This reestablishment of the Israelite divine sonship indicates that Israel's divine sonship was at stake because they not only abandoned God's commandments but also served

---

10. E.g., VanderKam, *Jubilees*, 263; Van Ruiten, "Visions of the Temple," 222–23; Jackson, *New Creation*, 47.

the nations' gods (Jub. 1:7–14). God, however, will establish an eternal father-son relationship between God and Israel by creating a holy spirit for them and purifying them. Jub. 1:23–25 depicts this renewal of Israel's divine sonship:

> [23] ... I will cut away the foreskins of their minds and the foreskins of their descendants' minds. I will *create a holy spirit for them* and will purify them in order that they may not turn away from me from that time forever. [24] Their souls will adhere to me and to all my commandments. They will perform my commandments. *I will be their Father and they will be my children.* [25] All of them will be called *children of the living god.* Every angel and every spirit will know them. They will know that they are *my children* and that I am their *Father* in a just and proper way and that I love them. (Jub. 1:23–25, emphasis added)

We should note that as in Jub. 1:28, the Israelite divine sonship is characterized by proclamation. God will publicly proclaim Israel's divine sonship in front of every angel and every spirit. It is not *acquired* by any human conditions but *created* by God's calling and election. God will also *create a holy spirit* for his people in order to secure the eternal relationship between God and them. Not all Israel will be blessed, but *all the elect ones* of Israel will be blessed in the time of new creation (Jub. 1:29).

In sum, in Jub. 1:27–29, the author of Jubilees uses the concept of new creation in the framework of the *Urzeit-Endzeit* correlation. Also, new creation relates to God's rebuilding of the temple in Jerusalem on Mount Zion and God's proclamation of Israel's divine sonship. The second mention of "new creation" in Jub. 4:26 has many affinities with the new creation in Jub. 1:29, as we shall below.

(2) Jub. 4:26

Jubilees 4:16–26, which deals with Enoch's birth and life, is one of the most interesting sections in Jubilees, since we can compare Enoch's character and life as depicted here with that of 1 Enoch as well as that of Gen 5:18–24.[11] In vv. 23–24, the author of Jubilees reinterprets "God's

---

11. The description of Enoch as a scribe in vv. 17–18 also appears in 1 Enoch (12:3–4; 13:4, 6; 15:1; 74:2; 82:1, 6; 83:1; 92:1; 104:12–13). In addition, many scholars argue that Enoch's night vision in v. 19, where Enoch saw in a vision regarding the day of judgment while he was sleeping, refers to the Book of Dreams (1 En. 83–90; Charles, Milik, Grelot) or the first part of the Epistle of Enoch (1 En. 91–107: VanderKam).

transposing Enoch" in Gen 5:24 as "the angels (the angels of presence) leading Enoch into the garden of Eden" (cf. 1 En. 12:1; 70:1–3). In spite of the fact that in Gen 7:21–23 the flood killed every living thing outside the ark, in Jub. 4:24 God did not bring the floodwaters into the garden of Eden because of his regard for Enoch. Enoch, then, offers "the evening incense of the sanctuary" in the garden of Eden. Just as Adam serves as a priestly figure when he was leaving the garden of Eden in Jub. 3:27 (see below), here Enoch plays the same role. In this context, the phrase "new creation" appears again:

> For there are four places on earth that belong to the Lord: the garden of Eden, the mountain of the east, this mountain on which you are today—Mount Sinai—and Mount Zion (which) will be sanctified in the new creation (በፍጥረት፡ ሐዳስ) for the sanctification of the earth. For this reason the earth will be sanctified from all its sins and from its uncleanness into the history of eternity. (Jub. 4:26)

Just as in Jub. 1:29 the time of new creation refers to the time when the cosmic renewal of the whole universe and the building of the eschatological temple on Mount Zion occur, so here the new creation refers not only to the eschatological sanctification of Mount Zion but also to that of the earth. We, again, find the connection between the theme of new creation and *the Urzeit-Endzeit* correlation since the context relates the garden of Eden to the eschatological sanctuary on Mount Zion.

Also, we should note that the concept of new creation in Jub. 4:26 is closely related to the sanctification or purification from sins and uncleanness. Since this purification from sins is related to not only the sanctuaries but also the whole earth, we can find the origin of sins and uncleanness mentioned here from the story of the "watchers," where their sins result in the corruption of everything on the earth from people to all animals (Jub. 5:2).

However, we should note that in a deeper level, the creation had been already influenced by Adam's disobedience to God's commandment in the garden of Eden (Jub. 3:17–25). God cursed not only the serpent (Jub. 3:23) but also the ground on account of Adam (Jub. 3:25). Just after his expulsion from the garden of Eden, Adam burned incense as a pleasing fragrance as a priestly figure: "On that day, as he was leaving

---

Moreover, along with Jub. 5:1–2, the story of the Watchers in v. 22 provides a very interesting parallel with 1 En. 6–11.

the garden of Eden, he burned incense as a pleasing fragrance—frankincense, galbanum, stacte, and aromatic spices—in the early morning when the sun rose at the time when he covered his shame" (Jub. 3:27). This verse is reminiscent of Exod 30:7–8,[12] which states an instruction for a priest (i.e., Aaron) in front of the mercy seat: "Aaron shall offer fragrant incense on it; every morning when he dresses the lamps he shall offer it." Also, the fact that the author connects this behavior to the time "when he covered his shame" suggests that the purpose of this sacrificial act relates to an atonement for Adam's transgression in the garden of Eden.[13] Moreover, on that day all animals became incapable of speaking and were also dismissed from the garden of Eden and were dispersed into the places that had been created for them (Jub. 4:28–29). This means that Adam's transgression in the garden of Eden was a sin which needs an act of atonement, and that all creation was influenced by Adam's sin. Finally, a few verses later from Jub. 4:26, the author of Jubilees describes the death of Adam in connection with his disobedience in the garden of Eden:

> [29] At the end of the nineteenth jubilee, during the seventh week—in this sixth year [930]—Adam died. All his children buried him in the land where he had been created. He was the first to be buried in the ground. [30] He lacked 70 years from 1000 years because 1000 years are one day in the testimony of heaven. For this reason it was written regarding the tree of knowledge: "On the day that you eat from it you will die." Therefore he did not complete the years of this day because he died during it. (Jub. 4:29–30)

Thus, we can reasonably conclude that sins and uncleanness of the creation in Jub. 4:26 can be traced to the Adamic sin and its influence on all creation in Gen 3. As VanderKam points out, the Adam expansion in the above text appears at a natural point in the sequence of Jubilees 4 since the explanation of Noah's name in v. 28 uses several terms which are reminiscent of God's judgment over Adam in Gen 3:17–19: grief, labor, and cursing the earth.[14] Thus, it is probable that the author uses

---

12. The fact that the three names of fragrant incense in Jub. 3:27 except the last one (aromatic spices, *sanbalta*) also appear in Exod 30:34 strengthens the connection between this verse and Exod 30 (cf. Num 16:39–40). See VanderKam, *Jubilees*, 228.

13. Adam's covering his shame also indicates Adam's priesthood. According to the law of sacrifice, the priest must cover their nakedness during their service (Exod 20:26; 28:42).

14. VanderKam, *Jubilees*, 264.

the theme of purification of sins in the time of new creation in connection with the Adamic sin in Gen 3.

In sum, as with Jub. 1:29, the concept of new creation in Jub. 4:26 refers not only to the eschatological sanctification of Mount Zion but also to the cosmic sanctification of the earth. This sanctification includes purification from the Adamic sin in the context of the *Urzeit-Endzeit* correlation.

(3) Jub. 19:15–30; Jub. 23:22–31

Although the term "new creation" does not occur in them, Jub. 19:15–30 and Jub. 23:22–31 are important texts for our discussion since both texts not only have the motif of new creation but also provide important clues to reveal the meaning of the new creation within the *Urzeit-Endzeit* correlation.

In Jub. 19:16–25, Abraham tells Rebekah that Jacob will be blessed forever as Abraham's special heir. Abraham's blessing for Jacob clearly uses creation language after his mention of Adam in the list of his fathers:

> [23] May all the blessings with which the Lord blessed me and my descendants belong to Jacob and his descendants for all time. [24] Through his descendants my name and the name of my ancestors Shem, Noah, Enoch, Malaleel, Enosh, Seth, and Adam be blessed. [25] May they serve (the purpose of) laying heaven's foundations, making the earth firm, and renewing all the luminaries which are above the firmament. (Jub. 19:23–25)

Here Abraham speaks of Jacob's descendants hoping that Abraham's ancestors, who can be traced back to Adam, may be blessed by Jacob's descendants and that they may serve to lay the foundations of heaven, to strengthen the earth, and to renew all the luminaries above the firmament. As VanderKam argues, this eschatological renewal of heaven, the earth, and all the luminaries above the firmament points to the new creation.[15] This text is particularly significant for our understanding of new creation in that here Jacob's descendants participate in God's new creation as the agency through which the order of creation is set right.

---

15. VanderKam argues that the description of Jacob's progeny, who will be involved in the eschatological renewal of heaven, the earth, and all the luminaries, clearly utilizes creation language. According to him, it is not surprising that this depiction appears just after a reference to Adam. He links this creation language with the new creation in Jub. 1:29 and 4:26 (VanderKam, *Jubilees*, 599–600).

After Abraham speaks to Rebecca about Jacob's descendants, he calls Jacob in the sight of Rebecca and blesses him:

> [27] My dear son Jacob whom I myself love, may God bless you from above the firmament. May he give you all the blessings with which he blessed Adam, Enoch, Noah, and Shem. Everything that he said to me and everything that he promised to give me may he attach to you and your descendants until eternity—like the days of heaven above the earth. [28] May the spirits of Mastema not rule over you and your descendants to remove you from following the Lord who is your God from now and forever. [29] May the Lord God be your Father and you his firstborn son and people for all the time. Go in peace my son. (Jub. 19:27–29)

God's blessing of Adam mentioned here by Abraham, probably refers to Gen 1:27–28, where God creates the first pair as the image of God to procreate and to rule over all creation. Thus, we can regard Abraham's blessing of Jacob as an extension of the original Adamic blessing; progeny and lordship. Moreover, as with Jub. 1:28–29, we can recognize the close connection between the motif of new creation and the language of the divine sonship. Just as Abraham mentions the eschatological blessing of the new creation after the reference to Adam in Jub. 19:23–25, so Abraham gives the blessing of the eternal sonship of God for Jacob after referring to Adam in Jub. 19:27–29: the acquisition of the eternal sonship of God parallels the eschatological blessing of new creation.

Finally, Jub. 23:22–31, which with Jub. 1:22–29 is perhaps the most eschatological text in Jubilees, expresses the hope for new creation by focusing on the restoration of human longevity. In preceding verses, the author contrasts "the days of the ancients" with "this evil generation" to point out that the pervasive sins in the land cause the shortening of lifespan (vv. 14–15). As seen above, humanity's original lifespan, as long as 1000 years, began to shorten due to the fall of Adam (Jub. 4:29–30). In vv. 28–29, the author of Jubilees depicts the hope for new creation with the theme of the restoration of human longevity:

> [28] There will be no old man, nor anyone who has lived out (his) lifetime, because all of them will be infants and children. [29] They will complete and live their entire lifetimes peacefully and joyfully. Here will be neither a satan nor any evil one who will destroy. For their entire lifetimes will be times of blessing and healing. (Jub. 23:28–29)

V. 28 clearly alludes to Isa 65:20, where the restoration of human longevity is described as a part of the blissful conditions of the new creation—the creation of new heavens and a new earth (Isa 65:17)—in Isa 65:17–25. Also, "times of blessing and healing" probably refers to "the time of the new creation" in Jub. 1:29, since the new creation in Jub. 1:29 includes the theme of "healing, health, and blessing for all the elect ones of Israel." Moreover, we should note that the restoration of human longevity resonates with the *Urzeit-Endzeit* correlation since it implies "a return of the world to its original, pristine condition before the fall of Adam."[16]

As seen above, the two occurrences of the phrase "new creation" (Jub. 1:29; 4:26) relate not only to the cosmic renewal of the world but also to the eschatological establishment of the temple on Mount Zion. Also, at the time of new creation, God will proclaim his elected people as His sons and will create a holy spirit for them. Jubilees describes this concept of new creation in relation to the creation account and the Adamic narrative in Gen 1–3. We can find these aspects of new creation in 1 Enoch also.

4. The concept of new creation in 1 Enoch

First Enoch is significant for the present study since it uses not only the phrase "new creation" itself (72:1) but also the concept of new creation with the *Urzeit-Endzeit* eschatology. First Enoch is a composite book written by numerous authors in different periods. After the discovery of its fragments among the Dead Sea Scrolls, Milik divides the Ethiopic version into five primary books,[17] which has been accepted by the majority of scholars. I will investigate the concept of new creation in each book of 1 Enoch as we shall see below.

(1) The concept of new creation in the Book of the Luminaries

Although the Book of the Luminaries (72–82) is not the first part of 1 Enoch (the Book of the Luminaries, however, is probably among the oldest sections of 1 Enoch corpus),[18] I will begin the discussion of the

---

16. Scott, *On Earth as in Heaven*, 8, 112–13; Doering, "*Urzeit-Endzeit* Correlation," 34.

17. Milik, "Problèmes de la littérature," 333–78; see also Black and Milik, *Books of Enoch*, 4–135.

18. Nickelsburg, *1 Enoch 1*, 7–8.

new creation motif in 1 Enoch with this book, since the phrase "new creation" itself only occurs in the first verse of the Book of the Luminaries in the whole range of 1 Enoch:

> The book about the motion of the heavenly luminaries all as they are in their kinds, their jurisdiction, their time, their name, their origins, and their months which Uriel, the holy angel who was with me (and) who is their leader, showed me. The entire book about them, as it is, he showed me and how every year of the world will be forever, until a new creation (ግብር፡ ሐዲስ) lasting forever is made. (1 En. 72:1)[19]

The notion of new creation here is clearly both eschatological and cosmological. It is eschatological since it is about the eschatological time which lasts forever and it is cosmological in that it relates to the motion, the time, the rule, and the destiny of the heavenly luminaries. The term translated "creation" is ግብር (*gebr*), a cognate of the verb ገብረ ("to do" or "to make"). As Nickelsburg argues, this noun ultimately relates to the Hebrew verb עשה which occurs in Gen 1 (vv. 7, 16, 25, 26, 31) alongside ברא to refer to God's act of creation.[20] Thus, the new creation in 1 En. 72:1 has a connection with God's original creation of the earth and the heavenly luminaries in Gen 1, but it is also a *new* one, which is distinct from the first creation, in the sense that it will last forever. The concept of new creation more clearly appears in other parts of 1 Enoch within the *Urzeit-Endzeit* eschatology, as we shall see below.

(2) The concept of new creation in the Book of the Watchers

In the Book of the Watchers, the new creation motif is most clearly expressed through the theme of transplanting the life-giving tree to the eschatological sanctuary in chapters 24–25. On his heavenly journey from the west through the center of the earth to the east (1 En. 21–36), Enoch views seven dignified mountains. The seventh mountain resembles the seat of a throne surrounded by fragrant trees. Among them Enoch finds one particularly beautiful and fragrant tree with magnificent leaves, blossoms, and fruits (1 En. 24:3–4). It is important to note that this passage

---

19. This translation is from Nickelsburg and VanderKam, *1 Enoch 2*. Unless otherwise indicated, I will use the translation of Hermeneia series (*1 Enoch 1* and *1 Enoch 2*) when I use a text from 1 Enoch.

20. Nickelsburg and VanderKam, *1 Enoch 2*, 414.

CHAPTER 2: THE CONCEPT OF NEW CREATION IN THE PARABIBLICAL TEXTS

has Eden traditions which clearly appear in Michael's answer to Enoch's question about the beautiful tree:

> [3] This high mountain that you saw, whose peak is like the throne of God, is the seat where the Great Holy One, the Lord of glory, the King of eternity, will sit, when he descends to visit the earth in goodness. [4] And (as for) this fragrant tree, no flesh has the right to touch it until the great judgment, in which there will be vengeance on all and a consummation forever. [5] Then it will be given to the righteous and the pious, and its fruit will be as food for the chosen. And it will be transplanted to the holy place, by the house of God, the King of eternity. [6] Then they will rejoice greatly and be glad, and they will enter into the sanctuary. Its fragrances will be in their bones, and they will live a long life upon the earth, such as your fathers lived also in their days, and torments and plagues and suffering will not touch them. (1 En. 25:3–6)

The seven dignified mountains are probably identical with the seven mountains in 1 En. 18:6–9, although 1 En. 18:6–9 describes the mountains with precious stones, not trees. The descriptions of the seven mountains in the two passages (1 En. 18:6–9 and 1 En. 24–25) are similar in their (1) orientations, (2) precious stones, (3) centrality, (4) towering height resembling God's throne, and (5) fire. The description of the paradise like mountains with precious stones is probably influenced by the Eden tradition in Ezek 28:13–19, where "Eden, the garden of God" (Ezek 28:13) appears as "the holy mountain of God" (Ezek 28:14, 16) filled with various precious stones including the stones of fire (Ezek 28:14, 16, 18). However, the origin of the description of the mountains filled with the precious stones and fragrant trees can also be traced to Gen 2:8–15, where God planted the garden of Eden for the first human beings. Eden and the lands around Eden are full of not only every fruitful tree but also precious stones (Gen 2:11–12).

The description of the life-giving tree is one more piece of evidence for the influence of the Eden tradition in this text. This tree reflects the characteristics of the tree of life in Gen 2–3 in the sense that (1) the tree is singled out among many trees (1 En. 24:4–5; cf. Gen 2:9); (2) its fruit provides a long life (1 En. 25:5–6; cf. Gen 3:22); (3) now it is inaccessible to human beings (1 En. 25:4; cf. Gen 3:24). Furthermore, the journey to God's mountain paradise filled with fragrant trees occurs again in 1 En. 32, which alludes to Gen 2–3 with more explicit language. That passage also describes Adam's corruption by saying that "your father of old and your mother of old, who were before you, ate and learned wisdom. And their eyes were opened, and they knew that they were naked, and they were driven from the garden" (1 En. 32:6). Thus, it is difficult to deny the influence of the Edenic tradition in 1 En. 25:3–6.

With this allusion to the Edenic narrative in Gen 2–3, 1 En. 25:3–6 expresses the eschatological hope for new creation in the framework of the *Urzeit-Endzeit* correlation; the life-giving tree will be transplanted to the house of God and its fruit will be accessible as food for the chosen at the eschaton.[21] God's chosen people will rejoice greatly in the eschatological sanctuary enjoying their restored long life span. As seen above, the establishment of the eschatological temple is one of the most important aspects of the new creation motif (Jub. 1:29; 4:26). Also, the recovery of a long life span is a typical theme of the new creation in parabiblical texts. According to Nickelsburg, here "the fragrance bringing new life to weary bones" may refer to a resurrection of the body.[22]

There is no language of divine sonship in 1 En. 25:3–6, but we should note that here the blessings of new creation are only given to *God's chosen people*, namely the righteous and the pious. As P. B. Decock points out, in 1 Enoch (62:11; 101:1) divine sonship refers to the righteous or to God's chosen people who have knowledge of the heavenly mysteries and will be vindicated on the day of judgement.[23] Particularly, in 1 En. 62:11, the author uses the language of divine sonship as a synonym for the righteous and for God's chosen people who will be delivered from the divine judgement. Accordingly, by indirect means, we can discern a connection between the new creation motif and divine sonship.

(3) The concept of new creation in the Book of Parables

We have seen that the theme of new creation is closely related to that of God's chosen people in the Book of Watchers. First Enoch 45:4–5, where the new creation motif most clearly occurs in the Book of Parables, is similarly related, but in 1 En. 45:4–6, it is not only God's chosen people but also God's Chosen One who appear in the context of new creation:

21. The inaccessibility of the life-giving tree until the final judgment also appears in other parabiblical texts which deal with the Adamic narrative (e.g., Apoc. Mos. 28:1–3; T. Levi 18:10–11; cf. Gen 3:22–24).
22. Nickelsburg, *1 Enoch 1*, 315.
23. Decock, "Holy Ones."

> On that day, I shall make my Chosen One dwell among them, and I shall transform heaven and make it a blessing and a light forever; and I shall transform the earth and make it a blessing. And my chosen ones I shall make to dwell on it, but those who commit sin and error will not set foot on it. For I have seen and satisfied my righteous ones with peace and have made them to dwell in my presence, But the judgment of the sinners has drawn near to me, that I may destroy them from the face of the earth. (1 En. 45:4–6)

Here the author describes the eschaton, where the judgment of the sinners occurs together with the blessing of the righteous. God's Chosen One, a messianic figure, will dwell among them as a judge (cf. 1 En. 45:3). God's chosen ones will *dwell in* the newly transformed earth. As Nickelsburg points out, the transformation of the earth alludes to the notion of a new heaven and a new earth in Isa 65–66 (65:17; 66:22).[24]

However, the transformation of the earth also alludes to God's creation of the heavens and the earth (and light) and the blessing of all creation in Gen 1–2. Interestingly, in 1 En. 60–61, *the dwelling place* for the righteous (or God's chosen ones) relates to a "garden" (60:8, 23; 61:12). Particularly, the two monsters, Behemoth and Leviathan which were created on the fifth day of creation (cf. 4 Ezra 6:49–52; 2 Bar. 29:4) appear with the "garden" in 60:7–8 and 60:23–24. On the great day of the Lord, the two monsters will be food for the righteous at the eschatological banquet. Thus, the hope of new creation that God's chosen people will dwell on the newly transformed earth or "the garden of the righteous ones" is depicted in connection with the *Urzeit-Endzeit* eschatology. Moreover, as seen above, 1 En. 62:11 identifies God's chosen ones or the righteous ones with *God's children*. They will be saved on that day (62:13) and will "rise up" from the earth putting on the garment of glory (62:14–15). As Nickelsburg argues, this seems to describe the resurrection of the righteous at the eschaton.[25] Thus, we can find the close connection between the theme of divine sonship and the new creation motif in 1 Enoch.

---

24. Nickelsburg and VanderKam, *1 Enoch 2*, 52, 151.
25. Nickelsburg, *1 Enoch 1*, 267–78; Decock, "Holy Ones," 72–73.

(4) The concept of new creation the Book of Dream Visions

The most relevant text for the theme of new creation in the Book of Dream Visions is 1 En. 90:28–29, where the new creation is expressed by the rebuilding of a *new* house (ቤተ ፡ ሐዲስ) for the sheep:

> [28] And I stood up to see, until that old house was folded up—and they removed all the pillars, and all the beams and ornaments of that house were folded up with it—and they removed it and put it in a place to the south of the land. [29] And I saw until the Lord of the sheep brought a new house, larger and higher than that first one, and he erected it on the site of the first one that had been rolled up. And all its pillars were new, and its beams were new, and its ornaments were new and larger than (those of) the first one, the old one that he had removed. And all the sheep were within it. (1 En. 90:28–29)

As Nickelsburg points out, the building of the new house which replaces the old one probably refers to the eschatological renewal of Jerusalem, although whether the New Jerusalem does include a temple is debatable.[26] Again, we can find a close connection between the theme of new creation and the *Urzeit-Endzeit* eschatology. However, here the author emphasizes the discontinuity between the old and the new houses since the new one will be established after the old one is totally removed. It is noteworthy that the hope for new creation is interwoven with the relationship between the Lord of the sheep and the sheep; the Lord of the sheep brought a new house in order that the sheep may be within in it.

This relationship between the messianic figure and his people in the context of new creation more clearly appears a few verses later:

> [37] And I saw how a white bull was born, and its horns were large. And all the wild beasts and all the birds of heaven were afraid of it and made petition to it continually. [38] And I saw until all their species were changed, and they all became white cattle. And the first one became leader among them (and that leader was a large animal), and there were large black horns on

---

26. In the Book of Dream Visions, usually the word "tower" (ማኅፈድ), not "house" refers to the temple. Thus, VanderKam argues that the new house here symbolizes "a restored Jerusalem devoid of a temple" (VanderKam, *Enoch and the Growth*, 168). The height of the house, however, parallels the previous reference to the high tower (1 En. 89:73), namely, the temple (Nickelsburg, *1 Enoch 1*, 404–5). For more discussion, see Tiller, *Commentary on the Animal Apocalypse*, 45–51.

its head. And the Lord of the sheep rejoiced over it and over all the cattle. (1 En. 90:37–38)

After all the beasts of the field and the birds of the heaven were gathered together in the new house (1 En. 90:33–36) and a white bull was born, all species were transformed into white bulls. The identity of the white bull is generally accepted as a messianic figure.[27] Also, this transformation of all species into white bulls probably refers to the eschatological hope for new creation that "in the end all the species representing the diversity of nations and people return to the primordial unity from which they diverged."[28] Thus, all enmities between Israel and the gentiles will be permanently eradicated under the rule of the messianic figure. Many scholars identify this messianic figure as a "new Adam," the head of a new human race in whom all nations return to their created unity.[29] The theme of the gentiles' conversion into God's people in the context of new creation appears in 1 En. 10:16–11:2, where "all the sons of men will become righteous and all the peoples will worship [God]" (1 En. 10:21) although in that passage a messianic figure does not occur. The theme of the gentiles' conversion into the righteous as well as the establishment of the eschatological temple also occurs in the last section of 1 Enoch, as we shall see below.

(5) The concept of new creation in 1 En. 91–108[30]

First Enoch 91:13–17, a part of the Apocalypse of Weeks, most clearly expresses the theme of new creation in the last section of 1 Enoch:

> [13] And at its conclusion, they will acquire possessions in righteousness; and the temple of the kingdom of the Great One will be built in the greatness of its glory for all the generations of eternity. [14] After this there will arise a ninth week, in which

---

27. Nickelsburg, *1 Enoch 1*, 406; Charles, *Book of Enoch*, 215–16; Dillmann, *Buch Henoch*, 286; Black et al., *Book of Enoch*, 279–80.

28. Nickelsburg, *1 Enoch 1*, 406.

29. Milik, "Problèmes de la littérature," 359; Nickelsburg, *1 Enoch 1*, 407; Black, "New Creation," 18–19.

30. The final section of 1 Enoch (91–108) is not written by one author, although it is written under the same pseudepigraphic name, "Enoch." The majority of scholars divide it into Apocalypse of Weeks (93:1–10; 91:11–17), Exhortation (91:1–10, 18–19), Epistle (92:1–5; 93:11—105:2), Birth of Noah (106:1—107:3) and Eschatological Admonition (108:1–15) based on its literary characteristics. See Stuckenbruck, *1 Enoch*, 1–2.

> righteous law will be revealed to all the sons of the whole earth; and all the deeds of wickedness will vanish from the whole earth and descend to the eternal pit, and all humankind will look to the path of eternal righteousness. [15] After this, in the tenth week, the seventh part, (will be) the eternal judgment; and it will be executed on the watchers of the eternal heaven, and a fixed time of the great judgment will be rendered in the midst of the holy ones. [16] And the first heaven will pass away in it, and a new heaven will appear; and all the powers of the heavens will shine forever with sevenfold (brightness). [17] After this there will be many weeks without number forever, in which they will do piety and righteousness, and from then on sin will never again be mentioned. (1 En. 91:13–17)

This passage is full of motifs related to new creation: (1) the building of the eschatological temple in v. 13; (2) the conversion of all humanity in v. 14; (3) the creation of a new heaven in v. 16.

We should note that here the author describes the new creation within the *Urzeit-Endzeit* framework. This is most clearly expressed in v. 16, where the appearance of a new heaven contrasts with the removal of the first heaven. Also, the vanishing of all deeds of wickedness (v. 14) and the description of the eternal sinlessness (v. 17) imply a return to the primordial state.[31] As seen above, the establishment of the eschatological temple can be understood in the *Urzeit-Endzeit* correlation.

In sum, as in Jubilees, the concept of new creation in 1 Enoch is expressed within the *Urzeit-Endzeit* correlation: it relates to the recovery of the blessings in the garden of Eden, the establishment of the eschatological sanctuary in Jerusalem, and the cosmological renewal of heaven and earth. Again, we can find a close relationship between the themes of new creation and divine sonship, because the language of divine sonship in 1 Enoch refers to God's chosen or righteous people who will be saved from the eschatological judgement at the time of new creation. Thus, we can conclude that the two very influential parabiblical texts, Jubilees and 1 Enoch, share many aspects of the concept of new creation. Similarly, other parabiblical texts also share these descriptions of new creation, particularly the portrait of the Adamic figure, as we shall see below.

---

31. Owens, *As It Was*, 62.

5. The concept of new creation in the Apocalypse of Moses

The Apocalypse of Moses is a creative explanation of the Adamic narrative in the early chapters of Genesis. Given the absence of apparent Christian allusions and its close affinities to the New Testament, particularly Paul's letters, the most probable date of composition would be anywhere between 100 BCE and 200 CE.[32]

The Apocalypse of Moses describes Adam as the archetypal sinner who brought sufferings to this world, but its narrative still retains a hope of new creation in the day of resurrection.[33] The author envisages the hope of new creation in terms of the restoration of Adam's glory, righteousness, the image of God, and life.

(1) The corruption of Adam in the *Urzeit*

The present world in the narrative of the Apocalypse of Moses is full of sufferings: (1) Adam and Eve have been expelled from the paradise and are staying in the East (Apoc. Mos. 1:1–2); (2) Adam's eldest son, Cain killed his brother Abel (Apoc. Mos. 2–3); (3) Adam is now dying because of his pain and illness (Apoc. Mos. 5:2–5); (4) the beast which was once subjected to the image of God is attacking and even ruling over the image of God (Apoc. Mos. 10–11).

All these present sufferings happened because of Adam and Eve's disobedience to God's commandment. In Apoc. Mos. 15–30, Eve is retelling the story of their transgression to their children in detail. Just after Eve ate the fruit of the tree of life, she found that she had lost her righteousness and glory:

> At that moment my eyes were opened, and I knew that I was stripped of the righteousness with which I had been clothed and

---

32. Jan Dochhorn recently argued that the date of the Apocalypse of Moses is around the birth of Jesus since the Assumption of Moses, which depends on the Apocalypse of Moses, was written in the time of Archelaus (Dochhorn, *Adammythos bei Paulus*, 252, 562–63). See also Johnson, "Life of Adam and Eve," 252; Merk and Meiser, *Leben Adams und Evas*, 769. Jonge and Tromp, however, give an alleged date between the second and fourth century CE according to their assumption of the Christian origin of the Apocalypse of Moses (Jonge and Tromp, *Life of Adam and Eve*, 77).

33. In 14:2, Adam says to Eve that her sin made death rule over all their race. Also, the fact that Adam's restoration at the eschaton entails the restoration of his all descendants (13:3–5; 41:3) indicates that the author of the Apocalypse of Moses regards Adam as a representative of all sinners.

I wept saying, "Why have you done this? I have been separated from my glory." (Apoc. Mos. 20:1–2)[34]

Here, the author identifies the loss of righteousness with the loss of glory. A few verses later, Adam repeats almost the same words after his transgression, saying to Eve: "O wicked woman! What have you done among us? You have separated me from the glory of God" (Apoc. Mos. 21:6). Unlike Apoc. Mos. 20:2, where the glory seems to refer to Eve's own glory, this verse describes the glory which Adam lost as "the glory of God," although it seems that there is no fundamental difference between them. This, however, shows that the source of this glory is God.

The meaning of the "glory" (δόξα) in Apoc. Mos. 20–21 (20:2; 21:2, 6) is not clear. It may refer to "righteousness," "visible splendor," "the image of God," "dwelling in paradise," or "immortality."[35] It is clear, however, that the loss of the glory is closely related to the entrance of death into the human condition. In Apoc. Mos. 14:2, when Seth and Eve came to the tent where Adam was lying, Adam said to Eve, "What have you done among us? You brought upon us great wrath, which is *death ruling over all our race*." Adam repeats the same reproach to Eve, "What have you done among us?" in 14:2 and 21:6. This indicates that the loss of the glory parallels death's ruling over all humanity. The fact that in 28:3, God forbids Adam from accessing the tree of life in order that Adam may not be immortal forever, supports this interpretation.

The loss of righteousness and glory is also related to humanity's loss of their authority as the image of God. In Apoc. Mos. 24:4, God's punishments of Adam include that the animals will rise up against Adam. As a

---

34. Text is from Dochhorn, *Apokalypse des Mose*, 325. In this book, all texts of the Apocalypse of Moses are from Dochhorn's critical edition with my English translation.

35. (1) "righteousness": righteousness is possible in light of 20:1–2, where it parallels "glory"; (2) "visible splendor": in 18:5 and 33:2, the glory refers to the "visible splendor" of the tree and the eagles. Thus, Brock argues that Adam and Eve's loss of glory refers to their loss of the "robe of light" (Brock, "Jewish Traditions," 221–22); (3) "the image of God": given the fact that the beast does not fear Eve as "the image of God," the glory which Eve lost in 20:1–2 can be regarded as "the image of God." Although there is no description regarding Adam and Eve's remarkable physical appearance in the Apocalypse of Moses, the physical appearance of Adam is described in terms of the *imago Dei* in *Vita Adae et Evae* (LAE 13:1; 21:3); (4) "dwelling in paradise": in light of the verb κατάγω in 21:2 and 39:1 (κατάγω is used in connection with the expulsion from paradise), Dochhorn argues that the glory indicates a place from which Adam and Eve fell (Dochhorn, *Apokalypse des Mose*, 360–61); (5) "immortality": see Sprinkle, "Afterlife in Romans," 204–7.

result, in Apoc. Mos. 10–12, when Eve and Seth went to the regions of paradise to bring some oil for Adam, a wild beast attacked them.

Eve cried out to the beast saying,

> Oh you evil beast, do you not fear to fight the image of God? How was your mouth opened? How did your teeth get strong? How did you not remember your subjection, for you were formerly subjected to the image of God? (Apoc. Mos. 10:3)

The beast replies to Eve saying,

> ... because the rule of the beasts has happened from you. How was your mouth opened to eat from the tree concerning which God commanded you not to eat from it? Because of this also our nature was changed. (Apoc. Mos. 11:1–2)

This text indicates that humanity's loss of the image of God and the inversion of the original created order occurred due to Adamic (Eve's) sin.

In sum, Adam and Eve were driven out from the garden of Eden and lost their righteousness, glory, and authority as the image of God because of their disobedience to God's commandment. This did not only affect themselves but also made death rule over all humanity. Additionally, their sin caused the change of creation's nature. However, the hope of restoration of Adam, his descendants, and creation in the *Endzeit* also appears in the Apocalypse of Moses.

(2) The hope for new creation in the *Endzeit*

A. THE RECOVERY OF ACCESS TO PARADISE IN THE *URZEIT-ENDZEIT* ESCHATOLOGY

In his recent article, Levison notes that the term παράδεισος, which occurs more than three dozen times in the Apocalypse of Moses, primarily refers to a terrestrial paradise, not a heavenly paradise. He also argues that "the relationship of paradise in the Greek Life of Adam and Eve to the *Urzeit-Endzeit* schema, in which what belonged to the primeval garden will be restored in the eschatological paradise, is tenuous."[36] As the title of the article "Terrestrial Paradise in the Greek Life of Adam and Eve" implies, his emphasis on the mundane elements of paradise

---

36. Levison, "Terrestrial Paradise," 42.

seems to try to minimize the eschatological elements of the paradise in the Apocalypse of Moses.[37]

However, although his argument that the term παράδεισος mainly refers to a terrestrial paradise is right, we should note that the divine revelation also occurs in this terrestrial paradise. For example, in Apoc. Mos. 22–29, God is coming into the terrestrial paradise with a trumpet sound of the archangel in order to judge Eve, the serpent, and Adam. Also, the fact that God casts Adam and Eve out of the paradise as soon as they disobeyed God's commandment shows that the author uses the term παράδεισος to refer to a sacred place, where the divine revelation and manifestation occur, rather than a mundane place.

Moreover, the author also uses the same term παράδεισος to refer to a heavenly paradise in 37:5 and 40:1 in an eschatological context. Particularly, in 37:5, the author uses παράδεισος for referring to a place, where Adam's soul will await the final judgment. This description of the heavenly paradise is a clear expression of an eschatological hope.

Finally, as Levison himself admits, the Apocalypse of Moses does use the theme of paradise in the context of the *Urzeit-Endzeit* eschatology[38]: (1) in chapter 13, Michael told Seth that although access to the oil of mercy in paradise is forbidden now, on the day of resurrection, Adam and his descendants will enjoy every joy of paradise (13:4); (2) similarly, in chapter 28, God expels Adam out of paradise, but God promises that in the time of resurrection, he will give the tree of life to Adam for Adam's eternal life (28:4). In these passages, access to paradise parallels Adam's bodily resurrection and his immortality. The recovery of access to paradise in the *Urzeit-Endzeit* eschatology is not a marginal theme of the Apocalypse of Moses; rather, it plays a central role in describing the hope of new creation in the Apocalypse of Moses in connection with the theme of resurrection.

---

37. In this context, Levison criticizes Jeremias's interpretation of the paradise in the Apocalypse of Moses by saying that "this analysis evinces a strident eschatological bias, which ignores the vast bulk of references to mundane elements of paradise, such as its windows and gates and regions and spices and deciduous trees" (Levison, "Terrestrial Paradise," 28).

38. Levison, "Terrestrial Paradise," 42–43.

B. The Restoration of Righteousness, Glory, the Image of God, and Immortality in Connection with the Theme of Resurrection

As Preston Sprinkle notes, the author does not use the language of righteousness and glory in the restoration passages of the Apocalypse of Moses (e.g., 13:3–5; 28:4; 39:2–3; 41:3; 43:2–3).[39] Rather, the theme of resurrection occurs in those passages to signify Adam's eventual restoration. However, given the fact that the themes of righteousness, glory, the image of God, and immortality are interwoven in the Apocalypse of Moses, Adam's eventual resurrection indicates the restoration of Adam's righteousness, glory, and the image of God.

The most important example of this tendency is Apoc. Mos. 13:2–5, where the theme of the resurrection at the eschaton indicates not only Adam's resurrection but also the resurrection of the holy people:

> [2] And God sent Michael the archangel, and he said to him, "Seth, man of God, do not labour, praying with this supplication about the tree from which the oil flows, to anoint your father, Adam. [3] It will not come to you now but at the end of times, when all flesh from Adam will be raised until that great day, who all will be a holy nation; [4] then to them will be given every joy of Paradise and God will be in their midst, and they will not be sinners before him anymore, because the evil heart will be removed from them, [5] and they will be given a heart that understands the good and worships God alone. (Apoc. Mos. 13:2–5)

Here the theme of resurrection is interwoven with the restoration of the joy of paradise, the forgiveness of sinners, the removal of the evil heart, and the presence of God among them. All these themes are closely related to the restoration of righteousness and the glory of Adam's descendants. In 28:4, God promises Adam that he will be able to access the tree of life and so be immortal forever. As seen above, the loss of Adam's glory parallels death's reign over humanity. Thus, God's promise of immortality can be linked to the restoration of Adam's glory. Similarly, in 39:2–3 God comforts Adam by saying that God will establish Adam's authority over Satan and his followers on the day of judgment and that they will see Adam sitting on a glorious throne. This also indicates the restoration of Adam's glory and his authority as the image of God. Finally, in 41:3

---

39. Sprinkle, "Afterlife in Romans," 206.

God promises to Adam that he will raise not only Adam but also all his descendants on the last day. All this evidence clearly shows that God will restore Adam's righteousness, glory, and the image of God on the day of resurrection in the frame of the *Urzeit-Endzeit* eschatology.

In sum, the Apocalypse of Moses portrays Adam as the archetypal sinner who brought death to the whole creation, but it expresses the eschatological hope for new creation with the theme of resurrection interwoven with other themes of the restoration of the accessibility of paradise, righteousness, glory, and the image of God. This portrait of Adam, not only as the archetypal sinner, but also as the bearer of the eschatological hope appears too in Liber Antiquitatum Biblicarum, 4 Ezra, and 2 Baruch.

6. The concept of new creation in Liber Antiquitatum Biblicarum

Liber Antiquitatum Biblicarum (LAB), which had been falsely attributed to Philo, describes God's unchangeable covenant and his mercy on Israel narrative in an haggadic manner, from the creation in Genesis to the death of Saul in 1 Samuel. The extant Latin text of LAB is probably translated from the Greek text, which is presumably also translated from a Hebrew original,[40] and the date of composition of the original Hebrew version seems to be around the first century CE.[41] The significance of LAB for the present study is that as in the Apocalypse of Moses, the author of LAB acknowledges the deep influence of Adamic sin on the whole creation. Also, it describes the eschatological hope of new creation in relation to the reversal of the curses in Gen 3:16–19 within the *Urzeit-Endzeit* correlation. Moreover, while speaking of the privileged status of Israel, the author understands Israel as an Adamic figure; at this point, we can find the relationship between Israel's divine sonship and the motif of new creation as we shall see below.

---

40. See Harrington, "Pseudo-Philo," 298–99.

41. Most scholars agree with this date based on LAB 19:7, which can be connected to Titus's capture of Jerusalem (70 CE), and the comparison with other Second Temple Jewish writings (4 Ezra and 2 Baruch, in particular). See Harrington, "Pseudo-Philo," 299; Murphy, *Pseudo-Philo*, 6; Barclay, *Paul and the Gift*, 266. Scholarly opinions, however, are divided whether it was written in a pre-70 date or a post-70 date. Jacobson, particularly, argues that the date of LAB could be much later than the middle of the second century. See Jacobson, *Commentary*, 199–210.

(1) The influence of Adamic sin and the *Urzeit-Endzeit* framework

Pseudo-Philo recognizes that Adam's sin in the garden of Eden deeply influences not only current Israel but also the whole creation. This understanding appears most prominently in 13:8–9, which describes Adamic sin at the garden of Eden, mentioning the period when Noah lived:

> [8] . . . And he said, "This is the place concerning which I taught the first-fashioned one, saying, 'If you do not transgress what I have commanded you, all things will be subject to you.' But that one transgressed my ways and was persuaded by his wife; she was deceived by the serpent. Then death was ordained for the generations of men." [9] The Lord proceeded to show him the ways of paradise and said to him, "These are the ways that men have lost by not walking in them, because they have sinned against me." (LAB 13:8–9)[42]

The "first-fashioned one," here, refers to Adam, who was disobedient to God's commandment despite the fact that he was granted the authority to rule over all creation (Gen 1:28–29). The effect of his disobedience was that death was ordained for the generations of men, not simply for himself. The "he" in v. 9 probably refers to Moses (cf. 2 Bar. 4:5), and v. 9 reminds us of the fact that God drove out Adam from the garden of Eden and placed the cherubim and a flaming sword to guard the way to the tree of life (Gen 3:24). In other words, God shows Moses the way to the paradise, which is hidden because of the Adamic sin, indicating that the way to the garden of Eden will be opened again to those who are faithful to the covenant with God and that the earth will recover its productivity by reversing the curses in Gen 3:16–19 (LAB 13:9–10).

Similarly, LAB 37, which deals with the parable of the trees in relation to the event when Abimelech killed his own brothers, portrays the effect of the Adamic sin at the garden of Eden. LAB 37:3, in particular, shows that the Adamic sin not only caused his death but also affected the whole created order by quoting Gen 3:18, where the earth was condemned to bring forth thorns and thistles. Interestingly, this text also indicates the close relationship between Adam and Israel by mentioning Moses just after describing the Adamic sin.

---

42. Translation is from Jacobson, *Commentary*. I will use Jacobson's translation of LAB in this chapter.

Moreover, the author describes the eschatological hope in the manner of the reversal of God's judgment in Gen 3:16–19. After the deluge in Noah's time, God describes the new creation at the eschaton as follows:

> But when the years of the world will be complete, then the light will cease and the darkness will be extinguished, and I will bring the dead to life and raise up from the earth those who are sleeping. The underworld will pay back its debt, and the place of perdition will return its deposit so that I will render to each according to his works and according to the fruits of his own deeds, until I judge between soul and flesh. And the world will be at rest, and death will be extinguished, and the underworld will close its mouth. The earth will not be without issue or sterile for those who dwell in it; and no one who has been vindicated by me will be polluted. There will be another earth and another heaven, an everlasting dwelling place. (LAB 3:10)

The eschatology expressed here relates to the protology in Gen 1–3; the expression "the light will cease and the darkness will be extinguished" parallels God's creation of light and darkness in Gen 1:3–5, and the new creation on the day of judgment is expressed in the fashion of the reversal of the curses in Gen 3:16–19. In other words, (1) death will disappear, and the dead will rise up from the earth (cf. Gen 2:17; 3:19); (2) the earth will recover its productivity (cf. Gen 3:17–18); (3) people who have been vindicated by God will obtain an everlasting dwelling place (cf. Gen 3:24). Again, the new creation at the eschaton here concerns not only the purification of human beings ("no one will be polluted") but also the renewal of the whole universe ("another earth and another heaven"). Also, it is noteworthy that the author states the new creation at the eschaton in relation to Noah's flood (cf. 1 En. 10:2; Matt 24:37–39; 2 Pet 3:5–7). This indicates that the author describes the new creation with the *Urzeit-Endzeit* correlation, and at the same time, it has a strong discontinuity with the first creation since the new creation destroys and purifies the previous things through the eschatological renewal like the deluge.

In LAB, therefore, the protology and the eschatology are closely related to each other, and thus Fredrick J. Murphy expresses this by stating that "everything within the work [LAB] is framed by the Creation and eschaton."[43] Another important point in relation to the *Urzeit-Endzeit* correlation in LAB is that this framework can also be applied to Israel, as we shall see below.

---

43. Murphy, *Pseudo-Philo*, 75.

(2) Adam and Israel

LAB 13:8–9, which we have seen above, is the first place where Adam appears in LAB. Its context is that Moses speaks of Israel's tabernacle and cultic regulations. Particularly, 13:7 relates Israel's festivals to the covenant given to Noah after the deluge, indicating that keeping Israel's festivals is the fulfillment of the Noachian covenant that the seasonal cycle will continue while the earth endures (Gen 8:22). In this cultic context, God promises that if the Israelites led by Moses are obedient to God's covenant, they will be liberated from the Adamic curse in Gen 3:16–19 (LAB 13:9–10).

Linking Israel to Adam in the cultic context more clearly occurs in LAB 26, where the judge Kenaz tried to remove seven precious stones which the tribe of Asher took from the Amorites. Those stones have an idolatrous character since they were used for the Amorite cult (LAB 25:12). Thus, God commanded Kenaz to place the stones on the top of the mountain beside the new altar since Kenaz cannot destroy them by himself. Kenaz, then, wished to test them with fire, an iron sword, and water, but he failed to destruct them. After seeing what happened, he said to God:

> "Blessed be God, who has done such great wonders for the sons of men, and he made Adam the first-fashioned one and showed him everything on condition that when Adam sinned thereby, he would deny the human race all he had shown, lest these things gain control over them." After saying this, he took the books and the stones and he placed them on the top of the mountain by the new altar as the Lord had commanded him. He brought a peace offering and offered the burnt offerings on the altar, 2000 burnt offerings in all. He gave them as a burnt offering on that day, and he and all the people together rejoiced greatly. (LAB 26:6–7)

This text is similar to LAB 13:8–9 in that the author mentions Adam's sin in a cultic context. Just as in LAB 13:8–10, God showed Moses the ways of the paradise from which Adam was expelled and promised him Israel's restoration from the Adamic curse, so here Kenaz performs a priestly role for Israel at the *new* altar in place of Adam.

As seen above, Jub. 3:27 describes Adam as a priestly figure who offered an incense sacrifice. Moreover, Jub. 8:19 portrays the garden of Eden as "the residence of the Lord" which parallels Mount Sinai and Mount

Zion. This Adamic tradition, which not only regards Adam as a priestly figure but also regards the garden of Eden as a sanctuary, is not uncommon in Second Temple Judaism. For example, Apoc. Mos. 29:3–6, where Adam asks the angels to take fragrances from the garden of Eden in order to offer God a sacrifice, follows this tradition.[44] This tradition in LAB 26:6–7 is even strengthened by the fact that the new precious stones from the land of Havilah which replace the original seven will be set on the ephod over against the twelve stones that Moses in the wilderness set on the breastplate (LAB 25:11; 26:4). As Robert Hayward rightly points out, the name of the first river going out from the garden of Eden is Pishon, which surrounds the land of Havilah. Pishon is full of precious stones (Gen 2:10–12) and in the early Jewish traditions, "Paradise with its river Pishon was the source of precious stones giving light of a miraculous kind, especially those oracle stones of the high priest's ephod and breastplate."[45] Thus, we can understand that the author of LAB describes Noah, Moses, and Kenaz as Adamic figures who replace Adam's priestly role in the garden of Eden: God shows them the paradise and they offered a new sacrifice in place of Adam (3:8–10; 13:7–10; 19:10; 26:6–7).

The connection between Adam, Israel, and their priestly role most clearly appears in LAB 32:15, where Deborah is urged to praise God's saving activities for Israel:

> And you, Deborah, begin to speak of what you saw in the field, how the people walked and went forth in safety and the stars fought for them. Rejoice, earth, over those dwelling upon you, because the congregation of the Lord that burns incense on you is present. Not unjustly did God take the rib of the primordial man who was fashioned from you, knowing that from his rib Israel would be born. That which is created from you will be a testimony to what the Lord has done for his people. (LAB 32:15)

Here, Israel, who springs from Adam's rib offers an incense sacrifice to God. Given the Adamic tradition in LAB which we have seen above, the connection between Adam and Israel in which Israel replaces Adam's priestly role at the garden of Eden is understandable. This shows that

---

44. This tradition is also found in Targum Pseudo-Jonathan of Gen 8:20; Genesis Rabbah 34:9. See Hayward, "Figure of Adam," 1–20.

45. Hayward, "Figure of Adam," 12. Hayward argues that LAB is one of the earliest witnesses to this tradition alongside Targum Pseudo-Jonathan of Exod 35:27; b. Yoma 75a; Exodus Rabbah 33:8. Josephus, *Antiquities* 3.215–18 and Philo, *De specialibus legibus* 1:88–90 also reflect this tradition.

Israel was already special to God when God created the universe in Gen 1–2 in the view of LAB.[46] Thus, it is not surprising that the author of LAB describes Israel's history, such as Israel's exodus from Egypt and the giving of the law at Mount Sinai, with the cosmological elements (11:2, 5; 15:6; 16:3; 23:10).[47] For example, in 32:7–8, the author describes the law as "the foundation of understanding that he had prepared from the creation of the world" and portrays the moment of giving of the law as like "Paradise giving off the scent of its fruit" as well as when "the terrestrial foundation was moved" and "the earth was shaken from its base." In other words, in 32:7–8, God's salvific activities and the giving of the law are interwoven with God's creation of the universe and planting of the paradise in Gen 1–2. Israel's special place within the whole universe, however, is best expressed by Israel's divine sonship in the context of new creation.

(3) Israel's divine sonship and new creation

Just after mentioning the connection between Adam and Israel in LAB 32:15, the author calls Israel God's own first-born and describes the eschatological hope of new creation:

> [16] . . . It will be like the night when God killed the first-born of the Egyptians on account of his own first-born. [17] Then I will cease my song, for the time will be readied for his righteous ones. I will sing praise to him at the renewal of creation. The people will remember this deliverance, and it will be a testimony for them. Let the sea with its deep be a witness, because not only has God dried it up before our fathers, but also he has overthrown the army from its stations and defeated our enemies. (LAB 32:16–17)

The night in v. 16, which will be like the Egyptian night of the Passover, probably refers to "a future eschatological night of redemption" (Tg. Ps.-J.

---

46. For the interpretation of Israel's unique place in LAB, see Barclay, *Paul and the Gift*, 272–78.

47. In LAB 11:2, 5, and 15:6, the giving of the law at Mount Sinai is interwoven with God's creation of the universe. With the "everlasting Law" God will judge not only Israel but also "the whole world" (11:2). LAB 15:6 designates the law as "laws for creation." In LAB 23:10, the author depicts God's redemption of Israel at the Red Sea and the giving of the law at Mount Sinai with many cosmic signs.

and Neof., Exod 12:42).[48] Israel, here, is described as "God's own firstborn," which derives from God's statement in Exod 4:22 ("Israel is my firstborn son"). It is interesting to note that in Exod 4:23, the purpose of Israel's exodus appears with further divine sonship language in God's subsequent statement to Pharaoh: "Let my son [Israel] go that he may worship me." That is, in Exod 4:22-23, Israel's divine sonship relates to Israel's priesthood. Thus, Israel's divine sonship in LAB 32:16 can refer to Israel's special status as an eschatological priest. The eschatological context of this passage goes one step further in v. 17, where the phrase "renewal of creation" occurs with cosmological language.[49]

The connection between divine sonship and the eschatological new creation also appears in LAB 16:2-5, where God himself warns against Korah and his followers' defiance (cf. Num 16). Pseudo-Philo combines together the stories of Korah, Cain's murder of Abel, and God's deliverance of Israel in the Red Sea through the motif of earth swallowing evil people. In the story of Cain (LAB 16:2), God "cursed the earth" (*maledixi terre*), but in Gen 4, when Cain murders Abel, God did not curse the earth. Rather, God cursed the earth after Adam's disobedience in Gen 3:17. The evil, like Korah and his men, will be swallowed up by the cursed earth and condemned to dwell in darkness until the day of judgment. The day of judgment, at the same time, is the day of new creation, where God will renew the earth and raise up all humanity except the evil from the earth:

> Behold I command the earth, and it will swallow up body and soul together. Their dwelling place will be in darkness and in the place of destruction. They will not die but waste away *until I remember the world and renew the earth*. Then they will die and not live, and their life will be taken away from the number of all men. The underworld will no longer spit them back . . . (LAB 16:3, emphasis added).

---

48. Jacobson, *Commentary*, 893-94.

49. In v. 17, the descriptions "God dried it [the sea] up before our fathers" and "has overthrown the army from its stations and defeated our enemies" are reminiscent of God's deliverance of Israel in the Red Sea (Exod 14:27, 29; 15:5). Thus, here the new creation motif is interwoven with God's exodus deliverance of Israel. The combination of the new creation and God's deliverance in the Red Sea also appears in LAB 15:5-6, where the author describes the division of the Red Sea with the language of the creation account in Gen 1:9: "And I commanded the sea, and the depths froze in front of them and walls of water stood forth. Nothing like this ever happened since the day I said, 'Let the waters beneath the heaven be gathered together into one place,' until that day" (LAB 15:5-6; cf. LAB 10:5).

Korah's seven sons, who had not joined in Korah's plot, rejected their bodily father's suggestion to join with him by saying, "Our father begot us, but the *Lord has fashioned us*. And now if we walk in his ways, we will be *his sons*" (LAB 16:5). Here, just after the author describes the day of new creation, the language of divine sonship appears again. As Fredrick J. Murphy well points out, 2 Macc 7:22b–23, where the mother of seven sons encourages her sons based on the fact that God is not only the Creator of the world but also will raise up them on the day of judgment, parallels this text.[50] Thus, the divine sonship in LAB 16:5 relates to both the Creator God and the hope of new creation in LAB 16:3, in which God will renew the world and raise up his people from the earth.

(4) The new womb and the new creation in LAB 60:3

Although the expression itself is slightly different from the divine sonship which we have seen above, in LAB 60:3, a very interesting phrase appears, namely, "the new womb." In LAB 60, Pseudo-Philo rewrites the narrative of 1 Sam 16:14–23, where David plays the lyre for Saul who suffers from an evil spirit. David's song in LAB 60:2–3, which does not occur in the original narrative in 1 Sam, demonstrates the origin of the evil spirit and David's supernatural power by reworking the creation account in Gen 1. After showing his knowledge of God's creation in the beginning and the origin of the evil spirit (LAB 60:2), David commands the spirit to stop being troublesome:

> "Now do not be troublesome, since you are a secondary creation. Otherwise, remember Tartarus wherein you walk. Or is it not enough for you to hear that by means of what resounds before you, I sing to many? Or do you not remember that your brood was created from an echo in the abyss? But the *new womb*, from which I was born, will rebuke you, from which in time one will be born from my loins and will rule over you." (LAB 60:3)

As Jacobson admits, the ambiguity of the meaning of "new womb" (*metra nova*) here might be such that "we should simply accept our inability to make sense out of the mysterious language."[51] Thus, Jacobson tentatively suggests that this means actually a "new age" by adopting a different reading from another manuscript family Δ here, which was not

50. Murphy, *Pseudo-Philo*, 82–83.
51. Jacobson, *Commentary*, 1179.

accepted by the majority of scholars.⁵² Also, another difficulty concerning the interpretation of this text is in identifying who is the "one will be born from my loins and will rule over you." Harrington and Murphy dismiss a messianic interpretation of this text because of Pseudo-Philo's lack of interest in a messiah.⁵³

However, this dismissal of the possibility of any messianic interpretation seems too hasty. There is a clear messianic implication in 2 Sam 7:12–14, which parallels this text in terms of the relationship between David and his offspring as well as his offspring's kingship:

> [12] When your days are fulfilled and you lie down with your ancestors, I will raise up your offspring after you, who shall come forth from your body (מֵעֶה), and I will establish his kingdom. [13] He shall build a house for my name, and I will establish the throne of his kingdom forever. [14] I will be a father to him, and he shall be a son to me. (2 Sam 2:12–14)

Very interestingly, the Hebrew term מֵעֶה has the meaning of "womb" (Gen 25:23; Isa 49:1; Ps 71:6; Ruth 1:11).⁵⁴ Also, the LXX and the Vulgate translate this term as κοιλία and *uterus* respectively, which mean "womb." One might point out the difference between the two wombs in LAB 60:3 and 2 Sam 7:12. That is, while the new womb in LAB 60:3 is not David's womb from which David himself was born, the womb in 2 Sam 7:12 is clearly David's "womb." However, we should note that in 2 Sam 7:14, another kinship appears: "I will be a father to him, and he shall be a son to me." Thus, given the parallelism between this text and 2 Sam 7:12–14, the new womb can refer to a close relationship between God and the Davidic lineage or simply, the *divine sonship* of the Davidic line.

Other occurrences of "womb" in LAB can support this interpretation. In LAB, it is God's power that can open or close women's wombs. For example, Hannah prayed and said, "Did you not, Lord, examine the heart of all generations before you formed the world? Now what womb is born opened or dies closed unless you wish it?" (LAB 50:4). The pattern that God opens a barren womb to give birth to a son can also be

---

52. He uses the reading of Δ "*arguet autem tempora nova unde natus sum*" and assumes a corruption of *arguent* to *arguet*. According to him, the corruption of *ent* to *et* is common. Then, the meaning of this verse will be "a new age will show from whom I am born" (Jacobson, *Commentary*, 1180).

53. They, thus, interpret this sentence as "an allusion to Solomon as exorcist." Harrington, "Pseudo-Philo," 373; Murphy, *Pseudo-Philo*, 209.

54. BDB, 589.

CHAPTER 2: THE CONCEPT OF NEW CREATION IN THE PARABIBLICAL TEXTS

applied to the births of Isaac, Jacob, Esau, and Samson (23:8; 32:1, 5; 42:1, 3). God's remark on Isaac's birth in 23:8 is particularly noteworthy since as Murphy observes, it uses not only the language of creation but also that of the eschaton[55]:

> I gave him Isaac and *formed him in the womb* of her who bore him and commanded <lacuna> to restore him quickly and to give him back to me in the seventh month. Therefore, every woman who gives birth in the seventh month, *her son will live, because upon him I summoned my glory and revealed the new age*. (emphasis added, LAB 23:8)

God himself, here, created Isaac in Sarah's womb and revealed the new age to the one who was born out of the womb in the seventh month. This strengthens the relationship between the womb and the divine power, which enables the divine gestation, in the eschatological context. As we shall see later (chapter 6, section 1), this tendency also is found in Rom 4:17, where Paul designates God as the one who "gives life to the dead and calls into existence the things that do not exist." This means that God's power enables Isaac's birth in spite of the state of Abraham's body ("already as good as dead") and "the barrenness of Sarah's womb" (Rom 4:19).

The new womb in LAB 60:3, therefore, implies the divine sonship between God and the Davidic line or at least the divine power which not only enables the divine gestation but also provides the ability to rule over evil spirits. Given the abundance of allusions to the creation account in LAB 60:2, the meaning of "new" in the phrase of "the new womb" probably refers to the "newness" or the "otherness" of this womb compared to ordinary wombs in the first creation.[56] In that sense, this new womb also indicates the concept of new creation.

To sum up, LAB describes the hope for new creation as a reversal of Adamic curses in Gen 3:16–19 within the *Urzeit-Endzeit* framework. Moreover, it not only focuses on the connection between Adam and

---

55. Murphy, *Pseudo-Philo*, 112.

56. In relation to this point, the concept of "Mother Earth or Womb Earth" is not uncommon in early Jewish writings (e.g., Gen 3:19; Job 1:21, 38:28–29; 4 Ezra 4:41–42, 5:48–49, 7:32, 8:8–11). Given the cosmological context of LAB 60:2–3, this understanding of the earth as womb in the first creation can be a counterpart of the concept of the new womb in the new creation. For more discussion regarding "Mother Earth or Womb Earth," see Dieterich, "Mutter Erde," 1–50; Hogan, "Mother Earth," 72–91.

Israel as a priestly figure but it also highlights the divine sonship of Israel and the Davidic line in the context of new creation.

7. The concept of new creation in 4 Ezra and 2 Baruch

The two famous Jewish apocalyptic writings, 4 Ezra and 2 Baruch, are so similar to each other that Michael Stone calls them a "matched pair" or "twins."[57] Both were written in response to the Roman destruction of Jerusalem in 70 CE through the voices of two pseudonymous characters, Ezra and Baruch, who lived at the time of the Babylonian destruction and exile. Also, they share the main structure that the two heroic figures are gradually being persuaded by Uriel (4 Ezra) and God (2 Baruch) regarding the meaning of the current catastrophe and the divine plan for Israel through the divine revelation and dialogue.[58] Both works are also significant for the present study since God's creation is one of the most important themes in both texts,[59] and Adam's role, in particular, is crucial not only for the current catastrophe but also for the eschatological hope for new creation.

(1) The concept of new creation in 4 Ezra

In 4 Ezra, the pessimistic world view of the present world and the hope for new creation of the world to come are expressed based on the Adamic narrative in Gen 1–3 within the *Urzeit-Endzeit* framework. The author's pessimism about this world is deeply rooted in his negative anthropology about human sinful nature. In 4 Ezra 7:11–12, God attributes the suffering of the present world to Adam's sin:

> For I made the world for their sake, and when Adam transgressed my statutes, what had been made was judged. And so the entrances of this world were made narrow and sorrowful and toilsome; they are few and evil, full of dangers and involved in great hardships. (4 Ezra 7:11–12)[60]

---

57. Stone and Henze, *4 Ezra and 2 Baruch*, 1.

58. For the close relationship between the two works, see Stone and Henze, *4 Ezra and 2 Baruch*, 1–2; Henze, "4 Ezra and 2 Baruch," 3–27.

59. For the theme of creation in 4 Ezra, see Moo, *Creation, Nature and Hope*. For the importance of the theme of creation in 2 Baruch, see, Klijn, "2 (Syriac Apocalypse of) Baruch," 618.

60. Translation is from Stone and Henze, *4 Ezra and 2 Baruch*, 40. All translations

Also, Ezra admits this fact by saying that "O Adam, what have you done? For though it was you who sinned, the fall was not yours alone, but ours also who are your descendants" (4 Ezra 7:118). Furthermore, in 4 Ezra 4:30, Uriel points out that the origin of humanity's evil heart was sown in Adam's heart: "For a grain of evil seed was sown in Adam's heart from the beginning, and how much ungodliness it has produced until now."

The hope for new creation at the eschaton, however, is depicted as the reversal of the curses caused by the Adamic sin. In 4 Ezra 7:13, Uriel contrasts the present world with the world to come whose "entrances are broad and safe, and really yield the fruit of immortality." "The fruit of immortality" implies, here, the reversal of the Adamic curse in Gen 3 (Gen 3:22–24; cf. Gen 2:17; 3:3). Again, we can find the *Urzeit-Endzeit* eschatology which restores Adam's right to freely access the tree of life at the garden of Eden. Moreover, the eventual purification of the world will occur after the temporary messianic kingdom:

> [30] And the world shall be turned back to primeval silence for seven days, as it was at the first beginnings; so that no one shall be left. [31] And after seven days the world, which is not yet awake, shall be roused, and that which is corruptible shall perish. [32] And the earth shall give back those who are asleep in it, and the dust those who rest in it; and the treasuries shall give up the souls which have been committed to them. (4 Ezra 7:30–32)

This text describes "the reversion of the age to primordial silence" and "a renewal of creation" at the eschaton. 7:75 designates this eschatological time as "those times . . . when thou wilt renew the creation." As Stone observes, here the Latin term *saeculum*, which corresponds to the Hebrew term עולם, can bear various meanings such as "world," "age," or "unlimited time," and evokes the language and context of creation.[61] After seven days, the world, which is not yet awake, shall be roused destroying the corruptibility of the original world. Thus, Doering describes this process as "de-creation and subsequent re-creation."[62] The bodily resurrection from the earth in v. 32 is a typical theme which implies the new creation at the eschaton in the Jewish apocalyptic tradition. Thus, this text depicts the new creation at the eschaton in connection with the *Urzeit-Endzeit* eschatology.

---

of 4 Ezra and 2 Baruch are from this book unless otherwise indicated.

61. Stone, *Fourth Ezra*, 217.
62. Doering, "*Urzeit-Endzeit* Correlation," 55.

The description of new creation as a reversal of the Adamic curse also appears in 4 Ezra 8:52–55, where Uriel speaks of the eschatological glory of the righteous that the righteous will enjoy: rest, goodness, wisdom, and immortality in the paradise where the tree of life is planted. The theme of the tree of life or the fruit of immortality, which appears in other verses of 4 Ezra (7:13, 123; 8:6), is the reversal of the inaccessibility of the paradise and the tree of life in Gen 3:22–24. As Stone points out, the term "delight" in v. 52 probably derives from "Eden," not only because the Hebrew term עדן means "bliss" but also because the phrase "paradise of delight" in 7:36 is probably a "literal translation of the rendering of 'garden of Eden' in Greek as παράδεισος τῆς τρυφῆς."[63] Moreover, "rest" and "goodness" are the technical terms for eschatological reward in connection with God's creation account in Gen 1–2. Thus, the eschatological hope of new creation in 4 Ezra 8:52–55 is expressed as the reversal of the Adamic curse in Gen 3, the reversal of affliction, labor, and death; that is, delight, rest, and immortality.

Another important passage in 4 Ezra for the present study is 6:38–59, where Ezra identifies Israel with Adam in the sense that God created this world for them. After Ezra describes God's creation of the world in six days, he highlights the fact that God placed Adam as ruler over all creation which God made for him and all Israel have come from Adam (vv. 38–54). Ezra, then, asks God why other nations oppress Israel and why Israel does not possess the world despite the fact that God created the world for Israel:

> [57] And now, O Lord, behold, these nations, which are reputed as nothing, domineer over us and trample upon us. [58] But we thy people, whom thou hast called thy firstborn, only-begotten, kin, and dear one, have been given into their hands. [59] If the world has indeed been created for us, why do we not possess our world as an inheritance? How long will this be so? (4 Ezra 6:57–59)

Given Adam's status as ruler of all creation and Ezra's identification of Israel with Adam in this text, we can envisage that the hope for the new creation concerns the restoration of Israel's status as ruler and heir of the whole creation. Here we should note that Israel's divine sonship ("firstborn, only-begotten son": cf. Exod 4:22; Gen 22:2) relates not only to Israel's inheritance of all creation but also to the hope for new creation.

---

63. Stone, *Fourth Ezra*, 221; 286. Cf. Joel 2:3; Ezek 36:35 LXX.

(2) The concept of new creation in 2 Baruch

Similar to 4 Ezra, the figure of Adam plays an important role to express the author's thought about the present sinful state of the world. Death came into this world and rules over all humanity because of Adam's sin (17:3; 19:8; 23:4; 48:42–43; 50:42–47). In the present world, "everything is in a state of dying" and this world is under the rule of the angel of death (21:22–23). Although the author of 2 Baruch argues that Adam does not cause his descendants to sin (54:19),[64] 56:5–6 evinces that Adam's sin deeply influenced all men:

> [5] . . . it is the transgression wherewith Adam, the first human, transgressed. [6] For when he transgressed, death [for those] not of his time came into being, mourning was named, sorrow was prepared, pain was created, labor was completed, pride began to be established, and Sheol sought to be renewed in blood, and the conception of children came into being, the fervor of parents was made, and the greatness of humanity was humiliated and goodness withered. (2 Bar. 56:5–6)

The sufferings from the consequences of Adam's transgression, however, will be remedied at the eschaton. The description of the messianic era in the angel Ramael's interpretation of the vision of the cloud (2 Bar. 73:1–74:3) envisages the reversal of the consequences of the Adamic sin. In 73:1–5, mourning, sorrow, pain, labor, pride, and death in 2 Bar. 56:5–6 will be removed and turn into joy, rest, healing, and immortality in the messianic era. Moreover, humanity will recover their authority as "the image of God" which Adam lost because of his disobedience at the garden of Eden; animals will come from their habitats and serve humans (73:6). Second Baruch 73:7—74:3, particularly indicates the reversal of the Adamic curse in Gen 3:16–19:[65]

> [73:7] Then women will no longer be in pain when they bear, nor will they be tormented when they give the fruits of the womb. [74:1] And in those days the harvesters will not grow tired, nor will the builders grow weary, for the works will progress quickly by themselves together with those who do them with much rest. [2] Because that time is the consummation of that which is

---

64. Levison argues that the author of 2 Baruch interprets Adam "as the 'spiritual' father of all the unrighteous who *imitate* his disobedience (18:1–2; 48:42–48)." Levison, *Portraits of Adam*, 130.

65. Doering, "*Urzeit-Endzeit* Correlation," 52.

> corruptible and the beginning of that which is not corruptible. [3] Therefore, these [things] that were said before will happen in it. Therefore, it is far away from the evils and near to those that do not die. (2 Bar. 73:7—74:3)

(1) Women will no longer suffer from their birth pangs (cf. Gen 3:16); (2) men will no longer toil to get their harvest due to the cursed ground (cf. Gen 3:17–18); (3) the era of incorruptibility will begin. That is, humanity will not need to return to the ground (cf. Gen 3:19).

The transition from the period of corruptibility to that of incorruptibility in 74:2 also appears in 2 Bar. 44:9–12, where Baruch makes the second public speech about God's judgment in the context of new creation:

> [9] For everything that is corruptible will pass by, and everything that is mortal goes away. All the present time will be forgotten, and there will be no memory of the present time, which is soiled by evils. [10] For he who runs now runs into emptiness, and he who prospers falls quickly and is humiliated. [11] For that which is yet to be will be desired, and that which is coming after this—we hope for it. For there is a time that does not pass, [12] and that season comes that remains forever, and that new world that does not return those to corruption who walk into its beginning, but upon those who walk toward torment, it does not show mercy. And those who live in it, it does not bring to corruption. (2 Bar. 44:9–12)

Here the sharp contrast between the present age and the age to come is highlighted by the former's corruptibility and the latter's incorruptibility. The coming *new* world is totally discontinuous with the present world since everything that is corruptible will pass away. As seen above, the corruptibility of the whole world was caused by the Adamic sin in 2 Baruch. Thus, the author describes the hope for the new world in the *Urzeit-Endzeit* framework.

In 2 Bar. 32, where the eternal building of Zion will be rebuilt, the author describes this transition from a different angle:

> [1] . . . the Mighty One will protect you in that time to come, who will shake up all of creation. [2] Because after a short time, the building of Zion will be shaken, in order to be built again. [3] But that building will not remain, but will again be uprooted after a time and will remain desolate until the time. [4] And after that, it must be renewed in glory and completed forever. [5] Therefore, we do not have to be saddened so much over the

> evil that has come now as over that which is yet to be. [6] For there will be a greater struggle than these two sorrows, when the Mighty One will renew his creation. (2 Bar. 32:1–6)

The time of new creation here is described as not only "when *the building of Zion* will *be renewed* in glory and completed *forever*" but also "when the Mighty One will *renew* his *creation*" (32:6; cf. 44:12; 57:2). As we have found in Jubilees and 1 Enoch, the concept of new creation in 2 Baruch relates both the eschatological renewal of the building of Zion and the cosmic renewal of all creation. The author already mentioned the building which God showed to Adam before he sinned (2 Bar. 4:3). God had prepared that building even before he intended to make the garden of Eden, but it is currently hidden from humanity because of the Adamic sin. However, that building is preserved with God now, and it will be revealed again at the eschaton together with the paradise (2 Bar. 4:6).[66]

Thus, we can notice that the author of 2 Baruch describes the hope for new creation which inaugurates the transition from the present world of corruptibility to the coming new world of incorruptibility, where God will rebuild the eschatological building and renew all creation within the *Urzeit-Endzeit* framework. This conclusion can be strengthened by the description of the messianic era in 2 Bar. 29:4–8, where the primordial beasts Leviathan and Behemoth which were created on the fifth day of creation serve as nourishment for the righteous. Not only these beasts but also the whole of creation including plentiful fruit-bearing plants and vine will be served as an eschatological feast for the righteous. This indicates a return to Adam's blissful life in the garden of Eden.

In sum, both 4 Ezra and 2 Baruch attribute the sufferings of the present world to the Adamic sin in the garden of Eden and describe the new creation as the reversal of the Adamic curses in Gen 3:16–19. Within this *Urzeit-Endzeit* framework, 4 Ezra and 2 Baruch develop the concept of new creation as found in Jubilees and 1 Enoch, which refers to the cosmic renewal of heaven and the earth and the eschatological establishment of the building of Zion.

8. Conclusion

In this chapter, we have investigated the concept of new creation in six parabiblical texts and have seen that the new creation motif is deeply

---

66. Doering, "*Urzeit-Endzeit* Correlation," 53.

rooted in the creation account and Adam narrative in Genesis 1–3 within the *Urzeit-Endzeit* framework. In other words, at many points, the *Endzeit* echoes and reverses key elements of the *Urzeit* (Gen 1–3), and thus implies a renewal and transformation of the original creation.

Two of the earliest and most influential parabiblical texts, Jubilees and 1 Enoch, express the new creation motif in connection with the themes of a renewal of creation (Jub. 1:29; 1 En. 91:13–17), building of a new temple (Jub. 1:29; 4:26; 1 En. 24:2–4; 91:13–17; cf. 2 Bar 32:1–6), establishment of a new Eden (Jub. 4:26; 1 En. 25:3–6). The Apocalypse of Moses is one of the earliest Second Temple Jewish writings that describes Adam's sin in the garden of Eden and its fatal influence on the whole world. The theme of resurrection in the Apocalypse of Moses implies the hope for new creation in which not only Adam but also Adam's descendants will recover Adamic glory, righteousness, and rulership over all creation (Apoc. Mos. 13:2–5; 28:4; 39:2–3; 41:3). LAB, 4 Ezra, and 2 Baruch also describe Adamic sin's influence on the whole world and express the hope for new creation as a reversal of Adamic curse in Gen 3:16–19 (LAB 3:10; 13:8–10; 4 Ezra 7:30–32; 8:52–55; 2 Bar. 73:1—74:3).

Another significant point we find in this chapter is that the theme of divine sonship in parabiblical texts often appears in the context of the new creation. For example, in Jub. 1:23–25 the elect of Israel are called sons of the living God, with receiving the Holy Spirit in the context of new creation. In Jub. 19:27–29, Abraham's eschatological blessings of the new creation include the acquisition of the eternal sonship of God. In LAB 32:16, Pseudo-Philo emphasizes the connection between Adam and Israel by mentioning that Israel was born from the rib of Adam (LAB 32:15), and then he calls Israel the firstborn of God in the context of new creation. Finally, in 4 Ezra 6:57–59, the new creation motif is related to the themes of Israel's divine sonship and inheritance of all creation.

Chapter 3: The Concept of New Creation in Qumran Literature

1. Introduction

SINCE THE DEAD SEA Scrolls were discovered near the site of Qumran in 1947, the Qumran literature has been one of the most important sources not only for understanding Second Temple Judaism but also for interpreting the New Testament,[1] although there are still ongoing debates regarding its origin[2] and its unity as a single library.[3] It also sheds light on the

---

1. For the huge impact of the discovery of the scrolls on New Testament scholarship, see Frey, "Critical Issues."

2. Since Eliezer Sukenik and Millar Burrows independently suggested the so-called "Essene hypothesis," most scholars still have regarded the Qumran-Essene identification as a valid hypothesis. Against "the Essene hypothesis," Norman Golb proposed the so-called "Jerusalem hypothesis," which argues that the scrolls originated in Jerusalem and were taken to the desert for hiding (Golb, *Who Wrote*). Other scholars (e.g., Hartmut Stegemann, Edward Cook, John Collins) argue for a revised version of the Essene hypothesis that the site of Qumran was a facility center for the larger Essene movement, not the headquarters of an autonomous Essene community, although they do not deny that Qumran was a religious center directly connected to the Dead Sea Scrolls. In this context, García Martínez proposed the "Groningen hypothesis," which distinguishes the origins of the Qumran group from the origins of the parent group, the Essene movement, and finds its origins from the apocalyptic tradition of the third century BCE (see García Martínez and van der Woude, "'Groningen' Hypothesis").

3. Since Frank Cross entitled his book *The Ancient Library of Qumran and Modern Biblical Studies* in 1958, most scholars have regarded the caves as the library of a religious community. Thus, they argue that the scrolls share a similar self-understanding as a community, legal traditions, and common interpretations of the Old Testament. However, some scholars (e.g., Sidnie White Crawford, Cecilia Wassen, Corrado Martone, Armin Lange, et al.) are doubtful that all of the Dead Sea manuscripts are part of a single library, since some of them seem to originate from different locations. See

diversity of Second Temple Judaism, even within Palestinian Judaism, before any "normative" Judaism was established. Thus, it is natural that we should include an investigation of Qumran literature in the present study to illuminate the concept of new creation in Second Temple Judaism.

In this chapter, I will deal with three important Qumran writings, the Hodayot, the Community Rule, and 4QInstruction. The reason for this selection is that the three texts not only contain the clear concept of new creation, but they also represent three important genres of Qumran texts, namely, hymn/poetic texts, the rule texts, and sapiential texts. The aim of this chapter is to demonstrate that: (1) the concept of new creation in Qumran literature is often expressed in connection with the Adamic narrative in Gen 1–3; (2) the concept of new creation has a close relationship with the language of divine sonship. These aims are the same as my previous investigation of the concept of new creation in the parabiblical texts. Also, I will try to reveal the meaning and the implications of the concept of new creation in Qumran literature.

2. The concept of new creation in the Hodayot

God's creation[4] is a prominent theme in the Dead Sea Scrolls.[5] Particularly, as Gordley argues, the motif of "God as creator of all things" is an overarching theme of the Hodayot,[6] as the author says in 1QH^a IX:22,

---

Schofield, "Dead Sea Scrolls," 152–53.

4. The theme of creation can refer to both the "creative act by God" and "the results of the divine act of creation." In the Qumran literature, the authors use the singular noun בריאה, a cognate of the verb ברא, to refer to the former while its plural בריאות refers to the latter. However, these nouns do not occur in the Old Testament except for Num 16:29–30, where God's act of creation refers to making the earth's mouth open to swallow Korah and his followers for their punishment. Moreover, in the Old Testament the participle of ברא is never used for the word "creator." Rather, the Old Testament uses the participles of other verbs such as יצר, עשׂה, פעל, and פעל to signify the meaning of "creator." Thus, we should not restrict our investigation of the concept of creation to the cognates of ברא. Rather, we should include other terms which can signify the meaning of creation in our investigation.

5. As Nitzan rightly observes, the theme of God's creation and God's eternal providence over his created world is apparent in the Qumran literature. According to him, this theme resonates with the biblical monotheistic concept of God's creation and relates all phenomena—cosmological, historical, and liturgical—to God's primordial decree (Nitzan, "Idea of Creation").

6. Gordley, "Creation Imagery," 266. In this article, Gordley also argues that the Hodayot goes beyond the biblical idea of creation in three points: (1) several creation passages in the Hodayot emphasise the weakness and impurity of humanity; (2) in spite

"According to your wi[ll] everything [comes] to pass; and without you nothing is made!" (ועל פי רצ[ונ]כה[] נ]היה כול ומבלעדיך לא יעשה). In what follows, I will investigate the theme of new creation in the Hodayot to find out its meaning and implications. Also, I will show that the concept of new creation in the Hodayot has a close relationship with the Adamic narrative in Gen 1–3 and the language of divine sonship.

(1) 1QH^a V:24–37

In connection with the theme of new creation, the most important text in the Hodayot is probably 1QH^a V:24–37 where the meaning of "new creation" clearly occurs:

> [24] And these are what [you] es[tablished from] ages [of old] to judge through them [25] all your creatures, before you created them together with the host of your spirits and the congregation of [the heavenly beings together wi]th your holy firmament and all [26] its hosts, together with the earth and all that springs from it, in the seas and in the deeps, according to all the plans for them for all eternal epochs [27] and the everlasting visitation. For you yourself established them from ages of old and the work [. . .] among them in order that [28] they might make known your glory in all your dominion, for you showed them what not y[. . .] which was of old, and creating [29] new things, destroying what was established of old, and [raising] up what will be forever. For you yourself have [established] them, and you yourself exist [30] for everlasting ages. In the mysteries of your understanding [you] apportioned all these in order to make known your glory. [But how i]s a spirit of flesh to understand [31] all these things and to discern [. . .] great [. . .]? What is one born of woman amid all your [gre]at fearful acts? He [32] is a thing constructed of dust and kneaded with water. Sin[ful gui]lt is his foundation, obscene shame, and a so[urce of im]purity. And a perverted spirit rules [33] him. If he acts wickedly, he will become [a sign for]ever and a portent for dis[ta]nt generations of flesh. Only through your goodness [34] can a person be righteous, and by [your] abundant compas[sion . . .]. By your splendour you glorify him, and you give [him] dominion [with] abundant delights together with

---

of the pervasive impurity of humanity, God's mercy and grace are highlighted in his redemptive act toward his creation; (3) God has predetermined the course of history before he established the whole creation.

eternal [35] peace and long life. For [. . . and] your word will not turn back. And I, your servant, know [36] by means of the spirit that you have placed in me [. . .] and all your deeds are righteousness. And your word will not turn back. And all [37] your ages are appoint[ted] . . . . (1QHª V:24–37)⁷

This text uses many terms for creation to highlight God's eternal plan, which has not been frustrated by any troubles that the community is undergoing. For example, the terminology of creation in ll. 24–26, such as "creature," "to create," "spirit," "firmament," "earth," and "sea" clearly allude to the account of God's creation in Gen 1. God established the destinies of all his creatures (כול מעשיך) before creating them (בטרם בראתם).

Particularly, God creates (לברוא) "new things" (חדשות) destroying what was established of old (להפר קימי קדם) and [raising] up what will be forever (ll. 28–29). In this statement of new creation, we can notice that the concept of new creation in the Hodayot does not merely refer to recovering the original state of the first creation. Rather, it is related to "destroying what was established of old." In other words, the difference between the new things and the old things is that the new things will be everlasting while the old things are not eternal. Thus, Mell rightly argues that God's eschatological new creation in 1QHª V:29 is not merely "antithetical" to the old world but also "beyond" it.⁸

As Holm-Nielsen observes, the contrast between the "former things" and the "new things" in 1QHª V:29 might allude to Isaianic texts (Isa 42:9; 43:19; 48:6–7).⁹ Isaiah 48:6–7 is particularly similar to 1QHª V:28–30 in that God shows formerly hidden things and creates new things now, and that God's glory is revealed in the community.¹⁰

At a deeper level, however, 1QHª V:24–37 also alludes to the account of God's creation and the Adamic narrative in Gen 1–3. In addition

---

7. Translation is from Schuller and Newsom, *Hodayot*, 21. This translation is almost the same as Newsom's translation in Stegemann, *1QHodayota* (DJD 40), with some minor revisions. All translations of the Hodayot are from this book unless otherwise indicated.

8. Mell, *Neue Schöpfung*, 100. "Die gesamte Schöpfung findet ihren Abschluß, wenn die vergängliche creatio originalis in die ewige creatio nova umgebrochen wird. Die verbal formulierte endzeitliche Neuschöpfungsaussage erscheint in Antithese zur bestehenden Welt. Die eschatologische Neuschöpfung ist Gottes Ziel jenseits der alten Welt."

9. Holm-Nielsen, *Hodayot*, 215.

10. Jackson, *New Creation*, 55. The theme of the revelation of God's glory to the community occurs in Isa 48:11.

to the creation vocabulary of ll. 24–26 aforementioned, the author uses the expression "born of woman" (ילוד אשה: v. 31) in connection with the phrase "a thing constructed of dust and kneaded with water" (מבנה עפר ומגבל מים). This alludes to Gen 2:7, where God formed man from the dust of the ground and breathed into his nostrils the breath of life. Some scholars regard the expressions such as "a thing constructed of dust and kneaded with water" or "a creature of clay and kneaded with water" (יצר החמר ומגבל המים)[11] as "technical terms in DSS for man's sinfulness as contrasted with the divine nature"[12] or "an idiom," doubting its allusion to Gen 2:7.[13] Although the direct verbal connection between 1QH[a] V:32 and Gen 2:7 is only עפר, given the importance of the Adamic themes in the Hodayot,[14] it is difficult to deny that the phrase "a thing constructed of dust" (מבנה עפר ומגבל מים) alludes to Gen 2:7. Also, the fact that Gen 2:22 uses the verb בנה (to build), a cognate of מבנה (structure), to describe Eve's creation supports 1QH[a] V:32's allusion to the creation narrative in Gen 2. Moreover, as Lichtenberger points out, the expression "kneaded with water" may indicate that God forms Adam from dust watered by the stream which rose from the earth in Gen 2:6.[15]

Similarly, other occurrences of "born of woman" in early Jewish writings (Job 14:1; 15:14; 25:4; 1QS XI:20–21) also have their origin in the Adamic narrative in Gen 1–3.[16] Particularly, in 1QS XI:20–22, the one born of woman parallels "the son of man":

11. This phrase repeatedly appears in the Hodayot (e.g., 1QH[a] IX:23; XI:25; XX:28).

12. Holm-Nielsen, *Hodayot*, 24n43.

13. Julie Hughes argues that "the creature of clay" in 1QH[a] XX:34–35 is the only allusion to Gen 2:7 while other occurrences of this phrase are best regarded as an idiom rather than an allusion since it occurs with the phrase "the one who returns to his dust," a clear evocation of Gen 3:19. See Hughes, *Scriptural Allusions*, 46–48.

14. For example, the description of trees, particularly the trees of life, in 1QH[a] XVI:6–7 is reminiscent of the tree of life in the garden of Eden in Gen 2:9. For more comparison between 1QH[a] XVI and Gen 2–3, see Yates, *Spirit and Creation in Paul*, 74–76. For more details of the Adamic themes in the Hodayot, see Meyer, *Adam's Dust*, 18–94.

15. Lichtenberger, *Studien zum Menschenbild*, 81–84.

16. In the Joban texts (14:1; 15:14; 25:4), "born of woman" refers to humanity's weakness and sinfulness. Particularly, 15:14 and 25:4 link this phrase to humanity's unrighteousness. We can trace the origin of humanity's unrighteousness to Adam and Eve's disobedience to God's commandment in the garden of Eden. Meyer and Maston argue that the phrase "born of woman" in the Hodayot has a direct connection with these Joban texts, although they admit that the origin of this phrase is the Adamic narrative in Gen 1–3. See Meyer, *Adam's Dust*, 51–53; Maston, *Divine and Human Agency*, 84. By contrast, Newsom argues that the language of loathing about humanity in the

> Who can endure your glory? What, indeed, is *the son of man* (בן האדם), among all your marvellous deeds? As what shall one *born of woman* (ילוד אשה) be considered in your presence? *Shaped from dust* has he been, maggots' food shall be his dwelling; he is spat saliva, *moulded clay*, and for dust is his longing. What will the clay reply and the one shaped by hand? And what advice will he be able to understand? (1QS XI:20–22)[17]

As Maston argues, "son(s) of man/Adam" (1QH[a] VII:19; cf. IX:29, 36; XII:31; IXX:9) and "born of woman" (1QH[a] V:31; XXI:2, 9; XXIII:13) may hint at "the first man and woman" and it is unclear whether the authors are referring to humanity in general or specifically to the first humans, Adam and Eve.[18] This ambiguity probably comes from the author's original intention to express the generality of all humanity. Thus, בן האדם and ילוד אשה in 1QS XI:20–22 can be translated as "son of Adam" and "born of Eve." This interpretation resonates with the Adamic narrative that "Adam named his wife Eve, because she was the mother of all living" (Gen 3:20). Moreover, the allusions to Gen 2:7, "shaped from dust" and "moulded clay," also support this interpretation.

Also, the author's description of humanity's sinful nature in 1QH[a] V:32–35 is reminiscent of Adam's fall in Gen 3. In particular, ערות קלן (obscene shame) in line 32 probably refers to Adam and Eve's shame they feel before God realizing their nakedness after their sin (Gen 3:7–11). The term עֵירָם (naked), a cognate of ערוה (nakedness)[19], occurs three times in Gen 3:7–11 (vv. 7, 10, 11).

Moreover, "a spirit of flesh" (רוח בשר) in l. 30, which refers to humanity's inability to understand God's eternal plan, can be understood in light of the Adamic narrative framework. This phrase also occurs in 1QH[a] IV:37–40, where the author contrasts it with God's holy spirit:

Hodayot has no direct connection with the Joban texts (4:17–21; 15:14–16; 25:4–6). See Newsom, *Self as Symbolic Space*, 220n44. Although she admits the Joban texts are one of the most important examples to show the negative anthropology of the Hebrew Bible, the pessimistic anthropology of the Hodayot comes from Gen 2–3. See Newsom, "Models of the Moral Self," 13–14, 23.

17. Translation is from García Martínez and Tigchelaar, *Dead Sea Scrolls*, 99. In this chapter, all translations of the Community Rule are from this edition unless otherwise indicated.

18. Maston, *Divine and Human Agency*, 84.

19. ערוה, *HALOT*, 882. This term also has the meaning of "genital area of a man or of a woman."

CHAPTER 3: THE CONCEPT OF NEW CREATION IN QUMRAN LITERATURE

[37] [...]their [domi]nion in his members; for your servant (is) a spirit of flesh. [...] *vacat* [...] *vacat* [38] [Blessed are you, God Most High, that]you have spread your holy spirit upon your servant[and you] have purified *m*[...]*t* his heart [39] [... hu] mankind, and to the whole covenant of Adam I will look[...] [...]*h* they will find it [40] [... w]*b* those who attain it and those who love it [... *yk*] for everlasting ages. (1QH^a IV:37-40)

Here God pours out the holy Spirit upon his servant and humankind to purify their heart. In other words, God pours out his Spirit to solve the problem of the "spirit of flesh" in their heart. God's saving activity here also relates to "the whole covenant of Adam" in line 39. The connection between a "spirit of flesh" and "the whole covenant of Adam" is uncertain, but it probably relates to God's blessings (Gen 1:28-30) and God's commandment to Adam, "you shall not eat the tree of the knowledge of good and evil, for in the day that you eat of it you shall die" in Gen 2:17 since other Second Temple Jewish writings describe this term in that way (e.g., 4QpHos^b 7-8; Apoc. Mos. 8:2; Sir 17:11-14). Also, in 4Q417 1 i 16-18, the spirit of flesh refers to humanity's inability to know the difference between good and evil in connection with the Adamic narrative in Gen 1-3, as we shall see later.

While "born of woman" and "a spirit of flesh" imply humanity's sinful nature which relates to Adam's ontological weakness as a creature fashioned from dust, the eschatological hope in 1QH^a V:33-35 seems to indicate the *reversal* of the miserable state caused by the Adamic sin and God's judgment in Gen 3:14-19. In other words, thanks to God's *goodness* and his abundant *compassion* (ll. 33-34), humanity will be restored to *glory, dominion* over all creation, *delight, eternal peace,* and *long-life* which Adam lost in the garden of Eden (ll. 34-35).[20] Here, we can see the sharp contrast between God's grace and humanity's sinful status in God's saving act of new creation.

The removal of sin and the restoration of Adam's glory within the *Urzeit-Endzeit* correlation also appears in 1QH^a IV:26-30:

[26] ... And [their] na[mes] you have *raised up* [27] [...] transgression and casting out all their iniquities and *giving them an inheritance in all the glory of Adam for long life.* [28] [...] *vacat*

---

20. As the Apocalypse of Moses describes, because of Adam's disobedience to God's commandment, Adam lost not only his *eternal life* but also his *glory, authority to rule over all creation* and the *peaceful relationship* with the creation (cf. Gen 3:14-19). See ch. 2, section 5.

> [29] [Blessed are you, O God of compassi]on on account of *the spirits that you have placed in me*. I will [f]ind a ready response, reciting your righteous acts and (your) patience [30] [. . .]k and the deeds of your strong right hand, and confessing the transgression of (my) previous (deeds), and p[rostr]ating myself, and begging for mercy . . . (1QH^a IV:26–30)

This passage implies inaugurated eschatology, which implies that God has already begun his salvific activity within the community, but the recovery of all the glory of Adam can also be connected to the hope for new creation in that it will continue until everlasting ages (1QH^a IV:32, 40). Also, as with 1QH^a V:33–37, God's compassion and mercy enable this process of new creation by placing His holy spirit in the community.

From the above discussion, it becomes clear that 1QH^a V:24–37 is full of the language and imagery in Gen 1–3. We, therefore, can conclude that the author makes the new creation statement in 1QH^a V:29 in connection with God's creation account and the Adamic narrative in Gen 1–3. Also, here the new creation is *God's* eschatological salvific activity: God planned it even before his first creation (ll. 25–26); God creates new things, destroying what was established of old; and God will raise up what will be forever (ll. 28–29); only through God's goodness, abundant compassion, and pouring of his spirit into humanity, can the Adamic curse on all creation be eschatologically reversed (ll. 33–37).

(2) 1QH^a XI:20–26

In the new creation statement in 1QH^a V:29, God's act of new creation includes not only "destroying what was established of old" but also "raising up what will be forever." What is the meaning of "raising up what will be forever" (להקים נהיות עולם)? We can find a parallel to this phrase in 1QH^a XI:20–26:

> [20] *vacat* I thank you, Lord, that you have redeemed my life from the pit and that from Sheol-Abaddon [21] you have lifted me up to an eternal height, so that I walk about on a limitless plain. I know that there is hope for one whom [22] you have formed from the dust for an eternal council. And a perverted spirit you have purified from great sin that it might take its place with [23] the host of the holy ones and enter into community with the congregation of the children of heaven. And you cast for a person an eternal lot with the spirits [24] of knowledge,

that he might praise your name in a common rejoicing and recount your wonderful acts before all your works. But I, a vessel [25] of clay, what am I? A thing kneaded with water. And as what am I regarded? What strength do I possess? For I have stationed myself in a wicked realm [26] and with the vile by lot . . .

The expression "from Sheol-Abaddon you have lifted me up to an eternal height" (משאול אבדון העליתני לרום עולם), which parallels "you have redeemed my life from the pit" in v. 20, signifies a similar concept to "raising up what will be forever" 1QH^a V:29 in terms of "raising up" and "eternity," although the two phrases use slightly different vocabularies. Here "God's lifting up one from Sheol-Abaddon to an eternal height" probably refer to "resurrection" from death.[21] The author already described the appearances of Sheol-Abaddon and the pit in the immediately preceding lines:

> [17] . . . And as they surge, Sh[eo]l [and A]badd[on] open up [and] all the arrows of the pit together with their retinue. [18] They make their sound heard to the deep, and break open the [eternal] gates [benea]th the works of venomous vanity. [19] And the doors of the pit close behind the one who is pregnant with iniquity, and the eternal bars behind all the spirits of venomous vanity. (1QH^a XI:17–19)

The אפעה (ll. 18–19)'s literal meaning is a "serpent" or "nothingness." Newsom translates it as "venomous vanity" since she argues that this term is probably a play on אפעה ("serpent") and אפעה/אפע ("nothingness").[22] Holm-Nielsen argues that here אפעה means "nothingness, wickedness" due to its parallelism with עול (iniquity).[23] This argument, however, seems unconvincing not only because "nothingness" and "wickedness" have different meanings, but also because lexically, אפעה/אפע do not have the sense of "wickedness." Rather, here אפעה seems to refer to a "serpent" since a "serpent" is more suitable for the subject of "the works" than "nothingness."[24] More specifically, the works of the serpent (מעשי אפעה)

---

21. In 1QH^a XVI:29–31, we can find a similar text where "pit" and "Sheol" together refers to a place of death: "[And dis]may [has come] upon me like those who go down to Sheol, and among the dead my spirit searches, for [my] life has reached the pit [. . .] my soul faints day and night without rest."

22. Newsom *Self as Symbolic Space*, 246.

23. Holm-Nielsen, *Hodayot*, 60n42; cf. Holm-Nielsen, *Hodayot*, 42–44n20.

24. Given the context of punishment here, a concrete noun "serpent" fits better than an abstract noun "nothingness" for an object of the divine judgment. The punishment over "the works of nothingness" is not only ambiguous but also unsuitable with the context.

probably refers to the serpent's evil deeds in the garden of Eden. The contrast between the two women's pregnancies—one is pregnant with a messianic figure (a wonderful counsellor in l. 11) and the other is pregnant with a serpent[25] (l. 13; cf. Gen 3:15)—and the themes of labor pains and death (cf. Gen 3:16; Gen 3:3-4) in the preceding lines (1QH^a X:8–13) also support this interpretation.

If this interpretation is correct, the phrase "raising up what will be forever" in 1QH^a V:29 can also refer to resurrection, and thus the statement of new creation in 1QH^a V:29 indicates hope for redemption from the Adamic death which was caused by Adam's disobedience in the garden of Eden.

Some scholars argue that the phrase "you have formed from the dust for an eternal council" (יצרתה מעפר לסוד עולם) in 1QH^a XI:22 implies the concept of new creation.[26] For example, Heinz-Wolfgang Kuhn, who interprets this verse as an expression that the eschatological salvation has already been inaugurated in the Qumran community, argues: "Daß die Heilszeit als schon gegenwärtig vorgestellt ist, kommt auch durch יצרתה in 3,21, das nur als 'Neuschöpfung' verstanden werden kann, zum Ausdruck."[27] According to Kuhn, although the phrase "you have formed from the dust for an eternal council" has no word for "new" in a literal sense, it can signify the concept of new creation because: (1) the following phrase "you have purified from great sin" (טהרתה מפשע רב) indicates that God's creative activity here is a *new* one in that it solves the previous human problem; (2) there are some parallels in the Old Testament[28] and

---

25. Newsom and Holm-Nielsen translate the phrase הרית אפעה in 1QH^a XI:13 as "she who is pregnant with venomous vanity" and "she that is pregnant with wickedness" respectively. Their interpretations are based on the fact that אפעה is parallel to שוא ("deception or worthlessness") in 1QH^a X:30: "Vanity and deception (אפעה ושוא) burst forth (יבקעו) toward the constellations when their waves mount up." As Holm-Nielsen argues, 1QH^a X:30 alludes to Isa 59:4b-5: "They rely on empty (תהו) pleas, they speak lies (שוא), conceiving mischief and begetting iniquity. They hatch adders' eggs, and weave the spider's web; whoever eats their eggs dies, and the crushed egg hatches out (בפע) a viper (אפעה)" (NRSV). As Newsom argues, although אפעה is probably a play on "serpent" and "nothingness," here its main meaning is "serpent," not "nothingness," as in Isa 59:4b-5 the combination of the terms בפע and אפעה indicates.

26. Sjöberg, "Neuschöpfung," 132–35; Schneider, "KAINH KTISIS," 82–83; Kuhn, "Gefundenen hebräischen Texte," 201.

27. Kuhn, *Enderwartung und gegenwärtiges Heil*, 48.

28. Kuhn argues that in Ps 102:18b ("so that a people yet to be created may praise the Lord") עם נברא has the meaning of "a newly created people" (Kuhn, *Enderwartung und gegenwärtiges Heil*, 48).

CHAPTER 3: THE CONCEPT OF NEW CREATION IN QUMRAN LITERATURE 81

rabbinical literature[29] where the meaning of "new creation" is expressed implicitly without the literal Hebrew phrase בריאה חדשה; (3) Given the theme of "salvation from death" in v. 20 and its parallelism with v. 22, עפר in v. 22 probably refers to "whereabouts of the dead" (cf. 1QH^a XIX:15). Accordingly, the creation from the dust implies the "abolition of the previous human existence" or "eschatological recreation of a pious community"; (4) the theme of participation in the eternal council resonates with the eschatological nuance of new creation that the new creation of the end times has already dawned.[30]

Mell, however, seems to be doubtful about Kuhn's interpretation of 1QH^a XI:22, which reads it as the eschatological new creation, on the following grounds. First, Mell claims that Kuhn's eschatological interpretation was made with the help of the late rabbinic literature which mainly relates to non-eschatological contexts, such as healing of people, deliverance from death, forgiveness of sins, and conversion to Judaism. Second, Mell points out that the verb of v. 22 is not ברא but יצר which, according to Mell, occurs nowhere in the Old Testament in the sense of "new creation." Third, Mell disagrees with Kuhn's interpretation of עפר which regards it as an equivalent of death. Rather, he argues that it refers to "humanity's sinful status" as a "structure of dust" in 1QH^a V:32. Fourth, Mell criticizes Kuhn's anthropological reading of new creation which connects 1QH^a XI:22 with the theme of "purification of sin," since it does not fit with the cosmological statement of new creation in 1QH^a V:29.[31]

Mell's criticism of Kuhn's interpretation, however, seems to be based on his false dichotomy between anthropology and cosmology in the concept of new creation. The connection between the phrase יצרתה מעפר לסוד עולם and the theme of "purification of sin" in this text cannot be evidence for the claim that this phrase has no reference to new creation. In fact, this passage has many verbal and thematic affinities with 1QH^a V:24-37. Apart from the connection between the theme of new creation and "raising up to eternity" aforementioned, the themes of "a perverted spirit" (v. 22; cf. 1QH^a V:32), "entering into the congregation of heavenly beings" (v. 23; cf. 1QH^a V:25), "the spirits of knowledge" (vv. 23-24; cf. 1QH^a V:36), "God's wonderful acts" (v. 24; cf. 1QH^a V:31), "a vessel of clay" (vv. 24-25; cf. 1QH^a V:32), and "a thing

---

29. E.g., Gen. Rab. 39; mShir 1:3, 8:5.
30. Kuhn, *Enderwartung und gegenwärtiges Heil*, 48-52.
31. Mell, *Neue Schöpfung*, 85-87.

kneaded with water" (v. 25; cf. 1QH^a V:32) also occur in 1QH^a V:24–37 with similar or even the same terms.

Moreover, just as 1QH^a V:24–37 has not only cosmological aspects but also anthropological aspects (descriptions of humanity's sinful nature), so 1QH^a XI:20–26 has cosmological dimensions as well. For example, the themes of "entering into the congregation of the children of heaven" and "recounting God's wonderful acts before all your works" have cosmological flavors. Also, a strong cosmological and apocalyptic context continues in 1QH^a XI:26–37.[32]

Mell's criticism that unlike ברא, there is no example in the Old Testament where יצר signifies the concept of *new* creation is partly true. However, we cannot exclude the possibility that in 1QH^a XI:20 יצר implies the meaning of new creation on the following grounds. First of all, in the Old Testament יצר often occurs with ברא to refer to God's act of creation without distinction (e.g., Gen 1:27; 2:3, 7, 19; Isa 43:7; 45:7, 18). As its cognate יֵצֶר metaphorically expresses the creator God as "potter," יצר refers to God's creative handiwork. Second, in the Old Testament, particularly Isaiah uses יצר almost exclusively to speak of God's creation of Israel in order to indicate God's *election* and *redemption* of Israel (Isa 43:1, 7; 44:21–24; 45:7; 49:5). This fits well with the context of God's redemption in 1QH^a XI:20–24. In that case, Isaiah uses יצר in the context of *new* creation in that God will restore Israel in spite of her current sinful status. Thus, Mell's claim that יצר cannot signify a concept of new creation based on its usage in the Old Testament is not convincing.

Mell's argument that עפר in the Hodayot refers to "humanity's sinful status" is right, but we should remember that "death" itself can *metaphorically* represent "humanity's sinful status" in the Adamic narrative in Gen 2–3.[33] In fact, in 1QH^a XIX:15 עפר is where God raises up "a corpse-infesting maggot." Thus, Kuhn's argument that עפר in v. 22 refers to "whereabouts of the dead" is right.

---

32. 1QH^a XI:26–37 describes a divine judgment over the wicked which involves the destruction of the cosmos. The destruction process is composed of the destruction of the watery areas with their vegetation and animals (l. 30), that of dry land and mountains (ll. 31–32), and that of the great deep and the underworld (ll. 32–33). This implies that the new creation event can accompany the destruction of the cosmos.

33. Recently, Chris W. Lee argued that the death warning in Gen 2:17 ("for in the day you eat of it, you shall surely die") itself does not provide textual support for its understanding in the sense of becoming mortal. Rather, he suggested that the death warning in Gen 2:17 should be read as introducing a death penalty within a legalistic setting, not a physical death. See Lee, *Death Warning*.

CHAPTER 3: THE CONCEPT OF NEW CREATION IN QUMRAN LITERATURE   83

In 1QH^a XI:20–24, the author describes a "transition" of status with several expressions in what follows:

From (metaphorically, death)	To (metaphorically, life)
vv. 20–21: from the pit and Sheol-Abaddon (משחת ומשאול אבדון)	to an eternal height (לרום עולם)
v. 22: from dust (מעפר)	to an eternal council (לסוד עולם)
vv. 22–23: from great sin (מפשע רב)	(enter) into community with the congregation of the sons of heaven (לבוא ביחד עם עדת בני שמים)

The recursive use of the prepositions מן and ל here clearly shows a sense of transition. This transition, which refers to redemption from death to life, is expressed as "creation from the dust to an eternal council" in v. 22. Thus, we can call this creation a *new* creation in that it accompanies the transition from death to life.

Also, the transition to the eternal council parallels "entering into community with the congregation of the sons of heaven" in v. 23. Although the phrase "the sons of heaven" (בני שמים, 1QS IV:22; 11:8; 4Q181 f1:2) does not appear in the OT, it seems to parallel the expression "the sons of God" in the Old Testament (cf. Gen 6:2, 4; Job 1:6; 2:1; 38:7; Ps 29:1; 82:6; 89:7; Dan 3:25) in the sense that it refers to heavenly beings or angelic beings. As Holm-Nielsen argues, here this phrase does not mean "an existence in the world to come," but it seems to refer to "the membership of the current community."[34] For the present study, it is crucial to note that the concept of new creation here has a connection with the theme of divine sonship. We can find this important relationship in 1QH^a XIX:12–17 as we shall see below.

(3) 1QH^a XIX:12–17

1QH^a XIX:12–17 has thematic affinities with 1QH^a XI:20–26 such as "purification of sin," "praises of God's wonderful acts," "self-denigration,"

---

34. Holm-Nielsen, *Hodayot*, 68n11.

"raising up from death (dust)," "entering into community with divine beings," and "new creation." This text, however, has more explicit language of new creation in l. 16:

> [12] but in your goodness is abundant forgiveness, and your compassion is for all the children of your good favour. Truly, you have made known to them the secret counsel of your truth [13] and given them insight into your wonderful mysteries. For the sake of your glory you have purified a mortal from sin, so that he may sanctify himself [14] for you from all impure abominations and from faithless guilt, so that he might be united with the children of your truth and in the lot with [15] your holy ones, so that a corpse-infesting maggot might be raised up from the dust to the council of [your] t[ruth], and from a spirit of perversion to the understanding that comes from you, [16] and so that he may take (his) place before you with the everlasting host and the [eternal] spirit[s], and so that he may be renewed together with all that i[s] [17] and will be and with those who have knowledge in a common rejoicing.

The statement "and so that he may be renewed together with all that is and will be" (ולהתחדש עם כול ה[וו]ה [ונהיה]) indicates the conception of new creation in terms of the use of the verb חדש (to make anew) and the theme of "the eternal spirit." In Ps 104:29–30, which evokes God's creation of Adam in Gen 2:7,[35] the psalmist uses this verb and the spirit to describe God's saving act of new creation: "When you take away their breath, they die and return to their dust. When you send forth your spirit, they are created (יבראון); and you renew (תחדש) the face of the ground" (Ps 104:29b–30; cf. Ps 51:12).

Here the person who God will renew is identified with "all the sons of your [God's] good favour" (כול בני רצונכה) in l. 12. The "sons of your truth" (בני אמתך) in l. 14 is another expression which implies divine sonship. According to Barclay, both are "a special sectarian self-label," which indicates that their identity is defined by God's "preference," neither by nationality as Israel nor by ethnicity as "children of Abraham."[36] As in 1QH[a] XI:20–24, here the phrase "being united with the sons of your

---

35. God's breath is the essence of the life, which animated Adam's body made out of dust (Gen 2:7). If God takes away his רוח from humanity, they will return to dust (Ps 104:29). See Allen, *Psalms*, 48.

36. Barclay, *Paul and the Gift*, 244. Here, "sons of your truth" (l. 14) and "your holy one" (l. 15) do not refer to angels although in Qumran literature "the saints" or "holy ones" often refers to angelic beings. See Holm-Nielsen, *Hodayot*, 187.

truth" signifies the transition of status, from "the dust" to "the council of your truth" (l. 15). This transition also indicates resurrection as the expression "a corpse-infesting maggot might be raised up from the dust" suggests. Thus again, we can find a close connection between the new creation motif and the theme of divine sonship.

As in 1QH^a V:33–35, God's goodness (טוב), compassion (רחמים) and favor (רצון) in l. 12 are the ultimate cause of the new creation of the sons of his favor and of all creation in 1. 16. This new creation is both eschatological and cosmological since it not only occurs with God's eternal presence ("the everlasting host" and "the eternal spirit"), but also with the renewal of the "sons of God's good favour"—a renewal which is part of the overall new creation of "all that is and will be" (ll. 16–17). At the same time, the concept of this new creation in this text is anthropological and soteriological since it relates to the themes of "purification of sin" and "sanctification from all impure abominations and faithless guilt" in ll. 13–14. This leaves no place for the false dichotomy between cosmology and anthropology in the concept of new creation which Mell and Hubbard devised.

In summary, the concept of new creation in the Hodayot and its implications are as follows. Firstly, the new creation in the Hodayot appears as a reversal of God's curse in Gen 3:16–19 within the *Urzeit-Endzeit* correspondence. In other words, the Hodayot describes God's new creation in the manner that the members of the community recover Adam's glory, rulership over the whole creation, and eternal peace in the garden of Eden. Secondly, the concept of new creation in the Hodayot highlights the sharp discontinuity and transition between the previous state and the newly restored state. Thirdly, this discontinuity in the concept of new creation is related to the change of the community member's status, which is newly given and is completely depending upon God's election and mercy. The new identity of the community is expressed by the language which implies divine sonship. This concept of new creation also appears in other Qumran writings, as we shall see in the next section.

3. The concept of new creation in the Community Rule

The Community Rule (סרך היחד, *Serek ha-Yahad*), which was among the first seven scrolls found, has been a critical document to reveal the life and self-understanding of the Qumran community behind the Dead

Sea Scrolls. The concept of new creation in the Community Rule relates to the eschatological destiny of the Qumran community and the world. I will analyze two passages of the Community Rule, 1QS IV:20–26 and 1QS XI:5–9, where the concept of new creation most prominently appears.

(1) 1QS IV:20–26

The Two Spirits Treatise (1QS III:13–IV:26) provides teaching for the Maskil regarding universal human nature in which the "spirit of truth" and "spirit of perversity" are struggling with each other. As Newsom rightly points out, Genesis 1 is "one identifiable text" with which the Two Spirits Treatise has "a particularly marked relationship."[37] The concept of new creation in the Community Rule most clearly appears in 1QS IV:20–26, a part of the Two Spirits Treatise:

> [20] . . . ripping out all spirit of injustice from the innermost part [21] of his flesh, and cleansing him with the spirit of holiness from every wicked deed. He will sprinkle over him the spirit of truth like lustral water (in order to cleanse him) from all the abhorrences of deceit and (from) the defilement [22] of the unclean spirit, in order to instruct the upright ones with knowledge of the Most High, and to make understand the wisdom of *the sons of heaven* to those of perfect behaviour. For those God has chosen for an everlasting covenant [23] and to them shall belong *all the glory of Adam*. There will be no more injustice and all the deeds of trickery will be a dishonour. Until now the spirits of truth and injustice feud in the heart of man: [24] they walk in wisdom or in folly. In agreement with man's *inheritance* in the truth, he shall be righteous and so abhor injustice; and according to his share in the lot of injustice, he shall act wickedly in it, and so [25] abhor the truth. For God has sorted them into equal parts *until the appointed end and the new creation*. He knows the result of their deeds for all times [26] [everlas]ting and has given them as a legacy to the sons of

---

37. Genesis 1–2 and 1QS 3–4 share many items of vocabulary such as "kind" (מין), "sign" (אות), "host" (צבא), "all" (כרא), "dominion" (ממשל), "plenitude" (מלא), "darkness" (חשך), "light" (אור), "generations" (תולדות). Newsom argues that although the text of 1QS 3–4 cannot be said to be "an exegesis of Genesis," the thick cross-referencing of vocabulary indicates that we should interpret 1QS 3–4 in connection with Gen 1. For example, the sharp contrast between light and darkness in one's heart (1QS 3:3, 19–21, 24–25) cannot fully be understood without understanding its relationship with God's creation of light and darkness in Gen 1. Newsom, *Self as Symbolic Space*, 86–87.

man so that they know good [and evil . . . and] to cast the lots of every living being according to his spirit in [. . . until the time of] the visitation. (1QS IV:20-26, emphasis added)

The concept of new creation, here, is interwoven with the themes of cleansing with the holy spirit, the recovery of Adam's glory, divine sonship, and inheritance.

Firstly, we should note that the eschatological time is expressed as "until the appointed end and the new creation" (עד קץ נחרצה ועשות חדשה) in l. 25. García Martínez translates עשות חדשה as "new creation,"[38] and this seems legitimate given the fact that Gen 1 uses עשה (vv. 7, 16, 25, 26, 31) alongside ברא to refer to God's act of creation. Also, this eschatological time parallels the famous phrase in Jub. 1:29, "the time of the new creation" (cf. 4Q225 1 7).[39]

Secondly, it is crucial to note that the hope for new creation is expressed as the recovery of all the glory of Adam (כול כבוד אדם) in l. 23. The glory of Adam here probably refers to Adam's status as a ruler over the whole creation since 1QS III:17-19, which is a part of The Two Spirits Treatise, alludes to Gen 1:27-28: "He [God] created man to rule all the world (הואה ברא אנוש לממשלת תבל וישם), and he assigned two spirits to him that he might walk by them until the appointed time of his visitation; they are spirits of truth and of injustice." John Collins, thus, argues that here אנוש is "none other than the Adam of Genesis 1:27."[40] The connection between Adam's glory and Adam's authority as "the image of God" ruling over all creation is also found in 4Q504 (4QDibHam\u1d43) Frag. 8 recto, which describes Adam as "the image of your [God's] glory" (l. 4; דמות כבודכה) to govern and to walk in "the land of glory" (l. 7; בארץ כבוד) namely, "the garden of Eden" (l. 6; גן עדן).

The phrase "all the glory of Adam," in fact, is a very important expression to signify the eschatological hope for new creation in Qumran literature, as we already have seen in 1QH\u1d43 IV:27. This phrase also appears in CD III:18-20, where God promises eternal life and all the glory of Adam for those who remained steadfast in God's commandments:

---

38. García Martínez and Tigchelaar, Dead Sea Scrolls, 80.

39. Mell translates עד קץ נחרצה ועשות חדשה as "until the end of all days determined by God when God will create something new" and calls it "the new creation statement" (Mell, Neue Schöpfung, 103).

40. Collins, Apocalypticism, 37-38.

[18] ... But God, in his wonderful mysteries, atoned for their iniquity and pardoned their sin. [19] And he built for them (ויבן להם) a safe house (בית נאמן) in Israel, such as there has not been since ancient times, not even till [20] now. Those who remained steadfast in it will acquire eternal life, and all the glory of Adam (כל כבוד אדם) is for them. (CD III:18–20)[41]

Wacholder interprets בית נאמן as an eschatological temple ("a new sanctuary") by reading ויבן not as a past consecutive (וַיִּבֶן, i.e., "and he built") but as a future tense verb (וְיִבֶן, i.e., "and he will build"). Grammatically, it is a legitimate reading. Also, this reading fits better with not only the context that the house (temple) "has not been since ancient times, not even till now" but also the eschatological context of acquiring eternal life.[42] If Wacholder's interpretation is correct, the recovery of Adam's glory in CD III:18–20 is interwoven with the establishment of an eschatological temple, a typical theme of new creation in Second Temple Judaism (cf. Jub. 1:29, 4:26; 1 En. 91:13–17). Given this relationship between "all the glory of Adam" and "new creation," it is at least clear that the theme of Adam's glory in 1QS IV:23 expresses the hope for new creation in connection with the *Urzeit-Endzeit* eschatology.

Thirdly, the phrase "the sons of heaven" in 1QS IV:22 indicates the fact that the theme of divine sonship is closely related to the theme of new creation as we already noticed above. As García Martínez points out, in Qumran literature the expression "the sons of heaven" is used as a collective name to designate angelic beings, replacing the expression "the sons of God."[43] The upright ones, who God cleansed with the spirit of holiness, now can participate in the communion with the angelic world (ll. 21–22). The theme of divine sonship, here, is also related to the theme of election (l. 22: "they [the upright ones] whom God has chosen for the eternal covenant") and inheritance (ll. 24–26). Intriguingly, the theme of new creation in 1QS XI:5–9 has many affinities with that of 1QS IV:20–26 in terms of the language of glory, divine sonship, election, and inheritance within the *Urzeit-Endzeit* correlation as I will discuss below.

---

41. Translation adapted from García Martínez and Tigchelaar, *Dead Sea Scrolls*, 555.

42. Wacholder also argues that the citation of Ezek 44:15 in CD 3:21–4:2a is supporting evidence for this reading since the last nine chapters of Ezekiel describe a new sanctuary, not the first temple built by Zadok for David and Solomon. Wacholder, *New Damascus Document*, 179–82.

43. García Martínez, *Qumranica Minora*, 263.

CHAPTER 3: THE CONCEPT OF NEW CREATION IN QUMRAN LITERATURE

(2) 1QS XI:5–9

The concluding psalm of the Community Rule describes the angelic world in which the members of the community are participating as the congregation of "the sons of heaven." Again, we can find a close relationship between the language of divine sonship and new creation within the Adamic narrative framework:

> [5] . . . My eyes have observed what always is, [6] wisdom that has been hidden from mankind, knowledge and prudent understanding (hidden) from the sons of man, fount of justice and well of [7] strength and spring of *glory* (hidden) from the assembly of flesh. To *those whom God has selected* he has given them as everlasting possession; and *he has given them an inheritance* in the lot of [8] the holy ones. He unites their assembly to *the sons of the heavens* in order (to form) the council of the Community and a foundation of the *building of holiness* to be an *everlasting plantation* throughout all [9] future ages . . . (1QS XI:5–9, emphasis added)

This text contrasts the hiddenness of divine gifts from the sons of man with the giving of divine gifts to God's selected people who are united to the sons of heavens: wisdom, knowledge, prudent understanding, justice, strength, and glory have been hidden from the "assembly of flesh," while all these gifts have been given to those whom God has chosen. We have seen that the participation in the congregation of the sons of heaven has a close relationship with the theme of new creation in the Adamic narrative framework (1QH[a] XI:23; 1QS IV:20; cf. 1QH[a] V:25). Here we can find that connection again. In addition, we can present several points in relation to the theme of new creation in the above text.

Firstly, the author says, "wisdom that has been hidden from mankind (אנוש)." As seen above, אנוש of the "Sapiential text" can refer to the Adam in Gen 1–3 (1QS 3:17; 4Q417 1 i 16). This tendency fits well with the theme of the "hiddenness of wisdom," which is reminiscent of Adam's expulsion from the garden of Eden, whereupon he became unable to access not only the tree of life but also the tree of the knowledge of good and evil. Moreover, the expression "knowledge (דעה) and prudent understanding (hidden) from the sons of man (אדם)" has the word אדם, which can have both meanings of humankind and the particular Adam of Gen 1–3. Also, the term דעה (*knowledge* or *wisdom*) here is a cognate of דעת,⁴⁴ which is used for "the tree of the *knowledge* of good and evil" (עץ הדעת טוב ורע) in Gen 2:17. Thus, this dual meaning of אנוש and אדם indicates that the theme of the hiddenness of wisdom or knowledge can be understood in the Adamic narrative of Gen 1–3.

Secondly, as Doering argues, the phrase "everlasting plantation" (למטעת עולם) evokes the garden of Eden in Gen 2:8: "And the Lord God planted a garden in Eden, in the east" (ויטע אלהים גן־בעדן מקדם). According to Doering, the phrase "building of holiness," which signifies temple, corroborates the link between the planting metaphor and Eden since many texts in Second Temple Jewish literature connect Eden to the eschatological temple (e.g., Jub. 1:29; 4:26, 8:19; 1 En. 24–25).⁴⁵ Doering's argument can be strengthened by the occurrences of the phrase למטעת עולם in the Hodayot. In 1QHᵃ XIV:17–19, this phrase appears with a description of Eden in an eschatological context:

> [17] . . . and they repent because of your glorious command, so that they become your princes in the [eternal] lo[t and] their [shoot] [18] opens as a flower [blooms, for] everlasting fragrance, making a sprout grow into the branches of an *eternal planting* (מטעת עולם). And it will cast shade over all the world, and its br[anches] [19] will reach to the clouds and its roots as far as the deep. *All the rivers of Eden* (כול נהרות עדן) [make] its [br]an[ches m]oist, and it will (extend) to the measure[less] seas . . . (1QHᵃ XIV:17–19, emphasis added)

Here we can find the clear connection between "everlasting plantation" and the garden of Eden in the eschatological context. This eschatological blessing of the "new Eden" will be given to the members of the community "in the midst of humankind" (בתוך בני אדם) in 1QHᵃ XIV:14. Newsom translates the phrase בתוך בני אדם as "in the midst of humankind," but given the Edenic context of this text, a more precise translation would be "in the midst of *the sons of Adam*" as García Martínez translates.⁴⁶ Similarly, the phrase "everlasting plantation" also occurs in 1QHᵃ XVI:5–7 with another allusion to Gen 2, namely "trees of life":

> [5] I thank [you, O Lo]rd, that you have placed me by the source of streams in a dry land, (by) a spring of water in a thirsty land, and (by) a watered [6] garden (גן), and a pool the field, a planting

---

44. *HALOT*, s.v. "דֵּעָה." Cf. *HALOT*, s.v. "דַּעַת."
45. Doering, "*Urzeit-Endzeit* Correlation," 46–47.
46. García Martínez and Tigchelaar, *Dead Sea Scrolls*, 176

of juniper and elm with cedar all together for your glory, *trees of [7] life* (עצי חיים) at a secret spring, hidden in the midst of all the trees by the water. And they were there so that a shoot might be made to sprout into an *eternal planting* (למטעת עולם). (1QH^a XVI:5–7, emphasis added)

A few verses later, the author, in fact, designates this eschatological garden as a glorious Eden (עדן כבוד, 1QH^a XVI:21). Moreover, 1QH^a XVI has plentiful allusions to Gen 2–3.[47] Thus, it is difficult to deny that "everlasting plantation" in 1QS X1:8 has a close connection to the Adamic (or Edenic) motif in Gen 2–3 in light of its usages in the Hodayot. The connection between "everlasting plantation" and "building of holiness" (or "temple") also appears in 1QS VIII:5–6, where the author equates למטעת עולם with a "holy house for Israel" (בית קודש לישראל) and "the holy of holies for Aaron" (קודש קודשים לאהרון). Thus, it is highly probable that the expression "a foundation of the building of holiness to be an *everlasting plantation*" in 1QS XI:8 refers to the establishment of the eschatological temple, which is one of the most important themes of new creation in Second Temple Judaism. Thus, we can conclude that the theme of divine sonship in 1QS XI:5–9 is associated with the new creation motif within the Adamic narrative framework in terms of the conjoining of the elect with the angelic beings.

The aforementioned affinity between 1QS IV:22 and 1QS XI:5–9 is that the language of divine sonship appears with the themes of election and inheritance in the context of new creation. The privilege of the participation in worship with the sons of heaven is *given* to God's *chosen* community as an *inheritance*. The emphasis on God's election, gift, and inheritance indicates God's initiative in his salvific activity. Thus, the author continues to confess, "By his knowledge everything shall come into being, and all that does exist he establishes with his calculations and nothing is done outside of him" (l. 11). In this context, 1QS XI:12–15 sharply contrasts God's mercy, compassion, and great goodness with humankind's transgressions, impurity, sinfulness. God's mercy will be "my everlasting salvation" (l. 12), justification comes by God's mercies and compassion (ll. 13–14), and in God's great goodness,

---

47. In addition to "trees of life" and "glorious Eden," there are other allusions to Gen 2–3 in 1QH^a XVI. For example, the verb שקה in "watered garden" (משקי גן) in ll. 4–5 appears in Gen 2:10, describing a river flows out of Eden "to water the garden" (להשקות את־הגן) (cf. Gen 2:6). Also, "the whirling flame of fire" (להט אש מתהפכת) in l. 13, which guards the spring of life and the everlasting trees clearly alludes to a "sword flaming and turning" (להט החרב המתהפכת) to guard the way to the tree of life in Gen 3:24.

God will atone for all transgression, impurity, and sinfulness (ll. 14–15). This is the theology of creation, in which everything comes into being by God's creation, and at the same time, this is the theology of new creation, in which God redeems the sons of Adam from the sinfulness of mortals to participate with the sons of heaven.

In sum, the concept of new creation in the Community Rule is very similar to that of the Hodayot. First, the Community Rule expresses the theme of new creation as the recovery of all the glory of Adam within the *Urzeit-Endzeit* framework. Second, the concept of new creation is interwoven with the theme of divine sonship in the manner that the elect participate in the communion with the angelic beings. Third, the theme of new creation as God's salvific activity highlights God's election and mercy for the chosen people.

4. The concept of new creation in 4QInstruction (Mûsār Lĕ Mēbîn)[48]

4QInstruction (1Q26, 4Q415–418, 4Q243) is the longest sapiential text in Qumran literature.[49] However, unlike other wisdom texts based on biblical wisdom tradition, it is famous for its affinities with apocalypses in terms of eschatology and the theme of revelation. The enigmatic phrase רז נהיה, which can be translated as "the mystery that is to be," appears more than twenty times in 4QInstruction in the context of eschatological judgment. Thus, Matthew Goff calls 4QInstruction "a wisdom text with an apocalyptic worldview."[50] 4QInstruction often starts a new discourse with a formula "ואתה מבין plus an imperative" particularly in 4Q416–4Q418. The addressee *mebin* (understanding one) is a term that describes a person who wants to learn as a member of the community, as other important Qumran texts use the same term to portray a member of the *yaḥad* (1QS 11:7–8; 1QH 19:14–15).[51] In relation to the pres-

---

48. Strugnell and Harrington named 4QInstruction Mûsār Lĕ Mēbîn (מוסר למבין), which means "instruction for a *mebin* (student)." Strugnell et al., *Qumran Cave 4*.

49. Proverbs, Job, and Ecclesiastes represent the wisdom tradition in the Old Testament, while Ben Sira and the Wisdom of Solomon in the Apocrypha also follow this tradition. Apart from 4QInstruction, other texts (e.g., 4Q184; 4Q185; The Two Spirits Treatise [1QS III:13–IV:26]; 4Q424; 4Q525) from Qumran have been also widely recognized as sapiential literature. See Goff, *Discerning Wisdom*, 3–6, 70.

50. Goff, *4QInstruction*, 19.

51. Goff, *4QInstruction*, 17.

CHAPTER 3: THE CONCEPT OF NEW CREATION IN QUMRAN LITERATURE 93

ent study, it is important to note that 4QInstrunction uses the Adamic narrative in Gen 1–3 to describe the elect status of the *mebin*.[52] In what follows, I will show how the author of 4QInstruction portrays the present and eschatological status of the *mebin* in parallel with Adam's status in Gen 1–3. In that process, I will also show that the author often uses language of divine sonship to highlight the *mebin*'s elect status. Lastly, I will demonstrate that the author expresses the eschatological hope for new creation within the *Urzeit-Endzeit* correlation.

(1) 4Q416 1:10–17

4Q416 1 is generally regarded as the opening text of 4QInstruction because of its remarkably wide right margin in the fragment. After discussing the orderly structure of the cosmos and God's dominion over the cosmos (ll. 1–9), the author describes the eschatological judgment in which the wicked will be destroyed while all the sons of God's truth will be saved:

> [10] in heaven he will judge over the work of wickedness. But all the sons of his truth will be favorably accepted b[*efore him* . . .] [11] its end. And all those who polluted themselves in it (wickedness) will be terrified and cry out, for heaven will be afraid; [*earth*] wi[ll shake from *its* place;] [12] [s]eas and depths are terrified. Every fleshly spirit will be laid bare but the sons of heav[en . . . on the day of] [13] its judgment. And all iniquity will come to an end forever and the period of tru[th] will be completed [*forever* . . .] [14] in all the periods of eternity, for he is a god of truth. From before the years of [*eternity* . . .] [15] to make a righteous person understand the difference between good and evil to . . . every judgme[*nt* . . .] [16] it is a fleshly [in]clination and understanding [*ones* . . .] [17] his creatures, for . . . [18] . . .[53]

---

52. Goff argues that "4Q423 1 makes the remarkable claim that the *mebin* is entrusted with the garden of Eden" using the story of Gen 2:15 where God took Adam and put him in the garden of Eden to till it and keep it. Also, the term אנוש and the theme of the knowledge of good and evil (4Q417 1 i 17–18) evoke Adam (Goff, *4QInstruction*, 18–19).

53. Translation is from Goff, *4QInstruction*, 44. In this chapter, all the translations from 4QInstruction are from Goff's edition. Regarding the usage of brackets and italics Goff explains, "Any letter within brackets that is in a shadow font (א) is not based on physical evidence but is rather supplemented on semantic grounds. In the translation this material is in italics" (Goff, *4QInstruction*, xvi).

The eschatological judgment depicted here is also a cosmological one in which heaven will fear and the earth will shake from its place. This implies that the divine judgment will accompany a cosmic renewal or a new creation. All the sons of God's truth, however, will be favorably accepted by God at the eschaton. The expression "all the sons of his truth" (כל בני אמתו) can be regarded as the language of divine sonship given the fact that the author designates God as a "god of truth" (אל אמת) in l. 14. Moreover, in l. 12 the language of divine sonship (i.e., "the sons of heaven") appears again although its reference is not clear; it can refer to angels,[54] but we cannot exclude the possibility that it refers to the righteous in l. 15 (or "all the sons of his truth" in l. 10) since 4QInstruction often expresses the *mebin*'s elect status with their special affinity with the angels.[55]

The phrase "the sons of heaven" also appears in 4Q418 69 ii:12–13: "And the s[ons of] heaven whose inheritance is eternal life, would they really say 'We are weary of deed of truth and [we] are tired of [*vacat* (?)].'" Here again "the sons of heaven" can refer to angels. However, as Fletcher-Louis well argued, it probably refers to the righteous since in Qumran literature or the early Jewish traditions "inheritance" is almost always the privilege of the human elect, not angels.[56]

Thus, it is at least clear that the phrase "the sons of heaven" (בני השמים) in 4Q416 1:12 is related to the theme of divine sonship whether it refers to the human elect's acquisition of divine sonship (in this case, "the sons of heaven" is identified with "the sons of his truth" in l. 10) or their participation in the congregation of the heavenly beings. At the same time, this confirms the inseparable relationship between the language of divine sonship and the theme of new creation.

In l. 15, the elect status of "the sons of his truth" is expressed as the possession of knowledge of good and evil: "to make a righteous person understand the difference between good and evil to ... every judgment." It does not merely refer to the elect's ability to live in a righteous manner but indicates that God reveals the knowledge of good and evil to the elect. As we shall see later, in 4Q423 1:1–2 the author highlights the

---

54. Goff argues that as in other early Jewish literature (e.g., 1QS 4:22; 1QapGen 2:16), this phrase refers to angels since it does not have a definite article (Goff, 4QInstruction, 52–53). The editors of DJD 34 argue that the same phrase in 4Q418 69 ii:12 refers to angels, although they do not leave any comments about the reference of בני משמים in 4Q416 1:12. See Strugnell et al., *Qumran Cave 4*, 290.

55. We will see the close relationship between the *mebin*'s elect status and their participation in the lot of angelic beings in other passages of 4QInstruction below.

56. Fletcher-Louis, *All the Glory of Adam*, 120.

CHAPTER 3: THE CONCEPT OF NEW CREATION IN QUMRAN LITERATURE 95

mebin's possession of Adam's stewardship over the garden of Eden and connects Adam's stewardship to "making one very wise." Thus, in light of this, here the ability to understand the difference between good and evil parallels Adam's possession of the knowledge of good and evil in the garden of Eden (cf. Gen 2:9, 17). This connection becomes clearer in 4Q417 1:16-18 as we shall see below.

(2) 4Q417 1:16-18

As 4Q416 1:10-17 contrasts fleshly spirit with the sons of heaven, in 4Q417 1:16-18 the author emphasizes the dichotomy between "spiritual people" and "people of the fleshly spirit" using the Adamic narrative of Gen 1-3:

> [16] ... He bequeathed it to Adam (אנוש) together with a spiritual people be[*cau*]se [17] according to the likeness of the holy ones he fashioned him. But no more did he give what is meditated upon to the fleshly spirit, for it did not distinguish between [18] [*go*]od and evil according to the judgment of its [*sp*]irit. *vacat* And you, understanding son, gaze *vacat* upon the mystery that is to be and know.

As seen above, and as Goff translates it, here the term אנוש can refer to Adam although there are other interpretative options.[57] Collins well observes that in the sapiential text, particularly in 4Q417 1:16-18, the authors associate אנוש with "in the likeness of the Holy Ones" (l. 17), which evokes "in the image of God" in Gen 1:27, while other Qumran writings (e.g., the Hodayot, the Community Rule) often use this term to highlight the sinful state of the human beings.[58] Collins argues further that these two tendencies of Qumran literature in terms of the usages of אנוש can be traced to the creation narrative in Gen 1-2, which signifies two dichotomous human

---

57. It can refer to either humankind or the proper name of the son of Seth (Gen 4:2,; 5:6-7). The editors of DJD 34 support the former option since they think here the אנוש is the same group of the spiritual people, which is contrasted with "the fleshly spirit." In other words, they argue that here וינחילה does not refer to "a heavenly transmission of learning to an individual in history," but it refers to "a general bestowal of gifts upon mankind" (Strugnell et al., *Qumran Cave 4*, 164-65). On the other hand, Lange claims that the אנוש, which is differentiated from "the fleshly spirit," cannot refer to humankind in general. Rather, the אנוש here refers to the proper name of the antediluvian patriarch Enosh, since the author mentions "the children of Seth" in l. 15 (Lange, *Weisheit und Prädestination*, 88).

58. Collins, *Jewish Wisdom*, 124; Collins, "In the Likeness," 609-18.

types, as Philo of Alexandria famously argued for "double creation of man" in Gen 1–2: as the image of God in Gen 1:27 and from the dust in Gen 2:7.[59] According to Collins, thus, the two types of humanity in this text, a spiritual people in the likeness of the Holy Ones and a "spirit of flesh," are based on the creation narrative in Gen 1–2.[60]

The language of creation in this text supports Collins's interpretation and indicates its background in Gen 1–2. For example, the verb יצר in l. 17 (cf. 1. 9) is the very term to describe God's creation of Adam in Gen 2:7. In addition to it, "dominion of its creature" (l. 9: ממשלת מעשיה) and "every creature" (l. 10: כול מעשה) also evoke God's creation of Adam as a ruler over all creation in Gen 1:27–30.[61]

In light of this interpretation, it is natural that we should understand the fleshly spirit's inability "to distinguish good and evil" in ll. 17–18 in connection with the Adamic narrative in Gen 2–3. Conversely, this implies the spiritual people's possession of knowledge of good and evil, as the author already mentioned the *mebin*'s eschatological possession of knowledge of good and evil in l. 8 (cf. 4Q416 1:15). Also, the likeness of the holy ones (תבנית קדושים) in l. 11 probably refers to the *mebin*'s affinity with angels. Thus, this text resonates with 4Q416 1:10–17 in that the author expresses the elect's high status with "their possession of knowledge of good and evil" and "their affinity with angels" in connection with Adam's glorious status in the garden of Eden. We can also find this connection in 4Q418 81:1–5.

(3) 4Q418 81:1–5

The theme of the *mebin*'s likeness to the holy ones (תבנית קדושים), one of the major themes of 4QInstruction, most clearly appears in 4Q418 81:1–5:

> [1] Your lips he has opened as a spring to bless the holy ones.
> So you, as an eternal spring, praise [his name, beca]use he has

---

59. *Opif.* 134–35; *Alleg.* 1.31. As seen above, recently Meyer describes this schema in Gen 1–2 and the Hodayot as "Adam's Dust and Adam's Glory."

60. Collins, *Jewish Wisdom*, 124–25.

61. Some scholars (e.g., García Martínez, Goff, et al.) translate ממשלת מעשיה as "the dominion of its deeds" since מעשה can refer to both meanings. However, given the fact that מעשה appears again in l. 10 with the meaning of "creature," it seems more reasonable to take ממשלת מעשיה as "the dominion of its creature" in connection with the creation narrative in Gen 1–2.

CHAPTER 3: THE CONCEPT OF NEW CREATION IN QUMRAN LITERATURE 97

> separated you from every [2] fleshly spirit. And you, separate yourself from all that he hates and keep away from all abominations of the soul, [beca]use he has made everyone [3] and has bequeathed to each man his inheritance. He is your portion and your inheritance among the sons of Adam, [and over] his [in]heritance he has given you dominion. So you [4] in this way glorify him, by making yourself holy to him, as he has established you as a holy of holies [over all the] earth. And among all the [a]n[gels] [5] he has cast your lot and your glory he has greatly magnified. He has established you for himself as a firstborn son among . . .

This paragraph begins with the elect's blessing of the angels and ends with their elect status as God's firstborn son among all the angels. Although Goff translates נחלתכה בתוך בני אדם in l. 3 as "your inheritance among humankind," it should be literally translated as "your inheritance among the sons of Adam." This translation can be supported by the fact that the author mentions this inheritance in connection with the dominion (or authority) that God gives (המשיל). In 4Q423 1:2 (cf. 4Q417 1:9), the same phrase (המשיל) appears again to signify Adam's authority in the garden of Eden (Gen 2:15), as we shall see below. This interpretation also resonates with the cosmological statement in l. 4, "he has established you as most holy [over all the] earth," which evokes Adam's rulership over the whole creation (Gen 1:27–30). Moreover, in ll. 13–14, the author mentions the *mebin*'s inheritance of the earth in connection with the eternal planting (מטעת עולם). As seen above, in Qumran literature this phrase often appears with the description of the garden of Eden (e.g., 1QH^a XIV:17–19; 1QH^a XVI:5–7; 1QS 11:8). Thus, it seems clear that this text describes the *mebin*'s elect status in comparison with Adam's status in the garden of Eden. This can be understood as an inaugurated eschatology in the Qumran community with the framework of *Urzeit-Endzeit* correlation.

Finally, we should note that the author expresses the *mebin*'s elect status with the language of divine sonship in l. 5: "He has established you for himself as *a firstborn son* among . . ." ([. . .]וישימכה לו בכור ב). The editors of DJD 34 regard this designation as "a little surprising"[62] since in the Old Testament it usually refers to Israel (Exod 4:22) or Israel's king (2 Sam 7:14). However, we already have seen that 4QInstruction often uses the language of divine sonship to emphasize the *mebin*'s elect status. Here the theme of divine sonship is interwoven with the participation in the lot of the angels in l. 4: "he has established you as a holy of holies

---

62. Strugnell et al., *Qumran Cave 4*, 305.

[over all the] earth" ([שמכה לקדוש קודשים] לכול [תבל ובכול] א[ל]ים]). The parallelism between l. 4 and l. 5 (שמכה ל~) indicates that the divine sonship also relates to the *mebin*'s rulership over all the earth. Now we will examine the *mebin*'s rulership in 4Q423, where that theme occurs most clearly in 4QInstruction.

(4) 4Q423

Although 4Q423 is a short fragment, it is significant for understanding early Jewish literature's interpretation of Gen 1–3. This text, in particular, is famous for its remarkable argument that the *mebin* has the stewardship over the garden of Eden, which was previously given to Adam:

> [1] . . . and every fruit of the produce and every delightful tree, desirable for making one wise. Is it not a de[lightful and desirable] garden . . . [2] . . . for [making] one v[er]y wise? He has given you authority over it to till it and keep it. *vacat* A [lush] gar[den . . .] [3] [. . . but the earth] will make thorn and thistle sprout for you and its strength will not yield to you . . . [4] . . . when you are disloyal. *vacat* . . . [5] . . . *vacat* she has given birth and all the wombs of pregnant [women . . .] [6] . . . in all your desires because it will make everything spro[ut for you . . .] [7] . . . and with the planting . . .

In ll. 1–2, the author uses many allusions to Gen 1–3 in order to describe the *mebin*'s elect status in connection with Adam's status in the garden of Eden. First, the descriptions of fruits and trees in the garden, "every delightful tree" (כל עץ נעים) and "desirable for making one wise" (נחמד להשכיל) are echoes of Gen 2:9 and 3:6 respectively. Second, as seen above, in 4Q418 81:3 the author already argued that God has given the *mebin* authority (המשיל) among the sons of Adam. Here the connection with Adam becomes clearer due to the further allusions to Gen 2:15. That authority is revealed as Adam's authority over the garden of Eden to till and to keep. The verbs עבד (to till) and שמר (to keep) are the same terms as found in Gen 2:15: "The Lord God took Adam and put him in the garden of Eden to till it and keep it." Thus, it seems clear that in ll. 1–2, the author highlights the *mebin*'s elect status and possession of wisdom by creatively utilizing the Adamic narrative in Gen 1–3.[63]

63. In ll. 1–2, the author indicates that the *mebin* can obtain wisdom by freely accessing the fruits desirable for making one wise. The author emphasizes that every fruit and every tree of the garden provide wisdom by modifying the original story (in Gen

It is difficult to interpret ll. 3–5 due to its fragmentary state, but these lines seem to describe the cursed condition of the earth and humanity after God's judgment in Gen 3:16–19.[64] The phrase קוץ ודרדר תצמיח לכה ("thorns and thistles it will bring forth for you") clearly alludes to Gen 3:18, where God curses the earth with the same phrase. Moreover, the phrase כוחה לא תתן לכה ("its strength will not yield to you") also alludes to Gen 4:12, where God curses Cain by making the earth unproductive. In ll. 4–5, the author probably expresses Adam and Eve's disloyalty to God's commandment and God's curse on Eve (Gen 3:16) in relation to childbirth,[65] although it is impossible to determine the exact meaning of these lines. This description might be related to a condition of unrighteous people, which makes a contrast with the elect status of the *mebin* in order to encourage the members of the community to study the mystery that is to be.

Lines 6–7 seem to describe again the abundance of blessings in the garden of Eden. As seen above, Qumran literature often uses the term "planting" (מטע) in connection with the garden of Eden. Elgvin's interpretation of מטע in 4QInstruction as an "eschatological community" is probably right given the author's use of "eternal planting" in 4Q418 81 13–14 (cf. 1QH[a] XVI:7; 1QS 8:5; 11:8).[66] This again expresses the *mebin*'s elect status as the restoration of Adam's stewardship in the garden of Eden in terms of inaugurated eschatology.

In sum, 4QInstruction describes the concept of new creation as the *mebin*'s elect status which recovers Adam's authority over the garden of Eden. It also relates to the eschatological judgment which involves the cosmic renewal of heaven and the earth, but its emphasis lies on the *mebin*'s privileged status, which God has already established within the community. The *mebin* possesses knowledge of good and evil and participates in the communion with the angelic beings. These privileges are often expressed with the language of divine sonship. This inaugurated eschatology of 4QInstruction is also expressed within the *Urzeit-Endzeit* correlation.

3:6, only the tree of the knowledge of good and evil, not every tree, looks desirable for making one wise).

64. Strugnell et al., *Qumran Cave 4*, 508.

65. Wold, *Women, Men, and Angels*, 116; Strugnell et al., *Qumran Cave 4*, 510.

66. Strugnell et al., *Qumran Cave 4*, 511; Goff, *4QInstruction*, 298.

5. Conclusion

We can summarize the concept of new creation in Qumran literature in what follows. Firstly, the new creation in these texts show that God takes the initiative to intervene in the disordered state of humanity and all creation: God not only elected and redeems his people by pouring out his spirit upon them, but also renews the whole creation according to his eternal plan. All these salvific activities are driven by God's abundant mercy and compassion under his initiative. Secondly, the new creation in Qumran literature is expressed in conjunction with the creation account and Adamic narrative in Gen 1–3. The righteous are restored to all the glory of Adam, and the whole creation is restored to the blessings and peace of the garden of Eden, by the reversal of the Adamic curse in Gen 3. Thirdly, the new creation in the Qumran writings has discontinuity with the first creation, although it is described in connection with the first creation. God destroys what was established of old and creates new things. The resurrection, which most dramatically expresses this discontinuity, signifies transition from death to eternal life. Lastly, the new creation in Qumran literature has a close relationship with the divine sonship of God's people. They will not only be granted the status of the sons of God at the eschaton, but also participate in the communion with the sons of heaven in the current pious community. These privileges are closely related to the theme of new creation.

This conclusion is not different from that of the previous chapter, the concept of new creation in parabiblical texts. Rather, the concept of new creation in Qumran literature shares many affinities with that of parabiblical texts. Two important points, in particular, have been highlighted: (1) the theme of new creation is expressed in connection with the creation account and Adamic narrative in Gen 1–3 within the *Urzeit-Endzeit* framework; (2) the language of divine sonship often occurs with the theme of new creation. Now, we are fully prepared to turn to Paul's letters to explore the concept of new creation in Paul.

Chapter 4: **The Concept of New Creation in Paul**

1. Introduction

PAUL WAS ONE OF the Jews living in the Second Temple period. Paul introduced himself as a member of the people of Israel, a Hebrew of Hebrews (Phil 3:5; cf. Rom 11:1; 2 Cor 11:22). He also treats other fellow Jews as his "kinsmen according to the flesh" (Rom 9:3). Therefore, even if the Pauline Epistles have a canonical position that distinguishes them from other Second Temple Jewish writings, it is natural to place them among his contemporary Jewish literature which shares social, cultural, and theological ideas. However, it is also true that the Pauline Epistles, written by Paul, who always introduces himself as an apostle (or servant) of Jesus Christ (Gal 1:1; Rom 1:1; 1 Cor 1:1; 2 Cor 1:1; etc.), have unique characteristics that distinguish them from other Second Temple Jewish literature. This is because when Paul quotes the Old Testament or speaks of the history of Israel, he reinterprets everything in light of Christ and the Spirit (e.g., Gal 3:14–16; Rom 4:23–25; Rom 9:1).

In this chapter, thus, first I will place Paul's epistles within Second Temple Jewish writings and try to discover Paul's concept of new creation through the exegesis of two Pauline texts (2 Cor 5:14–19 and Gal 6:14–16), where the phrase καινὴ κτίσις occurs, as I dealt with other Second Temple Jewish texts. Then, I will compare Paul's concept of new creation and that of other Jewish texts to summarize their similarities and differences. This process will be helpful for answering the following two questions: (1) What kind of emphasis does Paul have when he uses the new creation motif? (2) To what degree can we apply our findings of the previous chapters (the concept of new creation in Second Temple literature) to Paul's concept of new creation? To clarify Paul's concept of new creation will also illumine Paul's use of υἱοθεσία, as we shall see later.

2. The concept of new creation in 2 Cor 5:17

(1) The narrative of Gen 1–3 in 2 Corinthians

Paul's defense of his apostleship is one of the main themes of 2 Corinthians. Paul wrote this letter to defend himself from his adversaries who had greatly expanded their influence in the church at Corinth during his absence. The reason why this fact is important for the present study lies in what follows. First, the new creation statement in 5:17 also appears in the context of Paul's defense of his apostleship. Second, Paul uses the language and motifs of Gen 1–3 to establish the authenticity of himself and his message against his adversaries. To prove this fact, we will first analyze 2 Cor 4:4–6 and 2 Cor 11:2–5, where Paul defends his apostleship with the narrative of Gen 1–3.

A. 2 Cor 4:4–6

In 2 Cor 4:1–6, Paul contrasts the false teaching of his adversaries with his own gospel using similar language to 2:14–17, where he describes the opponents of his gospel: while Paul proclaims the gospel in the sight of God (4:2; cf. 2:17: "standing in God's presence"), "those who are perishing" (2:15; 4:3: οἱ ἀπολλύμενοι) falsify God's word (4:2; cf. 2:17: "peddlers of God's word").[1] In this context, Paul uses the Genesis creation narrative to highlight the sincerity of his gospel that he proclaims to the Corinthian church:

> [4] In their case the god of this world has blinded the minds of the unbelievers, to keep them from seeing the light of the gospel of the glory of Christ, who is the image of God. [5] For we do not proclaim ourselves; we proclaim Jesus Christ as Lord and ourselves as your slaves for Jesus' sake. [6] For it is the God who said, "Let light shine out of darkness," who has shone in our hearts to give the light of the knowledge of the glory of God in the face of Jesus Christ. (2 Cor 4:4–6)[2]

1. Martin, 2 Corinthians, 75.
2. In this study, all translations of referenced biblical passages are from the NRSV unless otherwise indicated.

As many commentators agree,[3] "the image of God" (εἰκὼν τοῦ θεοῦ) in v. 4 alludes to Gen 1:27, where God creates Adam in the image of God. Here Paul designates Christ as the image of God, which implies Paul's Adam-Christology (cf. Phil 2:6; Col 1:15). In 2 Cor 3:18, Paul already used the combination of image (εἰκών) and glory (δόξα) to refer to believers' glorified transformation into the Lord's image by the Spirit of the Lord. As we have seen above, the themes of "the image of God" and "glory" are interwoven in the reinterpreted Adamic narrative in the Apocalypse of Moses. We can find this tendency again in Rom 8:29–30 and 1 Cor 15:40–49, where Paul uses these themes together to signify believers' glorified transformation into the image of Christ (cf. Phil 3:21). First Corinthians 15:40–49, in particular, contrasts Adam and Christ by indicating that "as we have borne the image of the man of dust [Adam], so will we bear the image of the man of heaven [Christ]."

Also, we should note that in 2 Cor 4:5, Paul's gospel relates to his proclamation of Christ as the Lord (κύριος). In Gen 1:27–28, God's creation of Adam as the image of God relates to Adam's lordship over all of creation; God commanded Adam to have dominion (κατακυριεύω) over the whole creation (1:28). With the theme of "the form of God" in Phil 2.6 (μορφὴ θεοῦ, cf. ὁμοίωμα in Phil 2.7), which many scholars regard as an allusion to "the image of God" in Gen 1.27,[4] the recurring use of πᾶς and the designation of Jesus as κύριος in Phil 2:9–11 also resonates with this passage.

Finally, in v. 6 Paul uses the introductory formula "ὁ θεὸς ὁ εἰπών" to cite the divine voice "Let light shine out of darkness" (ἐκ σκότους φῶς λάμψει). Although it is not a direct citation of Gen 1:3–4, it seems clear that this is at least an allusion to Gen 1:3–4, where God spoke and created light and separated the light from the darkness.

At the same time, as the majority of scholars (e.g., Bornkamm, Barrett, Dunn, R. P. Martin, Newman, and others) argue, v. 6 as well as v. 4 may allude to the Damascus Christophany; Paul's description of "blindness" in v. 4 and "shining light" which illuminates God's glory in

---

3. For example, Furnish, *II Corinthians*, 222; Hubbard, *New Creation*, 158; Jackson, *New Creation*, 140–41; Jervell, *Imago Dei*, 174–75.

4. Despite the ongoing debate over the interpretation of μορφὴ θεοῦ in Phil 2:6, many scholars (e.g., Cullmann, Dunn, Murphy-O'Connor, Schweizer, Ridderbos, Caird, Hooker, et al.) equate μορφή with εἰκών in Gen 1:26, 27. For the reception history and the interpretative options of this phrase, see Reumann, *Philippians*, 342–44.

the face of Christ in v. 6 may allude to Paul's encounter with the risen Christ on the road to Damascus. Thus, 2 Cor 4:4-6 is a key passage to undergird Seyoon Kim's main thesis that Paul's conceptions of Christ as "the image of God" or "Last Adam" originated from the Damascus Christophany.[5] This argument fits well with the context of this passage, namely the defence of his apostleship and the sincerity of his gospel. In any case, it seems clear that Paul uses the Genesis creation narrative to defend his apostleship against his opponents.

B. 2 COR 11:2-5

As in 2 Cor 4:4-6, Paul uses the Adamic narrative again to attack his adversaries and to defend his apostleship in 2 Cor 11:2-5:

> [2] I feel a divine jealousy for you, for I promised you in marriage to one husband, to present you as a chaste virgin to Christ. [3] But I am afraid that as the serpent deceived Eve by its cunning, your thoughts will be led astray from a sincere and pure devotion to Christ. [4] For if someone comes and proclaims another Jesus than the one we proclaimed, or if you receive a different spirit from the one you received, or a different gospel from the one you accepted, you submit to it readily enough. [5] I think that I am not in the least inferior to these super-apostles. (2 Cor 11:2-5)

In v. 2, Paul uses the metaphor of betrothal to portray his apostolic ministry in which he presents the Corinthian congregation as "a chaste virgin" to "one husband" Christ. In v. 3, Paul uses the Adamic narrative in Gen 3 to criticize his opponents. In Paul's allegory, Eve represents the Corinthian church while the serpent symbolizes Paul's opponents, namely the super-apostles (ὑπερλίαν ἀπόστολοι) in v. 5, who can lead astray the Corinthian church from Christ by preaching a different gospel. This allegory indicates the Adam-Christology, since Christ as Eve's husband corresponds to Adam in the Genesis narrative.

The word "cunning" (πανουργία) is the same word that Paul used for describing his opponents in 2 Cor 4:2. Also, its cognate πανοῦργος was the term that Aquila and Symmachus use for translating ערום into Greek in Gen 3:1, which describes the characteristics of the serpent in the garden of Eden. What, then, does the "cunning" of the serpent refer

---

5. Kim, *Origin of Paul's Gospel*, 229-33.

to here, by which the serpent deceived (ἐξηπάτησεν) Eve? In the Genesis account, the serpent deceived (ἠπάτησεν, Gen 3:13 LXX) Eve by its cunning words. Here, thus, πανουργία probably refers to the false teachers' eloquent but deceitful words by which they mislead the Corinthian congregation with a different gospel. This meaning of πανουργία resonates with Paul's description of the false teaching as "smooth talk" and "flattery" in Rom 16:18, where the followers of Satan (cf. Rom 16:20) deceive (ἐξαπατῶσιν) the hearts of the simple-minded.[6]

Thus, in 2 Cor 11:13–14, Paul says that false apostles, namely deceitful workers, disguise themselves as apostles of Christ, just as Satan disguises himself as an "angel of light." Apocalypse of Moses 17 provides a fascinating parallel to this. In Apoc. Mos. 17:1, Satan, who controls the serpent to tempt Eve, appears to Eve in the form of an angel (ἐν εἴδει ἀγγέλου) singing hymns to God (cf. Apoc. Mos. 7:2; *Vita Adae et Evae* 9:1). In addition to this, the Apocalypse of Moses has several striking parallels with 2 Corinthians: (1) the idea that Eve brought sin and death to the world (Apoc. Mos. 14:2; cf. 2 Cor 11:3); (2) the location of a heavenly paradise in the third heaven (Apoc. Mos. 37:5; cf. 2 Cor 12:2); (3) the separation of one's soul from the body after death (Apoc. Mos. 37–38; cf. 2 Cor 5:1–9).[7] All these parallels enhance the probability that Paul uses the Adamic narrative in Gen 1–3 in his discussion in 2 Corinthians.

From the above discussion, it has become clear that when Paul continues the argument in defence of his apostleship and gospel in 2 Corinthians, he uses the language and motifs of Gen 1–3 comparing Christ with Adam. Now, we are fully prepared to analyze 2 Cor 5:14–17, where Paul uses the phrase "new creation" to defend his apostolic ministry.

(2) Exegesis of 2 Cor 5:14–17

The context of 5:14–17 is similar to that of 4:4–6 and 11:2–5. In 5:11–13, Paul again defends his apostolic ministry in contrast to that of his adversaries: (1) his ministry is controlled by the fear of the Lord and he is well known to God (v. 11); (2) unlike his opponents, who boast in outward

---

6. Barnett, *Second Epistle*, 501–2.

7. The concept that ἐπιθυμία is the origin of every sin (Apoc. Mos. 19:3) is also found in Rom 7:7 although it is not in 2 Corinthians. See M. D. Johnson, "Life of Adam and Eve," 255. For further study on the parallelism between Apoc. Mos. 19:3 and Rom 7:7, see Dochhorn, "Röm 7,7," 59–77. See also Dochhorn, *Adammythos bei Paulus*, 312–13, 376–77.

appearance (ἐν προσώπῳ), Paul gives the Corinthian congregation an opportunity to boast in Paul's ministry in the heart (ἐν καρδίᾳ) (v. 12); (3) his ministry is not only for God but also for the Corinthian believers. In this context, Paul says that the momentum of his ministry is the love of Christ, who died and was raised for all:

> [14] For the love of Christ urges us on, because we are convinced that one has died for all; therefore all have died. [15] And he died for all, so that those who live might live no longer for themselves, but for him who died and was raised for them. [16] From now on, therefore, we regard no one from a human point of view; even though we once knew Christ from a human point of view, we know him no longer in that way. [17] So if anyone is in Christ, there is a new creation: everything old has passed away; see, everything has become new! (2 Cor 5:14–17)

If Paul speaks of his apostolic ministry in this passage, then does he also use the Adamic motif here as in 4:4–6 and 11:2–5? In what follows, I will demonstrate that the answer to this question is "yes" through the exegesis of this passage.

A. vv. 14–15: The ΕΙΣ-ΠΑΝΤΕΣ motif and Adam-Christology

In vv. 14b–15a, Paul highlights Christ's death for *all*: "*one* has died for *all*; therefore *all* have died. And he died for all . . ." (εἷς ὑπὲρ πάντων ἀπέθανεν, ἄρα οἱ πάντες ἀπέθανον· καὶ ὑπὲρ πάντων ἀπέθανεν . . .). Paul uses the contrast between *one* and *all* in Rom 5:12–21 and 1 Cor 15:21–22, where Adam appears as a type of "the one who was to come" (Rom 5:14), namely Christ:

> Therefore, just as sin came into the world through *one man*, and death came through sin, and so death spread to *all* because *all* have sinned. (Rom 5:12)

> If, because of the *one man*'s trespass, death exercised dominion through *that one*, much more surely will those who receive the abundance of grace and the free gift of righteousness exercise dominion in life through *the one man*, Jesus Christ. Therefore just as *one man*'s trespass led to condemnation for *all*, so *one man*'s act of righteousness leads to justification and life for *all*. (Rom 5:17–18)

> For since death came through *a human being*, the resurrection of the dead has also come through *a human being*; for as *all* die in Adam, so *all* will be made alive in Christ. (1 Cor 15:21–22)

Two points are in common in the above passages: (1) one man's act affects all people; (2) Paul contrasts Adam with Christ; while Adam's sin brought death into the world, Christ's death and resurrection brought life to all.

Unlike Rom 5:12–21 and 1 Cor 15:21–22, an explicit contrast between Adam and Christ does not occur in 2 Cor 5:14–15, although 2 Cor 5:14–15 does use the concept of these two other texts that the death and resurrection of *one* man, Christ, effects *all*. However, given the fact that in 2 Corinthians, Paul defends his gospel and apostleship in connection with Adam-Christology, we cannot exclude the probability that the comparison between Adam and Christ also exists in 2 Cor 5:14–17 as a background. Rather, Paul's statement that Christ died for all in vv. 14–15 suggests that "Paul has the Adam-Christ or First Adam-Second Adam antithesis in mind."[8]

The context of 2 Cor 5:1–4 also supports this interpretation. In 2 Cor 5:1–4, Paul contrasts "our earthly house" (ἡ ἐπίγειος ἡμῶν οἰκία) with "a house in the heavens" (οἰκία ἐν τοῖς οὐρανοῖς) as well as "what is mortal" (τὸ θνητὸν) with "life" (ζωή). These contrasts are very similar to those of 1 Cor 15:47–54, where Paul not only contrasts Adam with Christ as "the man of dust" (ὁ χοϊκός) and "the man of heaven" (ὁ ἐπουράνιος) respectively but also contrasts "what is mortal" (τὸ θνητὸν) and "immortality" (ἀθανασία). Moreover, the contrast between "to take off" (ἐκδύσασθαι) or "being found naked (γυμνός)" and "to put on" (ἐπενδύσασθαι) in 2 Cor 5:3–4 evokes the narrative in Gen 3, where God clothed (ἐνέδυσεν: 3:21) Adam when Adam found himself naked (γυμνός: 3:7, 10) after he had eaten the forbidden fruit. Interestingly, Paul uses the verb ἐνδύειν to show that the resurrected body will put on imperishability and immortality in 1 Cor 15:53–54, where Paul describes Christ as the second Adam.[9]

---

8. Harris, *Second Epistle*, 440. Many commentators recognize Paul's implicit use of comparison between Adam and Christ in 2 Cor 5:14–15 (e.g., Barnett, *Second Epistle*, 290; Furnish, *II Corinthians*, 327–28; Martin, *2 Corinthians*, 131; Jackson, *New Creation*, 138–40; Hubbard, *New Creation*, 172–73).

9. The author of the Apocalypse of Moses uses the verb ἐνδύειν (to wear) in connection with the righteousness and the glory: Eve found that she had been separated from the righteousness and the glory with which she had been clothed after she ate the forbidden fruit (Apoc. Mos. 20:1–2). On the other hand, in Rom 5:12–21, where Paul contrasts Adam and Christ, believers can recover their righteousness and life thanks to Christ's act of righteousness.

Moreover, Paul also uses the concept of "to clothe (ἐνδύειν) oneself in Christ" in Rom 13:14 and Gal 3:27. This increases the likelihood that in 2 Cor 5:1–4, Paul already had in mind the contrast between Adam and Christ and continues this contrast in 2 Cor 5:14–15.

What, then, is Paul's intention in using this implicit contrast between Adam and Christ? Paul argues that the purpose of Christ's death and resurrection is to change the lifestyle of believers: *from their previous Adamic life* in which they lived for themselves *to the new life in Christ* in which they live for Christ who died and was raised for them.[10] This contrast fits well with the context of Paul's defence of his apostleship in that Paul indicates his apostolic ministry is not for himself but for Christ and for the Corinthian congregation (vv. 13–15). As Barnett notes, here "no longer" (v. 15, μηκέτι: "living *no longer* for themselves") signals the transition of the aeons from the "former" to the "new" creation.[11]

B. V. 16

The eschatological transition from the old era in Adam to the new era in Christ is also found in v. 16: "*From now on*, therefore, we know no one according to the flesh; even though we once knew Christ according to the flesh, *but now* we know him *no longer* in that way" (emphasis added). This new eschatological situation is more explicitly expressed in 6:2: "See, now is the acceptable time; see, now is the day of salvation!"

Just as Christ's death and resurrection changed believers' purpose and way of life (vv. 14–15), so their epistemological value system has been changed in this eschatological new era. Believers no longer know others and Christ according to the flesh (κατὰ σάρκα).[12] What, then,

---

10. Martin expresses this antithesis between Adam and Christ by saying that "Adam represents wayward man, living for himself; Jesus is the progenitor of a new race, the representative of the new humanity" (Martin, *2 Corinthians*, 131).

11. Barnett, *Second Epistle*, 293.

12. There has been a debate whether κατὰ σάρκα in v. 16 is adjectival, modifying "no one" and "Christ," or it is adverbial, modifying "we know" and "we knew." If we take the first option (e.g., Plummer, Bultmann, Dinkler, et al.), this verse implies a personal experience with the historical Jesus. However, as most scholars agree, this phrase should be interpreted as an adverbial use in terms of syntax, context, and even statistics (not only does Paul use this phrase adverbially in most cases, but he also uses it adverbially in all other four occurrences in 2 Corinthians). In his famous essay "Epistemology at the Turn," Martyn concludes that "he [Paul] is saying that there are two ways of knowing, and that what separates the two is the turn of the ages, the apocalyptic event of Christ's death/resurrection" after his argument for the adverbial reading. See Martyn, "Epistemology at the Turn," 90–95.

CHAPTER 4: THE CONCEPT OF NEW CREATION IN PAUL 109

does the flesh mean here? In the Pauline letters, Paul often uses the flesh/Spirit (σάρξ/πνεῦμα) antithesis (e.g., Gal 3:3; 4:29; 5:16–26; Rom 8:1–14). Thus, the flesh represents, according to Barclay, "the environment of all human agency untransformed by the Spirit—including life under the Torah, which was incapable of 'creating life' because of the power of sin (Gal 3:21–22)."[13] Also, in Phil 3:3–6, Paul uses the phrase "having confidence in the flesh" to refer to human achievements including outward faithfulness to the Torah. In this context, "knowing others and Christ according to the flesh" in v. 16 seems to refer to evaluating other people on the basis of worldly criteria or outward appearances regardless of the Spirit and Christ. Interestingly, in 1 Cor 15:50, Paul connects σάρξ to the Adamic body in contrast to Christ's spiritual body by stating that "flesh and blood cannot inherit the kingdom of God, nor does the perishable inherit the imperishable." Similarly, since the church father Origen viewed the "I" in Rom 7:7–25 as Paul's impersonation of Adam,[14] many scholars have interpreted the "I" as the Adamic "I," who is "of the flesh (σάρκινος), sold into slavery under sin" (Rom 7:14).[15] In this sense, the old era in Adam can be characterized by the flesh.

C. V. 17: THE STATEMENT OF "NEW CREATION"

In v. 17, Paul describes the positive result of Christ's representative death in vv. 14–15: ὥστε εἴ τις ἐν Χριστῷ, καινὴ κτίσις· τὰ ἀρχαῖα παρῆλθεν, ἰδοὺ γέγονεν καινά.

Although at first glance, the singular pronoun τις in the protasis of v. 17a seems to highlight the anthropological aspect of new creation, the apodosis does not have a verb but has only the phrase καινὴ κτίσις. Thus, the literal translation of v. 17a is: "If anyone is in Christ, a new creation." What, then, is the meaning of this terse apodosis? Two options exist:

---

13. Barclay, *Paul and the Gift*, 426.

14. Origen, *Commentary*, 30–34. For the history of interpretation of Rom 7:7–25, see Dochhorn, *Adammythos bei Paulus*, 93–147. Several church fathers saw Adam in that text.

15. Regarding the effect of the Adam narrative in Rom 7:7–25, Dunn says, "As most recognize, Paul is almost certainly speaking in typical terms, using the Adam narrative to characterize what is true of man (adam) in general, everyman—somewhat as 2 Apoc. Bar. 54.19, 'Each of us has been the Adam of his own soul'" (Dunn, *Romans 1–8*, 381). Recently Jan Dochhorn interprets the "Adamic I" in Rom 7:7–25 in light of the Adamic narrative in Apoc. Mos. 15–30. See Dochhorn, *Adammythos bei Paulus*, 367–84.

either "that person is a new creation" (in this case, the omitted subject refers to τις in the protasis)[16] or "there is a new creation."[17]

Both interpretative options are possible, but the latter is preferable. First, given the fact that the continuing sentence (τὰ ἀρχαῖα παρῆλθεν, ἰδοὺ γέγονεν καινά) has two neuter plural nouns (τὰ ἀρχαῖα and καινά), καινὴ κτίσις seems to refer to a new creation of the whole creation, not a human being only. Second, the latter is preferable given Paul's use of κτίσις in his letters. As Martin well observes, in Paul's letters, κτίσις almost always relates to the creation in its entirety (e.g., Rom 1:20, 25; 8:19, 20, 21, 22).[18] Third, the expression "the old has passed away; behold, the new has come" (τὰ ἀρχαῖα παρῆλθεν, ἰδοὺ γέγονεν καινά) is reminiscent of the recursive contrast of "former things/new things" in Isa 40–55 (e.g., 42:9; 43:18-19; 48:3-6; cf. 65:17-18; 66:22). Paul seems to allude to the Isaianic texts (particularly Isa 43:18-19 as recognized in the margins of Nestle-Aland),[19] which contain cosmological themes. Moreover, as seen above, the concept of new creation in Second Temple Jewish writings and Qumran literature often involves a cosmological renewal within the *Urzeit-Endzeit* framework. Thus, we can translate the phrase καινὴ κτίσις in 5:17a as "there is a new creation," which implies a cosmological renewal, although it does not exclude an anthropological sense. In other words, καινὴ κτίσις in 5:17 refers to *God*'s salvific act of creation, which inaugurates an eschatological *new* era, not just referring to a human creature.

It is crucial to note that this new creation occurs *in Christ* (ἐν Χριστῷ). As seen above, in 1 Cor 15:22, Paul contrasts the death *in Adam* with the life *in Christ* by saying, "as all die in Adam, so all will be made alive in Christ." In vv. 14-16, we have seen that Paul emphasizes believers' new life in Christ by contrasting their previous Adamic life according to the flesh. Since Christ's death and resurrection have had such a great effect on the

---

16. Many English translations follow this interpretation. In this case, καινὴ κτίσις is usually translated as "new creature." Not only many church fathers (e.g., Clement, Tertullian, Jerome, Augustine, et al.) but also Reformers including Calvin and Luther supported this reading.

17. As Hubbard points out, this interpretation has become more popular because of Käsemann's emphasis on apocalyptic as "die Mutter der christlichen Theologie" (Hubbard, *New Creation*, 4). Many modern commentators (e.g., Barnett, Dunn, Furnish, R. P. Martin, et al.) follow this reading.

18. Martin, *2 Corinthians*, 314.

19. Paul's use of ἰδού with καινά in 5:17 also seems to allude to the phrase "ἰδοὺ ποιῶ καινά" in Isa 43:19. Moreover, the fact that in 2 Cor 6:2, Paul cites Isa 49:8, which also contains the prophetic promise marker ἰδού, strengthens the probability of the allusion to the Isaianic text in 5:17.

life of the believers, they now live no longer for themselves, but for Christ, nor do they know other people according to the flesh. It is the *new creation in Christ* that has made such a radical change in the life of the believers. In this sense, καινὴ κτίσις in 2 Cor 5:17 does indeed have an anthropological dimension, but we should note that this fundamental transformation of one's whole situation is not merely an individual one, but is also a relational change which occurs in the relationship with others. This transformation not only relates to human relationships, but also concerns one's relationship with the whole world, as we shall see below.

D. VV. 18–19: THE MINISTRY OF RECONCILIATION

In vv. 18–20, Paul returns to the direct discussion about his ministry and apostleship, although in fact he still, in vv. 14–17, has this topic in mind:

> [18] All things are from God, who reconciled us to himself through Christ, and has given us the ministry of reconciliation; [19] that is, in Christ God was reconciling the world to himself, not counting their trespasses against them, and entrusting the message of reconciliation to us. [20] So we are ambassadors for Christ, since God is making his appeal through us; we entreat you on behalf of Christ, be reconciled to God. (2 Cor 5:18–20)

Paul, here, designates his ministry as "the ministry of reconciliation" in which God reconciles not only believers but also the world (κόσμος) to himself. Moreover, since all things (τὰ πάντα) can refer to the whole created universe (e.g., Phil 3:21; Col 1:16–17),[20] the theme of reconciliation in v. 18 indicates a cosmic reconciliation (cf. Rom 11:15). This ministry of reconciliation only occurs *through Christ* (v. 18) and *in Christ* (v. 19), just as the new creation only occurs *in Christ* (v. 17). This resonance between the new creation in v. 17 and the cosmic reconciliation in v. 18 enhances the cosmological and christological dimensions of the new creation. Also, Paul makes clear that both the new creation and the cosmic reconciliation are related to *God*'s sovereignty and action not only because all things are from *God* but also because *God himself* reconciled us to himself through Christ.

The theme of cosmic reconciliation in Christ more clearly occurs in Col 1:20: "through him [Christ] to reconcile (ἀποκαταλλάξαι) to himself [God] all things (τὰ πάντα), whether on earth or in heaven,

---

20. Harris, *Second Epistle*, 435.

making peace by the blood of his cross." The theme and language of Col 1:15–20 are similar to this passage in terms of the themes of creation and reconciliation. Particularly, Col 1:15–17 describes Christ as the image of the invisible God (εἰκὼν τοῦ θεοῦ τοῦ ἀοράτου) and the firstborn of all creation (πρωτότοκος πάσης κτίσεως), through whom all things were created. As we noted in the analysis of 2 Cor 4:4–6, the phrase "the image of God" evokes Adam in Gen 1:26–28 and can signify the Adam-Christology, although there is an ongoing debate on the influence of the Genesis narrative in this text.[21]

The theme of reconciliation (καταλλαγή) in Christ is also found in Rom 5:10–11, just before Paul uses the contrast between Adam and Christ in Rom 5:12–21. Paul describes Christ's death and resurrection as Christ's work of reconciliation through which believers were reconciled to God (5:10–11). In other words, the descendants of Adam had become God's enemies (v. 10: ἐχθροί) because of the influence of Adam's sin (v. 12), but now believers have received reconciliation (v. 11: καταλλαγή) through Christ's ministry of reconciliation. In this sense, Paul describes his apostolic office as that of an "ambassador" for Christ. Thus, we can conclude that in vv. 18–20, Paul still continues his implicit contrast between Adam and Christ through his discussion of the ministry of reconciliation.

Several important points become clear in Paul's concept of new creation in 2 Cor 5:17. First, Paul uses the phrase new creation in the context of Adam-Christology to defend his apostleship. Second, the concept of new creation highlights God's salvific and reconciling action through the Christ-event. Third, the concept of new creation here has mainly christological and cosmological dimensions, although it does not exclude an anthropological aspect. Can these findings be also applied to the concept of new creation in Gal 6:15? This question will be answered in the next section.

---

21. Some scholars (e.g., Dunn, Lohse, O'Brien, et al.) highlight the prominence of Hellenistic Judaism in this text, which regards divine Wisdom as the "image of God" (e.g., Prov 8:22; Wis 7:26; Philo, *Legum allegoriae* 1.43; Philo, *Migr. Abr.* 175) rather than the echo of Gen 1:26–28, since the combination of εἰκών and ἀόρατος can reflect Hellenistic understanding of "image of God" influenced by ancient Greek philosophy. See Dunn, *Epistles to the Colossians and to Philemon*, 87–89. However, the author's description of Christ as the dwelling of God's fullness within the *bodily* (σωματικῶς) form of Christ in Col 2:9 (cf. Col 1:19) rejects Gnostic or Platonic dualism. See Steenburg, "Worship of Adam," 99–106.

3. The concept of new creation in Gal 6:15

What is essential for the exegesis of Gal 6:14–16 is the parallelism between 6:14–16 and 3:27–29, which I, as a consequence, will discuss first.

(1) The parallelism between 6:14–16 and 3:27–29

Galatians 6:14–16 and Gal 3:27–29 have a striking similarity in terms of the logical flow in Paul's statements. In both passages, Paul develops his argument in the following sequences: (1) union with Christ (6:14: co-crucifixion with Christ; 3:27: baptism into Christ) → (2) the distinctions determined by the value system in the old age have become insignificant (6:15: circumcision/uncircumcision; 3:28: Jew/Greek, slave/free, and male/female) → (3) the emphasis on the new rule of "in Christ" (6:15: the new creation; 3:28: unity in Christ) → (4) the new identity of God's people and their blessings (6:16: "Israel of God" and "peace and mercy"; 3:29: "Abraham's offspring" and "heirs according to the promise"). I have laid out the logical flow, (1) → (2) → (3) → (4), in the table below.

Gal 6:14–16	Gal 3:27–29
(1) the union with Christ	
v. 14: May I never boast of anything except the cross of our Lord Jesus Christ, by which the world has been crucified to me, and I to the world	v. 27: As many of you as were baptized into Christ have clothed yourselves with Christ
(2) the invalidation of the distinctions in the old age	
v. 15a: For neither circumcision nor uncircumcision is anything	v. 28a: There is neither Jew nor Greek, there is neither slave nor free, there is no male and female
(3) the emphasis on the new rule of "in Christ"	
v. 15b: but a new creation	v. 28b: for all of you are one in Christ Jesus
(4) the new identity of God's people and their blessings	
v. 16: And as for all who will follow with this rule, peace and mercy be upon them, and upon the Israel of God	v. 29: And if you belong to Christ, then you are Abraham's offspring, heirs according to the promise

If this comparison is right, "the new creation" parallels "one in Christ Jesus," and "the Israel of God" parallels "Abraham's offspring" in Christ. Although there has been much debate on the meaning of "Israel of God" in 6:16, given the parallelism between the two passages, it can be identified with the phrase "all who will follow this rule," that is all who will follow the rule of "new creation," regardless of their ethnic identities.[22] I will discuss this in further detail in the exegesis of 6:16.

This parallelism can be strengthened by Paul's use of the phrase "οὐκ ἔνι ἄρσεν καὶ θῆλυ" in Gal 3:28. As many scholars note, this phrase alludes to Gen 1:27 where God creates humankind according to the image of God, male and female (ἄρσεν καὶ θῆλυ):

> And God made humankind; according to the image of God, he made him; male and female, he made them (καὶ ἐποίησεν ὁ θεὸς τὸν ἄνθρωπον, κατ' εἰκόνα θεοῦ ἐποίησεν αὐτόν· ἄρσεν καὶ θῆλυ ἐποίησεν αὐτούς). (Gen 1:27 LXX)[23]

Three points should be noted here. First, in Gal 3:28c Paul breaks the pattern of "there is neither ... nor ..." (οὐκ ἔνι ... οὐδὲ ...), which he uses in 28a and 28b, and replaces it with "there is not ... and ..." (οὐκ ἔνι ... καὶ ...). Second, although Paul often discusses themes pertaining to the relationship between *men and women*, Paul uses the terms ἄρσην and θῆλυς in only one other passage (Rom 1:26–27).[24] Third, the theme of "to put on Christ" (ἐνδύειν Χριστόν) in Gal 3:27 is reminiscent of Gen 3:21 where God made garments of skin for Adam and Eve and clothed them (ἐνέδυσεν αὐτούς). Thus, it is highly probable that in Gal 3:28, Paul alludes to Gen 1:27 or even that he is quoting that verse.[25]

---

22. Abraham's offspring (τοῦ Ἀβραὰμ σπέρμα) in Gal 3:29 clearly refers to those who belong to Christ regardless of their ethnic identities. Given the fact that Paul uses the expression "Abraham's offspring," with a metaphorical sense beyond its literal meaning (literally, "Abraham's offspring" can refer to ethnic Israel), it is highly probable that the Israel of God in Gal 6:16 also metaphorically refers to a new identity of believers in Christ. Similarly, Martyn notes the commonality of Gal 3:15–29 and Gal 6:15–16 and argues that Gal 6:15–16 is "the announcement of a totally new creation in which all religious distinctions are obliterated, coupled with the pronouncement of a blessing on the church as the Israel of God." See Martyn, *Galatians*, 576–77.

23. The LXX text is from H. B. Swete's edition of the Septuagint and the English translation is from Penner et al., *Lexham English Septuagint*. In this study, I will use Swete's edition and *Lexham English Septuagint* for the LXX text, unless otherwise noted.

24. In most cases, Paul uses ἀνήρ and γυνή for his discussion about the issues of men and women (e.g., Rom 7:1–3; 1 Cor 7:1–4, 10–16; 14:35; Gal 4:27. Cf. Eph 5:22–32; Col 3:18–19; 1 Tim 2:12).

25. See Litke, "Beyond Creation," 175. Litke argues that Gal 3:28 is Paul's deliberate

What, then, does the phrase "there is no male and female" mean? There are a number of interpretations of this phrase. For example, Wayne Meeks, who interprets the baptismal formula in Gal 3:27 as a "reunification formula," argues that this phrase indicates believers' restoration of the original androgynous state from the fateful division of male and female in the Adamic narrative (Gen 2:21–22).[26] Meeks's argument, however, is not convincing. As Litke rightly points out, Gal 3:28 negates not Gen 2:21–22, but Gen 1:27. Also, Gen 1:27, where God originally creates male and female (male and female he created *them*: ἄρσεν καὶ θῆλυ ἐποίησεν αὐτούς), indicates that the human race was originally created as male and female, not in an androgynous state. Others, such as Schüssler Fiorenza and Karin Neutel, interpret Gal 3:28c as "an eschatological end of male and female in procreation and marriage."[27] This is a possible interpretation, but it has difficulty in explaining the incompatible fact that there is no text in Galatians in which Paul discusses procreation and marriage.

Rather, given the striking parallelism between Gal 3:27–29 and Gal 6:14–16, Paul's allusion to God's creation of male and female in Gal 3:28 relates to the rule of new creation in Gal 6:15. All the pairings in Gal 3:28 imply the hierarchical systems of distinction. The rule of new creation, which invalidates the distinction between circumcision and uncircumcision, nullifies any hierarchical value systems in terms of ethnicity (neither Jew nor Greek), social status (neither slave nor free), and gender (no male and female). This does not mean that the differences between these categories are eradicated. It indicates the creation of a new community or world in Christ, where the old value system does not work anymore. With this parallelism in mind, I will begin the exegesis of Gal 6:14–16 in what follows.

---

quotation of Gen 1:27c, not simply an allusion, agreeing with Stendahl's argument that "we have good reason to put 'male and female' [Gal 3:28c] in quotation marks." See also Stendahl, *Bible and the Role of Women*, 32.

26. Meeks, "Image of the Androgyne," 185–86. Meeks also argues that myths of a bisexual progenitor of human race are very common in the ancient texts such as Aristophanes's tale in Plato's *Symposium* 189D–93D.

27. Neutel, *Cosmopolitan Ideal*, 232; Schüssler Fiorenza remarks on Gal 3:28, "Gal 3:28c does not assert that there are no longer men and women in Christ, but that patriarchal marriage—and sexual relationships between male and female—is no longer constitutive of the new community in Christ." See Schüssler Fiorenza, *In Memory of Her*, 211.

(2) Exegesis of Gal 6:14–16

In Gal 6:11–18, which Betz named "a postscript in his own handwriting,"[28] Paul summarizes the essentials of the whole letter and concludes with the blessings (v. 16) and the final "Amen" (v. 18). Particularly, in vv. 12–16, Paul contrasts the false teachers' message, which is characterized by the flesh (vv. 12–13), with his own message of new creation (vv. 14–16), as in 2 Cor 5:14–19.

A. V. 14: THE CROSS OF OUR LORD JESUS CHRIST

> May I never boast of anything except the cross of our Lord Jesus Christ, through which the world has been crucified to me, and I to the world

Paul contrasts himself with the agitators in that he boasts of the cross of Christ while they boast about the Galatian believers' flesh by compelling them to be circumcised (vv. 12–13). The agitators' boasting in the flesh refers to the phrase "to make a good showing in the flesh" (εὐπροσωπῆσαι ἐν σαρκί) through circumcision. Their boasting in the flesh is also contrasted with Paul's boasting in the cross in that the purpose of their boasting is to avoid persecution for the cross of Christ (v. 12). Paul's description of the agitators here is very similar to that of the false apostles in 2 Cor 5:12–16: (1) they boast in outward appearance (2 Cor 5:12); (2) they live for themselves, not for Christ (2 Cor 5:15); (3) their criteria for value are according to the flesh (2 Cor 5:16); (4) both descriptions appear just before the new creation statement.

In addition to these affinities, the most important point that the two passages share is that *the Christ-event* drives the change from the world of the flesh to the world of new creation: "the cross of our Lord Jesus Christ, by which the world has been crucified to me, and I to the world" (cf. 2 Cor 5:15–16). Hubbard interprets the term κόσμος here as "Paul's former way of life in Judaism" (cf. Gal 1:13) in light of his anthropological understanding of new creation.[29]

Hubbard's interpretation of κόσμος resonates with the immediate context which contrasts the two lifestyles in terms of boasting, but it wrongly seems to restrict the cosmological and eschatological meaning

---

28. Betz, *Galatians*, 312.
29. Hubbard, *New Creation*, 218.

CHAPTER 4: THE CONCEPT OF NEW CREATION IN PAUL

of κόσμος to an individual one: first, in Gal 4:3, the phrase στοιχεῖα τοῦ κόσμου has a cosmological meaning, namely "elements of the cosmos," to which the Galatians were enslaved, as we shall see in the exegesis of Gal 4:1–7 (chapter 7, section 3); second, this verse implies the theme of resurrection, which can be associated with the theme of the cosmic renewal in Second Temple Jewish literature, although there is no explicit language of resurrection here. As in Gal 2:19–20, where the theme of co-crucifixion with Christ occurs with the new resurrected life in Christ, this text's theme of co-crucifixion indicates a resulting new life in Christ in connection with the new creation in Gal 6:15; third, given the parallelism between the new creation passages in Gal 6 and 2 Cor 5,[30] it is highly probable that the κόσμος in Gal 6:14 also has a cosmological meaning, as in 2 Cor 5:19: "in Christ God was reconciling the world to himself." Thus, κόσμος here cannot be limited to Paul's previous lifestyle in Judaism.

B. V. 15: THE NEW CREATION

> For neither circumcision nor uncircumcision is anything, but a new creation (οὔτε γὰρ περιτομή τί ἐστιν οὔτε ἀκροβυστία ἀλλὰ καινὴ κτίσις).

The two parallel verses, which contrast the pair "circumcision and uncircumcision" with "faith working through love" (Gal 5:6), and "keeping God's commandments" (1 Cor 7:19) provide important hints for interpreting this verse:

> For in Christ Jesus neither circumcision nor uncircumcision means anything, but faith working through love (Gal 5:6: ἐν γὰρ Χριστῷ Ἰησοῦ οὔτε περιτομή τι ἰσχύει οὔτε ἀκροβυστία ἀλλὰ πίστις δι' ἀγάπης ἐνεργουμένη).

> Circumcision is nothing, and uncircumcision is nothing, but what matters is the keeping of the commandments of God

---

30. Mell points out three commonalities in the two passages: (1) The death of Christ has a radical effect on the whole universe (2 Cor 5:14b, 15: πᾶς; Gal 6:14: κόσμος). (2) The Christ event has a salvific effect enabling humanity to turn away from the world (2 Cor 5:15b; Gal 6:14b) in order to live a new life in Christ (2 Cor 5:15b; Gal 6:14a). (3) The soteriological conclusion is composed of two negative phrases (2 Cor 5:16: οὐδένα ~ οὐκέτι; Gal 6:15a: οὔτε ~ οὔτε) and the new creation statement (Mell, *Neue Schöpfung*, 350). We can add two more commonalities: first, Paul contrasts his apostolic ministry with his rival preachers; second, Paul connects his rival preachers' ministry to boasting about the flesh (2 Cor 5:12, 16; Gal 6:13–14).

(1 Cor 7:19: ἡ περιτομὴ οὐδέν ἐστιν καὶ ἡ ἀκροβυστία οὐδέν ἐστιν, ἀλλὰ τήρησις ἐντολῶν θεοῦ).

First, this formulaic antithesis (neither circumcision nor uncircumcision ~ but) shows that Paul wants to highlight a fundamentally more important matter than circumcision or uncircumcision. Second, the two verses indicate that the essential prerequisite of these statements is being "in Christ," as Gal 5:6 clearly shows. Also, in 1 Cor 7:22, Paul directly speaks of the precondition of 1 Cor 7:19, namely "for whoever was called *in the Lord*," although an explicit phrase "in Christ" does not appear in 1 Cor 7:19. For whoever was called in the Lord, it is not important whether the one was called as circumcised/uncircumcised (vv. 18–20) or a slave/freed person (vv. 21–24) or married/unmarried (vv. 25–27).

These points can be applicable to Gal 6:15. Paul's emphasis on the Christ-event (symbolically expressed as "the cross of Christ") in v. 14, "through which the cosmos has been crucified to me and I to the cosmos," indicates that the καινὴ κτίσις in v. 15 only occurs *in Christ*. Also, καινὴ κτίσις only has fundamental significance in Christ while circumcision *and* uncircumcision now lose their status as a standard criterion of value.[31] Given the parallelism between Gal 3:27–28 and Gal 6:14–16, the antithetical pair "circumcision or uncircumcision" can be broadened to "Jew or Greek," "slave or free," and "male and female." As seen above, the inclusion of the last pair, which alludes to the creation account in Gen 1:27, probably anticipates Paul's statement of καινὴ κτίσις in v. 15. The Christ-event has reconfigured the fundamental nature of the old fleshly world, namely the Adamic world.

What, then, does καινὴ κτίσις mean here? There are several interpretative options:

(1) καινὴ κτίσις as "new human existence" or "regeneration"; (2) καινὴ κτίσις as "new community"; (3) καινὴ κτίσις as "the new state of the world" or "transformation of the world." I will explain each interpretation respectively in what follows.

---

31. We should note that, for Paul, *both* circumcision and uncircumcision are of no ultimate significance. While Jews regard circumcision as "the sign of covenant" (Gen 17:11), non-Jews in the Greco-Roman tradition consider circumcision as "a barbaric disfigurement of the male body" (Barclay, *Paul and the Gift*, 392; see also Philo, *De specialibus legibus* 1.1–3; Josephus, *Against Apion* 2.137). For non-Jews in the Greco-Roman tradition, uncircumcision (or the foreskin) was rather an "ideal prepuce." For the understanding of uncircumcision in ancient Greece and Rome, see Hodges, "Ideal Prepuce"; Offord, "Restrictions Concerning Circumcision."

Scholars who follow the first option[32] usually prefer the term "creature" to "creation" as the translation of κτίσις, since they think this term refers to the inner change of an *individual person*. Hubbard, for example, relates καινὴ κτίσις to "the inner dynamic of the Christian life," contrasting with "outward state of circumcision or uncircumcision." Also, Hubbard connects the death-life (crucifixion-new creation) symbolism in vv. 14–15 to Paul's autobiographical experience, and this leads him to identify καινὴ κτίσις with "new birth."[33] In this sense, Betz claims that the "old creation" here simply refers to "ἄνθρωπος ('man') and σάρξ ('flesh')—human existence apart from God's redemption in Christ."[34]

The second option[35] is basically similar to the first option in terms of its relevance to humanity, but it is differentiated from the first option in that it highlights a corporate aspect of καινὴ κτίσις, which involves the establishment of a new community. Since the main issue of Galatians that Paul wants to address concerns the circumcision of gentile converts, καινὴ κτίσις in Gal 6:15, which appears with the phrase "neither circumcision nor uncircumcision is anything," can refer to a new transformative community irrespective of circumcision and uncircumcision.[36] This interpretation can be strengthened by the parallelism between Gal 3:28 and Gal 6:15, since Gal 3:28 emphasizes the oneness of believers' community in Christ regardless of their ethnicity, social status, and gender. Paul's benediction for the community, namely "Israel of God" in v. 16, also undergirds this interpretation.

Scholars who support option (3) note that καινὴ κτίσις in v. 15 stands in antithesis not only to the old world in v. 14 but also to the present evil age in 1:4.[37] Thus, the cosmological understanding of κόσμος as "the totality of the whole creation (human as well as nonhuman)"[38] and the antithetical relationship to αἰών lead us to understand καινὴ κτίσις as

---

32. E.g., Betz, *Galatians*, 319–20; Hubbard, *New Creation*, 225–29; Lightfoot, *Saint Paul's Epistle to the Galatians*, 224; Longenecker, *Galatians*, 296.

33. Hubbard, *New Creation*, 227.

34. Betz, *Galatians*, 319–20.

35. E.g., McKnight, *Galatians*, 302; Aymer, "Paul's Understanding," 181; Kraus, *Volk Gottes*, 247–52.

36. Aymer, Paul's Understanding, 103.

37. Dunn, *Epistle to the Galatians*, 342–43; Barclay, *Paul and the Gift*, 395; Jackson, *New Creation*, 96–106; Moo, *Galatians*, 397–98; Keener, *Galatians*, 574–75.

38. Dunn, *Theology of Paul's Letter*, 49.

"the new state of the whole creation that Christ's death and resurrection has inaugurated."[39]

Before we determine the best of these three options, we should note that they are not mutually exclusive but may be overlapping. Thus, even if we choose one option, that option can share some aspects of other options. What, then, is the most prominent characteristic of καινὴ κτίσις in v. 15, given its context and Paul's main argument in the whole letter? As seen above, the meaning of κόσμος in v. 14 should not be restricted to "Paul's former way of life in Judaism" as such, but its cosmological connotation still works here. This *cosmic* crucifixion in v. 14b, then, seems to be "rephrased" by the new creation statement in v. 15 as the explanatory conjunction γάρ indicates.[40] In this sense, the cosmological reading of καινὴ κτίσις seems to be the best option. In addition to this, there are other grounds for this interpretation.

Firstly, Paul uses here the language of "creation," not language of "birth." Hubbard argues that the language of new creation in v. 15 is the synonym of "new-birth" because of its parallelism with the new-birth imagery in 4:21–31, where Paul contrasts "the birth according to the flesh" with "the birth according to the Spirit."[41] However, we should note that the birth imagery in 4:21–31 does not refer to "new-birth," "conversion," or "regeneration" as such. Rather, that imagery focuses on the origin of the birth, whether one is born according to the flesh or according to the promise/Spirit (4:23, 29). There is no language of death and *new* birth. Moreover, strictly speaking, the language of creation is different from the language of birth. In the garden of Eden, God *created* Adam, not gave birth to him.

Secondly, in relation to the first point, the theme of new creation in v. 15 implies the theme of resurrection rather than new birth. As mentioned above, the parallel with 2:19–20 and the antithetical relationship with v. 14b lead us to take the new creation statement in v. 15 as an "intimation of the resurrection."[42] As seen in our investigation of Second Temple Jewish literature, the theme of resurrection often forms a part

---

39. Moo, *Galatians*, 397–98.

40. Dunn, *Epistle to the Galatians*, 342.

41. In other words, Hubbard identifies the language of new creation with the language of new birth, since the antithesis of 6:15 "neither circumcision nor uncircumcision, but new creation" reflects the fundamental contrast of Galatians (flesh/circumcision versus Spirit) as in Gal 4:21–31 (Hubbard, *New Creation*, 227).

42. Jackson, *New Creation*, 97.

of a cosmic renewal (e.g., 1 En. 25:3–6; Apoc. Mos. 13:2–5; 28:4; 4 Ezra 7:30–32; 1QH^a XI:17–19). Moreover, as seen above, the concept of new creation in the Second Temple period was mostly cosmological.

In this context, lastly, the cosmological understanding of καινὴ κτίσις can encompass not only an anthropological (the first option) but also an ecclesiological (the second option) understanding of new creation. This point can be strengthened by the comprehensive meaning of κόσμος in v. 14. As Adams well argued, in the Greco-Roman context, "human beings are related to the κόσμος as microcosm to macrocosm . . ., not only individually, but also collectively."[43] In other words, the meaning of the cosmos as microcosm can be extended to "the order of life and constitution which binds the citizens of a city-state."[44] It is, therefore, natural that we should understand καινὴ κτίσις in mainly a cosmological sense, recognizing that this does not exclude its anthropological and ecclesiological meanings.

The brevity of the phrase καινὴ κτίσις, however, still makes it difficult to determine its specific meaning, although we have recognized its cosmological significance. Again, the parallelism between Gal 3:28 and Gal 6:15 provides a hint for the interpretation of καινὴ κτίσις. In light of the allusion to Gen 1:27 in Gal 3:28, we can think that Paul uses the phrase καινὴ κτίσις in comparison with God's first creation. Just as all categories in Gal 3:28 are mainly primordial (natural or given by birth), so circumcision and uncircumcision basically belong to the fleshly world determined by the first creation (a female cannot be circumcised![45]). The fleshly value system, which is represented by circumcision or uncircumcision, is not important anymore as a result of Christ's death and resurrection. Thus, καινὴ κτίσις signifies the fundamental transformation of the cosmos which invalidates all previous fleshly/Adamic value systems.

C. V. 16: Israel of God

> And, as for all who will follow this rule—peace be upon them,
> and mercy, and upon the Israel of God (καὶ ὅσοι τῷ κανόνι

---

43. Adams, *Constructing the World*, 66. We can find this relationship between microcosm and macrocosm in ancient Greek philosophy and the Stoics such as Plato's *Timaeus* (30d; 44d–45b) and Cicero's *On the Nature of the Gods* (*De nat.* 2.11–14).

44. Sasse, "κόσμος," *TDNT* 3:868.

45. Female genital circumcision exists, but it is not of the "foreskin."

τούτῳ στοιχήσουσιν, εἰρήνη ἐπ' αὐτοὺς καὶ ἔλεος καὶ ἐπὶ τὸν Ἰσραὴλ τοῦ θεοῦ).

The fact that Paul uses the same verb στοιχεῖν in Gal 5:25, where the antithesis between the Spirit and the flesh appears, indicates that the life following the rule of new creation parallels the life led by the Spirit (5:18, 25). V. 16b has many exegetical issues concerning the identity of "the Israel of God," particularly because of its punctuation and the grammatical function of the καί before the last prepositional phrase. There are four most probable interpretative options as the referent of "the Israel of God":

1. Jewish believers in Christ who remain law observant

    Scholars who support this option[46] punctuate after "upon them" to highlight the symmetric structure, separating blessings for two distinct groups:

    εἰρήνη ἐπ' αὐτοὺς peace be upon them

    καί and

    ἔλεος καὶ ἐπὶ τὸν Ἰσραὴλ τοῦ θεοῦ mercy also upon the Israel of God

    That is to say, Paul is pronouncing two separate blessings, peace and mercy upon two different entities, namely "them" and "the Israel of God" respectively. Here "them" refers to "all who will follow this rule" in v. 16a, and the καί before the last prepositional phrase functions adverbially ("also"). The hypothesis[47] that Paul's rival teachers are using the term "the Israel of God" for referring to law-observant believers including themselves strengthens this interpretation since it explains why Paul suddenly uses this rare expression which does not seem to fit well with the context. Syntax also favors this option, since its punctuation provides a nicely symmetric structure, and it explains well why Paul uses the separate blessing "mercy" for "the Israel of God."

2. Ethnic Israel, specifically those who do not believe in Christ now

    The punctuation and the grammatical function of the last καί are the same as option (1), although an alternative case exists.[48] This

---

46. For example, de Boer, *Galatians*, 404–8.
47. Betz, *Galatians*, 323; Longenecker, *Galatians*, 298–99.
48. It is also possible that Paul is pronouncing the same combination of blessings,

CHAPTER 4: THE CONCEPT OF NEW CREATION IN PAUL 123

interpretation[49] argues that Paul pronounces a benediction of peace upon general believers in Christ who follow the rule of new creation *and* a prayer for mercy upon unbelieving ethnic Israel. This interpretation resonates with Paul's argument in Rom 9–11, where Israel receives God's mercy in spite of her disobedience. One would think that Paul's thought concerning Israel in Gal 6:16 is fully developed and articulated in Rom 9–11.[50] Also, this interpretation has an advantage given the occurrences of the term "Israel" in Paul's letters: Paul almost always uses "Israel" for referring to an ethnic/national Israel excepting two famously contested texts.[51]

3. Jewish believers in Christ who follow the standard of new creation

In this option,[52] "all who will follow this rule" in v. 16a mainly refers to gentile believers. This interpretation leads us to understand v. 16 like this: "And all Gentile believers in Christ who will henceforth follow this standard, peace be upon them, and mercy also upon God's Israel, Jewish believers in Christ who will henceforth follow this standard."[53] In other words, "the Israel of God" refers to "the righteous remnant" of Israel, and they are also included in the first blessing although they do not represent "all who will follow this rule." The advantage of this option is that it explains well why Paul adds the unique genitive phrase "of God" to Israel.

"peace and mercy," upon both Christians and ethnic Israel (the punctuation of the sentence in this case, is placed after mercy, and the last καί functions as "conjunctive" [and]). The special reason for the use of "mercy" for disobedient Israel, however, is weakened in this case.

49. For example, Eastman, "Israel and the Mercy of God," 367–95.

50. Eastman argues that in Gal 6:16, Paul pronounces a prayer for mercy on unbelieving Israel, having in mind that "there is an on-going mission to the circumcision led by Peter and the Jerusalem church." She also argues that in Rom 9–11, Paul again prays for his beloved kinsfolk after he found that the mission to the Jews was not successful contrary to what he originally had hoped for (Eastman, "Israel and the Mercy of God," 394).

51. In Rom 9:6b, Paul mentions two distinguishable "Israels": "For not all who are descended from Israel are Israel." Whether Paul here refers to the "true Israel," spiritual Israel or not is still debatable. Although most modern scholars take "all Israel" in Rom 11:26 to refer to ethnic Israel, this interpretation is still disputable.

52. For example, Betz, *Galatians*, 323. Bruce also interprets "the Israel of God" as "true Israel," but he adds an eschatological dimension to this verse by saying that "this remnant would increase until 'all Israel will be saved [Rom 11:26].'" See Bruce, *Epistle of Paul to the Galatians*, 274–75.

53. de Boer, *Galatians*, 407.

4. All believers in Christ made up of Jews and gentiles who follow the standard of new creation

This option[54] places punctuation after the word ἔλεος, presupposing that εἰρήνη and ἔλεος compose a double but unified blessing upon "all who will follow this rule" in v. 16a despite the intervening phrase (ἐπ' αὐτούς). Also, this interpretation takes the last καί as "epexegetic," in which "the Israel of God" is identified with "all who will follow this rule." The translation of this verse, which reflects this interpretation, would be: "And as for all who will follow this rule, peace and mercy be upon them, that is to say, upon the Israel of God." Although syntax does not favor this view because of the unusual sequence of "peace and mercy" and relatively rare occurrences of the epexegetic use of καί, the context of Galatians supports this interpretation. Given Paul's consistent argument in the whole letter that the soteriological importance of ethnic identity (Jews/gentiles or circumcision/uncircumcision) has been invalidated in Christ (e.g., 3:7, 16, 26, 28, 29; 4:26, 28, 31; 6:15; etc.), it is highly questionable that Paul suddenly draws attention to ethnic Israel just before closing the letter.

Since all these options have their own advantages and disadvantages, it is very difficult to select one option. Once more, the parallelism between 3:26–29 and 6:14–16 provides an important clue to determine the referent of "the Israel of God." As seen above, 6:16 corresponds to 3:29 in this parallelism:

> 6:16: And as for all who will follow this rule, peace and mercy be upon them, and upon the Israel of God
>
> 3:29: And if you belong to Christ, then you are Abraham's offspring, heirs according to the promise

The two verses are very similar in two points. First, the first part of each verse ("as for all who will follow this rule" and "if you belong to Christ") functions as a condition which leads to the result in the second part. Second, the result of the second part relates to "a change of identity" in those who satisfy the preceding condition.

---

54. This interpretation is not only a traditional view (e.g., Luther, Calvin, Lightfoot, et al.) of this verse, but also the majority of scholars still support it (e.g., Martyn, *Galatians*, 574–77; Barclay, *Obeying the Truth*, 98; Moo, *Galatians*, 402–3; Keener, *Galatians*, 578–81, etc.).

In light of this parallelism, "the Israel of God" perfectly matches the phrase "Abraham's offspring, heirs according to the promise." Paul clearly uses the expression "Abraham's offspring" in a metaphorical sense since he has already declared that "you are all one in Christ Jesus" regardless of their ethnicity (neither Jew nor Greek) in 3:28. This statement parallels the new creation statement in 6:15, and thus it is highly probable that Paul also uses the phrase "the Israel of God" in a metaphorical sense. Moreover, in light of this parallelism, we can explain why Paul adds the genitive phrase "of God" to Israel. Just as the appositive phrase "heirs according to the promise" (i.e., those not characterized according to the flesh) clarifies the metaphorical meaning of "Abraham's offspring," so the phrase "of God" clearly shows that the Israel in 6:16 is a *new* identity determined not by ethnicity but by God's new creation. Also, the fact that in 1 Cor 10:18, Paul mentions "the Israel according to the flesh" (ὁ Ἰσραὴλ κατὰ σάρκα) indicates that Paul can use the term Israel in a metaphorical sense to refer to "the Israel according to the promise," namely the Israel *of God*.

This point is crucial for the present study since it shows that Paul's concept of new creation closely relates to believers' new identity in Christ, regardless of their ethnicity. We should note that in 3:26, Paul uses another expression, the "sons of God," to refer to believers' new identity in Christ, which parallels "Abraham's offspring": "in Christ Jesus you are all sons of God, through faith." Here, the phrase "through faith" also corresponds to "of God" in "the Israel *of God*," in the sense that this new identity is given by God irrespective of one's ethnicity.

4. The concept of new creation in Paul and in Second Temple Judaism

We have analyzed 2 Cor 5:14–17 and Gal 6:14–16 to discover the concept of new creation in Paul. Now, I will summarize our findings regarding Paul's concept of new creation in comparison with the concept of new creation in Second Temple Jewish literature in terms of similarities and differences.

(1) Similarities

Paul's concept of new creation, which appears in 2 Cor 5:17 and Gal 6:15, is continuous with the concept of new creation in Second Temple Jewish literature in the following points. First of all, καινὴ κτίσις is *God's* redemptive work (cf. Jub. 1:29; 1 En. 24:3–6; Apoc. Mos. 13:2–5; LAB 3:10; 4 Ezra 7:30–32; 1QH^a V:24–37; 1QS IV:20–26; etc.). In both passages, the new creation is inseparably linked with the Christ-event, but we should recognize that God takes the initiative in planning and doing the work of new creation *through* the Christ-event. In the time predestined by *God* (Gal 4:2, 4), *God* sent his Son and the Spirit to redeem his people under the law (Gal 4:4–6). The new creation in Christ is closely related to God's redemptive action to liberate his people from slavery under the law, which invalidates the importance of circumcision and uncircumcision. Moreover, in 2 Cor 5:18–19, just after the new creation statement, Paul declares that "all these things are from God" and emphasizes God's reconciliation of the world in Christ. This indicates that the new creation is also God's work.

Secondly, Paul's concept of new creation is mainly a cosmological one which encompasses anthropological and ecclesiological dimensions (cf. Jub. 1:29; 1 En. 91:13–17; 4 Ezra 7:30–32; 2 Bar. 32:1–6; 73:1—74:1; LAB 32:16–17; 1QH^a V:24–37; 4Q416 1:10–17; etc.). It occurs with the term κόσμος and relates to a radical change in the relationship between humanity and the world (2 Cor 5:18–19; Gal 6:14).

Thirdly, the radical and cosmological change of the second point also involves eschatological discontinuity between the old and the new ages (cf. 1 En. 90:28–29; LAB 3:10; 4 Ezra 7:30–32; 2 Bar. 44:9–12; 1QH^a V:24–37; etc.). The new creation in 2 Cor 5:17 is identical to the fundamental change in which the old has passed away and the new has come. Also, God's sending of his Son and the Spirit has inaugurated an eschatological new age to redeem his people (Gal 4:4–6) from the present evil age (Gal 1:4). This new age is closely related to the new creation in Gal 6:15.

Fourthly, in the two new creation passages, the concept of new creation is closely related not only to *Christ's* death but also to *believers'* co-crucifixion and new life in Christ. Thus, Paul's concept of new creation implies the resurrection of believers as a part of the cosmic renewal (cf. Apoc. Mos. 13:2–5; 28:4; 41:3; LAB 3:10; 4 Ezra 7:30–32; 1QH^a V:29; XI:20–26; XIX:12–17; etc.).

Fifthly, Paul uses the concept of new creation in connection with the Adamic motif (cf. Jub. 4:26; 19:23–25; 1 En. 25:3–6; Apoc. Mos. 13:2–5; 41:3; LAB 26:6–7; 2 Bar. 73:1—74:3; 1QH^a IV: IV:26–30; V:24–37; 1QS IV:20–26; CD III:18–20; 4Q417 1:16–18; 4Q418 81:1–5; etc.). The εἷς-πάντες motif in 2 Cor 5:14–15 relates to the Adam-Christology, and the parallelism between Gal 6:15 and Gal 3:28, where Paul alludes to God's creation of male and female in Gen 1:27, indicates Paul uses καινὴ κτίσις in Gal 6:15 in connection with God's first creation.

Lastly, the concept of new creation in Paul relates to the change of God's people's identity (cf. Jub. 1:23–25; 19:27–29; LAB 16:2–5; 32:16–17; 4 Ezra 6:57–59; 1QH^a XI:20–24; XIX:12–17; 1QS IV:20–26; 4Q416 1:10–17; etc.). In Gal 6:16, believers' new identity in Christ is "the Israel of God." As seen above, this new identity is also closely linked to "Abraham's offspring according to the promise" (3:29) and "sons of God through faith" (3:26) in light of the parallelism between Gal 3:27–29 and Gal 6:14–16.

In spite of the fact that Paul's concept of new creation shares a number of features with the concept of new creation in Second Temple Judaism, there are also radical differences between them, as we shall see below.

(2) Differences

We have seen that Paul's concept of new creation highlights God's initiative just as that concept appears in Second Temple Jewish writings. Paul's concept of new creation, however, is radically distinctive from other Second Temple Jewish literature in that God's initiative in the new creation is decisively expressed *through the Christ-event*. The new creation statements appear just after Paul mentions the Christ-event (2 Cor 5:14–15; Gal 6:14) and even occurs with the phrase "in Christ" as a precondition of new creation (2 Cor 5:17; implicitly in Gal 6:15). In our investigation of the concept of new creation in Second Temple Jewish literature, we have seen a few cases in which the concept of new creation appears with a messianic figure as a "new Adam" (e.g., 1 En. 45:4–6; 90:37–38; LAB 60:3). However, nowhere in any Second Temple Jewish literature does the new creation motif so decisively relate to the Messiah as in the case of Paul. Thus, Paul seems to radically reinterpret the concept of new creation in light of the Christ-event. This is the first and the most important feature of Paul's concept of new creation, which is distinctive from other Second Temple Jewish literature.

This distinction of the Christ-event in Paul's concept of new creation leads to another distinction compared to the Jewish literature. In most cases, the new creation motif in Jewish literature appears as an eschatological event with a future focus, although sometimes it also occurs as a present blessing that has already come within God's chosen community (e.g., the Hodayot, the Community Rule, 4QInstruction). In contrast, the theme of the new creation in 2 Cor 5:17 and Gal 6:15 appears to be a present event, which can affect the current situation, rather than a future event. Especially in 2 Cor 5:16–17, the expressions "from now on," "the old has passed away," and "behold, the new has come" make it clear that the new creation is an event that has already happened in the present by the Christ-event.

Finally, Paul's concept of new creation is characterized by a strong contrast with the values according to the flesh. Both texts of the new creation appear in the context that Paul contrasts his ministry with those who boast about the values according to the flesh. Thus, the new creation in Christ appears to subvert this fleshly value system, which is determined by race, gender, status, and circumcision/uncircumcision.

5. Conclusion

In this chapter, we have examined the meaning of the new creation in Paul through the exegesis of the two texts where the phrase καινὴ κτίσις appears and have compared it with the new creation theme in other Jewish texts. Our conclusion from this analysis is that Paul shares many features of the concepts of the new creation in the Second Temple Jewish literature. In particular, Paul shares with other Jewish texts the two most important points related to our study: First, Paul, like other Second Temple Jewish texts, uses the concept of new creation in connection with the Adamic motif; Second, Paul uses the theme of the new creation in connection with the new identity of God's people. Paul's concept of the new creation, however, is distinctive from other Jewish literature in that God's sovereign work of new creation is expressed through the Christ-event that has already happened, in which the present meaning of new creation is further emphasized.

Part II: Paul's Use of Υἱοθεσία in Light of New Creation

Chapter 5: **Paul's Use of Υἱοθεσία in Romans 8 in Light of New Creation**

1. Introduction

ROMANS 8 IS PARTICULARLY important for the study of Paul's adoption metaphor. The reason is that only Rom 8 uses the adoption metaphor twice (Rom 8:15, 23) among Paul's letters, but it also shows both the present and future aspects of Paul's use of υἱοθεσία. When we explored the meaning of new creation in Part I, we found that the concept of new creation is closely related to the motif of divine sonship. Can this observation, then, be applicable to Paul's adoption metaphor in Rom 8? If so, what is Paul's intention in using the adoption metaphor in the context of new creation?

In this chapter, I will demonstrate that Paul uses the adoption metaphor in the context of new creation through the exegesis of Rom 8:14–17 and 8:19–23. To do this, I will focus particularly on three points: (1) I will show that each passage does bear the theme of new creation. Just as the allusion to Ezek 36–37 in Rom 8:1–17, which is eventually connected to the creation narrative in Gen 2, leads us to recognize the theme of new creation in Rom 8:14–17, so the allusion to Gen 3:16–19 in Rom 8:19–23 has the same function. (2) Through a close analysis of Paul's use of υἱοθεσία in Rom 8:15 and 8:23, I will highlight that Paul is actually using the adoption metaphor in connection with the new creation motif. (3) I will investigate how this new creation context sheds light on the meaning of Paul's use of υἱοθεσία in Rom 8.

2. Paul's use of υἱοθεσία in Rom 8:14–17 in light of new creation

Before offering an exegesis of Rom 8:14–17, I will investigate the allusion to Ezek 36–37 in Rom 8:1–11, since the themes of new creation and resurrection in Ezek 36–37 provide important context and background for the interpretation of Rom 8:14–17.

(1) The Echoes of Ezek 36–37 in Rom 8:1–11

As several scholars point out, Rom 8:1–11 has many echoes of Ezek 36–37.[1] In particular, it is highly probable that Rom 8:4 and 8:9–11 allude to Ezek 36:27 and Ezek 37:1–14 respectively. Romans 8:4 and Ezek 36:27 (LXX) are as follows:

> ἵνα τὸ δικαίωμα τοῦ νόμου πληρωθῇ ἐν ἡμῖν τοῖς μὴ κατὰ σάρκα περιπατοῦσιν ἀλλὰ κατὰ πνεῦμα (so that the righteous requirement of the law might be fulfilled in us who walk not according to the flesh, but according to the Spirit: Rom 8:4).

> καὶ τὸ πνεῦμά μου δώσω ἐν ὑμῖν, καὶ ποιήσω ἵνα ἐν τοῖς δικαιώμασίν μου πορεύησθε, καὶ τὰ κρίματά μου φυλάξησθε καὶ ποιήσητε (and I will put my Spirit in you, and I will work so that you may walk in my statutes and keep my ordinances and do them: Ezek 36:27).

There are many parallels between these two verses: (1) δικαίωμα/δικαιώμασιν; (2) περιπατοῦσιν/ πορεύησθε; (3) πνεῦμα; (4) the use of a ἵνα clause to signify the function of the Spirit, that is, the fulfillment of the law's requirement; (5) πληρωθῇ /φυλάξησθε καὶ ποιήσητε. In considering these parallels, we should note the following points.

First, the difference in number between δικαίωμα/δικαιώμασιν seems insignificant since, in the same letter, Paul uses the same word in

---

1. Hübner, *Biblische Theologie*, 300–304; Kim, *Paul and the New Perspective*, 159; Sprinkle, *Paul and Judaism Revisited*, 107–8; Yates, *Spirit and Creation*, 143–47; For example, Hübner summarizes the parallels between Rom 8:1–11 and Ezek 36–37 as follows: (1) God gives his Spirit to the people he has redeemed; (2) so God renews his people and frees them from their inability to keep the law; (3) the outpouring of the Spirit is in the context of fulfilling the requirement of the law (τὸ δικαίωμα τοῦ νόμου); (4) both texts describe the life in the context of the Spirit and the law (Ezek 37:5, 14; Rom 8:2, 6, 13); (5) both Ezekiel and Paul understand their sociological notions in the ecclesiological horizon; (6) both Ezekiel and Paul understand their *Heilsekklesia* as an eschatological community (Hübner, *Biblische Theologie*, 303).

the plural (δικαιώματα) with the same meaning (Rom 2:26a: if those who are uncircumcised keep *the requirements of the law*).[2]

Second, Ezek 36:27 (LXX) translates the Hebrew word חֹק and מִשְׁפָּט into δικαίωμα and κρίμα respectively. Ezekiel 11:20 (LXX), the parallel of Ezek 36:27, however, translates חֹק and מִשְׁפָּט into πρόσταγμα and δικαίωμα respectively:

> ὅπως ἐν τοῖς προστάγμασίν μου πορεύωνται, καὶ τὰ δικαιώματά μου φυλάσσωνται καὶ ποιῶσιν αὐτά, καὶ ἔσονταί μοι εἰς λαὸν καὶ ἐγὼ ἔσομαι αὐτοῖς εἰς θεόν (in order that they may walk in my commands and keep my ordinances and do them, and they will be my people and I will be their God: Ezek 11:20).

This means that τὰ κρίματά μου in Ezek 36:27 can be an equivalent of τὰ δικαιώματά μου. This fact strengthens the parallelism between Rom 8:4 and Ezek 36:27 since τὰ κρίματά μου as well as τὰ δικαιώματά μου can be regarded as the parallel of δικαίωμα in Rom 8:4.

Third, although the two passages use different words περιπατέω/πορεύομαι for the moral and religious meaning of "to walk," it is important to note that unlike the LXX, the New Testament uses πορεύομαι surprisingly infrequently for this sense.[3] As Yates observes, Paul, in particular, always uses περιπατέω for the moral and religious "walk" (e.g., Gal 5:16; 1 Thess 2:12; 4:1, 12; Rom 13:13; 14:15; 1 Cor 3:3; 7:17; 2 Cor 4:2; 10:2, 3; Phil 3:17).[4]

Fourth, as Cranfield points out, Paul seems to use the verb πληρόω instead of φυλάσσω and ποιέω in the ἵνα clause since he regards Rom 8:4 as the *fulfillment* of God's promise in Ezek 36:27 through the Christ-event.[5] Also, as Bertone rightly argues, "Paul intentionally avoids using these verbs [ποιεῖν, πράσσειν, or ὑποτάσσειν] in the contexts where he relates Christian behavior to the law. Instead, he uses the verb πληροῦν when he wants to mention the Mosaic law positively in his discussion of Christian ethics" (i.e., Rom 8:4; 13:8–10; Gal 5:14).[6] This tendency can also be applied to φυλάσσω since Paul uses this word two times with the meaning of "keeping the law," but he uses it for a negative meaning (Gal

---

2. Yates, *Spirit and Creation*, 144.

3. Friedrich Hauck and Seigfried Schulz, "πορεύομαι," *TDNT* 6:575.

4. Yates, *Spirit and Creation in Paul*, 144; Heinrich Seesemann, "πατέω," *TDNT* 5:944–45.

5. Cranfield, *Critical and Exegetical Commentary*, 1:384; Yates, *Spirit and Creation*, 145.

6. Bertone, *Law of the Spirit*, 239.

6:13) or a hypothetical situation (Rom 2:26), not a positive aspect of the Mosaic law. Also, in spite of the verbal difference in the ἵνα clauses, their meanings are strikingly similar in that the Spirit enables people to satisfy the requirement of the law.

The similarity in terms of context and theme reinforces the probability of Paul's allusion to Ezek 36–37 in Rom 8:1–11. In Rom 8:9–11, πνεῦμα θεοῦ in v. 9 stands parallel to πνεῦμα ζωή in v. 10. This follows the same pattern as Ezek 37:5–6 where πνεῦμα ζωῆς and πνεῦμά μου are parallel to one another.[7] Also, Rom 8:11 seems to summarize the imagery and language of Ezek 37:1–14:

> εἰ δὲ τὸ πνεῦμα τοῦ ἐγείραντος τὸν Ἰησοῦν ἐκ νεκρῶν οἰκεῖ ἐν ὑμῖν, ὁ ἐγείρας Χριστὸν ἐκ νεκρῶν ζωοποιήσει καὶ τὰ θνητὰ σώματα ὑμῶν διὰ τοῦ ἐνοικοῦντος αὐτοῦ πνεύματος ἐν ὑμῖν (If the Spirit of the one who raised Jesus from the dead dwells in you, he who raised Christ from the dead will give life to your mortal bodies also through his Spirit that dwells in you: Rom 8:11).

The core concept of 8:11 is that the Spirit will give life to dead bodies. That is to say, the keywords are the Spirit, the dead bodies, and the life. Ezek 37:1–14 figuratively repeats the same concept—bringing the Spirit to the dead bodies and they will live—as follows:

> This is what the Lord says to these bones: "Look, I am *bringing a living spirit into you*, and I will place tendons upon you, and bring flesh upon you, and stretch out skin over you, and *place my spirit into you, and you will live* and know that I am the Lord" (Ezek 37:5–6)

> "Come from the four *spirits*, and *blow into these corpses* and *they will live*" (Ezek 37:9)

> . . . and the *spirit entered into them, and they lived* and stood on their feet, an exceedingly great company (Ezek 37:10).

> and *I will place my spirit into you* and *you will live* . . . (Ezek 37:14)

In Ezek 37:8–9, YHWH calls the bones—with tendons, flesh, and skin but *without the Spirit* (πνεῦμα οὐκ ἦν ἐν αὐτοῖς)—"these corpses" (τοὺς νεκροὺς τούτους). In this sense, the νεκροὺς in Ezek 37:9 parallels "the mortal bodies" in Rom 8:11. The fact that the word νεκρός appears three times in Rom 8:9–11 also highlights this parallelism.

---

7. Yates, *Spirit and Creation*, 145.

In addition to the similarity of language use, the common theme of both texts is the eschatological restoration of God's people through the Spirit. Thus, it seems to be clear that Rom 8:1–11 alludes to Ezek 36–37 (particularly, Ezek 36:27 and Ezek 37:1–14). What, then, does this allusion mean for the interpretation of Paul's use of υἱοθεσία in Rom 8:15? To answer this question, we should understand the new creation motif of Ezek 36–37 first, which I will focus on in the next section.

(2) Ezek 36–37 and the new creation

As many scholars argue, Ezek 37:1–14 has strong links to the creation account of Gen 2.[8] This is seen most clearly in the prominence of the "breath of life" tradition: the process of the revivification of the dead is very similar to the process of the creation of man in two stages (man is formed but becomes a living being only after God breathes life into him). The verb, נפח (to blow: Ezek 37:9), is the same as that found in Gen 2:7. Ezek 37:1–14's connection with the creation narrative in Gen 1–2 can be strengthened by the fact that just prior to this passage, God promises that the land will be cultivated, coming to resemble the garden of Eden in its fruitfulness (36:34–35):

> "The land that was desolate shall be tilled (עבד), instead of being the desolation that it was in the sight of all who passed by. And they will say, 'This land that was desolate has become like *the garden of Eden* (גן־עדן); and the waste and desolate and ruined towns are now inhabited and fortified.'"

The Hebrew verb עבד[9] and the garden of Eden (גן־עדן) also occur together in Gen 2:15: "The Lord God took the man and set (נוח)[10] him in the garden of Eden (גן־עדן) to till (עבד) it and keep it." Thus, it is highly probable that Ezek 36:34–35 alludes to Gen 2:15. Regarding the Israelite creation traditions in Ezek 36:34–35 Kutsko puts it: "the ideological map

---

8. E.g., Zimmerli, *Ezekiel*, 261–65; Allen, *Ezekiel*, 185; Kutsko, *Between Heaven and Earth*, 133; Levenson, *Resurrection and the Restoration of Israel*, 159; Yates, *Spirit and Creation*, 31–35.

9. The use of עבד in relation with the theme of "desolateness" also occurs in Gen 2:5: "when no plant of the filed had yet in the earth and no herb of the field had yet sprung up—for the LORD God had not caused it to rain upon the earth and there was no one to *till* the ground."

10. נוח also occurs in Ezek 37:1, 14, particularly, in Ezek 37:14, YHWH promises to set (נוח) his people back in their own land (אדמה) in the context of Israel's restoration.

of the גן־עדן in Gen 2:10–14 portrays it at the headwaters of both the river Gihon (Jerusalem) and the rivers Tigris and Euphrates (Mesopotamia), the past and present residences of the audience of Ezekiel."[11] In addition, יטב (good) and ראשׁת (the former time) in Ezek 36:11 are also the language of the Genesis creation narrative (יטב appears in Gen 1:4, 10, 12, 18, 21, 25, 31; ראשׁת appears in Gen 1:1).

A number of allusions to the Genesis creation narrative in Ezek 36–37 lead us to read Israel's restoration in Ezek 36–37 in the context of new creation. The fact that Israel's renewal encompasses the restoration of creation such as the land of Israel (Ezek 36:6–8), animals (Ezek 36:11), the grain (Ezek 36:29), and the fruit of the tree and the produce of the field (Ezek 36:30) also highlights the new creation theme of this text. This indicates that Rom 8:1–11 which alludes to Ezek 36–37 can also be read in the context of new creation.

(3) The parallelism between God's people and the sons of God

As we have seen, Rom 8:4 and Rom 8:9–11 allude to God's two promises in Ezek 36–37. The first is that God will put his Spirit within Israel and make Israel obey the law (Ezek 36:27); the second is that God will put his Spirit within Israel, and Israel will live (Ezek 37:1–14). Ezek 36–37, however, repeatedly stresses another important promise in relation to the consequence of God's outpouring of his Spirit to Israel. That promise is: ἔσεσθέ μοι εἰς λαόν, κἀγὼ ἔσομαι ὑμῖν εἰς θεόν "you [Israel]will be my people and I will be your God" (Ezek 36:28; 37:23, 27). Where, then, does this relationship between God and his people occur in Romans 8? There is no literal expression of God's people (λαός) in Rom 8. Instead, the language of divine sonship occurs repeatedly in Rom 8:14–23 (vv. 14, 19: "sons of God"; vv. 15, 23: "adoption as sons"; vv. 16, 17: "children of God"; v. 17: "heirs of God"). Can we regard this father-son relationship as the parallel to the relationship between God and his people? In the early Jewish tradition, the term "the sons of God" often refers to Israel's special relationship with God as his people. For instance, in Hos 1:10, the parallelism between God's people and God's sons clearly occurs:

> . . . καὶ ἔσται ἐν τῷ τόπῳ, οὗ ἐρρέθη αὐτοῖς Οὐ λαός μου ὑμεῖς, ἐκεῖ κληθήσονται υἱοὶ θεοῦ ζῶντος (. . . and it will be, in the place

---

11. Kutsko, *Between Heaven and Earth*, 130.

where it was said to them, "You are not *my people*," they will also be called, "*Sons of the living God*": Hos 1:10)

God promises that the broken covenant relationship (not my people) will be restored to a new covenant relationship expressed with divine sonship (sons of the living God). Although there is no reference to the Spirit in this text, its context of Israel's eventual restoration is similar to Ezek 36–37.

Moreover, Jub. 1:23–25, which we have examined above (chapter 2, section 3), alludes to Ezek 36:26–27 and Hos 2:1 at the same time, combining the theme of the Spirit (also the changing of the heart and the obeying of the law) with the theme of divine sonship in the context of Israel's eventual restoration. In other words, the themes of "hearts and the spirit to keep God's commandments" (vv. 23–24) and "being called children of the living God" (v. 25) seem to allude to Ezek 36:26–27 and Hos 1:10 respectively. As Morales argues, the creation of a "holy spirit" in Jub. 1:23 may refer to "the purification of the human spirit or a change in the disposition of the recipients since nowhere in the passage does the author refer to God's own Spirit."[12] Yet, Ezek 36:26–27 says that the new spirit God put within the human heart is *God's* Spirit and this Spirit will make the Israelites observe *God's* commandments. This statement is very similar to Jub. 1:23–25, and thus we can regard the holy spirit in Jub. 1:23–25 as God's Spirit in light of the parallelism between the two passages.

Moreover, just before this text, the covenant formula also occurs in Jub. 1:17: "And I shall be their God, and they shall be my people truly and rightly." As Scott correctly observes, the "covenant formula" of v. 17 parallels the so-called the "adoption formula" ("I shall be a father to them, and they will be sons to me": the citation of 2 Sam 7:14) in Jub. 1:24.[13] This argument is undergirded by the fact that the parallelism

---

12. Morales, *Spirit and the Restoration of Israel*, 47.

13. Scott, *Adoption as Sons of God*, 107. In 2 Sam 7 itself, the adoption formula and the covenant formula occur together (although the adoption formula here is for the Davidic messiah, rather than for the people of Israel). Scott argues that 2 Sam 7 uses the covenant formula in v. 24 to contextualize the adoption formula in v. 14 in order to highlight the interrelationship between the king and the people of God (Scott, *Adoption as Sons of God*, 100). In the Old Testament, Israel is also declared as the sons of God (e.g., Exod 4:22; Hos 11:1; Jer 31:9). In this sense, Bertone argues that "within early Judaism, the promises of 2 Sam 7:14 [the adoption formula for the Davidic king] and Ezek 36:27 [the covenant formula for Israel] are amalgamated and applicable to every Jew" (Bertone, *Law of the Spirit*, 83).

appears again a little later in v. 28b: "And everyone will know that I am the *God of Israel* and *the father of all the children of Jacob* and king upon Mount Zion forever and ever."

It is important to note that Paul directly quotes Hos 2:1 in Rom 9:26 in the context of his discussion concerning the plight of his people Israel. Moreover, Paul himself uses the parallelism between the adoption formula and the covenant formula in 2 Cor 6:16–18. This confirms that the parallelism between God's people and God's sons also exists in Paul's mind. Thus, we can think that Paul's allusion to Ezek 36–37 continues in Rom 8:14–17. Also, we can regard the theme of divine sonship in Rom 8:14–17 as an equivalent to the covenant formula—you [Israel] will be my people and I will be your God—in Ezek 36–37. Now we are prepared to interpret Paul's use of υἱοθεσία in Rom 8:15 through the exegesis of Rom 8:14–17, in light of the theme of new creation in Ezek 36–37.

(4) Exegesis of Rom 8:14–17

A. V. 14

Romans 8:14 clearly shows the close relationship between the Spirit and being "sons of God": ὅσοι γὰρ πνεύματι θεοῦ ἄγονται, οὗτοι υἱοὶ θεοῦ εἰσιν ("for all who are led by the Spirit of God, they are sons of God"). The sequence of Israel's restoration Ezek 36:27–28 is that (1) God will establish his Spirit in Israel; (2) Israel will keep the law; (3) and Israel will be God's people. Compared to this sequence, Rom 8:14 seems to omit the second step, that is, the fulfillment of law's just requirement through the Spirit. It is probable that Paul omits this sequence since (1) he already mentioned this in Rom 8:4; or (2) "being led by the Spirit" itself implies this meaning. In Gal 5:18, Paul says: εἰ δὲ πνεύματι ἄγεσθε, οὐκ ἐστὲ ὑπὸ νόμον ("but if you are led by the Spirit, you are not under the law"). This indicates that in Paul's mind, the one who is led by the Spirit fulfils the requirement of the law as a consequence of Paul's statement in 8:4: "the righteous requirement of the law might be fulfilled in us, who walk not according to the flesh but according to the Spirit."[14] Thus, Rom 8:14 seems to effectively summarize the concept of Ezek 36:27–28.

14. The contrast between "to walk [live] according to the flesh" and "to walk according to the Spirit" in Rom 8:4 is clearly echoed in Rom 8:12–14: (1) in v. 12, τοῦ κατὰ σάρκα ζῆν (to live according to the flesh); (2) in v. 13, εἰ γὰρ κατὰ σάρκα ζῆτε (if you live according to the flesh) and εἰ δὲ πνεύματι τὰς πράξεις τοῦ σώματος θανατοῦτε (if by the

The language of ἄγειν (to lead) needs to be given more attention since its compounds εἰσάγειν (to lead into) and συνάγειν (to lead together) also occur in Ezek 36:24 and Ezek 37:21:

> "I shall take you from the nations and gather you from all the lands, and I will *lead* you *into* your land (εἰσάξω ὑμᾶς εἰς τὴν γῆν ὑμῶν)." (Ezek 36:24)

> "Look, I am taking all the house of Israel from the midst of the nations wherever they entered, and I shall *lead together* (συνάξω) them from all those surrounding them, and *lead them into* (εἰσάξω αὐτοὺς εἰς) the land of Israel." (Ezek 37:21)

It is worth noting that these two verses have the theme of "return from exile" or "new exodus." The new exodus theme in connection with covenant renewal is important within the book of Ezekiel as a whole (Ezek 11:16–21, 34:25–31, 36:24–38, 37:11–28, 39:22–29).[15]

Also, Levenson describes Israel's resurrection in Ezek 37:1–14 as "Israel's exodus from the grave" in that this recreation of Israel is associated with Israel's restoration to their ancestral and promised land:

> The verbs that denote God's lifting them (עלה) out of their graves and bringing (בוא) them into the land of Israel immediately recall the promise in Exodus to bring the enslaved Israelites out of the House of Bondage and into the land promised their fathers. העלה[16] ("to bring up") is a standard and ubiquitous term for God's involvement in the exodus. The use of הביא[17] ("to bring") in connection with the land promise, together with an emphasis on the recognition of the LORD as Israel's God in Ezek 37:12–14, is strikingly reminiscent of an oracle to Moses in Exodus 6.[18]

Thus, it appears that the theme of new creation is interwoven with the theme of new exodus in Ezek 36–37.

Can this usage of ἄγειν in the context of the new exodus, then, be applicable to ἄγειν in Rom 8:14 as well? La Potterie argues that "the verb ἄγειν (with its compounds ἐξάγειν/εἰσάγειν and its synonym ὁδηγεῖν) has

---

Spirit you put to death the deeds of the body). In this context, "being led by the Spirit" parallels "walking according to the Spirit."

15. Idestrom, "Echoes of the Book of Exodus," 502.
16. The hiphil of עלה.
17. The hiphil of בוא.
18. Levenson, *Resurrection and the Restoration of Israel*, 160–61. Particularly, Ezek 37:12, "I am going to open your graves, and bring you up from your graves, O my people; and I will bring you back to the land of Israel," expresses well Levenson's point.

become in the Greek Bible the technical terminology for the vocabulary of the exodus."[19] Similarly, Keesmaat argues that an examination of the context of these words in the LXX reveals that they do indeed occur most prominently in an exodus context (Exod 15:13; Ps 104:37, 42, 43; Ps 77:14, 53; Ps 22:3; Ps 30:4; Jer 38:9).[20] In spite of de la Potterie's extensive citation of and interaction with the LXX and the New Testament texts, Moo asserts that de la Potterie's argument lacks *clear* lexical support in the New Testament and LXX.[21]

However, as Keesmaat well argued, the combination of the themes "leading" and "sonship" makes the case much more persuasive. In early Jewish traditions, Israel's divine sonship is closely related to the exodus narrative (e.g., Exod 4:22-23; Deut 1:30-31; Hos 1:10-11; 11:1; Isa 43:6-7; 63:8-10a; Wis 11:10; 16:21, 26; 18:4, 18:13; 4Q504 III 5-10; Sir 36:1-17). Moreover, the conjunction of "leading" and "sonship" is often found in the Old Testament and Second Temple Jewish texts in the context of the new exodus (e.g., Isa 63:7-19; Jer 38:8-9; Tob 13:4-5; Bar 5:6; cf. Deut 32:6-20).[22]

This lexical evidence and the allusions to Ezek 36-37 in Rom 8:1-17 suggest that we can read the language of divine sonship in Rom 8:14-17 in light of the main theme of Ezek 36-37, new creation interwoven with new exodus. In this sense, the "sons of God" in v. 14 refers not merely to God's people, but to God's *newly created* people since God created his people from the dry bones by the reviving power of his Spirit in Ezek 37:1-14. The connection between v. 13 and v. 14 also supports this interpretation:

> v. 13: εἰ γὰρ κατὰ σάρκα ζῆτε, μέλλετε ἀποθνῄσκειν. εἰ δὲ πνεύματι τὰς πράξεις τοῦ σώματος θανατοῦτε, ζήσεσθε (For if you live according to the flesh you will die, but if by the Spirit you put to death the deeds of the body, you will live)

> v. 14: ὅσοι γὰρ πνεύματι θεοῦ ἄγονται, οὗτοι υἱοὶ θεοῦ εἰσιν (for all who are led by the Spirit of God, they are sons of God)

Since the γάρ in v. 14 is best interpreted in an explanatory sense, v. 14 seems to repeat the meaning of v. 13b in different terms.[23] Given this

---

19. La Potterie, "Chrétien conduit," 221.
20. Keesmaat, *Paul and His Story*, 55-59.
21. Moo, *Epistle to the Romans*, 498.
22. Keesmaat, *Paul and his Story*, 60-65.
23. Cranfield, *Critical and Exegetical Commentary*, 1:395.

relationship, "to live according to the Spirit putting to death the deeds of the body" can be equivalent to "being led by the Spirit of God," and "you will live" can be equivalent to "being sons of God." In this context, Rom 8:14 seems to include implicitly the statements of both Rom 8:4 ("the righteous requirement of the law is fulfilled in us, who walk according to the Spirit") and that of Rom 8:11 ("If God's Spirit dwells in you, God who raised Christ from the dead will also give life to your mortal bodies"). Thus, "being sons of God" in v. 14 indicates the spiritual transition from death under the law and sin to the new life in Christ.

B. V. 15

The contrast between "death" and "life" or "to walk according to the flesh" and "to walk according to the Spirit" continues in Rom 8:15 with the contrast between πνεῦμα δουλείας and πνεῦμα υἱοθεσίας: οὐ γὰρ ἐλάβετε πνεῦμα δουλείας πάλιν εἰς φόβον ἀλλ' ἐλάβετε πνεῦμα υἱοθεσίας ἐν ᾧ κράζομεν· αββα ὁ πατήρ (For you did not receive a spirit of slavery resulting again into fear, but you have received the Spirit of adoption by whom we cry, "Abba! Father!": Rom 8:15).The explanatory γάρ links this verse to the foregoing sentence as a confirmation of the statement in v. 14. That is to say, v. 15 describes the actualization of the familial relationship with God through receiving the spirit of adoption.

In the New Testament (Rom 8:21; Gal 4:24; 5:1; Heb 2:15), δουλεία[24] appears only with "figurative meanings for slavery to sin, law, and death, which continues wherever the redemption through Christ is not yet effective."[25] As with Gal 4:25 and 5:1, here δουλεία refers to slavery in relation to the law,[26] more specifically, slavery to "the law of sin and death" (Rom 8:2).

---

24. It is interesting to note that the LXX very commonly uses the word δουλεία for Israel's slavery in Egypt (e.g., Lev 26:42; Exod 6:6; 13:3, 14; 20:2; Deut 5:6; 6:12; 7:8; 13:5; 10:3; Jer 41:13; Mic 6:4). In these examples, δουλεία is almost always occurring with "lead out" (ἐξάγω). As we have seen, the word ἄγω already occurs in v. 14 and the combination of "leading" and "sonship" can be read in the context of the new exodus. Hence, just as the combination of "leading" and "sonship" establishes a matrix of the exodus motifs, so the conjunction of themes of "leading" and "slavery" strengthens the new exodus context. Thus, Rom 8:14-17 can be read in the context of new creation interwoven with new exodus.

25. A. Weiser, "δουλεία," *EDNT* 1:350.

26. Jewett, *Romans*, 497.

The slavery to sin and death can be connected to the Adam motif in Rom 5:12–21, where Paul argues that sin came into the world through Adam, and death came through sin, and so death exercised dominion over all sinners.²⁷ Although δουλεία does not occur in Rom 5:12–21, the repetitive use of βασιλεύειν (to rule) for death (vv. 14, 17) and sin (v. 21; cf. Rom 6:12) represents the slavery to death and sin.

The theme of slavery to sin and death (or sin/death's dominion over sinners) more clearly appears in Rom 6, where Paul uses the slavery imagery consistently. Paul says: "Our old self was crucified with him [Christ] . . . so that we would no longer be enslaved to sin (τοῦ μηκέτι δουλεύειν ἡμᾶς τῇ ἁμαρτίᾳ)" (6:6); "Christ, being raised from the dead, will never die again; death no longer has dominion over him (θάνατος αὐτοῦ οὐκέτι κυριεύει)" (6:9); "for sin will have no dominion over you (ἁμαρτία γὰρ ὑμῶν οὐ κυριεύσει)" (6:14); "you are slaves of the one whom you obey, either of sin resulting in death, or of obedience resulting in righteousness? (δοῦλοί ἐστε ᾧ ὑπακούετε, ἤτοι ἁμαρτίας εἰς θάνατον ἢ ὑπακοῆς εἰς δικαιοσύνην;)" (6:16); "you were slaves of sin" (ἦτε δοῦλοι τῆς ἁμαρτίας) (6:17, 20).

Paul's use of slavery imagery continues in Rom 7. While he uses the analogy from marriage to explain "being released from the law" (7:1–6), Paul says, "But now we *are released from the law*, having died to that which held us *captive*, so that we serve in the new way of the Spirit and not in the old way of the written code" (7:6). The slavery under sin is also the main theme of Rom 7:7–25, where the "Adamic I"²⁸ appears as a narrator. In 7:14, Paul describes the Adamic I as "I am of the flesh, sold under sin" (ἐγὼ δὲ σάρκινός εἰμι πεπραμένος ὑπὸ τὴν ἁμαρτίαν). The term "πιπράσκειν" here has a meaning of "sell someone as a slave" (cf. Matt 18:25).²⁹ Moreover, Paul concludes this section with the statement that "so then, on the one hand, I myself with my mind serve (δουλεύω) the law of God, but on the other, with my flesh the law of sin" (7:25).

---

27. Genesis 2:16–17 clearly shows the connection between Adam's sin and death: "And the LORD God commanded the man, 'You may freely eat of every tree of the garden; but of the tree of the knowledge of good and evil you shall not eat, for in the day that you eat of it *you shall die* (θανάτῳ ἀποθανεῖσθε).'" Here, Adam's sin refers to Adam's transgression of God's command. The warning of a death sentence does not refer to immediate execution but refers to ultimate death.

28. In the exegesis of 2 Cor 5:14–17 (ch. 4, section 1), we have already discussed this "Adamic I" in Rom 7:7–25.

29. BDAG, s.v. "πιπράσκω," 814–15.

Finally, the other reference to δουλεία in Rom 8:21 also uses the Adam motif as we shall see later. Thus, given the fact that in Rom 5–8, when slavery is associated with the past, or something now repudiated, it is always slavery to sin or death, "receiving πνεῦμα δουλείας" in Rom 8:15 seems to refer to slavery under sin and death.

What, then, does πνεῦμα υἱοθεσίας refer to and what is the meaning of this phrase? The verb λαμβάνειν (to receive) indicates that πνεῦμα υἱοθεσίας is something that a human being receives from outside of themselves. Also, given the close connection between the Holy Spirit and υἱοθεσία in Rom 8:23 (cf. Rom 8:14) and Gal 4:5–6, it is clear that πνεῦμα υἱοθεσίας refers to the Holy Spirit.

In Rom 8:1–17, the Spirit signifies "life" which is contrasted with "death" (vv. 2, 6, 11, 13). Particularly, v. 11 not only describes the Spirit as "the Spirit of him who raised Jesus from the dead" but also declares that "If the Spirit of him who raised Jesus from the dead dwells in you, he who raised Christ from the dead will give life to your mortal bodies also through his Spirit that dwells in you." The manifest relationship between the Spirit and Christ's resurrection also appears in Rom 1:4, where Christ was declared as the Son of God through *his resurrection* in the power of *the Holy Spirit*. This indicates that πνεῦμα υἱοθεσίας refers to the Spirit, which enables the transition from death to life in Christ. More specifically, πνεῦμα υἱοθεσίας refers to the Spirit of the one who not only delivers the "Adamic I" from the body of death (Rom 7:24) but who also gives life to believers' mortal bodies (Rom 8:11). The new creation context in Ezek 37:1–14 also links πνεῦμα υἱοθεσίας to the creation account of Gen 2:7–8, where Adam is formed but becomes a living being only after God breathes life into him. In this sense, πνεῦμα υἱοθεσίας enables believers' *new creation* in Christ, from death to the new life in Christ.

Why, then, does Paul use the technical term υἱοθεσία (v. 15) instead of the language of general sonship which he uses in the preceding sentence (v. 14: υἱός) and the next sentence (vv. 16–17: τέκνον)? As seen above, υἱοθεσία, a compound word of υἱός and θέσις, indicates a *transition of status*. Also, the phrase "not ~ again" (οὐ ~ πάλιν) in v. 15 suggests that here the second person plural "you" *was* in the condition of slavery under sin and death, but they *now* cry out "Abba, Father!" through receiving the Spirit of υἱοθεσία. Thus, the lexical meaning of υἱοθεσία fits well with this transition of status from slavery to sonship. Also, in light of the new creation motif, this transition can indicate the transition from death to life.

Roman adoption practices provide an important background for Paul's use of υἱοθεσία, particularly in terms of this transition of status.[30] The procedure of Roman adoption (*adoptio*)[31] required two steps: the first step is the destruction or release of the old *potestas*, the paternal power of the natural father. The second step is the adoptive father's acquisition of new *potestas* over the adoptee effected by the declaration of a magistrate.

The Twelve Tables had a provision that when a son had been sold three times, his father ceased to have any authority over him.[32] The first step of the ceremony was derived from this law. The natural father sold his son to a third party (not an adopting father), who intervened two times in an act of emancipation. The natural father restored his *potestas* over his son after two manumissions. Finally, after the third sale the natural father lost his *potestas*. In the second step, the adopter brought a fictitious claim of ownership against the third party, and the third party

---

30. Lyall asserts that Roman law is a more probable source of Paul's use of υἱοθεσία than the Greek adoption practice since (1) the Roman law is his personal law, the law of his citizenship; (2) the recipients of Romans and Galatians—the two letters that Paul uses the term υἱοθεσία—are directly under the rule of Roman law; (3) in the Roman law, unlike Greek law, there is a complete break between the adoptee and his former family, which fits better with the context of Paul's use of υἱοθεσία. See Lyall, *Slaves, Citizens, Sons*, 82–83, 95–99.

31. Roman adoption had three types of adoption: *adrogatio*, *adoptio*, and testamentary adoption. Both *adrogatio* and *adoptio* are *inter vivos* adoption, which were performed during the adopter's lifetime, and the testamentary adoption is not applicable to Paul's use of υἱοθεσία since in Paul's case the adopter is God, who is always alive. If the adoptee was *sui iuris* (legally independent), that is, not under the legal power and the authority of a *paterfamilias*, that adoptive act was called *adrogatio*. By contrast, *adoptio* was the adoption of a son who was under the legal power and authority of a *paterfamilias*. In the case of *adrogatio*, the adoptee lost *patria potestas* over his family, thus he, his family, and his property came under the *potestas* of his adoptive father. Since this entailed the termination of the adoptee's family line and its sacrum (sacred rites), *adrogatio* required public approval and pontifical sanction. According to Lyall, it is unlikely that Paul had *adrogatio* in mind when writing his letters, since its public approval and pontifical sanction were only possible in Rome. Consequently, the occurrences of adoption in Galatians and Ephesians might not be a reference to *adrogatio*. His argument seems persuasive since it was not until the time of Diocletian (284–305 CE) that *adrogatio* became possible throughout the Empire. Moreover, even in Vulgate (400 CE) *adoptio*, not *adrogatio* is the word used for adoption. Therefore, we should pay more attention to *adoptio*, although we cannot exclude the possibility that Paul refers to the concept of *adrogatio*. See Lyall, *Slaves, Citizens, Sons*, 85–86; Kuryłowicz, *Adoptio im klassischen römischen Recht*, 24–26, 78.

32. Twelve Tables had a provision to protect a son from his callous father who repeatedly sold his son into slavery: "si pater filium ter venum duit, filius a patre liber esto" (If a father gives his son in sale three times, let the son be free from his father, Table IV: 2). See Düll, *Zwölftafelgesetz*, 34.

made no defence, so the magistrate gave judgment in accordance with the adopter's claim. Therefore, the adopter became the adoptee's new *paterfamilias* and the adoptee was subject to the *patria potestas* of his adoptive father. All debts and obligations, from which the adopted son was freed, were in turn handed over to the adopting father.[33] Barclay describes this procedure with the language of creation:

> the legal procedure *created* a new person in the sense that from henceforth the adopted son was in every respect the son and heir of the father. He acquired thereby a new ancestry and a new set of kinship relations which redefined who he was, both objectively and in subjective truth (emphasis added).[34]

Roman adoption's complete break between the adoptee and his former family and the creation of a new kinship under his adoptive father's new *potestas* fits well with Paul's use of υἱοθεσία in Rom 8:15 in terms of the sharp transition of status. Thus, Paul's use of υἱοθεσία and its context of new creation in Rom 8:14–17 imply this transition of status from slavery to sonship as well as from death to life.

It is intriguing that Paul here cites an Aramaic prayer (Abba), which is associated specifically with Jesus in the gospel tradition (Mark 14:36 and parallels). If Paul was familiar with this tradition, the usage by believers here suggests that their sonship is related to Christ's. Certainly, whether or not he knew that gospel tradition, Paul indicates in the context of Rom 8 that sonship is a status shared with Christ. His statements in the proceeding verse (8:17), "we are children of God, and if children, then heirs—heirs of God and *fellow heirs with Christ*" square with this implication. Moreover, Paul continues his argument that Christ is the firstborn among many brothers whom God predestined to be conformed to the image of his Son (8:29). This christological emphasis on believers' divine sonship fits well with the context of new creation, given the fundamental significance of Christ's death and resurrection in Paul's concept of new creation.

---

33. For more details the Roman adoption practice, see Gardner, *Family and Familia*, 114–32.

34. Barclay, "Identity Received from God," 363.

C. VV. 16–17

> [16] αὐτὸ τὸ πνεῦμα συμμαρτυρεῖ τῷ πνεύματι ἡμῶν ὅτι ἐσμὲν τέκνα θεοῦ [17] εἰ δὲ τέκνα, καὶ κληρονόμοι· κληρονόμοι μὲν θεοῦ, συγκληρονόμοι δὲ Χριστοῦ, εἴπερ συμπάσχομεν ἵνα καὶ συνδοξασθῶμεν (The Spirit Himself testifies with our spirit that we are children of God, and if children, heirs also, heirs of God and fellow heirs with Christ, if indeed we suffer with Him so that we may also be glorified with Him).

The close relationship between the Spirit and believers' divine sonship appears again in v. 16. The compound συμμαρτυρεῖν is closely related to the use of μαρτυρεῖν in non-biblical Greek, which refers to "being a witness at a trial, or, in legal transactions of different kinds, a solemn witness" in a forensic sphere.[35] This confirmation of believers' divine sonship by the Spirit accords with the logical sequence of Gal 4:6: "And because *you are sons*, God has sent the Spirit of his Son into our hearts, crying, 'Abba! Father!'" That is, God has sent the Spirit to believers when they are already God's sons.

The role of the Spirit, a witness for believers' divine sonship, may imply the Roman adoption ceremony which was carried out in the presence of witnesses. Also, Roman adoption practices provide another reason why Paul uses the technical term υἱοθεσία here: Paul seems to use υἱοθεσία in connection with the theme of *inheritance*, which is related to the main purpose of Roman adoption (cf. Gal 4:1–7, where υἱοθεσία also occurs with the theme of inheritance). Childlessness appears to have been the commonest reason for adoption in Roman society, and adoption was practised to designate an heir.[36]

In addition to this Greco-Roman context, the theme of inheritance can be linked to Paul's previous discussion of heirs of the Abrahamic promise who inherit the world (Rom 4:13–14). Moreover, this theme is reiterated in Rom 8:32: "He who did not spare his own Son but gave him up for us all, how will he not also with him graciously *give us all things* (τὰ πάντα ἡμῖν χαρίσεται)?" As Jewett observes, τὰ πάντα here refers to the "entire creation rather than to the totality of salvation" since the article indicates that it refers to the previous argument (i.e., Rom 4:13–14; 8:17).[37] The common use of πᾶς for a cosmological sense in

---

35. Hermann Strathmann, "μαρτυρέω," *TDNT* 4:476.
36. Lindsay, *Adoption in the Roman World*, 103.
37. Jewett, *Romans*, 538.

Pauline epistles underpins this interpretation (e.g., Rom 11:36; 1 Cor 8:6; cf. Col 1:15–18a).[38]

Lastly, it is very interesting to note that the new creation motif in Ezek 36 is also interwoven with the theme of inheritance:

> And I will birth people upon you [the mountains of Israel], my people Israel, and they will inherit you, and you will be a possession for them, and you shall no longer continue to be made childless by them. (Ezek 36:12)

Despite its current desolation, God will renew the land of Israel like the garden of Eden (36:35) and Israel will inherit the land and the mountains of Israel. In this sense, Paul's use of υἱοθεσία and its new creation context in 8:14–17 perfectly fit with its allusion to Ezek 36–37. Can this close relationship between υἱοθεσία and the new creation motif be applicable to Paul's use of υἱοθεσία in Rom 8:19–23? In what follows, I will demonstrate that it is the case through the exegesis of that passage.

3. Paul's use of υἱοθεσία in Rom 8:19–23 in light of new creation

As seen above, the allusion to Ezek 36–37 in Rom 8:1–17 is connected to the creation account of Gen 1–2 in the context of new creation. This new creation context continues in Rom 8:19–23 through the allusion to Gen 3, as we shall see below. Also, Paul reiterates the language of divine sonship three times (v. 19: οἱ υἱοὶ τοῦ θεοῦ, v. 21: τὰ τέκνα τοῦ θεοῦ, v. 23: υἱοθεσία) in Rom 8:19–23. Paul, in particular, regards υἱοθεσία as redemption of our body (τὴν ἀπολύτρωσιν τοῦ σώματος ἡμῶν) which implies the resurrection of believers at the eschaton. The exegesis of Rom 8:19–23 is my attempt to demonstrate that: (1) Rom 8:19–23 alludes to Gen 3:16–19 in the new creation context; (2) Rom 8:19–23 uses a childbirth metaphor (including the theme of birth pangs); (3) the allusion to Gen 3:16–19 in Rom 8:19–23 and its childbirth context lead us to understand υἱοθεσία, namely the redemption of our body in v. 23, as believers' bodily resurrection; (4) thus, as in Rom 8:15, υἱοθεσία in Rom 8:23 indicates the transition from death to life; from the death originated from Adam's sin in the paradise to the life restored by Christ's crucifixion and resurrection. To begin with, we shall discuss the Adamic

---

38. H. Langkammer, "πᾶς," *EDNT* 3:48.

motif in Rom 1:18–25, since Rom 1:18–25 and Rom 8:19–23 seem to constitute a kind of *Urzeit-Endzeit* framework.

(1) Rom 1:18–25 and the influence of the Adamic sin

Since Hooker suggested that Paul had in mind the biblical narrative of Adam's fall in writing Rom 1:18–32, some scholars have accepted that Rom 1:18–25 contains allusions to the Adam narrative of Gen 1–3.[39] Hooker's argument is based on two observations: (1) the language of this section echoes that of Gen 1:20–27;[40] (2) the sequence of events of this text is reminiscent of the Genesis narrative of the creation and the fall.[41]

Although the connection between Gen 1–3 and Rom 1:18–25 is less explicit,[42] Rom 1:18–25 does have verbal links with Gen 1–3. For example, Rom 1:22 "claiming to be *wise*, they became fools" is reminiscent of the false promise of wisdom in Gen 3:6, where Eve saw that the tree was to be desired to make one *wise* (שׂכל). Moreover, "the image of a mortal human being" (εἰκὼν φθαρτοῦ ἀνθρώπου) in Rom 1:23 alludes not merely

---

39. Hooker, "Adam in Romans 1," 297–306; Barrett, *From First Adam to Last*, 17–29; Dunn, *Romans 1–8*, 72; Wright, "Letter to the Romans," 432–34; Jewett, *Romans*, 182.

40. Hooker, "Adam in Romans 1," 300. Hooker developed Hyldahl's brief article "A Reminiscence of the Old Testament at Romans 1:23" in which he observed that Paul mentions the creatures (τὰ πετεινά, τὰ τετράποδα, and τὰ ἑρπετά) in Rom 1:23 in the same order as they occur in Gen 1:20–25. Also, Hyldahl points out that ἄφθαρτος, εἰκών, and ὁμοίωμα in Rom 1:23 all occur in Gen 1:26–27 although the Genesis text uses ὁμοίωσις instead of ὁμοίωμα. See Hyldahl, "Reminiscence of the Old Testament," 285–88.

41. Hooker argues that the sequence of events outlined in Rom 1:18–32 reminds us of the story of Adam in Gen 1–3 in that: (1) God manifested himself to Adam in paradise as God has shown what can be known about God to humankind (Rom 1:19); (2) just as Adam's fall was the result of his desire to be as God, to attain knowledge of good and evil (Gen 3:5), so humankind became fools, claiming to be wise (Rom 1:22); (3) just as Adam believed and obeyed the serpent's lie, and thus gave his allegiance to a creature, the serpent, turning his back on the truth of God, so humankind exchanged the truth about God for a lie and served the creature rather than the Creator (Rom 1:25). Also, she argues that we can find another parallel between Rom 1:24–32 and the early chapters of Genesis in a broader context: (1) the worship of the creature in Rom 1:25 parallels Adam's sin in Gen 3; (2) the sexual perversion and unnatural intercourse in Rom 1:26–27 is found in Gen 6:1–4; (3) other forms of sin in Rom 1:28–31, which the sexual sins lead to, are parallel with the immediate result of lust in Gen 6:5, although the Genesis narrative describes this in a much more pithy manner (Hooker, "Adam in Romans 1," 300–302).

42. Fitzmyer refutes Hooker's argument by saying that "the alleged echoes of the Adam stories in Genesis are simply nonexistent," since Hooker depends on the rabbinic tradition dating from many centuries later than Paul. See Fitzmyer, *Romans*, 274.

to εἰκὼν θεοῦ in Gen 1:27 but to the creation of Adam in Gen 2:7, where God formed man from the dust of the ground. Paul uses a similar expression "the image of the man of dust" (εἰκὼν τοῦ χοϊκοῦ) in 1 Cor 15:49; "the man of dust" here refers to "the first man from the earth, a man of dust" (ὁ πρῶτος ἄνθρωπος ἐκ γῆς χοϊκός) in 1 Cor 15:47. It is difficult to deny that in writing 1 Cor 15:47–49 Paul had in mind the creation of Adam in Gen 2. Moreover, just several verses later the language of ἄφθαρτος and φθαρτός (immortal and mortal) also appears in 1 Cor 15:52–53. This striking similarity between Rom 1:18–25 and 1 Cor 15:47–53 in terms of terminology as well as themes indicates that εἰκὼν φθαρτοῦ ἀνθρώπου in Rom 1:23 can also refer to the creation story of Gen 1–2.

The Apocalypse of Moses provides more evidence for the background of the Adam narrative in Rom 1:18–25. Levison argues that "Rom 1:18–25 can be understood in light of the more expansive interpretative developments that characterize the Greek *Life of Adam and Eve*,"[43] namely, in terms of "the suppression of truth [Rom 1:18, 25], the advent of divine anger [Rom 1:18], the onset of death [Rom 1:23], and most notably, two related exchanges [Rom 1:23–26]—God's glory for mortality and natural dominion for unnatural subservience to animals."[44] All these themes of Rom 1:18–25 clearly occur in the Apocalypse of Moses, which retells the story in Gen 3 of Adam's and Eve's transgression of God's commandment and their expulsion from paradise. For example, the theme of exchange (v. 23: ἀλλάσσειν; vv. 25–26: μεταλλάσσειν) occurs in Apoc. Mos. 11:2, where a beast attacks Eve, saying that the rule of the beasts (ἡ ἀρχὴ τῶν θηρίων) has happened because of Eve's disobedience and that their natures *have been exchanged* (ἡμῶν αἱ φύσεις μετηλλάγησαν). Also, Eve and Adam found themselves estranged from *God's glory* after their disobedience to God's commandment (Apoc. Mos. 20:2; 21:5). Their loss of God's glory and the exchange of dominion for subservience in the Apocalypse of Moses seems to share the same theme with Rom 1:23.

Moreover, the parallelism between Adam's loss of glory and death's dominion over all humanity in the Apocalypse of Moses (14:2 and 21:6) also occurs in Rom 3:23 and 5:12. In Rom 3:23, Paul says "since all have sinned and fall short of the glory of God" (πάντες γὰρ ἥμαρτον καὶ ὑστεροῦνται τῆς δόξης τοῦ θεοῦ). The result of humanity's sin is their loss of God's glory. Paul reiterates a similar logic in 5:12b: "death spread to

---

43. Levison, "Adam and Eve," 521–22. For some scholars, the Greek *Life of Adam and Eve* (the abbreviation is LAE) is another title for Apocalypse of Moses.

44. Levison, "Adam and Eve," 519.

all because all have sinned" (εἰς πάντας ἀνθρώπους ὁ θάνατος διῆλθεν, ἐφ' ᾧ πάντες ἥμαρτον). The spread of death to all, here, parallels humanity's loss of God's glory in Rom 3:23. Furthermore, Rom 5:12a indicates that the current dominion of death over all humanity is originally caused by the Adamic sin.

Finally, as the conclusion of his argument in Rom 1:18–3:20, Paul says "no human being will be justified in his [God's] sight" in Rom 3:20. This indicates that the main theme of this section is the universal reign of sin and the unrighteousness of all humanity. Paul, therefore, depicts all humanity's Adamic sinful status in terms of the loss of glory, unrighteousness, and the reign of death as in the Apocalypse of Moses. Moreover, in Rom 8:18–39, Paul envisages believers' restoration of glory (vv. 18, 21, 30), righteousness (vv. 30, 33), and life (vv. 21, 23; cf. 8:1–13) in the context of new creation.

(2) The eschatological hope for new creation in Rom 8:18–23

Romans 8:18–23 shares many terms with Rom 1:18–32: apocalyptic "revelation" (1:18; cf. 8:18, 19), "creation" (1:20, 25; cf. 8:19, 20, 21, 22), "glory" or "to glorify" (1:21, 23; cf. 8:18, 21), "to become futile" or "futility" (1:21; cf. 8:20), and "body" (1:24; cf. 8:23). The *Urzeit-Endzeit* framework explains well why both passages share these terms; while Rom 1:18–32 describes the prevalence of human sin in the world under the influence of the Adamic sin, Rom 8:18–23 depicts the eschatological hope for new creation using the shared terms. Particularly, Paul uses the term "glory" as a keyword to express the eschatological hope for the age to come in contrast with the sufferings of this age in 8:18: "I consider that the sufferings of this present time are not worth comparing with the glory about to be revealed to us."

In what follows, I will demonstrate that the theme of resurrection is the climax of this eschatological hope, namely new creation. The reason that we can call this eschatological hope "new creation" is that the restoration in Rom 8:18–23 is expressed as a reversal of the Adamic curse in Gen 3:16–19. Again, the Apocalypse of Moses shares this eschatological hope for new creation with Rom 8:18–23 in that this hope for new creation is decisively expressed by the theme of resurrection, which also includes the restoration of glory, righteousness, and the image of God.

(3) Exegesis of Rom 8:19–23

A. V. 19: THE MEANING OF ΚΤΙΣΙΣ

ἡ γὰρ ἀποκαραδοκία τῆς κτίσεως τὴν ἀποκάλυψιν τῶν υἱῶν τοῦ θεοῦ ἀπεκδέχεται (For the creation waits with eager longing for the revealing of the sons of God).

Apart from Gal 6:15 and 2 Cor 5:17 where the phrase "new creation" (καινὴ κτίσις) occurs, κτίσις only appears in Rom 1 and 8 within Paul's undisputed letters (Rom 1:20, 25; 8:19–22, 39; cf. Col 1:15, 23). In Rom 1, the meaning of κτίσις is quite clear: (1) in Rom 1:20, κτίσις denotes "act of creation," which refers to God's creation of the world (κτίσεως κόσμου) in the beginning;[45] (2) in Rom 1:25, κτίσις denotes "the result of a creative act" or a particular "creature," given the fact that it can refer to "humans, birds, animals, and reptiles" in v. 23.[46] However, the meaning of κτίσις here can include both animate and inanimate beings since the object of idolatry is not restricted to animate beings. Also, the contrast between κτίσις and κτίσαντος (creator) in v. 25 supports this broad meaning of κτίσις, "the result of a creative act, *that which is created*."[47]

The meaning of the four occurrences of κτίσις in Rom 8:19–22, however, has been much debated. Hahne summarizes the interpretations of κτίσις in Rom 8:19–22 in five categories:[48] (1) *Universal*: κτίσις includes all creation;[49] (2) *Cosmic*: κτίσις refers to the subhuman creation, both animate and inanimate, or essentially what is called "nature" today;[50] (3) *Anthropological*: the Augustinian view that limits κτίσις to humanity,[51] with a few

---

45. BDAG, s.v. "κτίσις," 572–73.

46. Jewett, *Romans*, 171. The majority of scholars translate κτίσις in Rom 1:25 as "creature" (e.g., KJV, NRSV, Cranfield, Dunn, Fitzmyer, Moo, et al.).

47. BDAG, s.v. "κτίσις," 573. BDAG divides this definition of κτίσις into two subcategories: a. "individual things or beings created, *creature*"; b. "the sum total of everything created, *creation*, world." Also, BDAG categorizes the κτίσις in Rom 1:25 as the second subcategory. The first subcategory "individual creature," however, seems to fit better with the context of Rom 1:25, although this creature should include both animate and inanimate beings.

48. Hahne, *Corruption and Redemption of Creation*, 177–78.

49. E.g., Eastman, "Whose Apocalypse?" 273–76; Barrett, *Commentary on the Epistle to the Romans*, 166; Michel, *Brief an die Römer*, 173.

50. E.g., Longenecker, *Epistle to the Romans*, 719–22; Jewett, *Romans*, 511; Wolter, *Brief an Die Römer*, 1:509; Fitzmyer, *Romans*, 506; Moo, *Epistle to the Romans*, 551; Dunn, *Romans 1–8*, 469; Cranfield, *Critical and Exegetical Commentary*, 1:411–12.

51. Augustine writes about the creation in Rom 8:19–22: "This is not to be understood simply as meaning that trees, vegetables, stones and the like sorrow and sigh—this

limiting it (3A) only to believers,⁵² or (3B) only to unbelievers;⁵³ (4) *Cosmo-anthropological*: κτίσις refers to both the subhuman creation and unbelieving humanity excluding angels, demons, and believers;⁵⁴ (5) *Angelogical*: Fuchs takes the unusual position that it refers to angels.⁵⁵

Among these interpretative options, the second one is most persuasive since other options can be excluded in light of the context of Rom 8:19-22. For example, κτίσις cannot refer to unbelievers or demons here, since there is no probable reason that they will be glorified (v. 21) or that they long for the revealing of the sons of God (v. 19).⁵⁶ Likewise, believers must be excluded, since they are contrasted with creation in Rom 8:19-23: (1) creation eagerly awaits the revealing of the *sons of God* (v. 19); (2) and will obtain the eschatological "freedom of the glory" of the *children of God* (v. 21); (3) and most clearly, believers are not the same group of the rest of creation in v. 23, although they groan in a similar way.⁵⁷ Good angels are also excluded since they are hardly likely to be subjected to futility or corruption, either because of human sin or their own actions (vv. 20–21).⁵⁸

The only remaining option, therefore, is the cosmic view in which κτίσις refers to the subhuman creation (the universal view is of course excluded since κτίσις in this view contains humanity as well as the non-human order). The verbal links between Rom 1:18-25 and Rom 8:19-30 confirm the cosmic view. The two texts share a number of words; κτίσις (1:25, cf. 1:20; 8:20–22), ματαιότης (1:21; 8:20), δοξάζειν (1:21; 8:30), δόξα (1:23; 8:18, 21), εἰκών (1:23; 8:29), σώματα degraded (1:24) and redeemed

---

is the error of the Manichaeans—nor should we think that the holy angels are subject to vanity or that they will be set free from the slavery of death, since they are immortal. Here 'the creation' means the human race" (*Expositio quarundam propositionum ex epistola ad Romanos* prop. 53 [PL 35:2074]). See also Schlatter, *Gottes Gerechtigkeit*, 274; Manson, "Romans," 966.

52. Reumann, *Creation and New Creation*, 98–99; Hommel, *Schöpfer und Erhalter*, 7–23; Schmidt, *Brief des Paulus*, 145.

53. Brunner, *Revelation and Reason*, 72n16.

54. Käsemann, *Commentary on Romans*, 232–33; Foerster, "κτίζω, κτίσις," *TDNT* 3:1031.

55. Fuchs, *Freiheit des Glaubens*, 109.

56. Hahne, *Corruption and Redemption of Creation*, 179; Murray, *Epistle to the Romans*, 302; Cranfield, *Critical and Exegetical Commentary*, 1:411.

57. Hahne, *Corruption and Redemption of Creation*, 180; Cranfield, *Critical and Exegetical Commentary*, 1:411; Murray, *Epistle to the Romans*, 302.

58. Hahne, *Corruption and Redemption of Creation*, 179.

(8:23).⁵⁹ This is not a coincidence but reflects Paul's intention. In Rom 1:18–25, Paul describes the human predicament in terms of humanity's relationship with creation. God created Adam as an image of God to rule over all of creation, but after Adam's sin humankind exchanged the truth about God for a lie and worshiped and served creation (κτίσις) rather than Creator (Rom 1:25). With the shared terminology of Rom 1:18–25, Paul envisages the final restoration of the broken relationship between creation (κτίσις) and the sons of God (believers) in Rom 8:19–23 as a solution to the human problem of Rom 1:18–25.

Thus, we can conclude that the κτίσις in Rom 8:19–22 refers to sub-human creation as with Rom 1:25, both animate and inanimate.⁶⁰ This interpretation also enables us to find the Adamic motifs in Rom 8:20–23 as we shall see below.

B. V. 20: ΜΑΤΑΙΟΤΗΣ

While there is an ongoing debate on the Adamic motif in Rom 1:18–25, there is a wide scholarly consensus that in Rom 8:19–23 Paul has in mind the Adam narrative of Gen 3:16–19.⁶¹ Particularly, as Murray describes Rom 8:20 as "Paul's commentary on Gen 3:17–18,"⁶² the allusion to God's judgment scene in Gen 3 appears clearly in Rom 8:20:

τῇ γὰρ ματαιότητι ἡ κτίσις ὑπετάγη, οὐχ ἑκοῦσα ἀλλὰ διὰ τὸν ὑποτάξαντα, ἐφ᾽ ἐλπίδι (for the creation was subjected to futility, not willingly, but because of the one who subjected it, in hope).

Many scholars agree that "ὑπετάγη (v. 20) is a divine passive (subjected by God) with reference to Gen 3:17–18."⁶³ As Rom 5:12–21 says

59. Dunn, *Romans 1–8*, 467.

60. Cranfield also draws the same conclusion: "The only interpretation of ἡ κτίσις in these verses which is really probable is surely that which takes it to refer to the sum-total of sub-human nature both animate and inanimate" (Cranfield, *Critical and Exegetical Commentary*, 1:225).

61. E.g., Jewett, *Romans*, 513; Wolter, *Röm 1–8*, 510; Wright, "Letter to the Romans," 596; Dunn, *Romans 1–8*, 467–69; Brendan Byrne, *Romans*, 260; Moo, *Epistle to the Romans*, 515; Fitzmyer, *Romans*, 507; Cranfield, *Critical and Exegetical Commentary*, 1:416.

62. Murray, *Epistle to the Romans*, 303.

63. Dunn, *Romans 1–8*, 470; Jewett, *Romans*, 513. Hahne presents five interpretative options for the subject of the verb ὑπετάγη in Rom 8:20: God, Christ, Satan, humanity, and Adam (Hahne, *Corruption and Redemption of Creation*, 187–88). It should be noted that the active participle of this verb also appears in 8:20b, and that in the

that Adam's sin brought sin and death to the world and humanity, the sub-human creation is now enslaved to futility (ματαιότης: v. 20) due to Adam's sin. However, God, not Adam, subjected creation to this futility since God cursed the ground in his judicial pronouncement (Gen 3:17–18). Only God could subject creation to futility with a hope (ἐφ' ἐλπίδι: v. 20) for its future redemption since God pronounces a curse immediately following a promise of hope (Gen 3:15).[64]

As we have seen, the cognate of ματαιότης appears in Rom 1:21, where Paul describes humankind's sinful status in which they did not honor God or give thanks to God but became futile (ἐματαιώθησαν) in their thinking. The result of humankind's futility in their thinking was the idolatry of the subhuman creation (Rom 1:23). Thus, creation's subjection to futility seems closely related to humankind's futility. Μάταιος, a cognate of ματαιότης occurs in Apoc. Mos. 25:1, where God pronounces his sentence on Eve regarding her disobedience: "Since you have listened to the serpent and ignored my commandment, you shall be in futile toils and unendurable pains (ἔσῃ ἐν [καμάτοις] ματαίοις[65] καὶ ἐν πόνοις ἀφορήτοις)." It is important to note that here ματαίοις is used to describe the judgment scene of Gen 3. The word ματαιότης (or ματαίοις), however, does not occur in the sentence on Eve in Gen 3:16 of the LXX. Why, then, does the author of the Apocalypse of Moses use this word? It is interesting to note that the Hebrew equivalent of ματαιότης in the MT is הבל (e.g., Pss 30:6; 38:5; 61:9; 77:33; 118:37; Prov 22:8; Eccl 1:2, 14; 2:1–26; 3:19; 4:4–16; 5:6–9; 6:2–11; 7:1–16; 8:10–14; 9:9; 11:8–10; 12:8), which has a very similar form with the Hebrew word חבל (birth pang). Thus, Fuchs argues that the Greek μάταιος in Apoc. Mos. 25:1 is "follies," resulting from reading the Hebrew original חבל, "birth pangs," as הבל, "vanities [futilities]."[66]

---

other four undisputed Pauline occurrences of this verb in the active voice, the subject is God or Christ. This suggests that other options (Satan, humanity, and Adam) can be excluded. Of the two remaining alternatives, Christ should be excluded. Taking Christ as the subject in Rom 8:20 does not fit with the context since the Christ-event is the means of redemption, not the cause of corruption (Jackson, *New Creation*, 157).

64. Hahne, *Corruption and Redemption of Creation*, 188.

65. This reading "ματαίοις" is witnessed by the manuscripts St, B, A, and AC. Others read "ματαιότητι" (An2 and Pa) or "καμάτοις" (Ath). Dochhorn makes a probable conjecture by adding καμάτοις in front of ματαίοις here. See Dochhorn, *Apokalypse des Mose*, 391–92.

66. Fuchs, "Leben Adams und Evas," 511; Johnson supports this idea. See Johnson, "Life of Adam and Eve," 283.

Dochhorn, however, argues that the author of the Apocalypse of Moses uses μάταιος not by mistake, but makes a play on words on the Hebrew original חבל with its paronomasia הבל. By using μάταιος, the author reinterprets God's curse on Eve in Gen 3:16 more generally as futility, not merely about birth pangs. According to Dochhorn, the context of Apoc. Mos. 25:3–4 supports this idea because: (1) Eve swears she will never again turn to the sin of the flesh (οὐ μὴ ἐπιστρέψω εἰς τὴν ἁμαρτίαν τῆς σαρκός) in order not to suffer from birth pangs (v. 3); (2) however, she will return (στρέφειν) to her husband because of the enmity that the serpent has placed in her (v. 4); (3) the "enmity" refers to the poison of desire (ἐπιθυμία), the origin of every sin, with which the serpent has poisoned the woman (Apoc. Mos. 19:3); (4) thus, the meaning of "returning to her husband" implies that she will repeatedly have sexual intercourse with her husband and suffer from birth pangs again; (5) all these processes fit well with the meaning of μάταιος.[67]

Other evidence for the word play on חבל and הבל includes textual variants of Gen 3:16b:

> MT: your *desire* shall be for your husband, and he shall rule over you
>
> (ואל־אישך תשוקתך והוא ימשל־בך)
>
> LXX: your *return* will be to your husband, and he shall rule over you
>
> (καὶ πρὸς τὸν ἄνδρα σου ἡ ἀποστροφή σου, καὶ αὐτός σου κυριεύσει)

The Hebrew equivalent for ἀποστροφή (return) is תשובה, which makes another word play with תשוקה (desire). God's curse on Eve in Apoc. Mos. 25 contains both concepts (return and desire), which indicates that the author of Apoc. Mos. knew this play on the Hebrew word תשובה and תשוקה. Genesis Rabbah 20:7, a rabbinic parallel to Apoc. Mos. 25:2–4, also provides evidence for this play on the variants between תשובה and תשוקה. If this word play in the background of Apoc. Mos. 25:2–4 is the case, it is highly probable that the author of Apoc. Mos. also uses μάταιος as a word play on חבל and הבל.[68]

Furthermore, we cannot exclude the possibility that in Rom 8:20, Paul also knew the Hebrew word pun on חבל and הבל in the background

---

67. Dochhorn, "'Nichtigkeit" 70–71.
68. Dochhorn, "Nichtigkeit," 71–72.

of ματαιότης.⁶⁹ First, just as God's curse on Eve contains the futile toils (ἐν [καμάτοις] ματαίοις) and birth pangs (ὠδίνων) in Apoc. Mos. 25:1–2, so in Rom 8:20–22, Paul describes the sufferings of the creation as futility (ματαιότης) and birth pangs (v. 22: συνωδίνειν) with cognate words. We should note that the Hebrew equivalent of ὠδίνειν in the MT is חבל (Ps 7:15; Song 8:5). Second, just as the result of God's curse on Eve in Gen 3:16 and Apoc. Mos. 25:4 was her *subjection* to her sexual desire and her husband, the creation became *subjected* to ματαιότης in Rom 8:20. It should be noted that Paul uses ματαιόω, a cognate of ματαιότης in Rom 1:20 in order to describe humankind's guilt in their thinking which results in the lust (ἐπιθυμία) of their hearts and sexual sins (Rom 1:24). The connection between ματαιόω and ἐπιθυμία is reminiscent of Apoc. Mos. 25:2–4. Thus, this background of ματαιότης strengthens Rom 8:19–23's connection to Gen 3:16–19. Also, it provides additional evidence for this passage's childbirth context, which I will fully deal with in what follows.

C. V. 21: ΦΘΟΡΑ

The subjection to φθορά in v. 21 parallels the subjection to ματαιότης in v. 20:

> ὅτι καὶ αὐτὴ ἡ κτίσις ἐλευθερωθήσεται ἀπὸ τῆς δουλείας τῆς φθορᾶς εἰς τὴν ἐλευθερίαν τῆς δόξης τῶν τέκνων τοῦ θεοῦ (that the creation itself also will be set free from its slavery to corruption into the freedom of the glory of the children of God)

The basic meaning of φθορά is "breakdown of organic matter" or "corruption."⁷⁰ First Corinthians 15:42–44 uses this term to contrast the perishability of the present human body with the glory of the future resurrected body:

> So it is with the resurrection of the dead. What is sown is perishable (ἐν φθορᾷ); what is raised is imperishable (ἐν ἀσθενείᾳ). It is sown in dishonor; it is raised in glory. It is sown in weakness; it is raised in power. It is sown a physical body, it is raised a spiritual body. If there is a physical body, there is also a spiritual body.

The language of 1 Cor 15:42–44 is strikingly similar to Rom 8:18–23 in relation to perishability, glory, body, resurrection, and its use of the Adamic

---

69. Dochhorn, "Nichtigkeit," 74–75.
70. BDAG, s.v. "φθορά," 1054–55.

narrative. Notably, as in Rom 8:21, φθορά is used in contrast to glory and resurrection. A few verses later, it seems clear that φθορά in 1 Cor 15 refers to mortality (θνητός: vv. 53–54) and death (θάνατος: vv. 54–56). Given this parallelism between Rom 8:18–23 and 1 Cor 15:42–56, it is highly probable that φθορά in Rom 8:21 is also related to death.

Terms that have multiple meanings can gain particular connotations. In this regard, the childbirth metaphor in Rom 8:19–23 evokes an additional connotation of φθορά. It is noteworthy that φθορά can mean a rather specific form of death, namely "destruction of a fetus, abortion or miscarriage."[71] This meaning of φθορά fits very well with the childbirth context of Rom 8:19–23. Thus, φθορά might evoke the infertility or unproductivity of creation, like the destruction of a fetus in the process of childbirth.

In any case, it is clear that the slavery to φθορά relates to the theme of slavery to death, which Paul repeatedly mentions in Rom 5–8, as seen above. In this sense, the slavery to φθορά can also be connected to the spirit of slavery in Rom 8:15. Moreover, the transition from slavery to corruption into the freedom of the glory of the children of God resonates with Paul's use of υἱοθεσία in Rom 8:15, which signifies the transition of status not only from slavery to sonship but also from death to life. This remarkable sense of transition in this verse can also be linked to Paul's use of υἱοθεσία in Rom 8:23, as we shall see below.

D. V. 22: ΣΥΣΤΕΝΑΖΕΙΝ

> οἴδαμεν γὰρ ὅτι πᾶσα ἡ κτίσις συστενάζει καὶ συνωδίνει ἄχρι τοῦ νῦν (For we know that the whole creation groans and suffers the pains of childbirth together until now).

We should note that a cognate of συστενάζειν, στεναγμός (groaning) occurs in Gen 3:16a (LXX): "He said to the woman, 'Multiplying, I will multiply your pain and your groaning (στεναγμός). In pain you will bring forth children, and your recourse will be to your husband, and he will be master over you.'" The MT version of Gen 3:16a uses the term הריון (pregnancy) as a counterpart for στεναγμός. Also, although the term συνωδίνειν does not occur in Gen 3:16–19 (LXX), the pains of childbirth clearly occur in God's judgment on Eve. Thus, both συστενάζειν and

---

71. BDAG, 1055; for example, Barn. 19:5 and Did. 2:2 forbid abortion with the term φθορά: "you must not murder a child by abortion" (οὐ φονεύσεις τέκνον ἐν φθορᾷ).

συνωδίνειν in Rom 8:22 can be read together as part of the metaphor of childbirth in light of the allusion to Gen 3:16–19.

Moreover, in Isa 21:2–3 and Jer 4:31, στεναγμός occurs with the theme of birth pangs (ὠδίν) in the context of divine judgment. Particularly, in Jer 4:31 Zion is personified as a woman in birth pangs, whose groaning the prophet hears. The land became a desert because of God's judgment upon Israel and she is mourning like a woman in travail. This context is strikingly similar to the context of Rom 8:19–23 in light of its allusion to Gen 3:16–19. This is further evidence that συστενάζειν as well as συνωδίνειν in Rom 8:22 can be read in the context of birth pangs.

We should note that Paul uses the same word συστενάζειν to describe humanity's suffering in v. 23. This indicates that humanity and creation share the suffering caused by the Adamic sin. Moreover, Paul portrays creation's suffering as birth pangs, which were inflicted upon Eve in Gen 3:16. Accordingly, Rom 8:19–22 shares the vocabularies of God's judgment on Eve not only with Gen 3:16 (συστενάζειν) but also with Apoc. Mos. 25:1–2 (ματαιότης and συνωδίνειν).

E. V. 23: ADOPTION, THE REDEMPTION OF OUR BODY

> οὐ μόνον δέ, ἀλλὰ καὶ αὐτοὶ τὴν ἀπαρχὴν τοῦ πνεύματος ἔχοντες, ἡμεῖς καὶ αὐτοὶ ἐν ἑαυτοῖς στενάζομεν υἱοθεσίαν ἀπεκδεχόμενοι, τὴν ἀπολύτρωσιν τοῦ σώματος ἡμῶν (And not only this [creation], but also we ourselves, having the first fruits of the Spirit, even we ourselves groan within ourselves, waiting eagerly for our adoption as sons, the redemption of our body).

Just as creation eagerly awaits the revelation of the sons of God (v. 19), so believers themselves eagerly await adoption, the "redemption of our body" (v. 23). Here, the use of the same verb ἀπεκδέχομαι and the expression "not only the creation, but also we ourselves" (οὐ μόνον δέ, ἀλλὰ καὶ αὐτοί: v. 23) indicate that the objects of the verb ἀπεκδέχομαι are closely correlated in v. 19 and v. 23. In other words, creation's waiting for "the revelation of the sons of God" in v. 19 parallels believers' waiting for "adoption, the redemption of our body." Again, the solidarity between creation and humanity is clear, and they share the eschatological hope for redemption.

Also, creation's waiting for "the revelation of the sons of God" is closely related to creation's hope of "being set free from its slavery to corruption into the freedom of the glory of the children of God" in v.

21. As seen above, this connotation of transition from slavery to sonship perfectly matches the meaning of υἱοθεσία. What, then, does "the redemption of our body" (ἡ ἀπολύτρωσις τοῦ σώματος ἡμῶν), the phrase in apposition to υἱοθεσία in v. 23 mean?

Eastman claims that "redemption of our body" highlights the "redemption of Israel" noting Paul's use of the singular noun "body" not "bodies" and the occurrences of the divine sonship in Rom 9–11 and the LXX referring to Israel.[72] This reading is based on her interpretation of "the revelation of the sons of God" in v. 19. Contrary to the most common reading of Rom 8:19, which interprets the ἀποκάλυψις of sons of God as the public revelation of believers' hidden "status" as sons of God,[73] Eastman takes it as a "future rectification" of sons of God, which includes not only gentiles but also Israel according to the flesh. According to her, this interpretation fits well with not only the letter's thesis statement of the gospel as the ἀποκάλυψις of God's righteousness, which functions as God's saving power "for the Jew first, and also for the Greek" (Rom 1:16–17), but also Paul's argument concerning Israel's eventual salvation in Rom 9–11.[74]

Paul's focus in Rom 8, however, does not lie in Israel (unlike his emphasis in Rom 9–11). Rather, as the allusion to Gen 3:16–19 in 8:19–23 indicates, Paul deals with the redemption of all believers who were subjected to the power of Adamic sin, not specifically the people of Israel. Eastman attempts to separate "the redemption of our body" in 8:23 from the promise of 8:11 that "the one who raised Jesus from the dead will also give life to your mortal bodies through the Spirit dwelling in you" by noting the difference between the plural "bodies" in v. 19 and the singular "body" in v. 23. By doing so, she seems to avoid interpreting "redemption of our body" as "believers' individual bodily resurrection."[75] Wolter also argues that although "the redemption of our body" refers to the glorious transformation of "our body" at the parousia in Phil 3:21, it does not necessarily include the resurrection from

---

72. Eastman, "Whose Apocalypse?," 268–72. She focuses on a corporate sense of "body" and interprets "redemption of our body" as "the full redemption of the corporate body of Christ" which includes Israel according to the flesh.

73. E.g., Dunn, *Romans 1–8*, 470; Cranfield, *Critical and Exegetical Commentary*, 1:419; Byrne, *Romans*, 257; Fitzmyer, *Romans*, 507.

74. Eastman, "Whose Apocalypse?," 264–67.

75. Eastman, "Whose Apocalypse?," 263–64, 268.

the dead ("In diesem Geschehen kann die Auferstehung von den Toten eingeschlossen sein, sie muss es aber nicht").[76]

However, as a majority of scholars argue, the redemption of our body (τὴν ἀπολύτρωσιν τοῦ σώματος ἡμῶν) seems to refer to "the final resurrection of our bodies at the parousia, our complete and final liberation from the ματαιότης and φθορά to which we (like the sub-human creation) have been subjected."[77] As seen above, in 1 Cor 15:42–44, Paul contrasts φθορά of the present human body with the glory of the future resurrected body. Given the parallelism between Rom 8:19–23 and 1 Cor 15:42–44, the physical aspect of the human body, thus, should not be neglected in Rom 8:23.[78] Both believers' bodies and the sub-human creation will be delivered from enslavement to φθορά and will share in eternal glory (8:21).

The childbirth context of Rom 8:19–23 supports this interpretation of "the redemption of our body" as "believers' bodily resurrection." In the Old Testament and Second Temple Jewish literature, the earth often appears as the expectant mother of the dead, who will be reborn in the resurrection (e.g., Gen 3:19; Job 1:21a; Ps 139:13, 15; Sir 40:1; 4 Ezra 4:42–43).

For example, it is very interesting to note that in Isa 26:16–19, the theme of birth pangs, childbirth, and resurrection occur together in an eschatological context. Particularly, the resurrection from the dead parallels childbirth:

> O Lord, in distress they sought you, they poured out a prayer when your chastening was on them. Like a woman with child, who writhes and *cries out in her pangs* when she is near her time, so were we because of you, O Lord; we were with child, we writhed, but we *gave birth only to wind*. We have won no victories on earth, and no one is born to inhabit the world. *Your dead shall live, their corpses shall rise*. O dwellers in the dust,

---

76. Wolter, *Röm 1–8*, 519. Wolter interprets "the redemption of our body" in connection with Rom 8:18–19 in terms of "the *glory* that is to be revealed to us." His argument, however, seems unconvincing since Phil 3 itself mentions the resurrection from the dead (Phil 3:11).

77. Cranfield, *Critical and Exegetical Commentary*, 1:419. See also Longenecker, *Epistle to the Romans*, 727.

78. Lietzmann translates τὴν ἀπολύτρωσιν τοῦ σώματος ἡμῶν as "redemption *from* our bodies" which would be typical of a Greek anthropological dualism. See Lietzmann, *Einführung in die Textgeschichte*, 85. The genitive in this phrase is more likely objective than ablative.

awake and sing for joy! For your dew is a radiant dew, and *the earth will give birth* to *the shades* (וארץ רפאים תפיל).[79]

Isaiah metaphorically describes Israel's suffering as her severe birth pangs without a childbirth, contrasting YHWH's future work for Israel as raising the dead from the earth. Here, Isaiah depicts the resurrection as the earth's giving birth to the dead. Although some commentators argue that Isa 26 "does not necessarily involve an actual resurrection of dead Israelites,"[80] it is difficult to deny that the terms "corpses" and "shades" imply the physical and individual meaning of resurrection. Also, as Nickelsburg rightly notes, "the contrast between the raising of the dead of Israel and the fact that their dead overlords will not rise (v. 14)" makes the interpretation of a mere national restoration of Israel "untenable."[81]

Another example is 4 Ezra 7:30–32, which describes the general resurrection at the eschaton as the earth's giving birth to the dead: "And the earth shall give back those who are asleep in it, and the dust those who rest in it; and the treasuries shall give up the souls which have been committed to them" (7:32). As seen in our investigation of the concept of new creation in 4 Ezra (chapter 2, section 7), the theme of resurrection here appears in the context of new creation within the *Urzeit-Endzeit* eschatology. In other words, this apocalyptic resurrection occurs only after the cosmic renewal described in 7:30: "And the world shall be turned back to primeval silence for seven days, as it was at the first beginnings." Moreover, as seen above, this text attributes the suffering of the present world to Adam's sin (4 Ezra 7:11–12; cf. 7:70–74; 7:116–26). Particularly, when Ezra describes Adam's sin which brings death into the world in 4 Ezra 7:116–18, he regards the earth as at least a biological mother of Adam: "This is my first and last word: It would have been better if *the earth had not produced Adam*, or else, when *it had produced him*, had restrained him from sinning. For what

---

79. The literal meaning of נפל is "to fall," but as some translations indicate (NRSV, ESV, NIV, etc.), it can be translated into "to bring to life" (particularly in the hiph.); see BDB, 658. Also, as Gray notes, "the noun נֵפֶל means *an untimely birth*, and the Arabic سقط, *to fall*, also means *to be born*" (Gray, *Critical and Exegetical Commentary*, 446). Moreover, the word play between נבל (corpse) and נפל which signifies the contrast between infertility and fertility supports this interpretation. Finally, the childbirth context of Isa 26:16–19 strengthens this interpretation.

80. Collins, *Daniel*, 395; they usually argue that the resurrection in Isa 26:19 metaphorically refers to Israel's national restoration. E.g., Day, *Yahweh and the Gods*, 124; Schmitz, "Grammar of Resurrection," 148; Clements, *Isaiah*, 16.

81. Nickelsburg, *Resurrection, Immortality, and Eternal Life*, 31.

good is it to all that they live in sorrow now and expect punishment after death?" (4 Ezra 7:116–18, emphasis added).

Thus, in light of Isa 26:16–19 and 4 Ezra 7:30–32, the redemption of our body in Rom 8:23 can be understood as a "bodily resurrection" in its childbirth context. Moreover, given the fact that the meaning of καλύπτειν, a cognate of ἀποκάλυψις is "hiding or burying in the earth,"[82] "the revealing of the sons of God" (ἡ ἀποκάλυψις τῶν υἱῶν τοῦ θεοῦ) in v. 19 can refer to the revealing of sons of God *from the earth*, namely believers' bodily resurrection at the eschaton in v. 23.

Lastly, the phrase "the firstfruits of the Spirit" (ἡ ἀπαρχὴ τοῦ πνεύματος) supports the idea that v. 23 regards the resurrection as the earth's childbirth. As the literal meaning of ἀπαρχή (the firstfruits) implies, this word can refer to the product of the earth. Moreover, it is very interesting to note that ἀπαρχή has the meaning of "birth-certificate of a free person."[83] For example, *Gnomon des Idios Logos* (P11650 V, a papyrus of the second century CE)[84] contains a code regarding citizenship and a birth-certificate in Roman Egypt:

> If a woman, being a citizen [i.e., of Alexandria], marries an Egyptian in the mistaken belief that he is also a citizen, she is not liable to penalty; and if both parties present *birth-certificates*, their children preserve the status of citizens.

Here, this legal code uses ἀπαρχή as a "technical term for the birth-certificate of a free person, just as οἰκογένεια is for that of a slave."[85]

Although this perfectly fits the context of childbirth in Rom 8:19–23, it is striking that only very few scholars recognize this meaning of ἀπαρχή. What, then, is the meaning of "the birth-certificate of the Spirit"? It is probable that it refers to the spirit of υἱοθεσία in Rom 8:15. This interpretation explains well the eschatological tension of υἱοθεσία between "already" in v. 15 and "not yet" in v. 23; "you *have received* a spirit of υἱοθεσία" (v. 15), but "we *still wait* eagerly for υἱοθεσία" (v. 23).

---

82. Oepke, "καλύπτω," *TDNT* 3:556; BDAG, 505.

83. LSJ, 180; BDAG, 98.

84. In 1919 W. Schubart published *Gnomon des Idios Logos* as the first part of the fifth volume of the *Berliner Griechische Urkunden*, the papyrus collection of the Egyptian Museum of Berlin. *Gnomon des Idios Logos* refers to a collection of legal rules written for a procurator in the Roman province of Egypt.

85. This translation and explanation about the papyrus are from Jones, "ΣΠΙΛΑΣ-ΑΠΑΡΧΗ ΠΝΕΥΜΑΤΟΣ," 282–83. We can find similar examples in PTeb. 316 and PFlor. 57. See also Oke, "Suggestion."

CHAPTER 5: PAUL'S USE OF υἱοθεσία IN ROMANS 8 IN LIGHT OF NEW CREATION   163

As seen above, the spirit of υἱοθεσία in v. 15 probably refers to the Spirit through which "the one who raised Jesus from the dead" will give life to believers' mortal bodies (Rom 8:11). If this is the case, believers have already experienced the newness of life in Christ (Rom 6:4) through receiving the spirit of υἱοθεσία. In other words, believers already have the birth-certificate through the spirit of υἱοθεσία (v. 23a). Yet, they *will* experience their bodily resurrection (the redemption of their bodies) at the day to come. Also, the ἀπαρχή in 1 Cor 15 refers to Christ's resurrection (15:20, 23) which inaugurates the final harvest. Although the ἀπαρχή in 1 Cor 15 does not seem to refer to a birth certificate, this at least strengthens the close connection between the ἀπαρχή in Rom 8:23 and the event of resurrection.

Therefore, we can conclude that as with Rom 8:15, υἱοθεσία in v. 23 has a close relationship with the theme of resurrection, namely believers' bodily resurrection. In 8:19-23, the theme of resurrection appears as the core of the eschatological hope for new creation in the manner of reversing the Adamic curse in Gen 3:16-19. The childbirth context of Rom 8:19-23 maximizes not only the solidarity between humanity and creation but also the cosmological sense of new creation. The creation under its slavery to φθορά will obtain the freedom of the glory of the children of God (v. 21) by giving birth to the glorified sons of God. Paul, however, calls this context of childbirth "adoption" (v. 23), not "natural birth" since adoption well expresses the transition from death to life in resurrection. In this sense, believers in Rom 8 are not newly born children of the earth but newly *created* and *adopted* children of God.

(4) Christ's divine sonship and believers' υἱοθεσία

In 1 Cor 15:20-23, Paul uses the same term of the firstfruit (ἀπαρχή) in Rom 8:23 to signify that Christ's resurrection is a prototype of our future resurrection. This relationship can also be applied to Christ's divine sonship and believers' υἱοθεσία: in Rom 1:4, Christ *was declared to be the Son of God* in power *according to the Spirit* of holiness *from his resurrection of the dead*. Christ's divine sonship in Rom 1:4 has two similarities to believers' adoption in Rom 8:23: (1) as Christ's divine sonship was *reaffirmed* by his resurrection, believers' future adoption (believers already have received the Spirit of adoption) will be publicly displayed by their resurrection; (2) as Christ was declared to be the Son of God according to the Spirit, the Spirit is deeply involved in believers' future adoption as well as their present adoption. In this sense, Christ's divine sonship and resurrection are prototypical of the future adoption and resurrection of believers.

Romans 8:29 confirms this relationship: "For those whom he foreknew he also predestined *to be conformed to the image of his Son*, in order that he might *be the firstborn among many brothers*." The concepts of "the conforming of believers to the image of his Son" and "Christ's being the firstborn among many brothers" suggest that Christ's divine sonship—declared in power according to the Spirit at his resurrection—is a prototype of our adoption as God's sons. The language of "σύμμορφος" and "εἰκών" that occur in Phil 3:21 and 1 Cor 15:49, where Paul describes believers' transformation at the parousia, also suggests that "conforming to the image of his Son" eventually refers to the resurrection of the body, which he calls "adoption" in Rom 8:23.

In Rom 8:29 Paul almost certainly has in mind Adam when he uses the theme of humans bearing the image of God (Gen 1:26–27; cf. Ps 8:6–7; Sir 17:2–4).[86] As with the theme of new creation in Rom 8:19–23 which alludes to Gen 3:17–19, this Adamic motif indicates that υἱοθεσία should be interpreted in light of the new creation. Thus, the thought that the resurrected Christ is the prototype of the new humanity of the last age and the firstborn son of God's new adopted family is best explained in terms of the new creation motif. In other words, υἱοθεσία—which indicates the transition from death to life—can be interpreted as the believers' restoration in the image of God in creation, as well as participation in the resurrection of Christ, the last Adam (1 Cor 15:45).

4. Conclusion

The theme of new creation in Romans 8 has commonalities with the characteristics of the concept of new creation in Second Temple Jewish literature and Paul, which we found in Part I, in the following respects. First, the theme of the new creation in 8:14–17 and 8:19–23 is closely related to the Adam motif within the *Urzeit-Endzeit* framework. Second, it mainly has a cosmological aspect in relation to the eschatological restoration of all creation. Third, Christ's death and resurrection are central to the theme of the new creation (Gal 6:15, 2 Cor 5:17). Finally, and most

---

86. Jewett, *Romans*, 529; Dunn, *Romans 1–8*, 483.

CHAPTER 5: PAUL'S USE OF υἱοθεσία IN ROMANS 8 IN LIGHT OF NEW CREATION

importantly, the theme of the new creation is closely related to the theme of divine sonship. It is, therefore, natural that Paul's use of υἱοθεσία should be interpreted in the context of new creation.

In the light of this new creation motif, we can recognize that Paul's use of υἱοθεσία in Rom 8:15 and 8:23 refers to the theme of the resurrection. This indicates that Paul's adoption metaphor connotes the transition of status not only from slavery to sonship but also from death to newness of life in Christ. In the next chapter, we will turn to Paul's use of υἱοθεσία in Rom 9:4, and through the exegesis of Rom 9:4, we will dialogue with scholars belonging to the school of thought known as "Paul within Judaism."

Chapter 6: **Paul's Use of Υἱοθεσία in Romans 9 in Light of New Creation**

1. Introduction

SINCE STENDAHL ARGUED THAT "Rom 9–11 is not an appendix to chs. 1–8, but the climax of the letter,"[1] there has been a proliferation of studies on Rom 9–11.[2] The reason for this renewed interest in Rom 9–11 is that after the Holocaust more and more scholars have appreciated Paul's Jewishness, and for them, Rom 9–11 has become one of the most important passages to demonstrate their argument. Two years after the publication of E. P. Sanders's *Paul and Palestinian Judaism*, Lloyd Gaston's famous article "Paul and the Torah"[3] helped to establish a group of scholars who argue that Paul remained within Judaism even after he received the gospel of Christ. This group of scholars is known as "Paul within Judaism" or "the Radical New Perspective on Paul" since for them, E. P. Sanders "comes so close to a radical break with the traditional view, yet misses it by a mile," and Dunn's view is "a step backward from Sanders."[4]

The scholars who belong to the "Paul within Judaism" *Schule* have used υἱοθεσία in the list of Rom 9:4 as evidence for their argument that

---

1. Stendahl, "Apostle Paul," 205; cf. Stendahl, *Paul Among Jews and Gentiles*, 3–4; Munck, *Christ and Israel*; Munck, *Paul and the Salvation of Mankind*.

2. E.g., Wagner, *Heralds of the Good News*; Wagner's book is famous for its solid study on Paul's use of Scripture in Rom 9–11. For recent discussions on Rom 9–11, see Wilk et al., *Between Gospel and Election*. For "Paul within Judaism" *Schule*'s interpretation of Rom 9–11, see Lodge, *Romans 9–11*; Nanos, *Mystery of Romans*; Nanos, "'Gifts and the Calling,'" 1–17.

3. Gaston, "Paul and the Torah," 48–71.

4. Gager, *Reinventing Paul*, 49.

Israel does not need redemption in Christ because the nation *already* has the privilege of divine sonship. For example, Paula Fredriksen argues that "ethnic Israelites, quite apart from Christ, already have huiothesia (Rom 9.4; cf. Exod 4.22, 'Israel is my first-born son')."[5] Thus, they regard Paul as "the pagans' apostle," not an apostle for Jews, and some of them even argue that Paul's gospel message about Christ is only for gentiles. This argument, however, is questionable since (1) it does not explain why Paul, in spite of the fact that υἱοθεσία does not occur in the LXX and Second Temple Jewish writings, uses the term υἱοθεσία in Rom 9:4 rather than the general language of sonship; (2) the overall context of Rom 9–11 is about Israel's *future* salvation as Rom 11:26 says πᾶς Ἰσραὴλ σωθήσεται.

In conversation with the above argument of "Paul within Judaism," I will demonstrate two points in this chapter. First, in Rom 9:4, Paul radically reinterprets Israel's divine sonship tradition as υἱοθεσία in light of the Christ-event in order to highlight two aspects of the Christ-event: the *incongruous grace* and the *new creation*. This will be the answer to the question, "why does Paul use the term υἱοθεσία in Rom 9:4 rather than the general language of sonship?" Second, υἱοθεσία in Rom 9:4 is not evidence for the claim that Israel already has a *Sonderweg* for salvation. In other words, Israel still needs the gift of υἱοθεσία, namely redemption in Christ.

2. Why does Paul use the term υἱοθεσία rather than the general language of sonship?

(1) Israel's privileges in Rom 9:4–5 and Christ

Fredriksen's argument that "ethnic Israelites, quite *apart from* Christ, already have huiothesia" is doubtful since in Rom 9:4–5, Paul speaks of Israel's privileges *in connection with* Christ:

> [4] They are Israelites, and to them belong the adoption, the glory, the covenants, the giving of the law, the worship, and the promises; [5] to them belong the patriarchs, and from them,

---

5. Fredriksen, *Paul*, 150; Similarly, Caroline Johnson Hodge says, "Indeed, the whole analogy, in which the 'slaves' become adopted sons of God, makes no sense for Jews, who already enjoy this status (Rom 9:4)" (Hodge, *If Sons, Then Heirs*, 71); Thiessen, *Paul and the Gentile Problem*, 47; Nanos, "'Gifts and the Calling,'" 2; Stowers, *Rereading of Romans*, 284; Gaston, *Paul and the Torah*, 77.

according to the flesh, comes the Messiah, who is over all, God blessed forever. Amen.

The fact that Paul, here, ends his statement regarding Israel's privileges with the physical connection—expressed by the phrase "according to the flesh"—between Israel and Christ indicates that Paul regards it as the most important privilege of Israel. Moreover, just before this statement, Paul even says, "I could wish that I myself were accursed and cut off from *Christ* for the sake of my own people" (9:3). This hope, which is reminiscent of his closing statement in Rom 8:39 "nothing will be able to separate us from the love of God *in Christ* Jesus our Lord," ironically implies that now Paul sees the Israelite current crisis in light of the Christ-event and envisages that Israel *will* be grafted into Christ.

Also, unlike the two occurrences of υἱοθεσία in Rom 8, a definite article is attached to υἱοθεσία in Rom 9:4. This might suggest that Paul uses υἱοθεσία in Rom 9:4 in connection with his previous discussion about υἱοθεσία in Rom 8. We should note that the next privilege in 9:4, ἡ δόξα also appears in Rom 8 (vv. 17, 18, 21, 30); it is even a major theme of 8:17–30 as "sonship" by means of υἱοθεσία is a main theme of 8:12–17.[6]

Thus, it is probable that Paul mentions υἱοθεσία in Rom 9:4 in conjunction with his discussion about υἱοθεσία in Rom 8, where he speaks of believers' υἱοθεσία in connection with Christ and the Spirit.[7] In what follows, I will demonstrate that Paul radically reinterprets Israel's divine sonship as υἱοθεσία in light of the Christ-event.

---

6. Wright, *Paul and the Faithfulness of God*, 1012. The fact that other privileges in 9:4 can also be connected to Paul's arguments in the preceding chapters supports this interpretation: (1) αἱ διαθῆκαι and αἱ ἐπαγγελίαι can refer to God's promise to Abraham in Rom 4 (4:13, 16, 21), although the word "διαθήκη" itself does not occur in Rom 4; (2) ἡ νομοθεσία can refer to either the act of giving the law or the results of that act, "legislation," but in either case, it can be connected to the earlier passages where Paul talks about the law (e.g., 2:12–29; 3:19–31; 4:13–14; 5:12–21; 7:1–25); (3) ἡ λατρεία is what Paul mentioned in 1:9 (ὁ θεός, ᾧ λατρεύω ἐν τῷ πνεύματί μου ἐν τῷ εὐαγγελίῳ τοῦ υἱοῦ αὐτοῦ) as well as what the human race gave the creation rather than the creator in 1:25 (ἐλάτρευσαν τῇ κτίσει παρὰ τὸν κτίσαντα).

7. In Rom 8, Paul is talking about believers' υἱοθεσία; he begins Rom 8 with his declaration of believers' spiritual status: "There is therefore now no condemnation for those who are in Christ Jesus." Also, the two occurrences of υἱοθεσία in Rom 8 have strong connections with Christ and the Spirit: (1) the spirit of υἱοθεσία in v. 15 probably refers to "the Spirit of Christ" (v. 9; cf. Gal 4:6) or "the Spirit of him who raised Jesus from the dead" (v. 11); (2) as a result of the gift of υἱοθεσία, believers became joint-heirs with Christ (v. 17); (3) believers, who have the firstfruits of the Spirit, still wait for υἱοθεσία (v. 23); (4) Christ is the firstborn among many brothers who became sons of God through υἱοθεσία (v. 29).

(2) Paul's radical reinterpretation of Israel's divine sonship

As I mentioned before, the term υἱοθεσία does not occur in the LXX and Second Temple Jewish writings,[8] although the concept of Israel's divine sonship often occurs in the Old Testament and Second Temple Jewish literature. For example, we can find the *concept* of Israel's divine sonship in Exod 4:22, where YHWH instructs Moses:

> Then you shall say to Pharaoh, "Thus says YHWH: Israel is my firstborn son (בן בכור, LXX: υἱὸς πρωτότοκος). I said to you, 'Let my son go that he may worship me.' But you refused to let him go; now I will kill your firstborn son." (Exod 4:22–23)

The father-son relationship between God and Israel here seems metaphorical not biological since God is not the "progenitor" of Israel. In this sense, Cook argues that the concept of Israel's divine sonship of Exod 4:22 is adoption: "Yahweh has no consort, he has no theogony. Instead, he *adopts* or *elects* a historical people for his son."[9]

Also, the phrase כה אמר יהוה ("thus YHWH says") here indicates a *divine declaration* to Pharaoh that Israel is God's firstborn son. This divine announcement strengthens the metaphorical meaning of "firstborn son," God's election of Israel as his people.

Although the conception of Israel's divine sonship—and even the metaphorical meaning of *adoption*—exists in the Jewish tradition, Paul's use of υἱοθεσία in Rom 9:4 is radical in two points: (1) Paul is the first person to use υἱοθεσία for *Israel* rather than the language of natural sonship (e.g., υἱός, πρωτότοκος, μονογενής, etc.); (2) in Rom 8, Paul has used υἱοθεσία for believers—mainly the *gentile* converts (vv. 15, 23); given the fact that there is an insurmountable difference between the uncircumcised gentiles and Israel as sons of God in the early Jewish tradition, this is a radical reinterpretation of Israel's divine sonship.

What, then, makes it possible that Paul radically reinterprets Israel's divine sonship as υἱοθεσία? As the christological and pneumatological context of Paul's use of υἱοθεσία in Rom 8 implies, in Rom 9:4, Paul

---

8. Although Eduard Schweizer claims that υἱοθεσία is found in Philo for the relation of the wise to God without mentioning the exact text of Philo (Schweizer, "υἱοθεσία," *TDNT*, 8:399), a Thesaurus Linguae Graecae search shows that there is no occurrence of υἱοθεσία in Philo; cf. Jewett, *Romans*, 562. Although Philo can use the *conception* of υἱοθεσία and the language of sons of God, he does not use the term υἱοθεσία itself in his writings.

9. Cook, "Concept of Adoption," 138.

reinterprets Israel's divine sonship as υἱοθεσία in light of Christ and the Spirit; in other words, Paul reads Israel's divine sonship tradition backward from the Christ-event.

As the title of her article, "Thinking from Christ to Israel," indicates, Gaventa also argues the same point: "What Paul does in these chapters [Rom 9–11] is to *think backward from the cross and resurrection*, the event that inaugurates God's triumph. As he thinks backwards, he sees Israel as *God's adopted child*, recipient of a number of gifts" (emphasis added).[10] This argument can be supported by the fact that Paul begins his discussion about God's faithfulness to Israel in Rom 9–11 with saying, "I am speaking the truth *in Christ*." Paul, then, directly adds this statement: "my conscience bears me witness *in the Holy Spirit*" (Rom 9:1). This opening verse indicates that Paul speaks of the Israelite privileges in v. 4 in light of Christ and the Spirit.

However, Gaventa says nothing about the reason why "Paul sees Israel as God's *adopted* child" rather than the language of natural sonship while he thinks backward from the cross and resurrection. Which aspects of the Christ-event make Paul radically reinterpret Israel's divine sonship as adoption? In the following analysis, I will use the phrase "Paul's radical reinterpretation of Israel's divine sonship in light of the Christ-event" in two senses.

First, the Christ-event can refer to God's redemptive and merciful act for sinners, which is decisively expressed by Christ's death and resurrection. According to Barclay, the Christ-event is "a divine gift, given to all in the death of Christ, an act of love for the wholly unworthy," namely, "the Christ-gift, the ultimate incongruous gift"[11] (Rom 3:21–26; 5:1–11). In this sense, when I use the phrase "Paul's reinterpretation in light of the Christ-event," one of my intentions is to refer to Paul's reinterpretation of the Jewish tradition in light of the *God's merciful and incongruous gift in Christ*. Second, the Christ-event can operate in a manner that recalibrates or relativizes all systems of value including ethnic identities (Gal 6:15; Gal 3:28; Phil 3:7). In other words, while in the early Jewish tradition, only Israel was called "sons of God," υἱοθεσία is a gift for both Jews and gentiles.

These two important aspects of the Christ-event are closely related to the new creation motif. In our investigation of the concept of new

---

10. Gaventa, "Thinking from Christ to Israel," 241.
11. Barclay, *Paul and the Gift*, 479.

creation in Part I, we have seen that the theme of new creation often relates to God's merciful intervention to solve the human predicament caused by the Adamic sin. For example, in Qumran literature, the authors sharply contrast the worthlessness of humans with God's mercy and compassion in the context of new creation (e.g., 1QH^a IV:25–30; 1QH^a V:24–37; 1QS XI:12–15; cf. Jub. 4:26). Also, as Paul argues in 2 Cor 5:17, the Christ-event has inaugurated a new era, in which anyone in Christ can experience a *new creation in Christ*. In Gal 6:15, the new creation in Christ invalidates any value system which prioritizes a specific ethnic identity, namely, Jews or gentiles (cf. Gal 3:28). Thus, I will demonstrate that Paul reinterprets the Israelite divine sonship tradition as adoption in light of the *new creation in Christ*; (1) Paul highlights God's merciful and incongruous election of Israel by reinterpreting Israel's divine sonship as υἱοθεσία; (2) Paul uses the term υἱοθεσία for both gentiles (Rom 8:15, 23: for believers, mainly gentiles) and Israel (Rom 9:4), since anyone who experienced the new creation in Christ has been adopted as sons of God regardless of their ethnic identity. This approach is reasonable given the inseparable relationship between υἱοθεσία and the new creation motif in Romans 8.

(3) Υἱοθεσία as God's merciful act of election

We cannot totally neglect Byrne's claim that υἱοθεσία in Romans and Galatians should be translated as "sonship" or "adoptive sonship" rather than adoption,[12] since (1) the contrast is clear between the *status* of slavery (δουλεία) and that of sonship in Rom 8 and Gal 4; (2) υἱοθεσία always occurs with the language of divine sonship in Rom 8 and Gal 4 (Rom 8:14, 19, 29, 32; 9:9, 26; Gal 4:4, 6, 7, 22).

However, as Byrne himself notes, "lexical considerations require the translation of υἱοθεσία in the more strictly correct sense of 'adoption.'"[13] As seen above, the term υἱοθεσία etymologically signifies the *act* of placing (θέσις), or establishing, a new status as son (υἱός). Moreover, Scott's thorough research on the usage of υἱοθεσία in the Hellenistic period also shows that υἱοθεσία should be interpreted as "adoption as son," not merely "sonship."[14]

---

12. Byrne, *Romans*, 252; Byrne, review of *Adoption as Sons of God*, (Scott), 291–93.
13. Byrne, review of *Adoption as Sons of God*, (Scott), 293.
14. Scott, *Adoption as Sons of God*, 55. See n10 in ch. 1.

Paul's use of υἱοθεσία in Rom 8 has two implications. First, as we have seen in the previous chapter, υἱοθεσία in Rom 8 signifies the *transition* from "the slavery under sin and death" to "the sonship of God," which fits well with the shift of *patria potestas* in the Roman legal act of *adoptio*. Also, it is related to God's *action*, which makes the *transition* from death to life, as υἱοθεσία in Rom 8:23 refers to God's redemption of our body, namely, resurrection. Second, given the allusions to Ezek 36–37 and Gen 3:16–19—in Rom 8:1–11 and in Rom 8:19–23 respectively—υἱοθεσία in Rom 8 refers to God's restoration of *sinners* who are still under the influence of Adamic sin. Thus, υἱοθεσία in Rom 8 indicates God's *merciful* action for sinners.

These two implications of υἱοθεσία—the transition of status and God's merciful action—also appears in υἱοθεσία in Rom 9:4. By using the term υἱοθεσία, which indicates *action*, not mere *status*, Paul highlights God's merciful election of Israel as his son. The most famous Old Testament text, which describes God's election of Israel despite Israel's ineligibility, is Deut 7:6–9:

> [6] And the Lord your God *chose* (προείλατο) you so that you would be a special people for him compared to all the nations that are on the face of the earth. [7] It was not because you were more numerous than all the nations that the Lord *chose* (προείλατο) you and *elected* (ἐξελέξατο) you, for you were small compared to all the nations. [8] [But because] the Lord *loved* you (ἀλλὰ παρὰ τὸ ἀγαπᾶν κύριον ὑμᾶς), and he was keeping an oath that he swore to your fathers, that the Lord led out you with a strong hand, and he *redeemed* (ἐλυτρώσατο) you from the house of *slavery* (δουλεία) from the hand of Pharaoh, king of Egypt. [9] And you shall know today that the Lord your God, he is God, a faithful God, keeping the covenant and *mercy* (ἔλεος) to those that love him and who keep his commands to the thousandth generation. (Deut 7:6–9, emphasis added)

The reason for God's election of Israel, here, is not because of Israel's qualification but because of God's *love* and *mercy*. God *elected* and *redeemed* Israel when Israel was small compared to all the nations and even in a status of slavery, and in that sense God's election of Israel is merciful and incongruous. We should note that the theme of "redemption from slavery" is important for Paul's use of υἱοθεσία in Rom 8. Moreover, God's mercy on Israel is the main theme of Rom 9–11; Paul repeatedly uses the term ἔλεος and its cognate ἐλεέω in Rom 9–11 (9:15, 16, 18, 23; 11:30–32).

CHAPTER 6: PAUL'S USE OF υἱοθεσία IN ROMANS 9 IN LIGHT OF NEW CREATION   173

Romans 9:6–29, in particular, is very similar to Deut 7:6–9 in that Paul speaks of God's merciful election of Israel with the same language of election (ἐκλογή: v. 11), mercy (ἔλεος: v. 23; cf. ἐλεέω: vv. 15, 16, 18), and love (ἀγαπάω: vv. 13, 25). As Barclay notes, in Rom 9:6–29 Paul argues that "Israel has been constituted by the purposes of a *divine election* that pays no regard to criteria of fittingness or worth."[15] In this context, it is probable that υἱοθεσία, which implies God's election of Israel, is a keyword of Paul's discussion in Rom 9 since it opens Paul's discussion on the divine election in Rom 9:6–29. In other words, in Rom 9:6–29 Paul unfolds the sense of *merciful election* in υἱοθεσία: the divine election does not depend on any kind of human qualifications—ethnicity (vv. 7–8), birth (vv. 10–13), works (v. 12), and will or exertion (v. 16)—but only depends on God's election (v. 11), purpose (v. 11), calling (vv. 7, 12), love (v. 13) and mercy (vv. 15, 16). Particularly, in vv. 11–12 Paul underlines the *incongruity* between the divine election and the human condition of the elect:

> Though they were not yet born and had done nothing either good or bad—in order that God's purpose of election might continue, not because of works but because of him who calls—she [Rebecca] was told, "the greater will serve the inferior." (Rom 9:11–12)

Here, the divine election between Jacob and Esau is solely determined by God's purpose (πρόθεσις), not by human works (ἔργα) or "greatness"; God even selects "the inferior"[16] rather than the greater. This highlights the incongruity in God's election. Furthermore, we should note that in the original context of Gen 25:23, which Paul quotes in Rom 9:12, Jacob and Esau represent two *nations*; of course, Jacob represents Israel, as he will change his name to Israel (Gen 32:28). Thus, this example of divine election and its incongruous aspect have a connection with υἱοθεσία in Rom 9:4, the divine election of Israel.

Another important point of Paul's discussion in Rom 9:6–29 is that Paul expresses the divine election through the language of sonship (τέκνον: vv. 7–8; υἱός: vv. 9, 26–27; cf. σπέρμα: vv. 7–8, 29).[17] For example,

15. Barclay, *Paul and the Gift*, 524.
16. Although most English Bibles translate ἐλάσσων as "younger," I think a better translation is "inferior," given the main meaning of ἐλάσσων (less or inferior) and its Hebrew equivalent צָעִיר (little or insignificant) in Gen 25:23. In either translation, the incongruous meaning of the divine election does not change.
17. There is no language of sonship in Rom 9:12, in which Paul quotes Gen 25:23.

in Rom 9:8, Paul says, "it is not the children of the flesh who are children of God, but the children of the promise are regarded as descendants." In other words, the deciding factor in being "children of God" is not human qualification (i.e., lineage) but God's *promise*. The fact that ἐπαγγελία also appears in the list of Israel's privileges in Rom 9:4 indicates that here Paul uses the language of divine sonship in connection with υἱοθεσία in Rom 9:4 to highlight God's election of Israel as God's children. This strengthens my argument that υἱοθεσία in Rom 9:4 is a keyword to anticipate his discussion of the divine election in Rom 9:6–29.

(4) Paul's reinterpretation of Hosea in Rom 9:25–26

I have argued that Paul's use of υἱοθεσία rather than the language of natural sonship in Rom 9:4 highlights the transition of status and incongruity in God's election of Israel. In this regard, Paul's citation of Hosea in Rom 9:25–26 is crucial since it clearly shows the two important aspects of the divine election—transition of status and incongruity—with the language of divine sonship:

> As indeed he says in Hosea, "Those who were not my people I will call 'my people,' and her who was not beloved I will call 'beloved.'" "And in the very place where it was said to them, 'You are not my people,' there they shall be called sons of the living God." (Rom 9:25–26)

First of all, here Paul emphasizes the transition in the divine calling with three different expressions, namely, from "not my people" to "my people," from "not beloved" to "beloved," and from "not my people" to "sons of the living God." Second, Paul brings the incongruity of divine election to a climax by showing that God elects the people as "sons of the living God," who were not his beloved people before. Given the original context of Hosea, Israel's disobedience was the reason that God regards the nation as "not my people." This disqualification of the selected people highlights God's mercy and love in the divine election. In other words, here the reason for God's election is not any qualifications of the elect but God's calling and love. Thus, God's election of "sons of

---

However, as Stegner observes, we should note that υἱός is located in Gen 25:25. In midrashic discourse the rabbis frequently omit the important part or the keyword in citing the prooftext, since they assume that the audience knows these texts by heart (Stegner, "Romans 9:6–29," 40–41; cf. Jewett, *Romans*, 579).

CHAPTER 6: PAUL'S USE OF υἱοθεσία IN ROMANS 9 IN LIGHT OF NEW CREATION 175

the living God" indicates "transition of status" and "incongruity" at the same time, as υἱοθεσία in Rom 9:4 implies.

Also, we should note that while Paul quotes Hosea in Rom 9:25–26, Paul modifies not only some expressions but also Hosea's original context. Here, Paul combines two texts of Hosea, Hos 2:23 and Hos 1:10b LXX. The most striking adaptation of the first half of this combined citation (Hos 2:23 LXX) is that Paul reverses the order of clauses in Hos 2:23, locating the phrase "not my people" first.[18] By changing this order of phrases, Paul connects this citation to his argument concerning gentiles' inclusion in God's people in Rom 9:24: "he [God] called us, not from the Jews only but also from the Gentiles" (v. 24: ἐκάλεσεν ἡμᾶς οὐ μόνον ἐξ Ἰουδαίων ἀλλὰ καὶ ἐξ ἐθνῶν). Also, in citing Hos 2:23 he changes the verb ἐρῶ to καλέσω,[19] which he uses in Rom 9:24. This strengthens the connection between the gentiles in v. 24 and those who were not God's people in v. 25. The original context of Hos 2:23 is God's promise of Israel's return from exile and national restoration. Paul's modifications of the Hosea citations, however, shows that Paul radically reinterprets Hos 2:23 as "an announcement of God's embrace of Gentiles as his own people."[20]

The second half of this combined citation (Hos 1:10b LXX) reinforces this interpretation. Again, by quoting the verse which contains the phrase οὐ λαός μου and κληθήσονται, Paul connects this citation to the theme of the inclusion of gentiles in God's people in Rom 9:24. Furthermore, Paul uses the language of divine sonship ("sons of the living God") not only for Jews but also for gentiles in Rom 9:26.[21] This is a radical

---

18. Wagner, *Heralds of the Good News*, 81. In Hos 2:23 LXX, the phrase "not pitied" occurs first: "ἐλεήσω τὴν Οὐκ-ἠλεημένην καὶ ἐρῶ τῷ Οὐ-λαῷ-μου Λαός μου εἶ σύ." This order follows the order of Hosea's children's name (Lo-ruhamah and Lo-ammi in Hos 1:6, 9 respectively). Interestingly, the citation of Hosea 1:6, 9 in 1 Pet 2:10 follows Paul's modified order of clauses in Rom 9:25.

19. Paul's choice of the verb καλέω in Rom 9:25 also functions to combine two citations since his citation of Hos 1:10b in Rom 9:26 also uses this verb. Moreover, the previous occurrences of this verb (Rom 9:7, 12) signify the divine election.

20. Wagner, *Heralds of the Good News*, 81.

21. Some argue that the citation of Hosea in vv. 25–26 refers to God's calling of gentile believers not including Jews, since in vv. 27–29, Paul explicitly refers to God's calling of a remnant within ethnic Israel (e.g., Moo, *Epistle to the Romans*, 613; Morris, *Epistle to the Romans*, 370–71). However, given the original context of the Hosea texts and the overall context of Rom 9–11, which deals with Israel's future restoration, it is more probable that here "sons of the living God" refers to a mixed community of believers composed of both Jews and gentiles (See Jewett, *Romans*, 600; Dunn, *Romans 9–16*, 572; Cranfield, *Critical and Exegetical Commentary*, 2:499–500).

reinterpretation of the Jewish tradition since the language of divine sonship is exclusively used for Israel in the Jewish tradition.

The surprising inclusion of gentiles as God's sons sheds light on Paul's use of υἱοθεσία in Rom 9:4. By using the term υἱοθεσία for Israel, which Paul uses for believers (mainly gentiles) in Rom 8, Paul makes his audience anticipate his following argument that God has called Jews and gentiles together to be his sons (Rom 9:24–29). Thus, Paul's use of υἱοθεσία in Rom 9:4 is Paul's radical reinterpretation of Israel's divine sonship in light of the new creation in Christ, which means that there is no distinction between Jews and gentiles in God's calling of his sons (Gal 6:15; Rom 10:12).

The theme of divine calling in Rom 9:24–26 is particularly important since it strengthens this interpretation—Paul uses the term υἱοθεσία in light of the new creation in Christ—in that God's calling of Israel and gentiles together as his sons does not merely refer to God's election of his people, but also refers to God's *creation* of his people, as we shall see below.

(5) Ὑιοθεσία and God's new creation of his people from Jews and gentiles

The divine calling is one of the most important themes in Paul's argument in Rom 9:6–29 (vv. 7, 12, 24, 25, 26). The theme of "calling" in Rom 9:6–29 signifies the divine election of Isaac (v. 7), Jacob (v. 12), and God's sons, not from the Jews only but also from the gentiles (vv. 24–26).

The theme of divine calling, however, refers not only to the divine election; it also signifies God's act of *creation*. Chester rightly notes that in Isa 40–66, the theme of divine calling often emerges with God's character as creator; namely, the God who *calls* is the *creator* God (e.g., Isa 43:1; 46:11; 48:13–15; Isa 51:1–3).[22] For example, in Isa 43:1, where God encourages Israel with the word of assurance that he has *called* (ἐκάλεσα) Israel by name, God describes himself as a creator who created (ποιήσας)[23] and formed (πλάσας) Israel. The connection between God's act of creation and calling of his people occurs again a few verses later in Isa 43:6–7:

---

22. Chester, *Conversion at Corinth*, 64–69.

23. The LXX reads this verb "to make" (ποιεῖν) although the MT has ברא which means "to create." However, "to make" and "to form" clearly refer to God's act of creation.

> I will say to the north, "Bring them," and to the south, "Do not hinder them." Lead *my sons* from a far land, and *my daughters* from the ends of the earth, all who *are called* (ἐπικέχληνται)[24] by my name. For by my glory I have prepared him and *formed* (ἔπλασα) him and *made* (ἐποίησα) him.

God's act of creation here parallels his calling of Israel. It should be noted that the language of divine sonship (my sons and my daughters) occurs with God's act of calling of his people, as in Hos 1:10 which Paul cites in Rom 9:26.

Given the fact that nearly half of Paul's Old Testament citations in Romans are from Isaiah, the close relationship between the divine calling of Israel and God's creation of Israel cannot be neglected. Moreover, there is additional evidence that God's calling implies God's act of creation.

First of all, the imagery of the potter and his clay in Rom 9:20–23 supports this connection. Many of the Old Testament and Jewish texts which use this imagery highlight God as Creator (e.g., Isa 29:16; 45:9; Jer 18:6–10; Wis 15:7; Sir 33:13). Particularly, we should note that πλάσσειν in Rom 9:20 is the word which describes God's creative activity when he formed Adam from the dust of the ground in Gen 2:7–8 LXX. Also, as seen above, the combination of the verbs, πλάσσειν and ποιεῖν in Rom 9:20–21, also occurs in Isa 43:1 and Isa 43:6–7 in the context of the divine calling and creation of Israel. Another important text using the imagery of the potter and his clay is Isa 64:8: "O Lord, you are our Father; we are the clay, and you are our potter; we are all the work of your hand." The appellation אבינו, "our father," for God is rare in the Old Testament, appearing only here and in Isa 63:16; it refers to the creator God who created the nation, Israel. This indicates that the father-son relationship between YHWH and Israel or the divine sonship of Israel relates to God's act of creation.

Also, Paul already used the notion of God's act of creation as an effective "calling" in Rom 4:17:

> as it is written, "I have made you the father of many nations"—in the presence of the God in whom he believed, who gives life to the dead and calls into existence the things that do not exist.

---

24. We can take the verbal form ἐπικέκληνται as middle (*to call* upon my name) or passive voice (*to be called* by my name), but given the context that God brings and leads Israel from the ends of the earth, it is more natural to take the passive voice which signifies God's act of "calling." The niphal form of the Hebrew original (הנקרא) also supports this translation.

Here, Paul describes the divine calling as an act of creation, which parallels God's act of giving life to the dead. As Gaventa rightly observes, the calling in Rom 4:17 is not simply an act of selecting. The phrase "calling that which does not exist into existence" (καλοῦντος τὰ μὴ ὄντα ὡς ὄντα) itself clearly shows that this is a creative act, which makes things exist where they did not before.[25] As Cranfield argues that "there is little doubt that the reference is to God's *creatio ex nihilo*," the concept of "calling into existence the things that do not exist" in Rom 4:17 can be connected to the Jewish belief that God created "out of nothing" (e.g., 2 Macc 7:28; Jos. As. 12:2; 2 Bar. 21:4; 48:8; Philo, *Spec. Leg.* 4.187).[26]

Moreover, the description of God as "the one who gives life to the dead" which parallels "the one who calls into existence the things that do not exist" reinforces this interpretation since (1) this phrase is reminiscent of God's creative work in Gen 2:7–8, where God blew into Adam's lifeless body the breath of life; (2) in the Jewish tradition, God's *creative* power often parallels God's power to resurrect the dead.[27] This divine power also refers to God's power to make the dead womb of barren Sarah come to conceive Isaac (Rom 4:19). Thus, in Rom 4, God's promise to Abraham is not merely about *election* but about *creation*.

The idea of the divine calling as an act of creation in Rom 4:17 is particularly important for the understanding of calling and creation in Rom 9:24–26 in the following two points. First, the concept of the divine calling and creation in Rom 4:17 has commonality with that of Rom 9:24–26 in that God's act of creation in both texts indicates remarkable discontinuity or transition from the previous status. Just as God calls into "being" out of "nothing" in Rom 4:17, so God calls his

---

25. Gaventa, "On the Calling-Into-Being of Israel," 260.

26. E.g., Cranfield, *Critical and Exegetical Commentary*, 1:244–45; Dunn, *Romans 1–8*, 218; Jewett, *Romans*, 334. Cf. Moo, *Epistle to the Romans*, 281–82; although Moo admits the possibility that this text can refer to this tradition, he concludes "hesitantly" and "reluctantly" that Rom 4:17 cannot refer to God's creative power because Paul uses ὡς, not εἰς; here Paul speaks of God's calling things "as though" they existed, which does not fit well with the Jewish creatio ex nihilo tradition. However, as Moo himself admits, ὡς also has the meaning of "marker of result in connection with indication of purpose" (BDAG, 1105). We cannot neglect the possibility that here Paul uses ὡς with the meaning of result or purpose.

27. For example, this parallelism occurs in 2 Macc 7:23, where the mother of the seven martyred sons encourages her sons: "*The creator of the world*, who shaped the beginning of humankind and devised the origin of all things, will in his mercy *give life and breath back to you again*." Also, Paul himself uses this parallelism in 1 Cor 15:42, where he quotes Gen 2:7 to contrast Adam and Christ: "It is written, 'The first man Adam became a living being'; the last Adam became a life-giving spirit."

people from the status of "not my people" and "not beloved" to that of "my people" and "beloved." In this context, the concept of the divine calling in Rom 9:24–26 has the meaning of *new* creation. Paul also describes this transition with the language of divine sonship, namely, from "not my people" to "the sons of the living God."

Second, just as Rom 9:24–26 indicates the inclusion of gentiles in God's people, so the divine calling and creation in Rom 4:17 prophesies that gentiles also become the sons of Abraham. Thus, the purpose of divine calling and creation is to make Abraham "the father of many Gentiles" (πατέρα πολλῶν ἐθνῶν; v. 17, 18). Also, in Rom 4:16, Abraham appears as "the father of all of us" (πατὴρ πάντων ἡμῶν), namely, "not only to those who are of the law, but also to those who are of the faith of Abraham" (οὐ τῷ ἐκ τοῦ νόμου μόνον ἀλλὰ καὶ τῷ ἐκ πίστεως Ἀβραάμ). Although there is an ongoing debate on the meaning of the two groups, "those who are of the law" and "those who are of the faith of Abraham,"[28] it seems clear, at least, that the descendants of Abraham are composed of not only Jews but also gentiles. In Rom 4:9–12, Paul already mentioned this point by saying that Abraham became the father of both the uncircumcised (ἀκροβυστία) and the circumcised (περιτομή) who follow in the footsteps of Abraham's faith.[29]

Hodge argues that the preposition ἐκ in Rom 4:16 (ὁ ἐκ πίστεως Ἀβραάμ) and Gal 3:7 (οἱ ἐκ πίστεως) should be interpreted as "born out of" or "descend from" in terms of a lineage.[30] The purpose of this argument is to highlight the importance of ethnic identity in Pauline thought;[31] not

---

28. Some scholars argue that "those who are of the law" in Rom 4:16 refers to non-believing Jews in light of the contrast with "those who are of the faith of Abraham" and the fact that "those of the law" in v. 14 refers to non-believing Jews (e.g., Fitzmyer, *Romans*, 385; Gaston, "Abraham and the Righteousness of God," 58). Others argue that it refers to Jewish Christians based on the parallel in 4:12 or the structure of "not only ... but also" in v. 16 (i.e., not only Jewish believers but also "those out of the faith of Abraham" [in this interpretation, the latter refers to "Gentile believers"]) (e.g., Moo, *Epistle to the Romans*, 279; Cranfield, *Critical and Exegetical Commentary*, 1:242–43; Käsemann, *Commentary on Romans*, 121). Jewett, however, argues that it refers to Jews, whether believing or not (Jewett, *Romans*, 331). Similarly, some argue that "those who are of the faith of Abraham" refers to gentile Christians (e.g., Moo, Cranfield, Barrett, et al.), while others argue that it refers to both gentile and Jewish believers (e.g., Jewett, Fitzmyer, et al.).

29. In the Pauline letters, the circumcised and the uncircumcised can often refer to ethnic identities, namely, Jews and gentiles (e.g., 1 Cor 7:19; Gal 5:6; 6:15).

30. Hodge, *If Sons, Then Heirs*, 84–9.

31. Hodge, *If Sons, Then Heirs*, 9; She argues that even the "radical new perspective on Paul," which she supports, has neglected the ethnic categories such as "Jew" or

only "blood" but also πίστις can be a way to acquire the ethnic identity of Abraham's descendants. Also, by interpreting πίστις as "faithfulness" rather than "faith," she focuses more on "*Abraham's faithfulness* to God's promise" rather than *God's promise* itself. Thus, she argues that the phrase ὁ ἐκ πίστεως Ἀβραάμ refers to "progeny descending from the ancestor's trust and faithful actions."[32] Paul's argument here, however, is in the exact opposite direction: the ethnic identity or any kind of human actions is not important but irrelevant to "being Abraham's descendants." The critical factor to be Abraham's descendants is God's promise and calling itself rather than the ethnic identity and any kind of human conditions (Rom 4:13, 14, 16, 20; Gal 3:14, 16–19, 21–22, 29; 4:23, 28).

Romans 9:6–8 reiterates the same logic three times; Jewish ethnicity is irrelevant to God's calling of Abraham's descendants: (1) "they are not all Israel, which are of Israel" (v. 6); (2) "not all of Abraham's children are his descendants, but in Isaac shall your descendants be called" (v. 7); (3) "it is not the children of the flesh who are the children of God, but the children of promise are counted as descendants" (v. 8). Again, the necessary and sufficient condition to be Abraham's children is God's promise, not an ethnic condition as Jews. We should note that here Paul identifies "Abraham's children" with the children of God. This means that Paul uses this kinship language as a *metaphorical* expression to signify God's election of Israel (we will deal with this issue in more detail in the next chapter). Both Abraham's children and the children of God, not according to the flesh but according to the promise, are closely related to Paul's use of υἱοθεσία in 9:4.

Similarly, as seen above, Rom 9:24–26 describes the inclusion of gentile believers in God's people with the language of divine sonship. Moreover, in Rom 9:27–28, Paul quotes from Isa 10:22–23 to depict Israel's current situation and the salvation of a remnant within ethnic Israel. In Rom 9:27, however, Paul slightly modifies the subject of the first clause

---

"gentile" in the Pauline thought. Thus, she argues that the central insight of the "radical new perspective on Paul"—Paul is speaking to gentiles and not to humanity—requires "a rereading of Paul with *ethnicity and kinship as a central focus*." Although her argument that "Paul teaches the gospel using ethnic and kinship language to articulate God's plan for salvation" is true, it is questionable whether Paul focuses on the ethnic and kinship language itself. Paul's use of the ethnic and kinship language is a *metaphorical* expression which signifies God's salvation. Her tendency to interpret Paul's ethnic and kinship language *literally*, not *metaphorically*, makes her give too much focus on Paul's ethnic and kinship language itself.

32. Hodge, *If Sons, Then Heirs*, 89.

in the original LXX text, from "the people Israel" (ὁ λαὸς Ἰσραήλ) to "the number of the sons of Israel" (ὁ ἀριθμὸς τῶν υἱῶν Ἰσραήλ): "Though the number of the sons of Israel were like the sand of the sea, only a remnant of them will be saved." The fact that the same phrase "the number of the sons of Israel" occurs in Hos 1:10, which Paul has just cited in Rom 9:26, shows that Paul wants to connect this text to his preceding discussion about a new community of "sons of the living God," which is composed of both Jews and gentiles. Thus, the language of divine sonship in v. 26 ("sons of the living God") also indicates God's creation of his people regardless of any ethnic identities as Jews and gentiles.

Again, God's creation of his sons composed of both Jews and gentiles in Rom 9:6–29 helps to answer the question, "Why does Paul use the term υἱοθεσία in Rom 9:4 rather than the language of natural sonship?" By using the term υἱοθεσία, Paul not only highlights God's merciful election of Israel but also indicates God's calling and creation of his people not according to any ethnic identities but according to God's promise and election. In this sense, we can understand that Paul radically reinterprets Israel's divine sonship as υἱοθεσία in light of the new creation in Christ.

The next question to be answered is "Does Israel not need the gift of υἱοθεσία since the nation already has that privilege in Rom 9:4?" Paul's answer will be "μὴ γένοιτο" as we shall see below.

3. Israel still needs the gift of υἱοθεσία

As I mentioned above, the "Paul within Judaism" *Schule* has used υἱοθεσία in Rom 9:4 as supporting evidence for their argument that Israel does not need redemption in Christ since Israel already enjoys the privilege of υἱοθεσία. Thus, some of the "Paul within Judaism" *Schule* argue that there are two separate paths to salvation: the law for Jews and faith in Christ for gentiles.[33] Others, although they do not totally agree

---

33. In order to advocate the "two-way solution," Gager argues that for Paul, a special path is rather for gentiles, not for Jews: "As to the question of whether we can speak of Paul's *Sonderweg* or special path to salvation, I am rather of the view that it is the other way around. For Paul, Israel's salvation was never in doubt. What he taught and preached was instead a special path, a *Sonderweg*, for Gentiles" (Gager, *Reinventing Paul*, 146). Similarly, Gaston argues that "it is precisely Israel's universalistic perspective, which allows non-Jews to relate to God in their own way, which enables Israel to have her own particularity in relating to God through the Sinai covenant" (Gaston, *Paul and the Torah*, 23). Also, he argues that Paul did not think of Jesus as the messiah of Israel, but only of gentiles (Gaston, *Paul and the Torah*, 33).

with the "two-covenant" model of salvation, argue that the adoption in Christ (Gal 4:5; Rom 8:15, 23) is *only* for gentiles since Jews already have this privilege.³⁴

Their arguments, however, are dubious. If Israel already has a special way to salvation and thus does not need redemption in Christ, why does Paul have great sorrow and unceasing anguish in his heart because of Israel in Rom 9:2–4? In what follows, I will demonstrate that the Israelite privilege of υἱοθεσία does not mean that Israel currently possesses an absolute *right* as the sons of God, which is given regardless of their faith in Christ. Rather, I will show that Israel's *gift* of υἱοθεσία can only be confirmed and fulfilled in Christ.

To do so, I will discuss the following points: (1) υἱοθεσία in Rom 9:4 does not necessarily mean Israel currently possesses υἱοθεσία; rather, it can have a connection with an event in Israel's history; (2) In what sense, does υἱοθεσία belong to Israel? I will attempt to answer this question in connection with the olive tree metaphor in Rom 11, and I will show that Israel still needs redemption in Christ; (3) υἱοθεσία in Rom 9:4 anticipates Paul's argument on Israel's future salvation in Rom 11 in the context of new creation.

---

34. For example, Eisenbaum tries to keep a distance from the "two-covenant" model of salvation by answering to the question, "Does Paul really think there are two ways to salvation?" Her answer is "yes, for those who see Paul from within the traditional paradigm; it is no for those in the new paradigm" (Eisenbaum, *Paul Was Not a Christian*, 251). Although her answer attempts to point out the problem of the question itself, she seems to still remain in the frame of the dual-covenant theology; she argues that "Paul's critique of Israel is not that Torah observance has prevented her from having faith in Christ, but the problem is that Israel is not heeding the words of the Torah carefully enough" (Eisenbaum, *Paul Was Not a Christian*, 254). Similarly, Fredriksen's view is different from the *Sonderweg* interpretation in that she admits the following points: (1) Christ is the messiah son of David for Israel as well as for the gentiles; (2) not only gentiles but also Jews are "under sin" and the blessing of Abraham as "our father of faith" is pronounced on not only "the circumcised" but also "the uncircumcised" (Rom 4:1–25); (3) Christ's parousia coincides with the resurrection of the dead among whom certainly number Jews; (4) Paul himself supported other apostles' mission to Jews (Fredriksen, *Paul*, 234n64). However, as seen above, she argues that gentiles only need the privilege of adoption since Israel already has it. Thiessen also argues that the two-track scheme of Mussner, Gaston, and Gager fails to do justice to Paul's thought. From his exegesis of Rom 11:17–24 (the analogy of the olive tree), he argues that Jews also need to be in Christ and to have Christ's *pneuma* to remain connected to the cultivated olive tree (Thiessen, *Paul and the Gentile Problem*, 120). However, as we shall see in ch. 7, Thiessen claims that there are two types of the descendants of Abraham: the descendants of Abraham by birth (Jews) and the descendants of Abraham by adoption (gentiles). See Thiessen, *Paul and the Gentile Problem*, 87–91.

CHAPTER 6: PAUL'S USE OF υἱοθεσία IN ROMANS 9 IN LIGHT OF NEW CREATION 183

(1) The connection between υἱοθεσία in Rom 9:4 and an event in Israel's history

Grammatically, in Rom 9:4 Israel and υἱοθεσία are connected with a genitive relative pronoun:

οἵτινές εἰσιν Ἰσραηλῖται, ὧν ἡ υἱοθεσία καὶ ἡ δόξα καὶ αἱ διαθῆκαι καὶ ἡ νομοθεσία καὶ ἡ λατρεία καὶ αἱ ἐπαγγελίαι

Although the main verb (εἰσιν) of this sentence has the present tense, it does not necessarily guarantee that Israel currently has an *inalienable possession* or *status* as sons of God. First, as seen above, the lexical meaning of υἱοθεσία is closer to an *action* rather than a status. Second, it is important to note that each of the Israelite privileges in Rom 9:4 can be correlated with a specific moment in Israel's history. Erin Heim claims that υἱοθεσία is the only metaphorical predication among the list of privileges Paul gives in Rom 9:4, while the rest of the terms in the list directly refer to either a "historical event" or a "concrete object."[35] Her argument is right in that υἱοθεσία in Rom 9:4 is a metaphorical expression to refer to the covenantal relationship between YHWH and Israel, but we cannot exclude the possibility that υἱοθεσία can also be connected to a historical event of Israel. For instance, as seen above, υἱοθεσία can refer to YHWH's designation of Israel as his firstborn son in the exodus narrative (Exod 4:22–23). Erin Heim seems hesitant to connect υἱοθεσία in Rom 9:4 to God's proclamation that Israel is his firstborn son (Exod 4:22–23), since in Rom 8:29, Paul uses the term "firstborn" for Christ, who is the Davidic Messiah, not for Israel.[36] Also, she claims that connecting Israel's

---

35. Heim, *Adoption in Galatians and Romans*, 255–58; Her connections of the Israelite privileges to a historical event are: (1) "the glory" can be connected to the glory of God's presence during the exodus event (Exod 16:10, 24:15–17); (2) the plural covenants can refer to all of the various covenant between YHWH and Israel in the Old Testament (Gen 15:17; Exod 19:5–6; 2 Sam 23:5); (3) the giving of the law (νομοθεσία) refers to the Mosaic law which can be linked to "the giving of the Law on Mount Sinai"; (4) "the worship" likely refers to "the cultic observance and sacrificial system (Exod 12:25–26; Josh 21:27 LXX; 1 Chr 28:13)"; (5) "the promises" refers to YHWH's promises to Abraham regarding his inheritance of land and offspring (Gen 12:2–9; 15:5–7; 17:4–8; cf. Rom 4:1, 13, 16–17).

36. Heim, *Adoption in Galatians and Romans*, 294–97; she argues that "υἱοθεσία provides a noticeably different schema from 'firstborn,' which appears in several other versions of sonship metaphors (e.g., Exod 4:22; Jer 31:9; Sir 36:16–17; Pss. Sol. 18:1–4), but which Paul reserves for Christ alone (Rom 8:29)." She also claims that Paul's designation of Christ as firstborn is rooted in the Old Testament texts where the Davidic messiah is designated the "firstborn" (e.g., Ps 89:27).

adoption to the exodus event is unsatisfying since the exodus event is "not an installation of Israel to sonship, but rather an affirmation of Israel's current status as the son of YHWH."[37]

Of course, we cannot deny the Davidic Messiah tradition in Paul's use of "firstborn" in Rom 8:29, but its main emphasis is Christ as a representative of God's people rather than Christ as the Davidic Messiah. The πρωτότοκος in Rom 8:29, is the one who is *among many brothers* (ἐν πολλοῖς ἀδελφοῖς) and the one with whom believers should *share* the form (σύμμορφος). In this sense, the same language of πρωτότοκος in Rom 8:29 and Exod 4:22 rather enhances the probability that when Paul uses υἱοθεσία in Rom 9:4, he has in mind the historical event of the exodus, since he already used the term πρωτότοκος just after he mentioned believers' privilege of υἱοθεσία (8:15, 23). Furthermore, as seen in our exegesis of Rom 8:23, υἱοθεσία can connote "affirmation" or "public display" of sonship which has been already established. Also, as seen above, we can understand Exod 4:22 as a "divine declaration" to Pharaoh that Israel is God's firstborn son. Finally, the fact that the rest of the privileges of Rom 9:4 can also be linked to Israel's exodus tradition reinforces this interpretation.[38]

It is more probable, therefore, that υἱοθεσία in Rom 9:4 can also be connected to Israel's history, particularly God's redemption of Israel in the exodus event, than that it refers to "Israel's ongoing covenant relationship with YHWH" in a merely metaphorical sense. The connection between υἱοθεσία in Rom 9:4 and the event in Israel's history increases the probability that υἱοθεσία in Rom 9:4 does not necessarily

---

37. Heim, *Adoption in Galatians and Romans*, 259.

38. As Fitzmyer rightly notes, "The second prerogative [δόξα] is the resplendent manifestation of Yahweh's presence to Israel at the exodus and the crossing of the Reed Sea (Exod 15:6, 11), in the desert (Exod 16:10; 40:34)" (Fitzmyer, *Romans*, 546). The covenants (διαθῆκαι) would refer to the various covenants made at different points in Israel's history including the covenant at Mount Sinai (Exod 19:5–6) (Dunn, *Romans 9–16*, 527; Jewett, *Romans*, 563–64; Moo, *Epistle to the Romans*, 563), but it is equally probable that διαθῆκαι refers to the several ratifications of the Mosaic covenant in the exodus (Barrett, *Commentary on the Epistle to the Romans*, 166; Byrne, *Romans*, 287). νομοθεσία can be related to God's giving the law in the exodus. Regarding λατρεία, which can refer to either Israel's worship of God in a general sense or the Israelite sacrificial system, we should remember that the purpose of the exodus was Israel's worship of God (Exod 4:23: "Let my son [Israel] go that he may worship [λατρεύσῃ] me"). ἐπαγγελίαι, "a word that appeared in the singular four times in Rom 4 in reference to Abraham's promise to inherit the world" (Jewett, *Romans*, 565), can also be connected to Israel's exodus, given the fact that the Abrahamic covenant itself prophesies Israel's exodus (Gen 15:13–16).

mean that Israel currently possesses an inalienable status as sons of God. As in Rom 3:2, where Paul says that the first advantage of the Jew is the historical fact that the Jews *were entrusted* with the oracle of God (ἐπιστεύθησαν τὰ λόγια τοῦ θεοῦ), υἱοθεσία as the first privilege of Rom 9:4 can refer to a historical event.

(2) Υἱοθεσία as Israel's gift and redemption in Christ

I have argued that Paul's use of υἱοθεσία in Rom 9:4 is his radical *reinterpretation* of *Israel's divine sonship tradition* in light of the Christ-event. Paul's emphasis on the physical connection between Israel and Christ in Rom 9:5 indicates that Paul considers Israel's *history* in Rom 9:4–5 retrospectively from the vantage point of the present after the Christ-event.

Although υἱοθεσία in Rom 9:4 has a connection to Israel's history, here Paul says that the privilege υἱοθεσία is of (ὧν) Israel while Paul has already spoken about believers' υἱοθεσία in Rom 8. Most English translations interpret this genitive phrase as "υἱοθεσία *belongs* to Israel." In what sense, then, does υἱοθεσία "belong" to Israel? Or, in what sense is υἱοθεσία still Israel's privilege distinct from believers' υἱοθεσία? This question relates to the peculiar way in which Paul announces the gospel, the power of God in Rom 1:16. Although the gospel is the power of God for salvation to everyone who believes, Paul indicates that there is something special about Jews by interjecting "first" (πρῶτον) into the expression "to the Jew *first*, and also to the Greek" (Ἰουδαίῳ τε πρῶτον καὶ Ἕλληνι). Paul not only reiterates this formula in 2:9 and 2:10 but also says that the Jew has something extraordinary (περισσός) in every respect (3:1–2). In Rom 9:4, given the close relationship between υἱοθεσία and Christ (Rom 8:15, 23; Gal 4:5) Jews seem to have at least one advantage over gentiles in terms of υἱοθεσία although this gift has been extended to gentiles; they have a *physical* connection with Christ. In other words, "from them [Israelites], according to the flesh, comes Christ" (9:5: ἐξ ὧν ὁ Χριστὸς τὸ κατὰ σάρκα). This might suggest in what sense υἱοθεσία "belongs" to Israel.

Paul's use of the olive tree analogy in Rom 11:16–24 also sheds light on the meaning in which υἱοθεσία belongs to Israel. Paul describes Israel as "natural branches" (vv. 21, 24: κλάδοι κατὰ φύσιν) and refers to the tree as their "own olive tree" (v. 24: ἰδία ἐλαία) while he portrays gentiles as a wild olive tree grafted, contrary to nature (v. 24: παρὰ φύσιν), into a cultivated olive tree. The analogy that Jews are *natural* branches resonates with Paul's statement that υἱοθεσία "is of" or "belongs to" Israel. Again, however, it does not mean that Israel has an inalienable status as sons of God. In fact, currently they have been *broken off* because of their unbelief (11:20).

In Gal 4 and Rom 8, υἱοθεσία refers to believers' *redemption in Christ*: (1) in Gal 4:4–5, Paul parallels the gift of υἱοθεσία with the God's redeeming act (ἐξαγοράζειν) for those who are under the law, by the sending of Christ; (2) in Rom 8:23, υἱοθεσία refers to the redemption of our body (ἀπολύτρωσις τοῦ σώματος ἡμῶν). Paul uses the same term ἀπολύτρωσις to refer to redemption in Christ Jesus (ἀπολύτρωσις ἐν Χριστῷ Ἰησοῦ) in Rom 3:23–24: "for all have sinned and fall short of the glory of God; they are now justified by his grace as a *gift*, through the redemption in Christ." Thus, in this sense, υἱοθεσία, namely redemption in Christ is also God's *gift*, not an inalienable possession.

In Rom 9:4, υἱοθεσία refers to the privilege of Israel's divine sonship *before* the new era inaugurated by God's sending of Christ and the Spirit (Gal 4:4–6). But, as I have argued, υἱοθεσία in Rom 9:4 is Paul's radical reinterpretation of Israel's divine sonship tradition in light of the new creation in Christ. This indicates that Israel's gift υἱοθεσία has to be *confirmed* and *fulfilled* by redemption in Christ.

Moreover, Rom 9:30–32 clearly shows that the current plight of Israel is caused by the fact that Israel did not pursue the righteousness out of faith (ἐκ πίστεως), but as if it [righteousness] were out of works (ἀλλ' ὡς ἐξ ἔργων). Here, "the righteousness out of faith" means the righteousness by faith in Christ. Thus, Israel has stumbled over the stumbling stone, namely Christ, because Israel did not believe in Christ, as the combined citation (Isa 28:16 and Isa 8:14) in Rom 9:33 implies: "Behold, I am laying in Zion a stone of stumbling, and rock of offense; and whoever *believes in* him will not be put to shame." Moreover, Paul's emphasis on "faith in Christ" in Rom 10:1–13 confirms that "the righteousness out of faith" in Rom 9:30–32 refers to "righteousness by faith in Christ." The recurrent use of πᾶς with the language of faith (e.g., "everyone who believes": vv. 4, 11, 12, 13) here shows that Israel also needs the redemption by faith in Christ, as Rom 10:12 says, "For there is no distinction between Jew and Greek; the same Lord [Christ] is Lord of all and is generous to all who call on him."

Again, the parable of the olive tree provides evidence that Israel still needs salvation by faith in Christ. In Rom 11:20, Paul says, "They [Israel] were broken off because of their *unbelief*, but you [Gentiles] *stand only through faith*" (τῇ ἀπιστίᾳ ἐξεκλάσθησαν, σὺ δὲ τῇ πίστει ἕστηκας). Nanos interprets ἀπιστία in 11:23 as Israel's "lack of faithfulness" to carry out Israel's calling to announce the message to the nations rather than "unbelief" in Christ as Messiah.[39] Given the contrast between ἀπιστία of the Israelites and πίστις of gentiles in 11:20, his interpretation is unconvincing. If Israel's ἀπιστία refers to their unfaithfulness to the gentile mission, does πίστις of gentiles refer to gentiles' faithfulness to this mission? Rather, the faith in 11:20 seems to refer to "the faith in Christ" that Jesus is Lord and God raised him from the dead (Rom 10:9) or "conversion in response to the gospel."[40] The fact that the theme of "standing through faith" also occurs in Rom 5:2, where Christ is described as the one through whom believers have obtained access into grace, supports the interpretation that the faith in Rom 11:20 refers to the faith in Christ. Israel, therefore, still needs the fulfillment of Israel's gift of υἱοθεσία, the redemption in Christ, in order to be grafted back into the olive tree. Paul describes Israel's regrafting or eventual restoration with the theme of new creation as we shall see below.

(3) Israel's future salvation and the new creation motif

The overall context of Rom 9–11 is about Israel's *future* salvation. Thus, the desire of Paul's heart and prayer to God for Israel is that Israel may be saved (Rom 10:1; cf. 9:2). Moreover, although the phrase "all Israel" in Rom 11:26 can refer to either "the nation of Israel" or "the elect within Israel,"[41] it is clear that the future tense of this verse refers to Israel's future salvation: "all Israel will be saved" (πᾶς Ἰσραὴλ σωθήσεται).[42] The fact that

39. Nanos, "'Gifts and the Calling,'" 7.
40. Jewett, *Romans*, 688.

41. Given the fact that Paul uses Israel in Rom 9–11 for both meanings ("the nation generally" or "the elect from within Israel" particularly as in 9:6b, "not all who are from Israel are Israel"), the latter can be an interpretative option. However, this interpretation has a difficulty in explaining why Paul uses "Israel" with different meanings in v. 25b (here Israel clearly refers to the nation of Israel) and v. 26a. Thus, as Dunn observes, "there is now a strong consensus that πᾶς Ἰσραὴλ must mean Israel as a whole, as a people whose corporate identity and wholeness would not be lost even if in the event there were some (or indeed many) individual exceptions" (Dunn, *Romans 9–16*, 681).

42. Nanos translates this verse as "all Israel will be *protected*" in order to highlight the idea that "these Israelites are being and will continue to be *preserved safely* in their already *preexisting* covenantal standing." The ground for this argument is that a future form of σῴζω is not used to describe saving as in returning to life that which had died, but to keeping alive (Nanos, "'Gifts and the Calling,'" 4–5). However, we should note

the main theme of Rom 9–11 is about Israel's future destiny ironically indicates that the privilege of Israel's divine sonship is at stake.

In fact, Israel's current spiritual reality does not seem secure in Rom 9–11. They have stumbled over the stumbling stone (9:32), have not submitted to God's righteousness (10:3), have not obeyed the good news (10:16), and finally have been cut off from the olive tree because of their unbelief (11:20). Their stumbling and defeat, however, do not mean that God has rejected them (11:1). Israel's current spiritual status is summarized well in 11:28–29:

> As regards the *gospel* they are enemies for your sake; but as regards *election* they are beloved, for the sake of their ancestors; for the *gifts* and the *calling* of God are irrevocable.

I have argued that υἱοθεσία in Rom 9:4 is a keyword to anticipate Paul's argument in Rom 9:6–29 regarding God's election, calling, and creation of Israel, and that it highlights the incongruity of God's gift and the new creation in Christ. We should note that Paul reiterates these themes—election, incongruous gift, and calling—in Rom 11:28–29. This indicates that υἱοθεσία in Rom 9:4 anticipates not only Paul's argument in 9:6–29 but also his overall argument in Rom 9–11.

Since υἱοθεσία in Rom 9:4 signifies God's election, calling, even creation of Israel as "God's sons" and it is freely and graciously given by God, we can include it in the gifts (χαρίσματα) in 11:29. Again, this, however, does not mean that Israel possesses an inalienable privilege as "God's sons," since currently some in Israel (those in unbelief) seem to be cut off from the olive tree so as to lose their status as God's people.

Rather, the meaning that υἱοθεσία is of Israel is this: in terms of God's irrevocable calling and gift (Rom 11:29), υἱοθεσία will always be Israel's. However, at the same time, it can only be *confirmed and fulfilled in Christ*; although Israel is cut off from the olive tree because of their *unbelief* (11:20), the cut-off branches *will be* grafted back in if they do not persist in *unbelief* (11:23a: ἐὰν μὴ ἐπιμένωσιν τῇ ἀπιστίᾳ, ἐγκεντρισθήσονται).

---

that Paul describes Israel's future salvation as "life from the dead" in Rom 11:15. Also, as the thesis statement of Romans, Rom 1:16 (the gospel is the power of God for salvation to the Jew first and also to the Greek) shows, Paul uses σῴζω or its cognate σωτηρία not only for Jews but also gentiles who did not have any covenantal relationship with God before. In Rom 11:11, Paul directly mentions that through Israel's stumbling salvation (σωτηρία) has come to the gentiles. Finally, the terms "to cut off" and "to graft into" in the analogy of the olive tree in Rom 11 have a clear sense of "discontinuity," which his translation does not have (see below).

CHAPTER 6: PAUL'S USE OF υἱοθεσία IN ROMANS 9 IN LIGHT OF NEW CREATION

This is possible because God is able (δυνατὸς γάρ ἐστιν ὁ θεὸς) to graft them in again (11:23). In Rom 1:16–17, Paul says the gospel is the *power of God* (δύναμις θεοῦ) for salvation to everyone who has *faith*, to the Jew first and also to the Greek. The same theme of God's *power* for salvation in 11:23 and 1:16 indicates that Israel's regrafting will be possible only if Israel accepts the gospel through their faith in Christ.

Nanos translates the word ἐξεκλάσθησαν (11:17, 19) as "broken" or "dislocated," not "broken off" or "cut off," in order to imply that although the branches are injured, they remain on the tree.[43] He justifies this interpretation with two main reasons: (1) it fits well with Paul's argument that the Israelites have stumbled, but they have not fallen (11:11); (2) Paul's evident use of the term "cut off" (ἐκκόπτω) in 11:22–24 is just for a rhetorical purpose; in order to emphasise the severity of the threat to their well-being, Paul portrays some Israelites *as if* they were "cut off."[44]

Nanos's interpretation, however, does not seem convincing. First, the most natural meaning of ἐκκλάω is "to *separate* something from something," or "to break *off*," not merely "to bend" or "to break."[45] Second, as Nanos himself admits, Paul's warning to gentiles in 11:22, "otherwise you [Gentiles] *also* will be cut off" (ἐπεὶ καὶ σὺ ἐκκοπήσῃ), indicates that the Israelites were already cut off. Third, Paul says the Israelites will be grafted into (ἐγκεντρισθήσονται) the olive tree again vv. 23–24, which means that they are currently cut off. Finally, this concept of "grafting," which implies the meaning of "transition" of status, does fit well with Paul's previous descriptions of restoration, namely, from "not my people" to "my people," from "not beloved" to "beloved," and from "not my people" to "sons of the living God" (Rom 9:25–6). This also squares with Paul's use of υἱοθεσία (Rom 9:4) to signify the transition of status.[46]

Furthermore, we should note that Paul describes Israel's future salvation using the new creation motif in Rom 11:15, which again implies this sense of "discontinuity" in Israel's restoration:

43. Nanos, "'Gifts and the Calling,'" 6–7; Nanos, "'Broken Branches,'" 339–76.
44. Nanos, "'Broken Branches,'" 372.
45. BDAG, s.v. "ἐκκλάω," 303.
46. Interestingly, Philo compares "grafting" with "adoption" in that both processes share the characteristic of uniting things in order to improve their quality: "to improve such as yield poor crops by inserting grafts into the stem near the roots and joining them with it so that they grow together as one. The same thing happens, I may remark, in the case of men, when adopted sons become by reason of their native good qualities congenial to those who by birth are aliens from them, and so become firmly fitted into the family" (Philo, *De agricultura* 6).

"For if their rejection is the reconciliation of the world, what will the acceptance be but life from the dead!"

Paul here identifies Israel's acceptance with "life from the dead." Some scholars interpret "their rejection" (ἡ ἀποβολὴ αὐτῶν) as an objective genitive "God's rejection of the Jews."[47] However, as Fitzmyer rightly points out, Paul explicitly rebuts the idea that God has rejected his own people in Rom 11:1–2.[48] Moreover, the same causal relation between Israel's transgression and the salvation of the gentiles is also found in Rom 11:11–12:

> Through their [Israel's] transgression (παράπτωμα), salvation has come to the gentiles (11:11)
>
> Their [Israel's] transgression means riches of the world (πλοῦτος κόσμου) (11:12a)
>
> Their [Israel's] loss (ἥττημα) means riches of gentiles (πλοῦτος ἐθνῶν) (11:12b)

This clearly supports the interpretation of ἡ ἀποβολὴ αὐτῶν as a subjective genitive (Israel's rejection [of the gospel]). Particularly, the parallelism between 11:12 and 11:15 is striking: (1) the structure of a sentence is similar (v. 12: if (εἰ) A is B, how much more (πόσῳ μᾶλλον) C?; v. 15: if (εἰ) A′ is B′, what (τίς) will C′ be?); (2) "their transgression" (A) parallels "their rejection" (A′); (2) "riches of the world" (B) parallels "the reconciliation of the world" (B′); (3) "their fullness" (C: τὸ πλήρωμα αὐτῶν) parallels "the acceptance"(C′). We, therefore, should interpret both ἀποβολὴ and πρόσλημψις in a subjective sense, Israel's rejection and acceptance (of the gospel).[49] Thus, we can confirm that Israel's future salvation will be fulfilled only if they accept the gospel through their faith in Christ.

---

47. Moo, *Epistle to the Romans*, 693–94; Cranfield, *Critical and Exegetical Commentary*, 2:562; Longenecker, *Epistle to the Romans*, 887. For example, Moo argues that two points favor the objective genitive "their [the Jews'] rejection [by God]": (1) since its counterpart "the acceptance" (ἡ πρόσλημψις) probably refers to "God's acceptance of the Jews" in light of Rom 14:3 and 15:7, "their rejection" should also be interpreted as the objective genitive, given their contrasting relationship; (2) throughout this section, Paul puts the accent on God's responsibility for Israel's present stubbornness, for instance, in v. 8 ("God has given them a spirit of stupor") and in v. 17 (they have been "cut off [by God]").

48. Fitzmyer, *Romans*, 612.

49. The reason that Israel's rejection/acceptance means their rejection/acceptance of the gospel is that: (1) in Rom 10:16, Paul says, "all [Israel] have not obeyed *the gospel*" (οὐ πάντες ὑπήκουσαν τῷ εὐαγγελίῳ); (2) Israel's spiritual obduracy in Rom

CHAPTER 6: PAUL'S USE OF υἱοθεσία IN ROMANS 9 IN LIGHT OF NEW CREATION 191

The majority of scholars agree that the unparalleled "life from the dead" (ζωὴ ἐκ νεκρῶν) refers to the general resurrection at the eschaton.[50] As seen in the previous chapter, υἱοθεσία in Rom 8 has strong connection with resurrection. Particularly, υἱοθεσία in Rom 8:23 "the redemption of our body" refers to believers' bodily resurrection at the end of time. Thus, υἱοθεσία in Rom 9:4, which anticipates Paul's overall argument in Rom 9-11, can be connected to the apocalyptic hope for new creation in the sense that God's will (re)create Israel at the eschaton.

Also, it is crucial to note that the phrase "reconciliation of the world" (καταλλαγὴ κόσμου) in 11:15a can also be read in the context of the new creation. Paul uses a similar expression in 2 Cor 5:19, "God was in Christ, reconciling the world to himself" (θεὸς ἦν ἐν Χριστῷ κόσμον καταλλάσσων ἑαυτῷ), just after he mentioned the new creation in Christ (2 Cor 5:17). In both passages (Rom 11:13-15 and 2 Cor 5:17-21), Paul is talking about his apostolic ministry (διακονία: Rom 11:13; 2 Cor 5:18) in connection with the reconciliation in Christ.[51] Moreover, Col 1:20 says that "through him [Christ] God was pleased to reconcile (ἀποκαταλλάξαι) to himself all things, whether on earth or in heaven, by making peace through the blood of his cross." Given the fact that Col 1:15-20 describes God's work of creation in Christ, the reconciliation in Christ in Col 1:20 also signifies the new creation in Christ. Thus, Israel's future salvation—regrafting or resurrection at the eschaton—can be understood in the context of new creation.

From the above discussion, we can conclude that the privilege of υἱοθεσία in Rom 9:4 does not mean that Israel does not need redemption in Christ. The possession of that privilege itself does not guarantee their future salvation. Rather, this covenantal privilege will only be confirmed and fulfilled in Christ. Paul already mentioned the advantage of Israel's

---

11:7-10—their eyes' blindness, ears' deafness, and sluggish spirit—indicates their rejection of the gospel message; (3) Paul's designation of Israel as "enemies according to the gospel" in Rom 11:28 also supports this interpretation.

50. E.g., Jewett, *Romans*, 681; Moo, *Epistle to the Romans*, 695-96; Cranfield, *Critical and Exegetical Commentary*, 2:563; Dunn, *Romans 9-16*, 658; Käsemann, *Commentary on Romans*, 307.

51. In 2 Cor 5:18-19, Paul says that God reconciled us to himself *through Christ* and *in Christ* God was reconciling the world to himself. Although there is no occurrence of Christ in Rom 11, Paul uses the theme of reconciliation in connection with Christ in Rom 5:10-11, where he says that we were reconciled to God *through the death of his Son* and we even boast in God through our *Lord Jesus Christ*, through whom we have now received reconciliation.

privileges in Rom 3:1–2, where many commentators find commonality with Rom 9:4:

> "Then what advantage has the Jew? Or what is the value of circumcision?" "Much in every way. To begin with, the Jews were entrusted with the oracles of God."

Paul, however, adds the following statement a few verses later (Rom 3:9):

> "What then? Are we any better off? No, not all; for we have already charged that all, both Jews and Greeks, are under sin."

Since Jews are also under sin, they still need redemption in Christ. As Paul says in Rom 15:8, "Christ has become a *servant of the circumcised* (διάκονος περιτομῆς) on behalf of the truth of God in order that he might confirm the promises given to the patriarchs." In this sense, Israel still needs the fulfillment of the gift of υἱοθεσία in Christ.

4. Conclusion

In this chapter, I have argued that Paul's use of υἱοθεσία in Rom 9:4 represents Paul's radical reinterpretation of the Israelite divine sonship tradition in light of the Christ-event: Paul reads backwards from the Christ-event in terms of (1) the incongruity of grace in Christ and (2) the new creation in Christ which invalidates any ethnic superiority in God's calling and creation of his people. Thus, υἱοθεσία in Rom 9:4 highlights God's election of Israel as his sons regardless of their disqualification. Also, it indicates that God calls and creates his sons without distinction between Jews and gentiles. This interpretation explains well why Paul uses the term υἱοθεσία in Rom 9:4 rather than the language of natural sonship.

Additionally, I have argued that υἱοθεσία in Rom 9:4 is a keyword to open not only Paul's argument in 9:6–29 regarding God's incongruous election, calling, and creation of Israel but also his overall argument in Rom 9–11 regarding Israel's future salvation. The privilege of υἱοθεσία belongs to Israel in the sense of her physical connection to Christ and special status as "natural branches," but Israel still needs the fulfillment of υἱοθεσία through the redemption in Christ in the context of new creation.

Although the "Paul within Judaism" school attracts many recent Pauline scholars because of its rejection of anti-Semitism and its respect for ethnic identity, its interpretation of Paul's use of υἱοθεσία suffers from a failure to take account of incongruous grace and new creation *in Christ*. Moreover, unlike the argument of the "Paul within Judaism" school, υἱοθεσία in Rom 9:4 refers not to Israel's inalienable possession or status but to God's gift for Israel which has to be fulfilled in Christ. Thus, their argument seems to need more secure exegesis of the Pauline texts themselves.

Chapter 7: **Paul's Use of Υἱοθεσία in Galatians 4 in Light of New Creation**

1. Introduction

GALATIANS IS THE ONLY book of the New Testament, in which both the term υἱοθεσία (4:5) and the phrase καινὴ κτίσις (6:15)—which are crucial to the main thesis of the present study—occur. Although many scholars have emphasized the importance of 4:1–7 (the passage about adoption)[1] and 6:11–18 (the passage about new creation)[2] not only in the interpretation of Galatians but also in Pauline theology as a whole, it is striking that there has been no study that focuses on the close relationship between the two themes. However, as we have seen in Paul's use of υἱοθεσία in Romans, Paul uses the term υἱοθεσία in the context of new creation and the two themes have a close relationship.

The substantial question of this chapter, then, is "Are the themes of adoption and new creation related to each other in Galatians?" and the answer to this question is "Yes" as we shall see below. In order to demonstrate the close relationship between Paul's use of υἱοθεσία and the new creation motif, this chapter will use two exegetical methods. First, I will show that since the theme of new creation in 6:15 is a "hermeneutical key," Paul's use of υἱοθεσία in 4:1–7 can be interpreted in light

---

[1]. For example, de Boer claims "4:1–7 is probably the central theological passage of [Paul's] letter to the Galatians" (de Boer, "Meaning of the Phrase," 204). See also Martyn, *Galatians*, 388.

[2]. For example, Betz remarks, "Seen as a rhetorical feature, the *peroratio* [6:11–18] becomes most important for the interpretation of Galatians" (Betz, *Galatians*, 313). See also Lightfoot, *Saint Paul's Epistle to the Galatians*, 220; Deissmann, *Bible Studies*, 347–48.

of the new creation motif. Second, through the exegesis of 4:1–7, I will demonstrate that the passage itself has various echoes of the Adamic narrative in Gen 1–3. Thus, I will show that Paul's use of υἱοθεσία, which lies at the core of the Adamic narrative frame in 4:1–7, can be best explained in light of new creation.

The second aim of this chapter is to have a conversation with the "Paul within Judaism" school of scholars with the results revealed by the exegesis of 4:1–7. Although to some extent there are different voices among the scholars of "Paul within Judaism," the general opinions of this group of scholars on "the descendants of Abraham" and "the sons of God" in Galatians can be summarized as follows. (1) The scholars of "Paul within Judaism" interpret the descendants of Abraham mainly in a literal sense. By doing so, they highlight "ethnicity" or "bloodline" in Israel's identity. (2) Through adoption, gentiles can become descendants of Abraham materially by receiving the Spirit: based on the Greco-Roman understanding of a spirit as a material thing, they (e.g., Hodge and Thiessen) understand the Spirit as a material like blood, with a kind of DNA; for "Paul within Judaism," the ethnic "descendants of Abraham" and "the sons of God" are used as a synonym. (3) The grace of adoption in Gal 4:5 is only for gentiles. Since Jews, the ethnic descendants of Abraham, are already sons of God, the grace of adoption by which believers become sons of God through their faith in Christ is only applicable to gentiles.

These arguments of "Paul within Judaism" in relation to its interpretation of Galatians seem not to recognize the close relationship between the themes of adoption and new creation. Also, they seem to neglect the importance of the Christ-event for both Jews and gentiles. This chapter, therefore, will try to reveal the flaws in their argument through the exegesis of 4:1–7.

2. The theme of new creation as a hermeneutical key to Galatians

As seen above (chapter 4, section 2), the meaning of καινὴ κτίσις in Gal 6:15 has been much debated and is interwoven with anthropology, cosmology, and ecclesiology. Also, we have seen that all these dimensions are important, but the central element should be the cosmological one which can include other dimensions within its framework.

The concept of new creation is not only an important theme of Pauline theology, but it is also the "hermeneutical key" for understanding the main argument of the whole of the letter to the Galatians. According to Betz, who analyzed the argument of Galatians in terms of classical rhetorical theory, Gal 6:11–18 serves as the *peroratio*,[3] which contains "the interpretive clues to the understanding of Paul's major concerns in the letter as a whole" and plays a role as "the hermeneutical key to the intentions of the Apostle."[4] Particularly, Betz argues that the rule of new creation (Gal 6:15–16) represents "the cutting-edge of the letter."[5]

Why is the concept of new creation so crucial for the interpretation of Galatians? We can answer this question in terms of both soteriology (also cosmology) and eschatology. First, in terms of soteriology, the conception of new creation sums up Paul's soteriology of "in Christ" in Galatians. The new creation in Gal 6:15 is closely related to the christological statement of Gal 6:14: "May I never boast of anything except the cross of our Lord Jesus Christ, by which the world has been crucified to me, and I to the world." The cross of our Lord Jesus Christ, here, does not only indicate Christ's death on the cross but also refers to believers' co-crucifixion with Christ where the cosmic event occurs in relation to the relationship between I and the cosmos. Thus, the new creation in Gal 6:15, which is founded on the Christ-event, seems to relate to not only the redemption of humanity but also the redemption of the whole cosmos.

This meaning of new creation in Christ reiterates the christological and soteriological statement of Gal 2:19–20: "I have been crucified with Christ; and it is no longer I who live, but it is Christ who lives in me." The soteriology of "in Christ" also relates to the redemption in Christ from our sin (1:4; 4:4–5), justification by faith in Christ (2:16–17), believers' being children of God in Christ (3:26), baptism into Christ and putting on Christ (3:27), believers' being one in Christ regardless of race, social status and gender (3:28), belonging to Christ (5:24), and the new life in Spirit (5:25). All these new existential situations of believers

---

3. *Peroratio* is the final section of an ancient rhetorical speech and has the two main purposes: (1) to summarize the main points of the speech (*recapitulatio*); (2) to make a strong emotional impression upon them. See Quintilian, *Inst.* 6.1.1–2; Betz, *Galatians*, 313.

4. Betz, *Galatians*, 313. Similarly, many scholars agree that Gal 6:11–18 functions as a concluding summary of the main themes of the epistle (e.g., Mussner, Moo, Dunn, Weima, Bonnard, Becker, et al.). Particularly, Weima argues that "Gal 6:11–18 must be seen as a carefully constructed unit in which Paul adapts and expands the usual closing conventions of the day so that they point back to the key issues of Galatians as a whole" (Weima, *Neglected Endings*, 160).

5. Betz, *Galatians*, 320.

in terms of soteriology and cosmology are well summarized as the new creation in Christ.

Second, in terms of eschatology, the new creation in Christ represents the inauguration of the new age/world in the midst of the present evil age/world. According to Martyn, the central question of the Galatian letter is "What time is it?" He answers this question by saying that:

> It is the time after the apocalypse of the faith of Christ (3:23–25), the time of things being set right by that faith, the time of the presence of the Spirit, and thus the time of the war of liberation commenced by the Spirit. In a word, it is *the time of dawn of the new creation* with its new antinomies (emphasis added).[6]

The eschatological time-frame in Galatians first appears in the letter-opening: "Grace to you and peace from God our Father and the Lord Jesus Christ, who gave himself for our sins to set us free from *the present evil age*" (1:4). The redemption in Christ expressed in the context of the eschatological time-frame also appears in 4:4–5: "But when *the fullness of time* had come, God sent his Son, born of a woman, born under the law, in order to redeem those who were under the law." The eschatological new age has been inaugurated by God's sending his Son into the present evil age. Thus, Martyn calls the temporal contrast between "the present evil age" (1:4) and "the new creation" (6:15) "eschatological dualism."[7]

Similarly, B. Longenecker rightly notes that "for Paul, the two ages are defined only in relation to Christ, the one who rescues Christians from the age of evil (1:4) and has inaugurated a new sphere of existence [new creation] (6:15)." He also notes that both the letter-opening (1:4) and the letter-closing (6:15) have the same emphasis on "the dawning of the new age," and that "Galatians is clearly framed by an eschatological perspective that Paul expects his readers to grasp as being central to his message."[8] This indicates that the main body of Galatians can be interpreted in light of this eschatological frame of new creation.

Due to the significance of the new creation in soteriological, cosmological and eschatological senses for the interpretation of Galatians, we can regard the new creation in Christ as the hermeneutical key for Galatians.

---

6. Martyn, *Galatians*, 573.
7. Martyn, *Galatians*, 153.
8. Longenecker, *Triumph of Abraham's God*, 45–46.

3. Exegesis of Gal 4:1–7

In our investigation of the concept of new creation in Galatians (chapter 4, section 2), we have seen that there is a strong parallelism between Gal 6:14–16 and Gal 3:27–29, and that Gal 3:28 alludes to Gen 1:27. Also, in the above discussion, I have argued that the new creation in Gal 6:15 can be seen as the hermeneutical key for the whole letter.

In addition to this, as many scholars argue,[9] Gal 4:1–7 has strong connections with the immediately preceding paragraph 3:23–29. Gal 4:1–7 begins with the motif of inheritance (4:1), which develops the previous argument of 3:23–29, and also ends with the same motif as a conclusion of this paragraph (4:7).[10] The connection between 3:23–29 and 4:1–7 indicates that the contrast between the era under the law (3:23–25) and the new era in Christ (3:26–29)[11] is closely related to the contrast between the status of minors like slaves (4:1–3) and the status of God's adopted sons after the Christ-event (4:4–7). Thus, we can read 4:1–7 in light of 3:23–29, particularly 3:28, where Paul describes a new identity in Christ regardless of ethnicity, social status, and gender in connection with its allusion to Gen 1:27.

In what follows, I will analyze Gal 4:1–7, where Paul re-narrates the story of transition from slavery under the law to redemption in Christ, with the aim to find out the close connection between Paul's use of υἱοθεσία and the new creation motif. Then, I will interpret Paul's use of υἱοθεσία in Gal 4:5 in light of new creation.

(1) Paul's analogy in vv. 1–2: A Greco-Roman legal principle?

The traditional interpretation is that the inheritance analogy in Gal 4:1–2 refers to Greco-Roman inheritance practices, such as the Roman law *tutela impuberis* ("guardianship for a minor"), specifically the *tutela*

---

9. For example, Dunn, *Epistle to the Galatians*, 210; Moo, *Galatians*, 257; Byrne *Sons of God*, 174; Hays, "Letter to the Galatians," 281.

10. This connection can be strengthened by the parallelism between Gal 3:23–29 and Gal 4:1–7 in the following aspects: (1) the theme of enslavement under the law (3:23–24; cf. 4:1–3); (2) the fulfillment of time (3:25; cf. 4:4–5); (3) the theme of divine sonship (3:26; cf. 4:5–6).

11. Moo expresses this contrast as a "salvation-historical contrast" (Moo, *Galatians*, 257). See also Longenecker, *Galatians*, 161; Dunn, *Epistle to the Galatians*, 210.

testamentaria ("guardianship established by testament").[12] Betz describes the situation of Gal 4:1–2 based on this Roman legal system:

> According to this institution [*tutela testamentaria*] the paterfamilias appoints one or more guardians for his children who are entitled to inherit his property after his death. During the period of time in which the heir (ὁ κληρονόμος) is a minor (νήπιος) he is potentially the legal owner (ὁ κύριος) of the inheritance, but he is for the time being prevented from disposing of it. Although he is legally (potentially) the owner of it all, he appears not to be different from a slave (οὐδὲν διαφέρει δούλου).[13]

Greco-Roman practices, however, do not represent every aspect of the situation Paul describes in 4:1–2 in the following points: (1) although the heir can legally have more than one tutor, the combination of ἐπίτροπος and οἰκονόμος is awkward;[14] (2) while in Roman law the guardianship of a minor ends automatically when the child reaches the age of maturity, Paul says the guardianship lasts "until the time set by the father" (v. 2); (3) Paul's statement that the heir is no better off than a slave does not fit Greco-Roman laws.[15]

In order to explain the first issue—the combination of ἐπίτροπος and οἰκονόμος—Scott suggests that it refers to Egyptian taskmasters in Israel's pre-exodus enslavement, but his argument has no solid evidence.[16]

---

12. According to this law, the heir should be under the supervision of a tutor nominated by his father until fourteen years old and then under a curator appointed by the *praetor urbanus* until twenty-five (Justinian, *Inst.* 1.22–23).

13. Betz, *Galatians*, 202–3.

14. While ἐπίτροπος is often used for the meaning of "guardian of a minor" (e.g., 2 Macc 11:11, 13:2, 14:2), the typical meaning of οἰκονόμος is "manager of a household or estate." There is no certain example of the use of οἰκονόμος for one who has charge of the person or estate of a minor, nor any instance where ἐπίτροπος and οἰκονόμος are used together (Longenecker, *Galatians*, 162–63).

15. Betz, *Galatians*, 203–4; Longenecker, *Galatians*, 163; Moo, *Galatians*, 259; Scott, *Adoption as Sons of God*, 123.

16. To support his argument that the collaboration of ἐπίτροπος and οἰκονόμος refers to state officials, Scott presents three examples (*OGIS* 699; Aristotle, *Pol.* 1315B; *Anthologiarum libri* 9.73.7) (Scott, *Adoption as Sons of God*, 136–37). Even if that is the case, the terms, ἐπίτροπος and οἰκονόμος, do not have any connections to Israel's exodus event. To overcome this flaw in his argument, Scott additionally presents four strands of evidence for identifying the ἐπίτροπος and οἰκονόμος in Gal 4:2 with Egyptian taskmasters (Scott, *Adoption as Sons of God*, 145). These additional grounds for his argument, however, still do not provide any direct connections between the terms (ἐπίτροπος and οἰκονόμος) and Egyptian taskmasters. For detailed criticism of Scott's alleged evidence, see Goodrich, "Guardians, Not Taskmasters," 263–64.

Rather, as John Goodrich well argued, the combination of ἐπίτροπος and οἰκονόμος can be more securely explained by the Roman legal practice of Paul's day, although at first glance it seems awkward.[17] Moreover, the illustration need not be perfectly precise in legal details and its real application. As Moo rightly argues, Paul describes a situation using sufficient analogies to relate to the experience of his readers in order that the illustration he chooses may be effective and meaningful; however, Paul takes "liberties with some of the details of that experience in order to facilitate its application to their spiritual situation."[18] It may be that Paul takes some liberties with exact correspondence when he uses this analogy from Greco-Roman legal practice.

Regarding the second and the third issues ("Why are the minors no better than slaves?" and "Why does the guardianship last 'until the time set by the father' rather than until the minors reach a certain age in the Roman law?"), however, a narrative framework of new creation can provide a reasonable explanation for Paul's adaptation of *tutela impuberis* in 4:1–2. In what follows, I will demonstrate that the narrative in Gen 1–3 provides an important narrative framework for interpreting Gal 4:1–7.

(2) The echoes of Gen 1:28–29 in Gal 4:1 and κύριος πάντων

Most English Bible translations interpret κύριος in 4:1 as "an owner of property." For instance, the NRSV translation of 4:1 is as follows: "My point is this: heirs, as long as they are minors, are no better than slaves, though they are the owners of all the property" (Λέγω δέ, ἐφ' ὅσον χρόνον ὁ κληρονόμος νήπιός ἐστιν, οὐδὲν διαφέρει δούλου κύριος πάντων ὤν). Of course, this is a possible translation in light of Greco-Roman inheritance practice. However, given the fact that one of the main themes of both Gal 3:23–29 and Gal 4:1–7 is the liberation from slavery under the law, κύριος in 4:1 can refer to "lord" or "master" rather than "owner of property." This interpretation fits better with the contrast between "lord" and "slave" in 4:1. Moreover, 4:1 is reminiscent of Gen 1:28–30 in connection with Adam's lordship over the whole creation:

> And God blessed them, saying, "Increase and multiply, and fill the land, and *gain dominion over* (κατακυριεύσατε) it, and *rule*

---

17. See Goodrich, "Guardians, not Taskmasters," 265–73.

18. Moo, *Galatians*, 259; See also Hays, "Letter to the Galatians," 281; Betz, *Galatians*, 203–4; Longenecker, *Galatians*, 163–64.

> *over* (ἄρχετε) the fish of the sea and the winged things of the heaven and *all* the cattle and *all* the land and *all* the creeping things that creep upon the land." And God said, "Behold! I have given to you every herb fit for sowing that sows seed that is upon *all* the land, and *every* tree that has in itself fruit of seed fit for sowing will become your food, and for *all* the wild animals of the land and for *all* the winged things of the heaven and for *every* creeping thing that creeps upon the land that has in itself soul of life. And *all* green fodder will be for food." And it happened in this way. (Gen 1:28–30 LXX, emphasis added)

We should note that in Gal 3:28c, Paul alludes to Gen 1:27, where humankind is described as not only "male and female" but also as made in "the image of God." The phrase, "the image of God" also signifies Adam's lordship over the creation.[19] Also, Gen 1:28 uses the term "κατακυριεύω," a cognate of κύριος. Furthermore, Gen 1:28–30 reiterates πᾶς many times to highlight Adam's lordship over *all* creation. It is probable, therefore, that κύριος πάντων[20] in 4:1 alludes to the Adamic narrative in Gen 1:28–30.

The Adamic narrative in Gen 3 indicates humanity's loss of lordship over the creation: Adam did not only fail to rule over the serpent, but also was seduced by the serpent's deception. As a result, he was driven out from the paradise where he ruled over all creation. As seen above, the Apocalypse of Moses highlights Adam's loss of glory (Apoc. Mos. 20–21). Although there has been much debate about the meaning of the glory (δόξα, Apoc. Mos. 20:2; 21:2, 6) here, it is clear that Adam's loss of glory is related to humanity's loss of their authority as the image of God. In Apoc. Mos. 24:4, thus, God's punishments of Adam include that the animals will rise up against Adam: "And the animals which you

---

19. The term צלם (image) has an Akkadian background which means "the statue of a god or king," and in both Egypt and Mesopotamia "image of god" often refers to a deified king. Psalm 8 also uses similar royal terminology to describe humanity's dominion over the created order, although the term "image of God" does not occur in it. Thus, many scholars interpret the image of God in Gen 1:27 as "God's representatives on earth, commissioned with dominion over the nonhuman part of creation" (F. J. Stendebach, צלם, *TDOT* 12:392; see also E. M. Curtis, "Image of God [OT])," *ABD* 3:391).

20. The term κύριος πάντων can refer to a title of universal sovereignty in both the religious and political spheres in the Greco-Roman culture. For example, Zeus and Osiris are regarded as κύριος πάντων in Plut. *Mor.* 381E and Plut. *Mor.* 355E, respectively. Also, in Aristotle's *Politica*, κύριος πάντων often refers to kingship in a monarchy (e.g., 1286A, 1; 1287A, 11; 1288A, 2). See Scott, *Adoption as Sons of God*, 131–34. In the New Testament, κύριος πάντων is the title for Jesus Christ to signify his lordship over all humanity and the universe (Rom 10:12; Acts 10:36; cf. Phil 2:9–11; Col 1:15–18; Eph 1:20–22).

ruled over will rise up against you in disorder, because you did not keep my commandment" (Καὶ τῶν ἐκυρίευες θηρίων, ἐπαναστήσονταί σοι ἐν ἀκαταστασίᾳ, ὅτι τὴν ἐντολήν μου οὐκ ἐφύλαξας).

Similar to Gal 4:1, 4 Ezra 6:53–59 connects Israel's inheritance of the world to the fact that God created Adam as κύριος πάντων ruling over the creation order: "On the sixth day you commanded the earth to bring forth before you cattle, beasts, and creeping things; and over these you placed *Adam as ruler over all the works which you made*; and from him we have all come, the people from whom you have chosen" (4 Ezra 6:53–54). Ezra, then, asks Uriel why Israel is being oppressed by other nations in spite of the fact that God created this world as the inheritance for Israel, God's first-born son (4 Ezra 6:57–59). The answer to this question would be Adam's disobedience to God's commandment, as 4 Ezra's other passages indicate (4 Ezra 3:7, 20–27; 4:30–31; 7:10–12, 46–48).

Thus, we can confirm that Israel's current situation dominated by other nations is related to the sin of Adam, who is originally created as κύριος πάντων. It is important to note that the important themes, slavery, inheritance, creation, and divine sonship, which also occur in Gal 4:1–7, are interwoven together in 4 Ezra 6:57–59 (see chapter 2, section 7).

The theme that God's people should or will rule over or possess all also occurs in other passages in Paul's letters. For example, in 1 Cor 3:21–22, Paul says, "So let no one boast in men. For *all things are yours*, whether Paul or Apollos or Cephas or the world or life or death or the present or the future—*all are yours.*" Also, in Rom 8:31–39, Paul connects God's everlasting love to believers' prevailing over all spiritual beings and all creation. After Paul points out the fact that God graciously gives us *all things* (v. 33), he says with confidence that in all painful situations we overwhelmingly prevail (ὑπερνικῶμεν) through God who loved us and neither any angelic beings nor anything else in all creation can separate us from God's love (vv. 37–39).

The above discussion explains well why the minors in Gal 4:1 are no better than slaves in spite of their original status as κύριος πάντων. Also, we can find the theme of believers' lordship or ownership over all creation in other passages in Paul. In this context, we can also read the slavery under τὰ στοιχεῖα τοῦ κόσμου in 4:3 in terms of Adam's loss of his lordship over the creation.

CHAPTER 7: PAUL'S USE OF Υἱοθεσία IN GALATIANS 4 IN LIGHT OF NEW CREATION 203

(3) An interpretation of τὰ στοιχεῖα τοῦ κόσμου

Although the debate about the meaning of τὰ στοιχεῖα τοῦ κόσμου in v. 3 continues, as the majority of scholars argue, τὰ στοιχεῖα τοῦ κόσμου is most likely to refer to the physical elements of the world.[21] We should note that ancient Jewish literature often uses στοιχεῖον in connection with God's creation.[22] Particularly, Wisdom of Solomon, where στοιχεῖον occurs twice (7:17; 19:18; cf. 13:1–3) provides important insights for the present study in two respects.

Firstly, in Wis 19:18–21 στοιχεῖον refers to not only earth (γῆ), fire (πῦρ), and water (ὕδωρ) but also *animals* or *creatures* in the context of new creation:

> For the elements (τὰ στοιχεῖα) changed places with one another, as on a harp the notes vary the nature of the rhythm, while each note remains the same. This may be clearly inferred from the sight of what took place. For *land animals* were transformed into *water creatures*, and *creatures* that swim moved over to the *land*. *Fire* even in *water* retained its normal power, and *water* forgot its *fire*-quenching nature. Flames, on the contrary, failed to consume the flesh of perishable creatures that walked among them, nor did they melt the crystalline, quick-melting kind of heavenly food. (Wis 19:18–21 NRSV, emphasis added)

The author of Wisdom of Solomon, here, describes the transformation of the whole creation in the context of God's salvation of his people. The meaning of στοιχεῖον seems to extend to animals beyond earth, water, air, and fire. In Wis 19:6–12, he already mentioned the transformation of *the whole creation* in its nature in the context of new creation:

---

21. Particularly, de Boer demonstrates that "the phrase is a technical expression referring in the first instance to the four elements of the physical universe: earth, water, air, fire" (de Boer, "Meaning of the Phrase," 207). See also Moo, *Galatians*, 260–63; de Boer, *Galatians*, 252–56; Martyn, *Galatians*, 393–406; Hays, "Letter to the Galatians," 282–83; Scott, *Adoption as Sons of God*, 157–60; Hafemann, "Paul and the Exile," 346–48.

22. E.g., Philo, *On the Cherubim* 127; Josephus, *Antiquities* 3.183; Justin, *Dialogue with Trypho* 62.2. Justin's case is particularly interesting since he uses the term στοιχεῖον in connection with God's creation of Adam in Gen 1:26–28, where God creates Adam, the image of God, and gives the authority to rule over all creation. Cf. 2 Pet 3:10, 12: here, the author of 2 Peter uses conflagration for referring to the dissolution of the cosmos at the eschaton. However, within the *Urzeit-Endzeit* framework, this can also be connected to God's creation.

> *For the whole creation in its nature was fashioned anew, complying with your commands, so that your children might be kept unharmed.* The cloud was seen overshadowing the camp, and *dry land emerging where water had stood before, an unhindered way out of the Red Sea, and a grassy plain out of the raging waves,* where those protected by your hand passed through as one nation, after gazing on marvelous wonders. For they ranged like horses, and leaped like lambs, praising you, O Lord, who delivered them. For they still recalled the events of their sojourn, *how instead of producing animals the earth brought forth gnats, and instead of fish the river spewed out vast numbers of frogs. Afterward they saw also a new kind of birds,* when desire led them to ask for luxurious food; for, to give them relief, quails came up from the sea. (Wis 1:.6–12 NRSV, emphasis added)

The author describes the transformation of the whole creation during Israel's exodus event. This transformation includes not only the change of the environment of the world (earth, water, and air) but also the change of creatures living in this environment: the earth emerges where water stood before, and the earth brings forth gnats, and the river spewed out frogs instead of fish, and a new kind of birds appear from the sea rather than in the air.[23]

Secondly, Wis 13:1–3 suggests that non-Jews regard the elements as gods that rule the world:

> For all people who were ignorant of God were foolish by nature; and they were unable from the good things that are seen to know the one who exists, nor did they recognize the artisan while paying heed to his works; but they supposed that either *fire* or wind or swift *air*, or the circle of the stars, or turbulent *water*, or the luminaries of heaven were the *gods that rule the world*. If through delight in the beauty of these things people assumed them to be gods, let them know how much better than these is their Lord, for the author of beauty created them. (Wis 13:1–3 NRSV, emphasis added)

---

23. Similarly, Philo uses στοιχεῖον for describing an interchange of functions between elements (air and earth) in the miracle of manna in the context of new creation: "The copy reproduces the original very exactly: for, as God called up His most perfect work, the world, out of not being into being, so He called up plenty in the desert, changing round the elements (μεταβαλὼν τὰ στοιχεῖα) to meet the pressing need of the occasion, so that instead of the earth the air bore food for their nourishment, and that without labour or travail for those who had no chance of resorting to any deliberate process of providing sustenance" (*Mos.* 2.267).

Here, although the author does not use the term στοιχεῖον, three elements—fire, air, and water—out of the four elements of the physical universe do occur. This text evokes Rom 1:20–25, where humanity does not recognize God's eternal power and divine nature in the things God created but worships and serves the creature rather than the creator. In this regard, "while we were minors, we were enslaved to the elements of the cosmos" (ὅτε ἦμεν νήπιοι, ὑπὸ τὰ στοιχεῖα τοῦ κόσμου ἤμεθα δεδουλωμένοι) in v. 3 can indicate gentile converts' previous pagan religious practices serving idols.

For Jewish converts who do not venerate other gods, "the slavery under the elements of the cosmos" can relate to the Torah-observances (calendrical observances in v. 10, e.g., Sabbath, Passover, etc.). In 4:9–10, Paul identifies the enslavement to the weak and beggarly elements of the cosmos with observing special days, months, seasons, and years. This is because calendrical observances are closely linked to the elements of the cosmos and associated principles (the amount of rainfall, the flow of water/air/heat, the movements of sun, moon, stars, etc.). Second Temple Jewish literature supports this idea. In Jub. 2:8–9, the author connects God's creation of the sun, the moon, and the stars to the calendrical appointments of days, sabbaths, months, feast days, years, sabbaths of years, jubilees, and for all the times of the years (cf. 1 En. 82:7–9). Moreover, in Wis 7:17–19, where the term στοιχεῖα occurs, the activity of στοιχεῖα involves the appointments of times, the alternations of the solstices, the changes of the seasons, and the cycles of the year.

The parallelism between στοιχεῖα and the law is also found in Gal 4:3–5: after Paul talks about our *slavery under* στοιχεῖα, he continues his remark on God's sending of his son, born *under the law*, in order to redeem those who were *under the law*. Thus, Paul's rhetorical question in Gal 4:9, "How can you want to be enslaved to them [στοιχεῖα] again?," is applicable to both gentile converts and Jewish converts: for gentile converts, who worshiped non-gods, they are coming *back* under these elements by coming under the authority of the law; for Jewish converts, they are returning to the slavery under the law, although they were liberated from that slavery by redemption in Christ.

Within the Adamic narrative framework, enslavement under the elements of the cosmos can refer to an inversion of the original created order. Although Adam was created as the image of God who has dominion over the natural world (Gen 1:27–30), he seems to lose this authority after his disobedience to God's commandment as seen above. Also, the

Adamic sin is the cause for God's curse against the earth, resulting in the earth's producing "thorns and thistles" for humanity (Gen 3:17–18). This indicates a change in the creation's nature.

The Apocalypse of Moses rewrites this situation in an interesting manner. As seen above (chapter 2, section 5), when Eve and Seth went to Eden to retrieve some oil for soothing Adam's suffering, a beast attacked them (Apoc. Mos. 10–12). So Eve cried out to the beast, saying, "O you evil beast, do you not fear to attack the image of God?" (10:3). The beast answered back to Eve that the rule of beasts and the change of their nature happened because of Eve's sin (11:1–2). This indicates that Paul's contemporaries could understand the subjection to the elements of the cosmos as the inversion of the original created order within the Adamic narrative framework.

Second Baruch 48:42–43 also indicates the inversion of the created order triggered by Eve's disobedience of God's commandments; Eve obeyed the serpent rather than God: "O what have you done, Adam, to all those who were born of you? And what will be said to the first Eve who obeyed the snake? For this entire multitude is going to corruption." The whole creation's corruption here implies the inversion of the original created order since it is caused by Eve's obedience to the serpent. The descendants of Adam, who had been created as the lord of all [creation] (4:1: κύριος πάντων), became enslaved to the elements of the cosmos (4:2).

Thus, "the slavery under the elements of the cosmos" in v. 3 is relevant to both Jewish and gentile converts. The Adamic narrative framework provides the universality of existence "under the elements of the cosmos" since all humanity are the descendants of Adam. This squares with Paul's statement, "the Scripture imprisoned *all things* under sin" (Gal 3:22: συνέκλεισεν ἡ γραφὴ τὰ πάντα ὑπὸ ἁμαρτίαν).

(4) Who are the "we" and "you" in Gal 4:1–7?

The above reading of "ὑπὸ τὰ στοιχεῖα τοῦ κόσμου" within the Adamic narrative framework offers significant insight into the identification of the personal pronouns "we" and "you" in Gal 4:3–7, which has been hugely debated. The grammatical shifts of personal pronouns in 4:3–7 are very complicated: (1) in vv. 3–5, Paul uses the emphatic καὶ ἡμεῖς in v. 3 and first person plural subject ("*we* were minors," "*we* were enslaved to the elements of the cosmos," and "so that *we* might receive adoption as children"); (2) he, then, changes the subject to second person plural ("*you are sons*") and again changes to first person plural pronoun ("*our hearts*") in the same verse (v. 6: Ὅτι δέ ἐστε υἱοί, ἐξαπέστειλεν ὁ θεὸς τὸ πνεῦμα τοῦ υἱοῦ αὐτοῦ εἰς τὰς καρδίας ἡμῶν κρᾶζον· Αββα ὁ πατήρ); (3) finally, he changes the personal pronoun to second person singular subject in v. 7 ("so *you* are no longer a slave, but a son").

If the above interpretation of "ὑπὸ τὰ στοιχεῖα τοῦ κόσμου" is correct, we can interpret ἡμεῖς in v. 3 in an inclusive sense which refers to both Jewish and gentile believers. Many commentators,[24] however, argue that the first person plural in vv. 3–5 refers to Paul's fellow Jews since (1) in the three earlier passages, where ἡμεῖς occurs, it refers to Jewish Christians (2:15–16; 3:13–14, 23–25).[25] Particularly, in 2:15, Paul explicitly identifies ἡμεῖς with "Jews by birth," (φύσει Ἰουδαῖοι) not gentile sinners (ἐξ ἐθνῶν ἁμαρτωλοί). (2) The unnecessary pronoun ἡμεῖς is intentionally emphatic, suggesting that Paul is speaking especially in the context of his being part of the Jewish community;[26] and (3) Paul's use of "you" in v. 6 suggests that "we" in this verse should be taken in an exclusive sense (Jewish Christian only).[27]

It may be that "we" is used here exclusively for Jewish believers. It is important to note, however, that Paul most commonly uses "we" to include both Jewish and gentile believers in Galatians. For example, Paul uses ὑμῖν and ἡμῶν together without distinction in the salutation of Gal 1:3–4. Given the universality of the gospel message and the fact that Paul calls Galatian believers "sons of God" (Gal 3:27, 4:6–7), we should read πατρὸς ἡμῶν (1:3) and ἁμαρτιῶν ἡμῶν (1:4) in an inclusive sense. Even in 3:13–14 and 3:23–25, it is more probable that ἡμᾶς includes both Jewish and gentile believers. In 3:13–14, ἡμᾶς seems to include the gentiles, since Christ redeemed "us" in order that "in Christ the blessing of Abraham might come to the *Gentiles*" (3:14a). Moreover, the "we" in verse 14b, "*we* might receive (λάβωμεν) the promise of the Spirit through faith," must

---

24. E.g., Longenecker, *Galatians*, 164; Hafemann, "Paul and the Exile," 340–41; Morales, *Spirit and the Restoration*, 121–22; Bergmeier, *Gerechtigkeit, Gesetz und Glaube*, 61–64; Fee, *Galatians*, 146; Bruce, *Epistle of Paul to the Galatians*, 193.

25. Longenecker, *Galatians*, 164; see also Fee, *Galatians*, 146.

26. Fee, *Galatians*, 146; Matera, however, argues that καὶ ἡμεῖς can be understood in either an exclusive sense ("we Jewish Christians") or an inclusive sense ("we Jewish and Gentile Christians") (Matera and Harrington, *Galatians*, 249).

27. Morales, *Spirit and the Restoration*, 121n151. Morales also argues that since νήπιος (v. 3), an allusion to Hos 11:1, connotes Israel's history, "we" refers to Jewish Christians.

include gentile believers since receiving the Spirit forms an *inclusio* with 3:1–5, where Paul refers to the Galatians' experience of the Spirit.[28] In 3:25 (following on from vv. 23–24), "the ἐσμεν includes the Galatians because Paul's substantiation (γὰρ) in v. 26 applies to 'you all' πάντες ἐστε."[29]

We can argue that this tendency, that in Galatians Paul often uses personal pronouns "we" and "you" without distinction in an inclusive sense, is also found in 4:3–7 on the following grounds. First of all, the consistent theme of vv. 5–7 is the divine sonship of believers in an inclusive sense. God sent (ἐξαπέστειλεν) his Son in order that *we* might receive *adoption as sons* (vv. 4–5), and because *you* are *sons*, God sent (ἐξαπέστειλεν) the Spirit of his Son into *our* hearts, crying, "*Abba! Father!*" (v. 6). So *you* are no longer a slave but a *son*, and if a *son* then also an heir, through God (v. 7). Thus, given the theme of believers' divine sonship in vv. 4–7 and the fact that God's sending of his Son and the Spirit is for all believers in salvation history, it is highly probable that both "we" and "you" in vv. 5–7 refer to believers in an inclusive sense.

Secondly, we can explain the reason that Paul uses "you" in vv. 6–7 although it refers to the same object (believers) which the first person plural refers to; in Galatians, Paul often uses "you" in the end of paragraph in order to draw the audience's attention when he says something important to the audience. For example, just after Paul uses the first person plural in 5:1 (For freedom Christ has set *us* free), he uses "you" to gain audience's attention: "Look: I, Paul, say to *you* that if *you* accept circumcision, Christ will be of no advantage to *you*" (5:2: "Ἴδε ἐγὼ Παῦλος λέγω ὑμῖν ὅτι ἐὰν περιτέμνησθε, Χριστὸς ὑμᾶς οὐδὲν ὠφελήσει).

This pattern (the change from the first person plural to the second person plural) also occurs in the paragraph Gal 3:23–29, where Paul is talking about the before and after of the coming of faith. In the first half of the paragraph (3:23–25), Paul uses the first person plural "we": before faith came, *we* were imprisoned (ἐφρουρούμεθα) under the law. Therefore, the law was *our* disciplinarian (παιδαγωγὸς ἡμῶν) until Christ came, so that *we* might be justified (δικαιωθῶμεν) by faith. But now that faith has come, *we* are (ἐσμεν) no longer subject to a disciplinarian.

In the second half of the paragraph (3:26–29), however, Paul concludes this section with the second person plural to make the general point specific to the audience: *you are* (ἐστε) all sons of God through faith

---

28. Moo, *Galatians*, 212.
29. Scott, *Adoption as Sons of God*, 156.

CHAPTER 7: PAUL'S USE OF ΥἱΟΘΕΣΊΑ IN GALATIANS 4 IN LIGHT OF NEW CREATION 209

in Christ. As many of *you* as were baptized (ἐβαπτίσθητε) into Christ have *clothed yourselves* (ἐνεδύσασθε) with Christ. There is no longer Jew or Greek, there is no longer slave or free, there is no longer male and female; for all of *you are* (ὑμεῖς ἐστε) one in Christ Jesus. And if you (ὑμεῖς) belong to Christ, then *you are* (ἐστέ) Abraham's offspring, heirs according to the promise. Particularly, in vv. 26–29, we should note three important points: (1) in v. 26, Paul uses the second person plural for the divine sonship (υἱοὶ θεοῦ ἐστε), the main theme of Gal 4:4–7; (2) in v. 28, the new rule that "there is no longer Jew or Greek" indicates that the second person pronoun ὑμεῖς in v. 28 includes both Jews and gentiles; (3) The two occurrences of ὑμεῖς in the end of the paragraph (vv. 28–29) in particular highlight Paul's intention to speak directly to the Galatian believers for rhetorical purposes. As in Gal 4:1–7, thus, Paul seems to use both "we" and "you" in an inclusive sense.

From the above discussion, at least it becomes clear that the first person pronoun "we" in Gal 4:3–7 may refer only to Jewish believers, but more likely refers to both Jewish and gentile believers. In any case, there is little possibility that "we" refers exclusively to gentile believers.

(5) Paul's allusion to Gen 3:15 in Gal 4:4

We can also interpret Gal 4:4 in the Adamic narrative framework discussed above:

> ὅτε δὲ ἦλθεν τὸ πλήρωμα τοῦ χρόνου, ἐξαπέστειλεν ὁ θεὸς τὸν υἱὸν αὐτοῦ, γενόμενον ἐκ γυναικός, γενόμενον ὑπὸ νόμον (But when the fullness of time had come, God sent his Son, born of woman, born under the law).

The fullness of time (τὸ πλήρωμα τοῦ χρόνου), which parallels "the date set by the father" in v. 3, can refer to God's prophecy about the seed of the woman (τό σπέρμα τῆς γυναικός) in Gen 3:15:

> And I will place enmity between you and the woman, and between your seed and her seed; he will watch carefully your head, and you will watch carefully his heel (καὶ ἔχθραν θήσω ἀνὰ μέσον σου καὶ ἀνὰ μέσον τῆς γυναικὸς καὶ ἀνὰ μέσον τοῦ σπέρματός σου καὶ ἀνὰ μέσον τοῦ σπέρματος αὐτῆς, αὐτός σου τηρήσει κεφαλήν, καὶ σὺ τηρήσεις αὐτοῦ πτέρναν).

Although many modern scholars argue that the text of Gen 3:15 itself does not have any "messianic" implications,[30] the fact that Rom 16:20 alludes to Gen 3:15 in an eschatological sense shows that Paul himself probably knows the messianic connotation of Gen 3:15, as we shall see later. Also, its reception history shows that the messianic interpretation of Gen 3:15 has already existed even before the beginning of early Christianity.

For example, as R. A. Martin argues, the LXX translation of Gen 3:15 indicates the messianic interpretation of Gen 3:15 in relation to its use of the masculine pronoun αὐτός for the seed of the woman. The LXX translator uses αὐτός [the seed of the woman] in spite of the fact that its antecedent is the neuter noun σπέρμα. It is the only case in Genesis, where the LXX literally translates הוא as αὐτός with violence to the gender agreement in Greek between the pronoun and its antecedent.[31] This probably indicates that the LXX supports the messianic interpretation of Gen 3:15.[32] The Jewish references to the messianic significance of Gen 3:15 are also found in the two Palestinian targums (Pseudo-Jonathan and the so-called Fragment Targum).[33] Moreover, the early apologists Justin Martyr and Irenaeus follow this tradition which regards Gen 3:15 as a protevangelium.[34] Particularly, Irenaeus mentions Gal 3:19 and Gal 4:4 in connection with Gen 3:15. Just after quoting Gen 3:15, he identifies the seed in Gen 3:15 with the seed in Gal 3:19 and the Son born of a woman in Gal 4:4:

> For from that time, He who should be born of a woman, [namely] from the Virgin, after the likeness of Adam, was preached as keeping watch for the head of the serpent. This is the seed of which the apostle says in the Epistle to the Galatians, "that

---

30. For example, von Rad puts it, "The exegesis of the early church which finds a messianic prophecy here, a reference to a final victory of the woman's seed, does not agree with the sense of the passage" (von Rad, *Genesis*, 81). See also Westermann, *Genesis*, 260–61; Wenham, *Genesis*, 80–81; Skinner, *Critical and Exegetical Commentary*, 80–82.

31. See Martin, "Earliest Messianic Interpretation," 425–27.

32. Also, in the royal Psalms (Pss 8, 89, 110) and the key text of the Davidic covenant (i.e., 2 Sam 7:1–17), we can find messianic allusions to Gen 3:15 in terms of the themes of "seed" (2 Sam 7:12; Ps 89:5, 30, 37) and "enemies under the messianic king's feet" (Pss 8:6, 89:24, 110:1).

33. Although these Targums interpret the "seed" in Gen 3:15 as the nation Israel, the phrase "in the days of the King Messiah" clearly shows that they take a messianic interpretation of Gen 3:15. See Maher, *Targum Pseudo-Jonathan, Genesis*, 27–28.

34. Justin Martyr, *Dialogue with Trypho* 100; Irenaeus, *Against Heresies* 5.21.1.

> the law of works was established until the seed should come to whom the promise was made." This fact is exhibited in a still clearer light in the same Epistle, where he thus speaks: "But when the fullness of time was come, God sent forth His Son, made of a woman." For indeed the enemy would not have been fairly vanquished, unless it had been a man [born] of a woman who conquered him. (*Against Heresies* 5.21.1)[35]

Here, Irenaeus interprets Gal 4:4 as the fulfillment of the prophecy in Gen 3:15, Christ's conquest over the seed of the serpent. His interpretation is based on the fact that Gal 3:19 and Gal 4:4 use the terms σπέρμα and γυνή which appear in Gen 3:15. Given the Adamic narrative framework of Gal 4:1–3 which I discussed above and also the tradition of the messianic interpretation of Gen 3:15, it is possible that Gal 4:4 alludes to Gen 3:15 in the Adamic narrative framework.

The phrase "born of woman" in Gal 4:4 increases the possibility that Gal 4:4 alludes to the Adamic narrative. Although many scholars argue that the expression "born of woman" in Gal 4:4 is simply "a Jewish locution for a human birth or idiom for being human" (e.g., Job 14:1; 15:14; 25:4; 1QH^a V:30–31; 1QS XI:20–21; cf. Matt 11:1; Luke 7:28),[36] a close look at the occurrences of "born of woman" in early Jewish writings leads us to find a connection between "born of woman" and the Adamic narrative in Gen 1–3, as we have seen in our investigation of the concept of new creation in Qumran literature (chapter 3, section 1).

Particularly, the context of new creation in 1QH^a V:24–37, which we have analyzed in chapter 3, is very similar to Gal 4:1–7 in terms of: (1) the use of the phrase "born of woman" (l. 31). Cf. Gal 4:4; (2) the eschatological dualism between the old age (l. 24: ages of old) and the new age (l. 29: everlasting ages). Cf. Galatians' eschatological dualism between the present evil age and the new creation; (3) God's recovering of humankind's dominion (l. 34). Cf. Gal 4:1–3; (4) God's placing his Spirit in humankind (l. 35). Cf. Gal 4:6; (5) God's appointing the ages (l. 37). Cf. "the date set by the father" in Gal 4:2 and "the fullness of time" in Gal 4:4.

---

35. Coxe et al., *Ante-Nicene Fathers*, 1:548.

36. E.g., Longenecker, *Galatians*, 171; Martyn, *Galatians*, 390; cf. Dunn, *Christology in the Making*, 40–41. Dunn, however, argues that this phrase finds "its answering echo" in Gal 4:5, "in order that we might receive adoption." In other words, for Dunn, Paul's use of "born of woman" in Gal 4:4 indicates Paul's Adam Christology—"Christ as the man who retraced the course of Adam through his fallenness to death," although Dunn agrees with the general argument that the phrase "born of woman" denotes simply "man" (see also Dunn, *Epistle to the Galatians*, 215).

Thus, when Paul was writing Gal 4:1–7, he probably was aware that the phrase "born of woman" can indicate humanity's sinful nature and weakness in the Adamic narrative framework. However, in Gal 4:4 Paul also connects this phrase to the messianic interpretation of Gen 3:15 and uses it in the context of new creation, as in 1QH^a V:24–37.

(6) Christ as the last Adam who recovers Adam's lost authority

As seen above, "born of woman" in Gal 4:4 has close connections with the Adamic narrative in two senses: (1) the messianic implications of the seed of the woman (τό σπέρμα τῆς γυναικός) in Gen 3:15; (2) humanity's sinfulness or weakness in relation to God's creation of Adam from dust in Gen 2:7. This dual meaning of "born of woman" clearly appears in Gal 4:4: (1) God sent his Son as the messiah (the seed of the woman) to redeem his people; (2) For this purpose, the messiah himself should come to this world as the one "born of woman" in the flesh under the law. The messianic theme of "born of woman" is also related to recovering Adam's authority as the image of God to rule over the whole creation (Gen 1:27–28).[37] As the image of God implies Adam's lordship over all creation, believers' new adopted sonship in Gal 4:4–7 can indicate the recovery of this authority. In this regard, Dunn argues that "born of woman" in Gal 4:4 implies the Adam Christology-soteriology:

> "Jesus wholly shared man's frailty and bondage to the law, shared, that is, man's condition as a child of Eve, a descendant of fallen Adam, in order that through his death fallen man might come to share his liberation from the law and sin (cf. Rom 6:5–11), might come to share the Spirit of his sonship. We may paraphrase Paul's underlying thought at this point as follows: Adam was the son of God (cf. Luke 3:38) whose sonship

---

37. Meyer's book title *Adam's Dust and Adam's Glory* expresses well this dual meaning of Adam in Gen 1–3. He argues the use of anthropogonic traditions in the Hodayot and the Pauline letters is dichotomous: "On the hand, the adam-of-dust motif (Gen 2:6–7) forms the basis for the trope of self-abasement and severely problematizes the enjoyment of the privileges involved in election; on the other hand, traditions which are associated with the creation of humanity after the divine image (Gen 1:26–28) or a little lower than elohim (Ps 8) undergird a vision of an exalted, eschatological humanity which is able to enjoy the glory intended for it" (Meyer, *Adam's Dust*, 91–92). His dichotomous explanation of a human nature is interesting and partly true, but his excessive focus on the ontological weakness of humanity based on Gen 2:7 has a tendency to undermine the seriousness of Adam's disobedience itself and the unity of the Adamic narrative in Gen 1–3.

was distorted if not destroyed by the fall; Israel was the son of God whose sonship was something inferior, no better than slavery (Gal 4:1); but Jesus is the son of God who shared that distorted and inferior sonship to the full and to death and by his resurrection made it possible for others to share the full sonship of his risen life"[38]

Although Dunn does not recognize the allusion to the Adamic narrative in Gal 4:1–3, he persuasively describes Paul's underlying thought which appears in Gal 4:4.[39] If Dunn's above argument and my exegesis of Gal 4:1–3 are correct, we can understand Jesus as the last Adam (cf. 1 Cor 15:45, 47) who recovers Adam's lost authority as "the lord of all creation" (Gen 1:26–28; Gal 4:1) and redeems God's people under the law. The last Adam who recovers the authority to rule over all things also appears in 1 Cor 15:21–28:

> For since death came through a human being, the resurrection of the dead has also come through a human being; for as all die in Adam, so all will be made alive in Christ. But each in his own order. Christ the first fruits, then at his coming those who belong to Christ. Then comes the end, when he hands over the kingdom to God the Father, after he has destroyed *every* ruler and *every* authority and power. For he must reign until he has put *all* his enemies under his feet. The last enemy to be destroyed is death. For "God has put *all* things in subjection under his feet." But when it says, "*All* things are put in subjection," it is plain that this does not include the one who put *all* things in subjection under him. When *all* things are subjected to him, then the Son himself will also be subjected to the one who put *all* things in subjection under him, so that God may be *all* in *all* (emphasis added).

Here, Paul contrasts Adam and Christ (cf. Rom 5:12–21; 1 Cor 15:45–49), highlighting Christ's victory against all his enemies and his lordship over all things. Particularly, in vv. 25–27 Paul alludes to Ps 110:1[40]

---

38. Dunn, *Christology in the Making*, 112.

39. His notice of the Lukan genealogy, which traces Christ's ancestors to Adam and ultimately God, is important (Dunn, *Christology in the Making*, 112–13). This does not only describe Christ as Adam's descendant but also indicates Adam's divine sonship. In the Lukan birth narrative, the angel said to Mary about Jesus' lordship and divine sonship: "He will reign over the house of Jacob forever . . . he will be called Son of God" (Luke 1:33–35).

40. The LXX Ps 110:1 reads: Εἶπεν ὁ κύριος τῷ κυρίῳ μου Κάθου ἐκ δεξιῶν μου, ἕως ἂν θῶ τοὺς ἐχθρούς σου ὑποπόδιον τῶν ποδῶν σου. First Corinthians 15:25 (δεῖ γὰρ αὐτὸν

and Ps 8:6[41] to signify Christ's ultimate authority over all creation. It is important to note that these two verses from the Psalms also allude to Gen 3:15 and Gen 1:26–30.[42]

The theme of "putting enemies in subjection under one's feet" or "victory over an evil power" also occurs in Rom 16:20:

> The God of peace will shortly crush Satan under your feet. The grace of our Lord Jesus Christ be with you (ὁ δὲ θεὸς τῆς εἰρήνης συντρίψει τὸν Σατανᾶν ὑπὸ τοὺς πόδας ὑμῶν ἐν τάχει. ἡ χάρις τοῦ κυρίου ἡμῶν Ἰησοῦ μεθ' ὑμῶν).

As many scholars admit, this verse also alludes to Gen 3:15.[43] One important difference of Rom 16:20a from other texts which use the theme of putting enemies under one's feet (e.g., Ps 8:6; 110:1; 1 Cor 15:25–27) is that the enemy is put under the feet of *believers*, not a messianic figure. Rom 16:20b where Paul prays for Christ's grace, however, implies that this victory over Satan is shared by Jesus Christ. This notion clearly

---

βασιλεύειν ἄχρι οὗ θῇ πάντας τοὺς ἐχθροὺς ὑπὸ τοὺς πόδας αὐτοῦ) adapts this verse, replacing his "sitting at God's right hand" with Christ's reign and using the "apocalyptic impersonal δεῖ" to signify a necessity that the prophecy of Scripture should come true (Fitzmyer, *First Corinthians*, 573).

41. The LXX Ps 8:6 reads: κατέστησας αὐτὸν ἐπὶ τὰ ἔργα τῶν χειρῶν σου, πάντα ὑπέταξας ὑποκάτω τῶν ποδῶν αὐτοῦ. First Corinthians 15:27a (πάντα γὰρ ὑπέταξεν ὑπὸ τοὺς πόδας αὐτοῦ) alludes to Ps 8:6b, changing the second person verb of the LXX to the third person verb and replacing ὑποκάτω τῶν ποδῶν with ὑπὸ τοὺς πόδας αὐτοῦ. According to Stanley, this slight change is only for "conforming to Paul's own linguistic usage" (Stanley, *Paul and the Language of Scripture*, 206–7).

42. As Wifall well observes, some "royal" Psalms and "messianic" Psalms have the Davidic background of the messianic portrait in Gen 3:15. In Ps 72:9, the enemies of the Davidic king appear as "bowing down before him" and "licking the dust." Similarly, Ps 8:6b portrays God as having put "all things under his feet" and Ps 110:1 expresses the final destruction of God's foes using the imagery of "making your enemies your footstool" (Wifall, "Gen 3:15," 363). Also, the expression in Ps 8:6a, "giving them dominion over the works of your hands" alludes to Gen 1:26–30.

43. For example, Dochhorn provides several grounds for thinking that Rom 16:20a alludes to Gen 3:15: (1) in both texts, a nonhuman actor is a victim of a man; particularly, the victim's position is under the feet of the man; (2) since the victim is a single actor, Gen 3:15 is more probable background than other texts, for example, Ps 91:13, where the enemies under a man's feet are a multitude of dangerous animals; (3) Paul is one of the earliest authors in early Judaism and Christianity, who use Gen 3 in their writings (e.g., Rom 5:12–21; 7:7–13; 1 Cor 15:22–23; 2 Cor 11:3; cf. Apoc. Mos. as a whole; 4 Ezra 3:6–7, 3:21–22, 7:10–12; 2 Bar. 17:2–3; 23:4; 48:42–43; 54:15–19; 56:5–7); (4) in the early Christian milieu, Gen 3:15 was often understood as a protevangelium, such as Irenaeus (*Against Heresies* 4.40.3; 5.21.1) and Cyprian (*Ad Quir.* 11.9) (Dochhorn, "Paulus und die polyglotte Schriftgelehrsamkeit," 194–95). See also Brown, "'God of Peace,'" 1–14.

CHAPTER 7: PAUL'S USE OF υἱοθεσία IN GALATIANS 4 IN LIGHT OF NEW CREATION   215

appears in 1 Cor 15:56–57: "The sting of death is sin, and the power of sin is the law. But thanks be to God, who gives us the victory *through our Lord Jesus Christ.*"

In 1 Cor 15:21–28, the enemies are every ruler, every authority, power, and ultimately death (vv. 24, 26; cf. 15:56). In Rom 16:20, the enemy is Satan, an evil power, which probably refers to the power of sin and death.[44] In Gal 4:1–7, humanity, who lost the status of the lord of all, is under the slavery of the elements of cosmos. As I argued above, this indicates the inversion of the original created order and it also relates to the Torah-observances. As Rom 16:20, where Paul uses Satan rather than the serpent in Gen 3:15, indicates, a creature can be an agent of an evil power and even can represent it. Thus, Ps 91:13 describes the enemies as creatures: "You will tread on the lion and the adder, the young lion and the serpent you will trample under foot." In a similar manner, the elements of the cosmos in Gal 4:3 can refer to an evil power which controls all creation and dominates humanity.

Although Galatians is less explicit for expressing the power of sin and death, in Gal 3:22, Paul describes this evil power as sin: συνέκλεισεν ἡ γραφὴ τὰ πάντα ὑπὸ ἁμαρτίαν, "the scripture has imprisoned all things under the power of sin." Thus, the ultimate enemy that Christ will destroy in Gal 4:1–7 is not different from that of 1 Cor 15:56 (sin and death).

Lastly, Phil 2:9–11 most clearly expresses Christ's lordship as κύριος πάντων which was originally given to the first Adam:

> Therefore God also highly exalted him and gave him the name that is above *every* name, so that at the name of Jesus *every* knee should bend, in heaven and on earth and under the earth, and *every* tongue should confess that Jesus Christ is *Lord*, to the glory of God the Father (emphasis added).

With the theme of "the form of God" in Phil 2:6 (μορφὴ θεοῦ, cf. ὁμοίωμα in Phil 2:7), which many scholars regard as an allusion to "the image of God" in Gen 1.27,[45] the recurring use of πᾶς and the designation of Jesus

44. In the New Testament, Satan is described as the one who "reigns over an empire of self-enclosed, anti-divine power" (Mark 3:23; Matt 12:26; Luke 11:18), controls "the spirits of disease (Luke 13:16; 2 Cor 12:7; 1 Thess 2:18; 1 Tim 1:20) and death (1 Cor 5:5; cf. 15:26; Heb 2:14)," or "the originator of both sin and wickedness (Mark 4:15; Luke 22:3; John 13:27; Acts 5:3; 1 Tim 5:15; cf. Matt 16:23; Mark 8:33)" (O. Böcher, "σατανᾶς," *EDNT* 3:234). In Romans, Paul often personalizes sin and death as an evil power (e.g., Rom 3:9; 5:12, 21; 6:9; 7:13–14, 24; 8:2–3, 38).

45. Despite the ongoing debate over the interpretation of μορφὴ θεοῦ in Phil 2:6, many scholars (e.g., Cullmann, Dunn, Murphy-O'Connor, Schweizer, Ridderbos,

as κύριος here indicate a Pauline Adam-Christology which resonates with "Lord of all" and "born of woman" in Gal 4:1–7.

In sum, we can interpret Gal 4:1–4 in light of the Adamic narrative in Gen 1–3. Because of the Adamic sin, humanity lost their authority as the image of God to rule over the whole creation. They are no better than slaves under the oppression of the elements of the cosmos, which means an inversion of the original created order. God, however, sent his Son, the *last Adam* to redeem his people from slavery under sin and the law and to recover their authority as the lord of all.

(7) Adoption and new creation

As seen above, the theme of divine sonship in Gal 4:4–7 can relate to the recovery of Adam's authority as the lord of all creation. This context of new creation can be applied to υἱοθεσία in Gal 4:5:

> ἵνα τοὺς ὑπὸ νόμον ἐξαγοράσῃ, ἵνα τὴν υἱοθεσίαν ἀπολάβωμεν (in order to redeem those who were under the law, so that we might receive adoption as sons).

Here, "our receiving υἱοθεσία" parallels "the redemption of those who were under the law." As Martyn well argued, "the law" is "the major enslaving power" in Galatians[46] and is closely related to the power of στοιχεῖα (4:3) and the power of sin (3:22). The term ἐξαγοράζειν (to redeem), which also appears in Gal 3:13,[47] can mean "to deliver or to liberate from something"[48] or "the sacral manumission of slaves" in Greco-Roman culture.[49] Thus, given the parallelism between Gal 4:5a and Gal 4:5b, υἱοθεσία in Gal 4:5 refers to believers' liberation from slavery

---

Caird, Hooker, et al.) equate μορφή with εἰκών in Gen 1:26, 27. For the reception history and the interpretative options of this phrase, see Reumann, *Philippians*, 342–44.

46. Among ten Galatians passages of "under the power of . . ." (ὑπὸ . . .: 3:10, 22, 23, 24–25; 4:2, 3, 4, 5, 21; 5:18), seven are "under the power of the law." According to Martyn, due to the remarkable success of the teachers and their false teaching, Paul should repreach the gospel to the Galatians "only by speaking of the Law as the major enslaving power from which Christ has liberated us" (Martyn, *Galatians*, 371–72).

47. Galatians 3:13 is very similar to Gal 4:5 in that Christ redeems believers from the slavery under the law: "Christ redeemed us from the curse of the law by becoming a curse for us." The curse, here, probably refers to the curse in Gal 3:10: "For all who rely on the works of the law are under a curse; for it is written, 'Cursed is everyone who does not observe and obey all the things written in the book of the law.'"

48. BDAG, s.v. "ἐξαγοράζω," 343.

49. Friedrich Büchsel, "ἐξαγοράζω," *TDNT* 1:124.

under the law. Also, given the close relationship between slavery under the law and slavery under στοιχεῖα, υἱοθεσία in Gal 4:5 can refer to believers' liberation from slavery under στοιχεῖα or their recovery of Adam's lordship over all creation and evil powers.

The theme of inheritance (vv. 1, 7) can support this cosmological interpretation of υἱοθεσία. As seen above, in the Greco-Roman legal practice υἱοθεσία relates to inheritance laws for a childless testator and his adopted heir. This means that υἱοθεσία always entails inheritance. What, then, do the adoptees in Gal 4:5 inherit from God? If my interpretation of κύριος πάντων in Gal 4:1 is correct, believers' inheritance from God would be the whole creation.

Also, Paul reinforces the theme of inheritance in Gal 4:7b: "if a son then also an heir, through God" (εἰ δὲ υἱός, καὶ κληρονόμος διὰ θεοῦ). Paul, then, encourages the Galatians not to return to the slavery under στοιχεῖα in Gal 4:8–9:

> [8] Formerly, when you did not know God [Ἀλλὰ τότε μὲν οὐκ εἰδότες θεὸν], you were enslaved to beings that by nature are not gods. [9] Now, however, that you have come to know God, or rather to be known by God, how can you turn back again to the weak and beggarly elemental spirits? How can you want to be enslaved to them again?

Although the NRSV does not explicitly translate the ἀλλά the first word in v. 8, its role is important to understand the theme of inheritance in v. 7. Contra de Boer's argument that the ἀλλά signals a broad contrast between "the preceding passage (and section) and arguably heads the whole section, extending to 5:12,"[50] Moo rightly argues that we need to have "a narrower focus, contrasting Paul's claim about Christians being 'sons of God' in 4:1–7 with their former life"[51] in v. 8. However, more specifically, the ἀλλά implies the direct contrast between believers' current status as "an heir through God" in v. 7b and their former slavery under "those which by nature are no gods" or στοιχεῖα in vv. 8–9. This contrast indicates that believers' current status as "an heir through God" refers to believers' inheritance of the whole cosmos or their recovered status as the lord of all creation. We can, then, paraphrase Paul's rhetorical question in v. 9 like this: "How can you, who will inherit the whole cosmos, return to your former slavery under στοιχεῖα?" That fact that the theme of "inheritance

---

50. De Boer, *Galatians*, 269.
51. Moo, *Galatians*, 275.

of the whole cosmos" also appears in Rom 4:13 and many parabiblical texts (e.g., Sir 44:21; Jub. 17:3; 22:14; 32:19; 1 En. 5:7; 4 Ezra 6:58–59; Apoc. Sedr. 6:1–2) undergirds this interpretation.

Moreover, Paul's statement in Gal 5:21, "those who do such things [the works of the flesh] will not *inherit* the kingdom of God" (οἱ τὰ τοιαῦτα πράσσοντες βασιλείαν θεοῦ οὐ κληρονομήσουσιν), resonates with the theme of inheritance of the whole cosmos since "the kingdom of God" invokes Christ's lordship over all creation (1 Cor 15:24–28; cf. Col 1:13).

Thus, we can confirm that "receiving υἱοθεσία" in Gal 4:5 indicates believers' liberation from slavery under στοιχεῖα and their recovery of the status as the heir of all creation. This interpretation of υἱοθεσία resonates with my interpretation of υἱοθεσία in Rom 8:23, where υἱοθεσία refers to "redemption of our body" or "believers' bodily resurrection." I underlined the cosmological sense of υἱοθεσία in Rom 8:23, interpreting it as liberation from the slavery under death, or believers' restoration of the image of God in creation, as well as participation in the resurrection of Christ. Also, I argued that Paul's use of υἱοθεσία rather than the language of natural sonship highlights (1) the transition of status and (2) God's incongruous grace in electing his people. This is applicable to υἱοθεσία in Gal 4:5 in the following points.

First, in Gal 4:1–7, Paul describes the transition from the condition of being slaves to the condition of being sons. Particularly, the shift of status in Gal 4:7, "you are no longer a slave but a son" (οὐκέτι εἶ δοῦλος ἀλλ' υἱός) clearly reflects the meaning of transition in υἱοθεσία.

Second, in Gal 4:1–7, Paul's emphasis is on the divine initiative in granting the gift of adoption to his people: (1) it occurs at God's appointed time (v. 2: the date set by the father; v. 4: the fullness of the time); (2) God sent forth (ἐξαπέστειλεν) His Son (v. 4) and the Spirit of His Son (v. 6); (3) believers became an heir through God (διὰ θεοῦ) (v. 7); (4) finally, we "receive" υἱοθεσία in v. 5; that is, υἱοθεσία is given by God. Also, in the Adamic narrative framework in Gal 4:1–7, all human beings are slaves under the law and στοιχεῖα by the influence of the Adamic sin. In this context, υἱοθεσία is God's incongruous gift.

We, therefore, can conclude that as in Romans, Paul uses υἱοθεσία in Gal 4:5 in the context of new creation. We can summarize the close relationship between υἱοθεσία and the new creation motif as follows. First, υἱοθεσία implies the recovery of the Adamic lordship over all creation. This means that υἱοθεσία relates not only to human salvation but also to the restoration of the whole creation. Second, υἱοθεσία conveys the transition of believers' status from slavery to sonship. This transition of status is also closely related to the transition of era, from an era of oppression to an era of new creation, inaugurated by God's sending of his Son and the Spirit. Third, υἱοθεσία as God's incongruous gift means that this is given by God regardless of existing human conditions such as ethnicity, gender, and social status. This fits well with the conception of new creation in Gal 6:15 as well as Paul's statement in Gal 3:28.

(8) The echoes of Ezek 36:26–27 and Jer 31:33–34 in v. 6 and new creation

In v. 6, Paul continues the theme of divine sonship in the context of new creation:

> Ὅτι δέ ἐστε υἱοί, ἐξαπέστειλεν ὁ θεὸς τὸ πνεῦμα τοῦ υἱοῦ αὐτοῦ εἰς τὰς καρδίας ἡμῶν κρᾶζον· Αββα ὁ πατήρ (And because you are sons, God has sent the Spirit of his Son into our hearts, crying, "Abba! Father!").

As many scholars recognize, themes of "Spirit" and "hearts" are echoes of Ezek 36:26–27 and Jer 31:33–34.[52] These two prophetic passages, which are part of the "new covenant,"[53] have many new creation motifs.[54]

We should note that in both passages the purpose of God's action is to make God's people follow the law.[55] This context squares with Gal

---

52. E.g., Martyn, *Galatians*, 391–92; de Boer, *Galatians*, 265; Moo, *Galatians*, 269.

53. Although Ezekiel does not use the term "new covenant" (he uses the term a "covenant of peace" and an "everlasting covenant"; Ezek 16:60; 34:25; 37:26), we can largely regard Ezek 36:26–28 as the new covenant since it is very similar to the new covenant in Jer 31:31–34.

54. We have seen a number of new creation motifs of Ezek 36–37 in ch. 5. Jeremiah 31 also has many new creation and new exodus motifs. Apart from the new exodus motif, we can enumerate the examples of the new creation motifs in Jer 31 as follows: (1) v. 22, "For the Lord has created a new thing on the earth: a woman encompasses a man." Although there are many interpretations of this puzzling verse, some scholars understand it as a new creation motif like that of Isa 65–66 (see Keown, *Jeremiah*, 122); (2) In vv. 12–13, "the plentiful grain, new wine, oil, and the young of flocks and herds," "a well-watered garden," and "no more mourning and sorrow" are typical examples of the bliss of a new heaven and a new earth; (3) v. 35 describes God's creative activities and power: "Thus says the Lord, who gives the sun for light by day and the fixed order of the moon and the stars for light by night, who stirs up the sea so that its waves roar—the Lord of hosts is his name."

55. "I will put my spirit within you, and make you follow my statutes and be careful to observe my ordinances" (Ezek 36:27); "I will put my law within them, and I will

4:1-7 in that Galatian believers have been *liberated from the curse of the law* by God's sending of his Son and the Spirit (Gal 4:4-6). Also, just as Israel shall all *know God* by God's writing the law on Israel's hearts (Jer 31:33-34), so the Galatian believers have come to *know God* in the new era (Gal 4:9) by their liberation from the law. Given the fact that the Adamic sin was Adam's disobedience towards God's commandment, God's sending of the Spirit into believers' hearts is a solution for humanity's plight in the Adamic narrative framework. Thus, in Gal 5:13—6:10, Paul highlights believers' actual life in the Spirit and their liberation from the law by being led by the Spirit (Gal 5:18). The fulfillment of the new covenant, however, is not by following the Torah but by following "the eschatological Torah," "the law of Christ" (Gal 6:2; cf. Gal 5:14).[56]

Thus, the allusions to Ezek 36:26-27 and Jer 31:33-34 in Gal 4:6 do not only fit well with Paul's overall argument but also strengthen the new creation context of υἱοθεσία. The fact that in parabiblical texts the theme of the outpouring of the Spirit often occurs in the context of new creation also undergirds this interpretation (e.g., Jub. 1:23-25; Jos. Asen. 8:9-11; 12:1; 1QH^a V:24-37; 8:14-22; T. Levi 18:1-14).

Another important point of v. 6 is that the Spirit in v. 6 is the Spirit of Christ. Why does Paul highlight that the Spirit God sent is the Spirit of Christ? The answer is probably that Paul wants to emphasize the fact that believers' divine sonship is derivative from Christ's sonship. The exclamation "Αββα ὁ πατήρ," which is reminiscent of Christ's cry in the garden of Gethsemane (Mark 14:36),[57] strengthens this interpretation. Thus, the

---

write it on their hearts" (Jer 31:33). Both passages have emphasis on the divine action to make God's people keep the law.

56. Moo, *Galatians*, 269-70.

57. Scholars have long debated the nature of the "Abba-cry." Some have suggested that this "crying out to God as Father" should be understood as grateful praise or an ecstatic acclamation (e.g., Jewett, *Romans*, 499; Wolter, *Röm 1-8*, 497; Fitzmyer, *Romans*, 501; Meeks, *First Urban Christians*, 88), while others argue that it is an anguished prayer in time of crisis or oppression (e.g., Longenecker, *Epistle to the Romans*, 705; Dunn, *Romans 1-8*, 453; Cranfield, *Critical and Exegetical Commentary*, 1:399; Keesmaat, *Paul and His Story*, 74-75; Byrne, *Romans*, 251). As Cranfield rightly points out, the lexical evidence favors the latter interpretation since κράζειν is often used in the LXX of urgent prayer, particularly in Psalms alone more than forty times (Cranfield, *Critical and Exegetical Commentary*, 1:399). Also, the context of the other occurrence of "Abba-cry" in Rom 8:15 is related to not only the language of suffering in vv. 17-18 (particularly, "the suffering of this present time" in v. 18) but also the groaning of the whole creation (v. 22) and the sons of God (v. 23). This context of suffering in the "Abba-cry" strengthens the relationship between the "Abba-cry" in the Pauline letters (Rom 8:15 and Gal 4:6) and Christ's "Abba-cry" in the garden of Gethsemane (Mark 14:36). For the theme of suffering in Galatians, see Dunne, *Persecution and Participation in Galatians*.

fact that the agent of the believers' cry is the Spirit of Christ (τὸ πνεῦμα τοῦ υἱοῦ αὐτοῦ ... κρᾶζον) indicates that υἱοθεσία constitutes the believers' participation in the sonship of Christ (cf. Rom 8:17, 29).

As seen above, the new creation in Gal 6:15 is "new creation in Christ" since it is founded on the Christ-event (co-crucifixion with Christ in Gal 6:14; cf. 2 Cor 5:17). This reinforces the new creation context of υἱοθεσία in Gal 4:5 since (1) υἱοθεσία has become available to believers only after God's sending of Christ; (2) believers participate in Christ's sonship. Thus, we can conclude that the cosmological and christological meaning of new creation in Gal 6:15 squares with the new creation context of υἱοθεσία in Gal 4:5.

4. Conversation with "Paul within Judaism"

In the introduction of this chapter, I mentioned three general arguments of the "Paul within Judaism" school regarding the meaning of descendants of Abraham, the role of the Spirit in being adopted sons of God, and the beneficiaries of the gift of adoption. With the results of my exegesis of Gal 4:1–7, I will examine the legitimacy of their arguments in what follows.

(1) The meaning of the descendants of Abraham: literal or metaphorical?

Hodge and Thiessen argue that there are two sorts of descendants of Abraham in Paul's use of this phrase; the descendants of Abraham by birth (Jews) and the descendants of Abraham by adoption (gentiles).[58] They understand the descendants of Abraham in a literal sense rather than a mere metaphorical sense. For example, Hodge highlights the literal meaning of this phrase by saying that "for Paul, kinship and ethnicity cannot be merely metaphorical, for lineage, paternity, and peoplehood are the salient categories for describing one's status before the God of Israel."[59] This literal understanding of "the descendants of Abraham" leads her to interpret υἱοθεσία as a mechanism to make a gentile believer a descendant of Abraham in a genealogical sense by sharing blood, the Spirit

---

58. Hodge, *If Sons, Then Heirs*, 146–47; Thiessen, *Paul and the Gentile Problem*, 87–91, 121.

59. Hodge, *If Sons, Then Heirs*, 4.

of Christ, who is the seed of Abraham. Also, she regards the descendants of Abraham as a synonym of the sons of God:

> In Paul the spirit serves as a version of "shared blood" in that it provides a tangible, organic connection between Christ and the gentiles. By the incorporation of Christ's spirit in their bodies, the gentiles inherit his ancestry: they "belong to Christ" (or more literally, they are "of Christ," or "a part of Christ") and are thus descendants of Abraham and adopted sons of God (Gal 3:29).

This literal understanding of "the descendants of Abraham," however, has some logical flaws in relation to Paul's use of υἱοθεσία. First of all, in Paul's passages of adoption (Rom 8:14–17, 19–23; 9:1–5; Gal 4:1–7), there is no occurrence of Abraham. Rather, as I have argued, Paul uses υἱοθεσία in connection with the Adamic narrative in the context of new creation. Thus, the argument that υἱοθεσία is a mechanism to make a gentile a descendant of Abraham is questionable. Furthermore, the Adamic narrative strengthens the generality in the Pauline soteriology, which can be applicable to all humanity, not the ethnic particularity in it.

Second, υἱοθεσία concerns how to become a child and heir of God. It is not about adoption into the Abrahamic family, but adoption into the family of God. Also, Christ is important in Gal 4:1–7 not as a seed of Abraham but as the Son of God. We should not conflate these two, parallel, lines of argument in Galatians, as if being the seed of Abraham was *the same as* being a child of God, or Abraham *equivalent to* God.

Thus, it seems more probable that Paul uses the phrase "the sons of Abraham" in a metaphorical sense. Wolter argues that in Gal 3 and Rom 4, Paul uses all ethnic expressions, which refer to the Abrahamic ethnicity, in a metaphorical sense.[60] He presents interesting evidence for this argument. In 1 Cor 10:1, Paul calls the exodus generation the *fathers* of Corinthian believers (οἱ πατέρες ἡμῶν). Here the gentile addresses of 1 Corinthians have no ethnic connection to the exodus generation of Israel. The only way that Paul can describe this exodus generation as the gentile believers' fathers is that they share the salvation of Christ. The rock from which the exodus generation drank the same spiritual drink

---

60. Wolter, "Ethnizität und Identität," 349–51. For example, Wolter argues that Paul uses the expressions such as "our father Abraham" (πατήρ ἡμῶν Ἀβραάμ; Rom 4:12), "sons of Abraham" (υἱοί Ἀβραάμ; Gal 3:7), and "Abraham's offspring" (τοῦ Ἀβραάμ σπέρμα; Gal 3:29) in a metaphorical sense.

was Christ (1 Cor 10:4).⁶¹ Thus, Paul uses the notion of their Israelite ethnicity in a metaphorical sense.

Also, in Rom 9:7–8 and Gal 4:22–31, what determines someone to be included amongst the "sons of God" is not their Abrahamic bloodline but God's promise. In other words, "it is not the children of the flesh who are the children of God, but the children of the promise are counted as descendants" (Rom 9:8). Similarly, Sarah, not Hagar, is believers' mother not according to flesh but according to God's promise (Gal 4:23, 26, 31). Here Paul speaks not literally but allegorically (Gal 4:24: ἀλληγορεῖν). Sarah is our mother (μήτηρ ἡμῶν) in a metaphorical sense.

(2) The role of the Spirit in adoption as the sons of God

As seen above, Hodge interprets Paul's concept of the Spirit as a material thing like blood. She summarizes her material understanding of "spirit" and its role for gentiles' adoption as follows:

> In Romans 8:14–17 and Galatians 4:1–7, Paul seems to be playing on characteristics of *pneuma* assumed by a range of his contemporaries, especially in his representation of *pneuma* as a binding agent which unites the gentiles to Christ. That is the gentiles join Christ by taking his *pneuma* into their hearts, incorporating his substance into theirs. In this way, this procreative *pneuma* creates new kinship, and does so materially.⁶²

Again, she understands Paul's language of kinship literally and argues that this material transformation of gentile believers is enabled by the injection of a material entity, the spirit which operates as a binding agent. Here her understanding of the role of the Spirit is to *create* new kinship, which means that the father-son relationship between God and believers has not been established until the *pneuma* is injected into believers.

Building on Hodge's argument, Thiessen also argues that the Spirit is "the very DNA" of Abraham's seed. He adds, "In receiving the *pneuma*, then, gentiles undergo a material transformation—again, to use a modern analogy, they undergo gene therapy—which addresses their genealogical deficiencies as Gentiles."⁶³ In order to support this argument, he argues that the second purpose clause in Gal 3:14, "so that we might receive the

---

61. Wolter, "Ethnizität und Identität," 250.
62. Hodge, *If Sons, Then Heirs*, 75.
63. Thiessen, *Paul and the Gentile Problem*, 117.

promise of the Spirit through faith" functions as an explication of the first purpose clause in Gal 3:14, "so that in Christ Jesus the blessing of Abraham might come to the Gentiles." He, then, newly interprets the blessing of Abraham (Gen 15:5; 22:16-18) as the promise of the *pneuma*. That is, he interprets the promise that Abraham's seed would be like the stars as the promise that Abraham's seed will be angelic beings or spiritual beings.[64] Thus, he argues that believers' receiving the Spirit in Gal 4:6 indicates believers' material transformation to spiritual beings by the injection of the *pneuma* as a fulfillment of the Abrahamic covenant.

This interpretation of the role of the Spirit in believers' adoption is questionable, however. First of all, Hodge and Thiessen argue that the *pneuma* is a means of establishing a rapport with God which materially creates a *new* kinship.[65] In Gal 4:6, however, Paul says, "because you are sons, God has sent the Spirit of his Son into our hearts, crying, 'Abba! Father!'" That is to say, the father-son relationship between God and his people was already established before God's sending of the Spirit. Thus, the role of the Spirit is important for believers' adoptive sonship of God because of the Spirit's *confirmation* of the kinship, not because of its *creation* of the kinship.

We can find a similar logical relationship between the adoptive sonship and the Spirit in Rom 8:16: "The Spirit himself bears witness with our spirit that we are children of God." Here the role of the Spirit is συμμαρτυρέιν, which means "to testify" or "to confirm" according to BDAG.[66] Paul's adoption passages themselves, therefore, do not support Hodge and Thiessen's argument that the role of the pneuma is to create a new kinship. Rather, the role of the Spirit for believers' adoptive sonship of God is *confirmation* of the divine sonship which is already established before.

---

64. Thiessen, *Paul and the Gentile Problem*, 129–47; To demonstrate this claim he presents three steps. (1) He argues that many early readers of Gen 15:5 and 22:16–18 took the promise to multiply seed like the stars of heaven not merely as a statement of numerical increase of descendants, but also as a statement of qualitative transformation (cf. Sir 44:21; Philo, *Heir* 86–87; QG 4.181). (2) He also argues that many early readers of the Old Testament understood the stars to be angelic or divine beings (e.g., Ps 148:1–3; Job 38:4–7; 1QH[a] IX:11b–14a; Jos. Asen 14:1–4). (3) Finally, he argues that in Paul's day many people thought angelic beings to be pneumatic beings, thus justifying Paul's use of the Abrahamic promise to talk about the promise of the *pneuma* (e.g., Ps 104:4; Jub. 2:2; 1 En. 15:4–6; 1QS III:13–4:26).

65. Hodge, *If Sons, Then Heirs*, 73–75; Thiessen, *Paul and the Gentile Problem*, 115–16.

66. BDAG, s.v. "συμμαρτυρέω," 957.

Secondly, Hodge and Thiessen's understanding of the material *pneuma* is mainly based on Stoic thinking on the *pneuma*.[67] We cannot completely deny the Stoic influence on Paul's thought, but it is more probable that Paul's understanding of the Spirit in the adoption passages is mainly based on the Jewish tradition.[68] As seen above (chapter 5, section 1), Paul uses the theme of the Spirit in Rom 8:14–17 in light of Ezek 36:26–27 and Ezek 37:1–14. Also, themes of "Spirit" and "hearts" in Gal 4:6 allude to Ezek 36:26–27 and Jer 31:33–34. Furthermore, we can find the theme of outpouring of the Spirit in the Jewish apocalyptic literature, where God restores Israel in the context of new creation. In this Jewish tradition of the Spirit in Rom 8:14–17 and Gal 4:6, the Spirit refers to a *power* or an *agent* to enable God's people to obey God's commandants (e.g., Ezek 36:26–27; Jer 31:33–34; Jub. 1:24–25; 1QS IV:2–3; 4Q504 5:17–18) and to rise from the dead (e.g., Gen 2:7; Ezek 37:1–14; 1 En. 47–51; 1 En. 62:15–16; T. Jud. 23–25), not merely a material entity. Also, this Jewish understanding of the Spirit implies a new, future divine gift not part of the already existing structure of the cosmos (in the form of stars or angels).

Finally, Hodge and Thiessen's emphasis on the materiality of *pneuma* seems to intend to highlight the Abrahamic ethnicity in Paul's adoption passages. In Paul's adoption passages, however, Paul highlights God's gift and God's saving activity, not any human qualifications or human

---

67. Hodge, *If Sons, Then Heirs*, 74–75; Thiessen, *Paul and the Gentile Problem*, 115–18. Their material understanding of the *pneuma* seems to be influenced by the studies of Dale Martin and Troels Engberg-Pedersen (See Hodge, *If Sons, Then Heirs*, 185n40; Thiessen, *Paul and the Gentile Problem*, 116).

68. In order to argue for the Stoic influence on Paul's pneumatology, Engberg-Pedersen points out the false dichotomies in Pauline scholarship (e.g., Jewish versus Greco-Roman influence) (Engberg-Pedersen, *Cosmology and Self*, 14–15). However, as John Levison well argues, Engberg-Pedersen "has rehabilitated this Jewish-Hellenistic dichotomy by including Greco-Roman literature to the exclusion of the Jewish tradition" (Levison, "Paul in the *Stoa Poecile*," 427). Compared to his many references to Epictetus, Cicero, the Stoic fragments, Alexander of Aphrodisias, Diogenes Laertius and Galen, Engberg-Pedersen refers to only eleven Jewish biblical texts in his book (*Cosmology and Self*). Hodge's and Thiessen's understanding of the material *pneuma* is heavily indebted to Engberg-Pedersen's study and seems to follow this dichotomy. It is ironic that "Paul within Judaism," which emphasizes Paul's Jewish ancestry, neglects the Jewish tradition in understanding of the Spirit. In the case of Hodge, she refers to a few Jewish texts to support her argument that the Spirit functions to create a new kinship relationship between God and Israel, but she does not use these texts to demonstrate her argument of the material understanding of the *pneuma*. She solely depends on the Greco-Roman context for her argument on the material *pneuma*.

activities. Moreover, what is given here is not a relationship to Abraham, but a relationship to God.

As seen above, Thiessen argues that the Abrahamic covenant in Gen 15:5 and Gen 22:16–18 refers to the promise that the sons of Abraham will be spiritual beings like the stars in heaven. By doing so, Thiessen connects believers' receiving the Spirit in Paul's adoption passages to the Abrahamic covenant and emphasizes the Abrahamic ethnicity. His new interpretation of Gen 15:5 and Gen 22:16–18 as a promise for qualitative transformation to spiritual beings is not convincing, however. If God's promise that Abraham's offspring will be like the stars of heaven would refer to the qualitative transformation of Abraham's offspring, what does the promise that they will be like the sand on the seashore refer to? God's promise in Gen 15:5 and Gen 22:16–18 is not about a qualitative transformation but about a quantitative multiplication. The text itself clearly supports this quantitative interpretation. In Gen 15:5, God brought Abraham outside and ordered him to count the stars if he can count them. God, then, gave the promise that Abraham's descendants would be like the stars. This obviously indicates that God's promise is about the numerical increase of Abraham's descendants. Thus, the theme of the Spirit in Rom 8:14–17 and Gal 4:4–7 has no explicit connection to the Abrahamic covenant. In other words, at no point does Paul make the connection Thiessen presupposes, between the promise in Gen 15:5 and Gen 22:16–18 and the "spiritual" nature of believers in Paul's adoption passages. Rather, in 1 Cor 2:12, Paul contrasts the Spirit of God with the spirit of the world: "Now we have received not the spirit of the world, but the Spirit who is from God, that we might understand the things freely given us by God." Here the Spirit is not a cosmic or natural phenomenon, part of the structure of cosmos, such as stars or heavenly bodies, but a free gift given by God.

Even in Rom 4 and Gal 3, where Paul is talking about the Abrahamic covenant, the main focus is Abraham's faith in *God's promise*, not the Abrahamic ethnicity or any other human capacities. Hodge reads πίστις in Gal 3 as "faithful characteristics and actions": "Abraham's trustworthy response to God constitutes the human action which generates this lineage."[69] This is a typical example of the emphasis in the "Paul within Judaism" school on "keeping the law" or "ethical behavior." The πίστις in Rom 4 and Gal 3, however, should be interpreted as "trust"

---

69. Hodge, *If Sons, Then Heirs*, 79–91 (see n6).

in God's promise rather than as "faithfulness."⁷⁰ Also, as the contrast between children born κατὰ σάρκα (Gal 4:23, 29) and children of the promise (Gal 4:23, 28; or children born κατὰ πνεῦμα in Gal 4:29) clearly shows, Paul emphasizes God's promise, not Abrahamic ethnicity in the allegory in Gal 4:21–5:1.

In the same vein, the new creation context in Gal 4:1–7 highlights God's redemptive activities to intervene in the human plight by sending Christ (4:4) and the Spirit (4:6). Paul's use of υἱοθεσία in Gal 4:5 also highlights God's redemption, not any human qualifications. The identity as God's adoptive sons does not mean a particular ethnic identity κατὰ σάρκα or an identity attained by a religious behavior, but a divine identity based on faith in God's promise. As the term υἱοθεσία underlines a concept of incongruity in God's election, the identity as sons of God acquired by υἱοθεσία refers to a divine identity granted by God, not an ethnic or cultural identity.⁷¹

(3) The beneficiaries of the gift of adoption in Gal 4:5

In the above exegesis of Gal 4:1–7, I have argued that the first person pronoun "we" in Gal 4:3–7 refers to both Jewish and gentile believers. This means that in Gal 4:4–5, God sent Christ to redeem those who were under the law, so that we (both Jewish and gentile believers) might receive adoption as sons (ἵνα τὴν υἱοθεσίαν ἀπολάβωμεν). The scholars of "Paul within Judaism," however, argue that the υἱοθεσία in Gal 4:5 is only applicable to gentile believers. For example, Fredriksen's following statement shows well the typical understanding in the "Paul within Judaism" school regarding υἱοθεσία in Gal 4:5:

> Especially in Galatians 3–4, arguing against apostolic competitors who want male believers to be circumcised, Paul stresses that this sonship, *huiothesia*, comes through spirit (thus *pistis*, faithfulness to or confidence in the good news, Gal 3:2–5), not through flesh (the site of circumcision; thus, through the Law).

70. In Rom 4:3, 5 and Gal 3:6, Paul quotes Gen 15:6, where Abraham trusted in (ἐπίστευσεν) God's promise that his descendants will be as countless as the stars in the sky and God reckoned it to him as righteousness. The meaning of πίστις in Rom 4 and Gal 3 follows the meaning of this lead verb πιστεύειν. As Barclay well points out, "the verb πιστεύειν does not and cannot mean 'to be faithful' in the sense of 'to be trustworthy'" (Barclay, "Identity Received from God," 359n16).

71. See Barclay, "Identity Received from God." In particular, see the conclusion of this article.

Spirit binds the believer in and to Abraham's *sperma*, Christ, bringing the gentile into the same family as a son and, thus, as an heir (4:7; cf. 3:26, 29). The ex-pagan gentile thereby becomes a "son of Abraham" apart from the Law, apart from the flesh, and can inherit the promised redemption (3:6–9).[72]

Here Fredriksen argues that υἱοθεσία in Gal 4:5 is only for the ex-pagan gentiles to make them the "sons of Abraham" apart from the law. Similarly to Hodge and Thiessen, she also puts emphasis on the Abrahamic ethnicity in spite of the fact that υἱοθεσία involves being the sons of God, not the sons of Abraham. What, then, is the other way for Jewish believers to be a son of God? She continues her argument on the family unity between redeemed gentiles and ethnic Israelites:

> Paul's kinship language, however, does indeed put his different gentiles all on the same basis: they are siblings together with and through Christ, who is "the first born of many *adelphoi*" (Rom 8:29). But within this family unity, Paul nonetheless asserts his own people's singular, enduring identity. Ethnic Israelites, quite apart from Christ, already have *huiothesia* (Rom 9:4; cf. Exod 4:22, "Israel is my first-born son"); they are already in a family relationship with Christ (Rom 9:5, the Christ is from Israel *kata sarka*); and the *ethnē*—the redeemed nations—rejoice *with* God's people, his *laos*, Israel (Rom 11:1, 15:10; Deut 32:43).[73]

In the above statement, she argues that ethnic Israelites already have υἱοθεσία, quite apart from Christ. In the phrase "apart from Christ," Christ seems to refer to "Christ's death and resurrection" which enable sinners to be sons of God through υἱοθεσία in Gal 4:5. She adds, using another "already," ethnic Israelites are in a family relationship with Christ *kata sarka*. Fredriksen argues that although she was deeply influenced by Gaston and Gager, she cannot follow the argument of *Sonderweg* scholars on two discrete paths to salvation, Torah for Jews and Christ for gentiles.[74] In the above argument, however, she seems to suggest another two paths to be sons of God: Christ for gentiles and *Jewish ethnicity* for Jews.

We can find a similar logic in Hodge and Thiessen's interpretation of υἱοθεσία in Gal 4:5. Both scholars argue that υἱοθεσία in Gal 4 is only for gentile believers. For instance, Hodge remarks: "This adoption, which is foretold in scripture (Gal 3:8) and realized by receiving

72. Fredriksen, *Paul*, 149.
73. Fredriksen, *Paul*, 150.
74. Fredriksen, *Paul*, 234n64.

the spirit of Christ (4:6), aggregatively links these gentiles to Israel."[75] Unlike *Sonderweg* scholars, she argues that both Jews and gentiles need the gospel of Christ. At the same time, however, she claims that what the gospel means for each group differs:

> The relevance of the gospel for gentiles is obvious: through Christ, they receive Abrahamic ancestry and blessings, and therefore establish a new and salvific relationship with God. The relevance of this good news for *Ioudaioi*, who already have these things that the gentiles have recently gained, is that it signals arrival of the awaited time. Through Christ, the nations are coming to Israel, and with Christ's return, the world will soon be God's. Thus Christ's death and resurrection are the first steps in a series of events described in Romans 9–11 (including gentiles coming to God and Israel stumbling) that leads to the final goal: the salvation of "all Israel" (Rom 11:26).[76]

Similarly to Fredriksen, Hodge here claims that Jews *already* have Abrahamic blessings and a salvific relationship with God without the redemption in Christ. The above statement, however, seems self-contradictory; if *Ioudaioi* already have the salvific relationship with God, why do they need to wait for the salvation of "all Israel"? Probably, she means two different ways for Jews and gentiles to have the salvific relationship with God. Two different ways for justification appear in Hodge's argument of *pistis* in Rom 3:30 (εἴπερ εἷς ὁ θεὸς ὃς δικαιώσει περιτομὴν ἐκ πίστεως καὶ ἀκροβυστίαν διὰ τῆς πίστεως):

> In Romans 3:30, Paul argues that both groups are justified through faithfulness, typically understood as the faith of the believer. As I argue in chapter 4, this faithfulness is better understood as belonging to Abraham and Christ and refers to the way God establishes relationships with peoples. It is not a uniform faith of the believer, whether Jew or gentile, that justifies, but the salvific, generative, obedient faithfulness of Christ—modeled in part after Abraham—that justifies. Thus we might paraphrase the verse above: he who makes the circumcised just out of Abraham's faithfulness (and God's faithfulness to Abraham) also makes the uncircumcised just through Christ's faithfulness.[77]

---

75. Hodge, *If Sons, Then Heirs*, 130.
76. Hodge, *If Sons, Then Heirs*, 139.
77. Hodge, *If Sons, Then Heirs*, 139–40.

Here we can find two different types of justification: the justification through Abraham's faithfulness for Jews and the justification through Christ's faithfulness for gentiles. Again, the former type of justification seems to be based on the Abrahamic ethnicity. Although Thiessen argues that *Sonderweg* scholars' two-track scheme fails to do justice to Paul's thought,[78] he seems to basically follow Hodge's new two-track: Abrahamic ethnicity for Jews and Christ's redemption for gentiles.[79]

This emphasis on Abrahamic ethnicity, however, is never Paul's own emphasis in his use of υἱοθεσία. As seen above, the context of new creation in Paul's adoption passages is more relevant to the Adamic descendants under the power of sin, rather than the Abrahamic descendants. In other words, Paul's use of υἱοθεσία signifies the recovery of the divine sonship as the image of God, rather than the acquisition of the Abrahamic ethnicity. Of course, Paul's use of the sons of God and that of the sons of Abraham are closely related to each other, but they are not equivalent.

Also, even when Paul directly deals with the theme of Abraham's dependants (e.g., Rom 4; Rom 9:6–9; Gal 3; Gal 4:21–5:1), Paul's focus lies in God's promise or Abraham's faith in God's promise, not Abrahamic ethnicity. Moreover, the Abrahamic family in these passages is constituted by God's promise through faith, not Abrahamic bloodline: (1) Abraham became the ancestor of all who believe (πατέρα πάντων τῶν πιστευόντων), the circumcised and the uncircumcised alike, through his faith (Rom 4:11–12); (2) those who out of faith (οἱ ἐκ πίστεως) are the descendants of Abraham (Gal 3:7). Furthermore, in Gal 3:26, Paul says that "you are all sons of God through faith in Christ Jesus" (πάντες υἱοὶ θεοῦ ἐστε διὰ τῆς πίστεως ἐν Χριστῷ Ἰησοῦ). Thus, in Paul, Abraham's

---

78. Thiessen, *Paul and the Gentile Problem*, 120, 235n17. He argues that Paul divides humanity into four categories: (1) sarkic Jews who have Christ's *pneuma*; (2) sarkic Jews who lack Christ's *pneuma*; (3) sarkic gentiles who have Christ's *pneuma*; (4) sarkic gentiles who lack Christ's *pneuma*. Based on this new categorization, he argues that sarkic Jews who lack Christ's pneuma also need the good news about Christ Jesus. At the same time, he adds that Jews need the gospel for somewhat different reasons than gentiles do. However, he argues that Paul does not explicitly talk about why Jews also need the gospel of Jesus. Also, Thiessen does not explain how Jews can acquire Christ's *pneuma*. In other words, Thiessen argues that Paul is talking about only the gentile problem and solution, not explicitly talking about the Jewish problem and solution. If Jews also need Christ's *pneuma*, how they can receive the *pneuma*? Thiessen does not say anything about it.

79. As he admits, when Thiessen analyzes Abrahamic sonship in Gal 3 and υἱοθεσία in Gal 4 he follows Hodge's exegesis of Gal 3–4 (Thiessen, *Paul and the Gentile Problem*, 105, 114). Also, as the book title implies, υἱοθεσία in Gal 4 is a solution only for gentiles, which solves the gentile problem by receiving the blood-like pneuma and makes them the sons of Abraham as well as the sons of God (Thiessen, *Paul and the Gentile Problem*, 155).

family is constituted by God's promise through believers' faith in Christ, Jews and gentiles alike. The sons of Abraham can be synonymous with sons of God in this metaphorical sense.

The inclusive meaning of the first person pronoun "we" in Gal 4:3–7 and Paul's metaphorical use of Abraham's descendants not emphasizing the Abrahamic ethnicity in a literal sense, lead us to conclude that υἱοθεσία in Gal 4:5 is applicable to both Jews and gentiles through the redemption in Christ.

5. Conclusion

In this chapter, I have demonstrated that Paul's use of the adoption metaphor in Gal 4:5 is closely related to the new creation motif in Gal 6:15. Since the new creation motif is the hermeneutical key for the interpretation of Galatians as a whole, it is natural that we should interpret Paul's use of υἱοθεσία in light of new creation. In particular, in Gal 4:1–7, Paul continues his discussion on the themes of divine sonship and inheritance in Gal 3:26–29. Since Gal 3:26–29 has clear parallelism with Gal 6:14–16, υἱοθεσία in Gal 4:5 and the new creation motif have a close relationship in terms of the context as well. Furthermore, I argued that Paul wrote Gal 4:1–7 within the Adamic narrative framework in Gen 1–3. Within this narrative framework, I interpreted κύριος πάντων, στοιχεῖα τοῦ κόσμου, γενόμενον ἐκ γυναικός, and υἱοθεσία.

Also, with the results of the exegesis of Gal 4:1–7, I had a conversation with scholars of "Paul within Judaism" (Hodge, Fredriksen, and Thiessen). Keeping a cautious distance from the two-track scheme of *Sonderweg* scholars, they argue that Jews also need the gospel of Jesus Christ, but they do not sufficiently explicate why Jews need it and how the redemption in Christ can be applicable to Jews. Rather, their literal interpretation of the Abrahamic bloodline and overemphasis on it seem to cause them to make a new two-track scheme for salvation: the Abrahamic ethnicity for Jews and the redemption in Christ through υἱοθεσία for gentiles. The close relationship between Paul's adoption metaphor and the new creation motif, however, reveals the flaws in their interpretation. Paul does not use the adoption metaphor to show that gentile converts can acquire the status as the sons of Abraham in a literal sense. Rather, he uses υἱοθεσία to signify that all descendants of Adam, Jews and gentiles alike, can recover the image of God or the status of sons of God, only in Christ.

Chapter 8: Conclusions

IN THE PRESENT STUDY, we have investigated various Second Temple Jewish writings and have analyzed the relevant Pauline texts not only to demonstrate the close relationship between the new creation motif and Paul's adoption metaphor but also to interpret Paul's use of υἱοθεσία in light of the new creation motif. With the results of our investigation and analysis, we are now able to provide answers for the questions raised in the introduction and to summarize their implications for Pauline theology, particularly in relation to the "Paul within Judaism" school.

1. The meaning of new creation in Second Temple Jewish literature and in Paul

It is difficult to define the meaning of new creation in a single sentence since in Second Temple Jewish literature the new creation motif appears with various themes and in various contexts. Thus, it is more reasonable to find shared patterns or characteristics of the new creation motif and to decide its implications for Paul's concept of new creation, as we shall see below.

The most important conclusion on the meaning of new creation motif in Part I of the present study is that the new creation motif is often expressed within the *Urzeit-Endzeit* scheme. As seen in the introduction, the studies of Paul's concept of new creation so far have mainly focused on deciding whether it is cosmological or anthropological. Depending on this decision, they have regarded its background as the Isaianic tradition or the Ezekiel/Jeremianic tradition respectively.

CHAPTER 8: CONCLUSIONS

However, through the investigation of parabiblical texts (chapter 2) and Qumran literature (chapter 3), the present study has demonstrated that the concept of new creation in the Second Temple period is more fundamentally based on the creation account and the Adam narrative in Gen 1–3 than on the prophetic traditions, and that it is often described within the *Urzeit-Endzeit* framework. In other words, although at first glance, the concept of new creation in the Second Temple period seems to relate to the themes of Isaiah and Ezekiel/Jeremiah—the creation of "a new heaven and a new earth" or "a new heart and a new spirit"—it is more deeply rooted in the creation account and the Adam narrative in Gen 1–3. Within this *Urzeit-Endzeit* framework, the new creation motif relates to various themes—cosmic renewal (e.g., Jub. 1:29; 1 En. 91:13–17; 2 Bar. 32:1–6; 73:1—74:1; 4 Ezra 7:30–32; LAB 32:16–17), building of a new temple (e.g., Jub. 1:29; 4:26; 1 En. 24:2–4; 91:13–17; 2 Bar. 32:1–6), establishment of a new Eden (e.g., Jub. 4:26; 1 En. 25:3–6; 4 Ezra 7:13, 123; 8:6; LAB 13:9–10), restoration of Adamic glory (e.g., Apoc. Mos. 13:2–5; 39:2–3; 1QS 4:20–23; 1QH^a 4:26f), outpouring of the Spirit (e.g., Jub. 1:23–25; 1QH^a V:24–37; XIX:11–17), and divine sonship (e.g., Jub. 1:23–25; 19:15–30; LAB 16:2–5; 32:16–17; 4 Ezra 6:57–59; 1QS IV:23; 1QS XI:5–9; 4Q418 81:1–5)—in an eschatological context.

This, however, does not mean that the new creation simply repeats the things that happened in the original creation. Rather, the concept of new creation in the early Jewish tradition has strong elements of discontinuity with the first creation in that it often appears in the manner of destroying the former things (e.g., 1 En. 90:28–29; 2 Bar. 44:9–12; LAB 3:10). The strong discontinuity between the previous state and the new creation indicates that the new creation motif occurs in the form of God's intervention in the present sufferings of the world caused by human sin which originally goes back to Adam. In other words, the new creation is God's salvific act for humanity, and it does not mean a simple restoration to the first creation, but an eschatological renewal of the whole creation.

Paul's concept of new creation shares these characteristics of the new creation motif in the Second Temple Jewish literature—the *Urzeit-Endzeit* correlation, Adamic motifs, cosmological renewal, the strong elements of discontinuity, etc. However, what is distinctive in Paul's concept of new creation is that God intervenes in the present sufferings of humankind and the world *through the works of his Son, Christ's death and resurrection*. In this context, Paul describes the new creation as an event which has been *already inaugurated* through the Christ-event, highlighting the present aspect of the new creation.

Christ's death and resurrection not only lead believers to have a new mode of life in its purpose and knowledge (2 Cor 5:15–16) but also bring a new creation to all things in Christ (2 Cor 5:17). Similarly, in Gal 6:14–15, Paul describes the cross of Christ as an event by which "the world has been crucified to me, and I to the world" in connection with a new creation. In other words, the new creation enables the whole world (including humanity) to experience a radical change through the Christ-event, from death to a new life. This concept of new creation, which indicates the fundamental transition from death to life, resonates with the concept of *creatio ex nihilo* which appears in Paul's description of Abraham's faith as directed towards "the God who gives life to the dead and calls into existence the things that do not exist" (Rom 4:17).

2. The close relationship between the adoption metaphor and new creation

The most important conclusion of the present study is that there is a strong connection between Paul's adoption metaphor and the new creation motif. In other words, Paul understands the metaphor of "adoption" within the frame of the "new creation" in Christ, and this affects both the *form* and the *content* of the adoption metaphor. The present study contributes to Pauline scholarship in that there has been no study that correctly recognizes this relationship between Paul's adoption metaphor and the new creation motif. For example, Erin Heim interprets Paul's adoption metaphor as if there were no consistent meaning in it, focusing on different contexts with regard to each of the texts where Paul uses the adoption metaphor. This seems to reflect the fact that she does not correctly recognize the close relationship between Paul's adoption metaphor and the new creation motif.

In order to rightly interpret Paul's adoption metaphor, therefore, we should note the close relationship between the two themes and interpret Paul's use of υἱοθεσία in light of the new creation motif. In what follows, I will summarize the key aspects of the new creation motif in Paul's adoption metaphor in terms of its form and content.

CHAPTER 8: CONCLUSIONS

(1) The form of Paul's adoption metaphor as new creation

A. The new creation eschatology

As Paul's concept of new creation has both present and future aspects in its eschatology, Paul's adoption metaphor can have both present and future meanings at the same time in the eschatological tension between "already" and "not yet." That is, in Rom 8:15 and Gal 4:15, believers are called sons of God since they have *already* received the spirit of adoption through Christ's death and resurrection, while Rom 8:23 describes the situation that believers are *still waiting* for adoption, the bodily resurrection, while they groan inwardly. Also, given the close relationship between Paul's adoption metaphor and the new creation motif and the eschatological context in Rom 9–11, we should regard Israel's privilege of υἱοθεσία in Rom 9:4 as an eschatological privilege, which will be fulfilled in Christ, rather than simply take it as a privilege that Israel already has. The new creation eschatology in Paul's adoption metaphor also relates to the *Urzeit-Endzeit* eschatology, which will be mentioned again when I summarize the content of new creation in the adoption metaphor.

B. A transition of status, from slave to son, with strong elements of discontinuity

Paul's adoption metaphor involves a transition from a previous status, as the new creation motif implies a strong discontinuity with "former things"; it indicates a transition of status from slavery under sin and death to sonship of God. In other words, people who were no better than slaves under the law and στοιχεῖα (Gal 4:1–3) have experienced a dramatic change of status to the status of the sons of God by receiving the spirit of adoption (Rom 8:15; Gal 4:5–6). Byrne's interpretation of υἱοθεσία as simple sonship, not adoption, does not properly catch the sense of transition and discontinuity.

This aspect of discontinuity in Paul's adoption metaphor indicates God's sovereign intervention in the sufferings of humanity and the world. The son, who appears as a slave in Gal 4:1–7, would have to remain in slavery to στοιχεῖα unless he went through the process of adoption. But God sent the Son and his Spirit to redeem and adopt those who had suffered under sin and the law, so they have been newly created as sons of God. In this sense, Paul's use of the adoption metaphor suggests God's apocalyptic intervention for the descendants of Adam who were suffering in the present evil age (Gal 1:4), rather than the gradual fulfillment of the Abrahamic covenant or the climax of the covenant.

C. A Form of *Creatio Ex Nihilo*, a Resurrection/New Life

The sense of discontinuity in Paul's adoption metaphor indicates not simply a transition of status from slavery to sonship but also a transition from death to life. The adoption metaphor in Rom 8:15 well captures this transition from death to life, which consistently appears in Rom 8:1–13. Also, the adoption metaphor in Rom 8:23 points to the redemption of our body, our bodily *resurrection* at the eschaton. In this context, Paul's adoption metaphor indicates God's power which creates life from death, existence from the things that do not exist; it occurs in a form of *creatio ex nihilo*. Scott, unlike Byrne, properly catches the sense of transition in Paul's adoption metaphor, namely from slavery to sonship, but he fails in grasping the meaning of new creation in the adoption metaphor, namely the transition from death to life. This is because he overly depends on the statement in 2 Sam 7:14, "I will be a father to him, and he shall be a son to me," which he regards as the background of the adoption metaphor.

D. An Act of God (as any *Creation* Must Be) and Not a Natural Form of Progression or a Development within the Frame of Human Possibility

The new creation is a salvific act of God which creates life from death, existence from nothing. Thus, when Paul uses the adoption metaphor in the context of new creation, he highlights not only God's calling and election (Rom 9:4; cf. Rom 9:6–29) but also God's power which raised Christ from the dead (Rom 8:15; cf. Rom 8:1–11). Here, any forms of human possibility—any kinds of symbolic capital, for instance, ethnicity or observance of the law—do not work. *God sent his Son and the Spirit in order to redeem those who were under the law, so that they might receive the gift of* υἱοθεσία (Gal 4:4–6). In the context of new creation, what believers should do for adoption is to receive the spirit of adoption (Rom 8:15) and to wait for adoption, the redemption of our body (Rom 8:23). In this sense, υἱοθεσία is God's incongruous gift to sinners by which believers have been given a new identity as sons of God.

(2) The content of Paul's adoption metaphor as new creation

The new creation motif does not only concern the form of Paul's adoption metaphor, but it also affects the content of Paul's adoption metaphor in the following aspects.

A. Multiple echoes of the Genesis narrative within the *Urzeit-Endzeit* framework

Just as the new creation motif appears with various allusions to the narrative in Gen 1–3 within the *Urzeit-Endzeit* framework, so Paul's adoption metaphor occurs in connection with the creation account and Adam narrative: (1) the spirit of adoption in Rom 8:15 is connected to Gen 2:7, where God breathed into Adam's nostrils the breath of life, via its allusions to Ezek 36–37 (chapter 5, section 1); (2) the adoption metaphor in Rom 8:23 appears with many echoes of Gen 3:16–19 in Rom 8:19–23 (chapter 5, section 2); (3) the adoption metaphor in Gal 4:5 can be linked to Gen 1:26–30 in that it relates to the restoration of Adam's lordship over all creation (chapter 7, section 3). Paul's adoption metaphor in Rom 8 and Gal 4, therefore, is expressed within the *Urzeit-Endzeit* eschatology in that it indicates believers' restoration of glory (Rom 8:17, 18, 21, 30; cf. Rom 9:4), righteousness (Rom 8:30, 33), and lordship as the image of God (Gal 4:1–7; Rom 8:29).

B. The cosmological sense of Paul's adoption metaphor

The fact that Paul uses the adoption metaphor in connection with the narrative in Gen 1–3 in the context of new creation implies that υἱοθεσία is not only about humanity but also about the whole of creation; it concerns not only human salvation but also cosmic renewal. The cosmological dimension of Paul's adoption metaphor most evidently appears in Rom 8:19–23, where it is not only the believers but the entire creation that awaits the revealing of the sons of God and υἱοθεσία, i.e., believers' eschatological resurrection. Also, in Rom 8:14–17 and Gal 4:1–7, the adoption metaphor relates to the theme of inheritance, and in this case, what believers will inherit appears to refer to "everything" (Gal 4:1; Rom 8:32; cf. Rom 4:13; Gal 5:21), the whole restored creation. The fact that Paul's adoption metaphor has both anthropological and cosmological aspects in connection with the new creation motif supports Jackson's cosmological interpretation of new creation, which encompasses the anthropological dimension, rather than Hubbard's anthropological interpretation of new creation.

c. It concerns divine sonship, the restoration or fulfillment of Adamic destiny

The most essential content of Paul's adoption metaphor is that it concerns *divine sonship*. This means that it is different from the metaphor of "sons of Abraham" or "sons of Jacob." Rather, Paul's use of υἱοθεσία closely relates to the restoration or fulfillment of Adamic destiny in Christ. Thus, Paul's adoption metaphor is not particular to any one ethnicity, but it incorporates both Jews and gentiles. In this sense, it resonates with Paul's statement that the gospel is the power of God for salvation to *everyone* who believes (Rom 1:16), and that there is *neither Jew nor Greek* since believers are all one in Christ (Gal 3:28). In other words, Paul's use of υἱοθεσία concerns universal humanity as the descendants of Adam rather than Jewish ethnicity as the descendants of Abraham.

d. Christ as new Adam

According to Paul, the new creation occurs in Christ (2 Cor 5:17) only after believers and the world have been crucified by the cross of Christ (Gal 6:14–15). In other words, for Paul, the new creation cannot be correctly understood apart from Christ. Similarly, Paul's adoption metaphor has an inseparable relationship with Christ. First, the spirit of adoption (Rom 8:15) can be connected to "the Spirit of him who raised Jesus from the dead" in Rom 8:11, while Paul identifies it with the Spirit of Christ in Gal 4:6. Also, God sent Christ so that believers might receive adoption as sons (Gal 4:5). Further, the adoption in Rom 8:23, which refers to believers' bodily resurrection, can be linked to Christ since Christ is not only the firstfruits of the resurrection (1 Cor 15:20, 23) but also the firstborn among many brothers (Rom 8:29). Similarly, the purpose of adoption in Rom 8:15 is to make believers heirs of God and joint heirs with Christ (Rom 8:17). Even when Paul speaks of Israel's adoption in Rom 9:4, he is speaking in Christ (Rom 9:1) and emphasizes the physical connection between Israel and Christ (Rom 9:5).

In light of the new creation motif, the close relationship between Paul's adoption metaphor and Christ can be best explained by the fact that Christ plays a role as the last Adam (1 Cor 15:45–47). This provides the answer to the question, "If Paul's adoption metaphor is an Adamic motif, why does Paul not call Adam son of God?" We can answer this question: because adoption to sonship is a feature of the eschatological new creation, that elevates Adamic humanity into a *new sonship* status for which it is fitted, but which it can only attain via the Son, Christ as the new Adam.

3. Conversation with Paul within Judaism

Our interpretation of Paul's adoption metaphor in light of the new creation motif provides the following responses to the main arguments of Paul within Judaism.

(1) Paul—apostle to the nations (pagans): an issue of audience

One of the most important arguments, which the Paul within Judaism scholars share, is that Paul was the pagans' apostle and Paul's audience were not Jews but gentiles. They also argue that the target audience of Paul's discussion about υἱοθεσία in Rom 8 and Gal 4 is gentiles since Israel already possesses the privilege of υἱοθεσία (cf. Rom 9:4). Against this claim, I have demonstrated that Paul's audience in Gal 4:1–7 includes both Jews and gentiles (chapter 7, section 3). Also, I have argued that Israel's privilege of υἱοθεσία in Rom 9:4 does not refer to a permanent *possession* or *right* but indicates a concept of *gift* which will be eschatologically fulfilled in Christ (chapter 6, section 2).

It is uncontroversial that Paul was an apostle for gentiles and that Paul wrote his letters mainly for gentile believers. However, some scholars of Paul within Judaism go one step further and claim that the *gospel of Christ* is *only* for gentiles.[1] That is a totally different story from the fact that Paul was an apostle of gentiles. As Paul had been entrusted with the gospel for the uncircumcised, Peter had been entrusted with the gospel

---

1. For example, Zetterholm argues that "if Paul's gospel concerns the whole of humanity, this perspective [Paul within Judaism] is simply incorrect," highlighting that Paul deals with "the gentile problem." He regards this point ("Paul—Apostle to the Nations") as one of the most important arguments of Paul within Judaism. See Zetterholm, "Paul Within Judaism Perspective," 187.

for the circumcised (Gal 2:7). Moreover, Paul often emphasizes the universality of the gospel by saying that "it [the gospel] is the power of God for salvation to *everyone* who has faith" including both Jews and gentiles (Rom 1:16; 3:9, 23–24; 10:12; 11:32; Gal 3:28; 6:15; 1 Cor 1:23). In this sense, the fact that Paul's adoption metaphor has a deep relationship with the Adam motif in the context of new creation confirms that the gospel concerns the whole of humanity. This is because: just as Adam as a representative of humanity brought sin into the world and death came through sin, so Christ as the new Adam came to the world to save all people who believe in him (Rom 5:12–21; 1 Cor 15:22).

(2) Emphasis on law observance and ethnicity

Another important emphasis of the Paul within Judaism scholars is Paul's "Jewishness," and in this regard, they tend to underscore Torah observance and Jewish ethnicity. For example, Gaston highlights the significance of Torah by saying that "For Paul the Torah is the great privilege of Israel (Rom 2:17–20; 3:1–2; 9:4–5), which, seen in the context of the promises to the Patriarchs and the Sinai covenant, should lead to obedience as the life of faith."[2] As seen above (chapter 7, section 4), this emphasis on Torah observance of the Paul within Judaism appears in their tendency to prefer to understand *pistis* as faithfulness, loyalty, and steadfastness rather than faith.[3] More recently, some of the Paul within Judaism scholars have focused on Jewish ethnicity (e.g., Hodge, Thiessen, et al.). In this context, they understand υἱοθεσία as a means that gentiles can acquire a form of Jewish ethnic identity as the descendants of Abraham (see chapter 7, section 4).

Of course, it is natural that they should emphasize the Jewishness of Paul, who calls himself "a Hebrew of Hebrews" (Phil 3:5). This, however, does not mean that Paul regards law observance or ethnicity as an absolute value. For Paul, what has an ultimate value is neither circumcision nor uncircumcision but a new creation in Christ (Gal 6:15) or knowing Christ, gaining Christ, and being found in Christ (Phil 3:7–9).

As Paul says in Gal 4:5, God sent his Son, born *under the law*, in order that Christ might redeem those who were *under the law*, and that

---

2. Gaston, *Paul and the Torah*, 30.

3. Recently, Nanos himself confirms this tendency of the Paul within Judaism scholars to introduce their main arguments. See Nanos, "Introduction," in *Paul within Judaism*, 8.

believers (both Jews and gentiles) might receive adoption as sons. Also, as the term "adoption" itself indicates, it has nothing to do with any human bloodlines or ethnicities. From the beginning, Israel's adoption (Rom 9:4) came only from God's election, and it indicates that God called those who were "not my people" and "not beloved," and in the very place God created "the sons of the living God" (Rom 9:6–29). In a nutshell, υἱοθεσία is the gift of God, who creates divine sonship from human "nothing" or "undeservedness."

(3) The "two-way solution"

The stress on Torah observance and Jewish ethnicity by Paul within Judaism scholars leads them to suggest a two-way solution model for salvation. For the early Paul within Judaism scholars, this two-way solution means: one path for the salvation of the Jews, through the Torah, and the other path for gentiles, through Christ (see chapter 6, section 2). Some of the recent Paul within Judaism scholars tend to keep a distance from this "two-covenant" model, but they seem to make a new two-track scheme which can be expressed as: the Abrahamic ethnicity for Jews and the redemption in Christ through υἱοθεσία for gentiles (see chapter 7, section 4).

According to Paul's expression, however, Torah observance or the Abrahamic ethnicity belong to "boasting about one's flesh" and have lost their significance as standards of value in the new creation in Christ (Gal 4:23, 29; 6:13; 2 Cor 5:12, 16). The gift of υἱοθεσία is important not only to gentiles but also to Jews in that it will be eschatologically fulfilled in Christ (see chapter 6, section 2). As argued in this study, the fact that Paul's adoption metaphor has a close relationship with Christ, the new Adam, confirms that the grace of υἱοθεσία is necessary for all humanity, as descendants of Adam.

Although here and elsewhere many of my comments about the Paul within Judaism have been critical, I acknowledge the stimulus I have gained by interacting with this new trend in scholarship. As I often use the expression "conversation with Paul within Judaism," the spirit of this study is that of open conversation, which I hope will be continued in the future.

Bibliography

Adams, Edward. *Constructing the World: A Study in Paul's Cosmological Language.* Studies of the New Testament and Its World. Edinburgh: T&T Clark, 2000.
Aland, Barbara, et al., eds. *Novum Testamentum Graece* (Nestle-Aland). 28th ed. Stuttgart: Deutsche Bibelgesellschaft, 2012.
Allen, Leslie C. *Ezekiel 20–48.* Word Biblical Commentary 29. Dallas: Word, 1990.
———. *Psalms 101–150.* 2nd ed. Word Biblical Commentary 21. Nashville: Thomas Nelson, 2002.
Anchor Bible Dictionary (ABD). Edited by David Noel Freedman. 6 vols. New York: Doubleday, 1992.
Attridge, Harold W., et al. *Qumrân Cave 4. VIII: Parabiblical Texts, Part I.* Discoveries in the Judaean Desert 13. Oxford: Oxford University Press, 1994.
Aymer, Albert J. D. "Paul's Understanding of 'Kaine Ktisis': Continuity and Discontinuity in Pauline Eschatology." PhD diss., Drew University, 1983.
Baltzer, Klaus, et al. *Deutero-Isaiah: A Commentary on Isaiah 40–55.* Hermeneia. Minneapolis: Fortress, 2001.
Barclay, John M. G. "An Identity Received from God: The Theological Configuration of Paul's Kinship Discourse." *Early Christianity* 8:3 (2017) 354–72.
———. *Obeying the Truth: A Study of Paul's Ethics in Galatians.* Edinburgh: T&T Clark, 1988.
———. *Paul and the Gift.* Grand Rapids: Eerdmans, 2015.
———. *Pauline Churches and Diaspora Jews.* Wissenschaftliche Untersuchungen zum Neuen Testament 275. Tübingen: Mohr Siebeck, 2011.
Barnett, Paul. *The Second Epistle to the Corinthians.* The New International Commentary on the New Testament. Grand Rapids: Eerdmans, 1997.
Barrett, Charles Kingsley. *A Commentary on the Epistle to the Romans.* Black's New Testament Commentaries. London: Black, 1991.
———. *From First Adam to Last: A Study in Pauline Theology.* 1961 Hewett Lectures. New York: Scribner, 1962.
Bergmeier, Roland. *Gerechtigkeit, Gesetz und Glaube bei Paulus: Der judenchristliche Heidenapostel im Streit um das Gesetz und seine Werke.* Biblisch-theologische Studien 115. Neukirchen-Vluyn: Neukirchener Theologie, 2010.

Bertone, John A. *"The Law of the Spirit": Experience of the Spirit and Displacement of the Law in Romans 8:1–16*. Studies in Biblical Literature 86. New York: Peter Lang, 2005.

Betz, Hans Dieter. *Galatians: A Commentary on Paul's Letter to the Churches in Galatia*. Hermeneia. Philadelphia: Fortress, 1979.

———. "Literary Composition and Function of Paul's Letter to the Galatians." *New Testament Studies* 21:3 (Apr. 1975) 353–79.

Black, Matthew. "The New Creation in 1 Enoch." In *Creation, Christ, and Culture*, edited by Richard W. A. McKinney, 13–21. Edinburgh: T&T Clark.

Black, Matthew, and J. T. Milik. *The Books of Enoch: Aramaic Fragments of Qumrân Cave 4*. Oxford: Clarendon, 1976.

Black, Matthew, et al. *The Book of Enoch or I Enoch: A New English Edition*. Studia in Veteris Testamenti Pseudepigrapha 7. Leiden: Brill, 1985.

Boccaccini, Gabriele. *Beyond the Essene Hypothesis: The Parting of the Ways Between Qumran and Enochic Judaism*. Grand Rapids: Eerdmans, 1998.

———. *Paul's Three Paths to Salvation*. Grand Rapids: Eerdmans, 2020.

Boccaccini, Gabriele, and Jason Zurawski. *Interpreting 4 Ezra and 2 Baruch: International Studies*. Library of Second Temple Studies 87. London: Bloomsbury T&T Clark, 2014.

Brock, S. P. "Jewish Traditions in Syriac Sources." *Journal of Jewish Studies* 30 (1979) 212–32.

Brooke, George J. "Esoteric Wisdom Texts from Qumran." *Journal for the Study of the Pseudepigrapha* 30:2 (Dec. 2020) 101–14.

Brown, Derek R. "'The God of Peace Will Shortly Crush Satan Under Your Feet': Paul's Eschatological Reminder in Romans 16:20a." *Neotestamentica* 44:1 (2010) 1–14.

Brown, Francis, et al. *A Hebrew and English Lexicon of the Old Testament* (BDB). Peabody, MA: Hendrickson, 1979.

Bruce, F. F. *The Epistle of Paul to the Galatians: A Commentary on the Greek Text*. The New International Greek Testament Commentary. Grand Rapids: Eerdmans, 1982.

Brunner, Emil. *Revelation and Reason: The Christian Doctrine of Faith and Knowledge*. Philadelphia: Westminster, 1946.

Burke, Trevor J. *Adopted into God's Family: Exploring a Pauline Metaphor*. New Studies in Biblical Theology 22. Nottingham: InterVarsity, 2006.

Byrne, Brendan. Review of *Adoption as Sons of God: An Exegetical Investigation into the Background of Yiothesia in the Pauline Corpus*, by James M. Scott. *Journal of Theological Studies* 44:1 (Apr. 1993) 288–94.

———. *Romans*. Sacra Pagina 6. Collegeville, MN: Liturgical, 1996.

———. *Sons of God, Seed of Abraham: A Study of the Idea of the Sonship of God of All Christians in Paul Against the Jewish Background*. Analecta Biblica 83. Rome: Biblical Institute, 1979.

Charles, R. H. *The Book of Enoch: Or I Enoch*. Oxford: Clarendon, 1912.

Charlesworth, James H., ed. *The Old Testament Pseudepigrapha*. Vol. 1: *Apocalyptic Literature and Testaments*. Garden City, NY: Doubleday, 1983.

———. *The Old Testament Pseudepigrapha*. Vol. 2: *Expansions of the "Old Testament" and Legends, Wisdom and Philosophical Literature, Prayers, Psalms, and Odes, Fragments of Lost Judeo-Hellenistic Works*. Garden City, NY: Doubleday, 1985.

Chester, Stephen J. *Conversion at Corinth: Perspectives on Conversion in Paul's Theology and the Corinthian Church*. Studies of the New Testament and Its World. Edinburgh: T&T Clark, 2003.

Childs, Brevard S. *Myth and Reality in the Old Testament*. Studies in Biblical Theology 27. London: SCM, 1960.

Clements, R. E. *Isaiah 1–39: Based on the Revised Standard Version*. New Century Bible Commentary. Grand Rapids: Eerdmans, 1980.

Collins, John J. *Apocalypticism in the Dead Sea Scrolls*. The Literature of the Dead Sea Scrolls. London: Routledge, 1997.

———. *Daniel: A Commentary on the Book of Daniel*. Hermeneia. Minneapolis: Fortress, 1993.

———. "In the Likeness of the Holy Ones: The Creation of Humankind in a Wisdom Text from Qumran." In *The Provo International Conference on the Dead Sea Scrolls*, edited by D. W. Parry and E. Ulrich, 609–18. Studies on the Texts of the Desert of Judah 30. Leiden: Brill, 1999.

———. *Jewish Wisdom in the Hellenistic Age*. Old Testament Library. Louisville: Westminster John Knox, 1997.

Cook, James I. "The Concept of Adoption in the Theology of Paul." In *Saved by Hope: Essays in Honor of Richard C. Oudersluys*, edited by James I. Cook, 133–44. Grand Rapids: Eerdmans, 1978.

Coxe, Arthur Cleveland, et al., eds. *Ante-Nicene Fathers*. Vol. 1: *The Apostolic Fathers with Justin Martyr and Irenaeus*. Edinburgh: T&T Clark, 1887.

Cranfield, C. E. B. *A Critical and Exegetical Commentary on the Epistle to The Romans*. 2 vols. 6th ed. The International Critical Commentary. Edinburgh: T&T Clark, 1975.

———. "Some Observations on Romans 8:19–21." In *Reconciliation and Hope: New Testament Essays on Atonement and Eschatology Presented to L. L. Morris on His 60th Birthday*, edited by Robert Banks, 224–30. Grand Rapids: Eerdmans, 1974.

Cross, Frank Moore. *The Ancient Library of Qumrân and Modern Biblical Studies*. London: Duckworth, 1958.

Cullmann, Oscar. *The Christology of the New Testament*. London: SCM, 1959.

———. *Salvation in History*. The New Testament Library. London: SCM, 1967.

Dahl, Nils A. "Christ, Creation, and the Church." In *The Background of the New Testament and Its Eschatology*, edited by W. D. Davies and D. Daube, 422–43. Cambridge: Cambridge University Press, 1956.

Danker, Frederick W., et al. *Greek-English Lexicon of the New Testament and Other Early Christian Literature* (BDAG). 3rd ed. Chicago: University of Chicago Press, 2000.

Day, John. *Yahweh and the Gods and Goddesses of Canaan*. Journal for the Study of the Old Testament Supplement Series 265. Sheffield: Academic Press, 2000.

de Boer, Martinus C. *The Defeat of Death: Apocalyptic Eschatology in 1 Corinthians 15 and Romans 5*. Journal for the Study of the New Testament 22. Sheffield: JSOT Press, 1988.

———. *Galatians: A Commentary*. The New Testament Library. Louisville: Westminster John Knox, 2011.

———. "The Meaning of the Phrase τὰ στοιχεῖα τοῦ κόσμου in Galatians." *New Testament Studies* 53:2 (Apr. 2007) 204–24.

———. "Salvation History in Galatians? A Response to Bruce W. Longenecker and Jason Maston." *Journal for the Study of Paul and His Letters* 2:2 (Sept. 2012) 105–14.

Decock, P. B. "Holy Ones, Sons of God, and the Transcendent Future of the Righteous in 1 Enoch and the New Testament." *Neotestamentica* 17 (1983) 70–82.

Deissmann, Adolf. *Bible Studies: Contributions, Chiefly from Papyri and Inscriptions, to the History of the Language, the Literature, and the Religion of Hellenistic Judaism and Primitive Christianity*. 2nd ed. Edinburgh: T&T Clark, 1903.

Dieterich, Albrecht. "Mutter Erde." *Archiv für Religionswissenschaft* 8 (1905) 1–50.

Dillmann, August. *Das Buch Henoch*. Leipzig: Vogel, 1853.

Dochhorn, Jan. *Der Adammythos bei Paulus und im hellenistischen Judentum Jerusalems*. Wissenschaftliche Untersuchungen zum Neuen Testament 469. Tübingen: Mohr Siebeck, 2021.

———. *Die Apokalypse des Mose: Text, Übersetzung, Kommentar*. Texte und Studien zum antiken Judentum 106. Tübingen: Mohr Siebeck, 2005.

———. "'Denn der Nichtigkeit ist die Schöpfung untergeordnet worden?' (Röm 8,20): Eine kosmologische Aussage des Paulus und ihre exegetischen Hintergründe." In *Paulinische Schriftrezeption*, edited by Markus Öhler Florian Wilk, 57–80. Forschungen zur Religion und Literatur des Alten und Neuen Testaments 268. Göttingen: Vandenhoeck & Ruprecht, 2017.

———. "Paulus und die polyglotte Schriftgelehrsamkeit seiner Zeit: Eine Studie zu den exegetischen Hintergründen von Röm 16,20a." *Zeitschrift für die neutestamentliche Wissenschaft* 98:3–4 (2007) 189–212.

———. "Röm 7,7 und das zehnte Gebot: Ein Beitrag zur Schriftauslegung und zur jüdischen Vorgeschichte des Paulus." *Zeitschrift für die neutestamentliche Wissenschaft* 100:1 (2009) 59–77.

Dodd, C. H., et al. *The Background of the New Testament and Its Eschatology*. Cambridge: Cambridge University Press, 1956.

Doering, Lutz. "*Urzeit-Endzeit* Correlation in the Dead Sea Scrolls and Pseudepigrapha." In *Eschatologie—Eschatology: The Sixth Durham-Tübingen Research Symposium; Eschatology in the Old Testament, Ancient Judaism and Early Christianity*, edited by Hans-Joachim Eckstein et al., 19–58. Wissenschaftliche Untersuchungen zum Neuen Testament 272. Tübingen: Mohr Siebeck, 2011.

Donner, Herbert. "Adoption oder Legitimation? Erwägungen zur Adoption im Alten Testament auf dem Hintergrund der altorientalischen Rechte." *Oriens Antiquus* 8 (1969) 87–119.

Düll, Rudolf. *Das Zwölftafelgesetz: Texte, Übersetzungen und Erläuterungen*. Tusculum-Bücherei. München: EHeimeran, 1971.

Dunn, James D. G. *Christology in the Making: A New Testament Inquiry into the Origins of the Doctrine of the Incarnation*. 2nd ed. London: SCM, 1989.

———. *The Epistles to the Colossians and to Philemon: A Commentary on the Greek Text*. The New International Greek Testament Commentary. Grand Rapids: Eerdmans, 1996.

———. *The Epistle to the Galatians*. Black's New Testament Commentary 9. Peabody, MA: Hendrickson, 1993.

———. "How New Was Paul's Gospel? The Problem of Continuity and Discontinuity." In *Gospel in Paul: Studies on Corinthians, Galatians and Romans for Richard N Longenecker*, edited by L. Ann Jervis and Peter Richardson, 367–88. Sheffield: Sheffield Academic Press, 1994.

———. "Paul and the New Perspective: Second Thoughts on the Origin of Paul's Gospel." *Journal of Theological Studies* 55:1 (Apr. 2004) 266–69.
———. *Romans 1–8.* Word Biblical Commentary 38A. Dallas: Word, 1988.
———. *Romans 9–16.* Word Biblical Commentary 38B. Dallas: Word, 1988.
———. *The Theology of Paul the Apostle.* London: T&T Clark, 2003.
———. *The Theology of Paul's Letter to the Galatians.* New Testament Theology. Cambridge: Cambridge University Press, 1993.
Dunne, John Anthony. *Persecution and Participation in Galatians.* Wissenschaftliche Untersuchungen Zum Neuen Testament 2:454. Tübingen: Mohr Siebeck, 2017.
Eastman, Susan Grove. "Israel and the Mercy of God: A Re-Reading of Galatians 6.16 and Romans 9–11." *New Testament Studies* 56:3 (July 2010) 367–95.
———. "Whose Apocalypse? The Identity of the Sons of God in Romans 8:19." *Journal of Biblical Literature* 121:2 (2002) 263–77.
Eisenbaum, Pamela Michelle. *Paul Was Not a Christian: The Original Message of a Misunderstood Apostle.* New York: HarperOne, 2009.
Elliger, K., and W. Rudolf, eds. *Biblia Hebraica Stuttgartensia.* 5th ed. Stuttgart: Deutsche Bibelgesellschaft, 1997.
Elliott, Mark W., et al., eds. *Galatians and Christian Theology: Justification, the Gospel, and Ethics in Paul's Letter.* Grand Rapids: Baker Academic, 2014.
Engberg-Pedersen, Troels. *Cosmology and Self in the Apostle Paul: The Material Spirit.* Oxford: Oxford University Press, 2010.
Exegetical Dictionary of the New Testament (EDNT). Edited by Horst Balz and Gerhard Schneider. 3 vols. Grand Rapids: Eerdmans, 1990–1993.
Fee, Gordon D. *Galatians: Pentecostal Commentary.* Blandford Forum, UK: Deo, 2007.
Fitzmyer, Joseph A. *First Corinthians: A New Translation with Introduction and Commentary.* Anchor Yale Bible 32. New Haven: Yale University Press, 2008.
———. *Romans: A New Translation and Commentary.* Anchor Bible 33. New York: Doubleday, 1993.
Fletcher-Louis, Crispin H. T. *All the Glory of Adam: Liturgical Anthropology in the Dead Sea Scrolls.* Studies on the Texts of the Desert of Judah 42. Leiden: Brill, 2002.
Fredriksen, Paula. *Paul: The Pagans' Apostle.* New Haven: Yale University Press, 2017.
Frey, Jörg. "Critical Issues in the Investigation of the Scrolls and the New Testament." In *Oxford Handbook of the Dead Sea Scrolls*, edited by J. J. Collins and T. H. Lim, 517–45. Oxford: Oxford University Press, 2010.
Fuchs, C. "Das Leben Adams und Evas." *Die Apokryphen und Pseudepigraphen des Alten Testaments* 2 (1900) 506–28.
Fuchs, Ernst. *Die Freiheit des Glaubens: Römer 5–8 ausgelegt.* Beiträge zur evangelischen Theologie 14. München: Kaiser, 1949.
Furnish, Victor Paul. *II Corinthians.* Anchor Bible 32A. Garden City, NY: Doubleday, 1984.
Gager, John G. *Reinventing Paul.* Oxford: Oxford University Press, 2000.
García Martínez, Florentino. *Qumranica Minora.* Vol. 2: *Thematic Studies on the Dead Sea Scrolls.* Studies on the Texts of the Desert of Judah 64. Leiden: Brill, 2007.
García Martínez, Florentino, and Eibert J. C. Tigchelaar. *The Dead Sea Scrolls: Study Edition.* Grand Rapids: Eerdmans, 1997.
García Martínez, Florentino, and Adam S. van der Woude. "A 'Groningen' Hypothesis of Qumran Origins and Early History." *Revue de Qumran* 14:4 (Apr. 1990) 521–41.
Gardner, Jane F. *Family and Familia in Roman Law and Life.* Oxford: Clarendon, 1998.

Gaston, Lloyd. "Abraham and the Righteousness of God." *Horizons in Biblical Theology* 2 (1980) 39–68.

———. "Paul and the Torah." In *Antisemitism and the Foundations of Christianity*, edited by A. T. Davies, 48–71. New York: Paulist, 1979.

———. *Paul and the Torah*. Vancouver: University of British Columbia Press, 1987.

Gaventa, Beverly. "On the Calling-Into-Being of Israel: Rom 9:6–29." In *Between Gospel and Election: Explorations in the Interpretation of Romans 9–11*, edited by Florian Wilket al., 255–69. Wissenschaftliche Untersuchungen zum Neuen Testament 257. Tübingen: Mohr Siebeck, 2010.

———. "Thinking from Christ to Israel: Romans 9–11 in Apocalyptic Context." In *Paul and the Apocalyptic Imagination*, edited by Ben C. Blackwell et al., 239–56. Minneapolis: Fortress, 2016.

Gibbs, John G. *Creation and Redemption: A Study in Pauline Theology*. Supplements to Novum Testamentum 26. Leiden: Brill, 1971.

Goff, Matthew J. *4QInstruction*. Wisdom Literature from the Ancient World 2. Atlanta: SBL, 2013.

———. *Discerning Wisdom: The Sapiential Literature of the Dead Sea Scrolls*. Supplements to Vetus Testamentum 116. Leiden: Brill, 2007.

Golb, Norman. *Who Wrote the Dead Sea Scrolls? The Search for the Secret of Qumran*. New York: Simon & Schuster, 1996.

Goodrich, John K. "Guardians, Not Taskmasters: The Cultural Resonances of Paul's Metaphor in Galatians 4.1–2." *Journal for the Study of the New Testament* 32:3 (Mar. 2010) 251–84.

Gordley, Matthew E. "Creation Imagery in Qumran Hymns and Prayers." *Journal of Jewish Studies* 59 (2008) 252–72.

Gorman, Michael J. "The Apocalyptic New Covenant and the Shape of Life in the Spirit According to Galatians." In *Paul and the Apocalyptic Imagination*, edited by Ben C. Blackwell et al., 317–37. Minneapolis: Fortress, 2016.

Gray, George Buchanan. *A Critical and Exegetical Commentary on the Book of Isaiah, I–XXXIX*. International Critical Commentary on the Holy Scriptures of the Old and New Testaments. Edinburgh: T&T Clark, 1912.

Gunkel, Hermann. *Schöpfung und Chaos in Urzeit und Endzeit: Eine religionsgeschichtliche Untersuchung über Gen 1 und Ap Joh 12*. Göttingen: Vandenhoeck und Ruprecht, 1895.

Hafemann, Scott J. "Paul and the Exile of Israel in Galatians 3–4." In *Exile: Old Testament, Jewish, and Christian Conceptions*, edited by James Scott, 329–71. Supplements to the Journal for the Study of Judaism 56. Leiden: Brill, 1997.

Hahne, Harry Alan. *The Corruption and Redemption of Creation: Nature in Romans 8.19–22 and Jewish Apocalyptic Literature*. Library of New Testament Studies 336. London: T&T Clark, 2006.

The Hebrew and Aramaic Lexicon of the Old Testament (HALOT). Edited by Ludwig Koehler, et al. Translated under the supervision of Mervyn E. J. Richardson. 4 vols. Leiden: Brill, 1994–1999.

Harrington, Daniel J. "Pseudo-Philo: A New Translation and Introduction." In *Old Testament Pseudepigrapha*, edited by James H. Charlesworth, 2:297–377. London: Yale University Press, 1985.

Harris, Murray J. *The Second Epistle to the Corinthians: A Commentary on the Greek Text*. The New International Greek Testament Commentary. Grand Rapids: Eerdmans, 2005.

Hays, Richard B. "The Letter to the Galatians: Introduction, Commentary, and Reflections." In *The New Interpreter's Bible*, edited by Leander E. Keck, 11:181–348. Nashville: Abingdon, 2000.

Hayward, Robert. "The Figure of Adam in Pseudo-Philo's Biblical Antiquities." *Journal for the Study of Judaism in the Persian, Hellenistic and Roman Period* 23:1 (June 1992) 1–20.

Heim, Erin M. *Adoption in Galatians and Romans: Contemporary Metaphor Theories and the Pauline Huiothesia Metaphors*. Biblical Interpretation Series 153. Leiden: Brill, 2017.

Henze, Matthias. "4 Ezra and 2 Baruch: The Status Quaestionis." In *Interpreting 4 Ezra and 2 Baruch: International Studies*, edited by Gabriele Boccaccini and Jason M. Zurawski, 3–27. Library of Second Temple Studies 87. London: Bloomsbury T&T Clark, 2014.

Hester, James D. *Paul's Concept of Inheritance: A Contribution to the Understanding of Heilsgeschichte*. Scottish Journal of Theology Occasional Papers 14. London: Oliver & Boyd, 1968.

Higgins, A. J. B. *New Testament Essays: Studies in Memory of Thomas Walter Manson, 1893–1958; Sponsored by Pupils, Colleagues and Friends*. Manchester: Manchester University Press, 1959.

Hodge, Caroline E. Johnson. *If Sons, Then Heirs: A Study of Kinship and Ethnicity in the Letters of Paul*. New York: Oxford University Press, 2007.

Hodges, Frederick Mansfield. "The Ideal Prepuce in Ancient Greece and Rome: Male Genital Aesthetics and Their Relation to Lipodermos, Circumcision, Foreskin Restoration, and the Kynodesme." *Bulletin of the History of Medicine* 75:3 (2001) 375–405.

Hogan, Karina Martin. "Mother Earth as a Conceptual Metaphor in 4 Ezra." *Catholic Bible Quarterly* 73 (2011) 72–91.

Holm-Nielsen, Svend. *Hodayot: Psalms from Qumran*. Acta Theologica Danica 2. Aarhus: Universitetsforlaget, 1960.

Hommel, Hildebrecht. *Schöpfer und Erhalter: Studien zum Problem Christentum und Antike*. Berlin: Lettner-Verlag, 1956.

Hooker, Morna D. "Adam in Romans 1." *New Testament Studies* 6:4 (July 1960) 297–306.

Horrell, David G. *Greening Paul: Rereading the Apostle in a Time of Ecological Crisis*. Waco, TX: Baylor University Press, 2010.

———. "A New Perspective on Paul? Rereading Paul in a Time of Ecological Crisis." *Journal for the Study of the New Testament* 33:1 (Sept. 2010) 3–30.

Hubbard, Moyer V. *New Creation in Paul's Letters and Thought*. Society for New Testament Studies Monograph Series 119. Cambridge: Cambridge University Press, 2002.

Hübner, Hans. *Biblische Theologie des Neuen Testaments*. Göttingen: Vandenhoek & Ruprecht, 1993.

Hughes, Julie A. *Scriptural Allusions and Exegesis in the Hodayot*. Studies on the Texts of the Desert of Judah 59. Leiden: Brill, 2006.

Hyldahl, Niels. "A Reminiscence of the Old Testament at Romans i. 23." *New Testament Studies* 2:4 (1956) 285–88.
Idestrom, Rebecca G. S. "Echoes of the Book of Exodus in Ezekiel." *Journal for the Study of the Old Testament* 33:4 (2009) 489–510.
Jackson, T. Ryan. *New Creation in Paul's Letters: A Study of the Historical and Social Setting of a Pauline Concept*. Wissenschaftliche Untersuchungen zum Neuen Testament 2:272. Tübingen: Mohr Siebeck, 2010.
Jacobson, Howard. *A Commentary on Pseudo-Philo's Liber Antiquitatum Biblicarum, with Latin Text and English Translation*. Arbeiten zur Geschichte des antiken Judentums und des Urchristentums 31. Leiden: Brill, 1996.
Jervell, Jacob. *Imago Dei: Gen 1, 26f. im Spätjudentum, in der Gnosis und in den paulinischen Briefen*. Forschungen zur Religion und Literatur des Alten und Neuen Testaments 76. Göttingen: Vandenhoeck & Ruprecht, 1960.
Jewett, Robert. *Romans: A Commentary*. Hermeneia. Minneapolis: Fortress, 2007.
Johnson, M. D. "Life of Adam and Eve: A New Translation and Introduction." In *Old Testament Pseudepigrapha*, edited by James H. Charlesworth, 2:249–95. London: Yale University Press, 1985.
Johnson Leese, J. J. *Christ, Creation, and the Cosmic Goal of Redemption: A Study of Pauline Creation Theology as Read by Irenaeus and Applied to Ecotheology*. Library of New Testament Studies 580. London: T&T Clark, 2018.
Jones, H. Stuart. "ΣΠΙΛΑΣ-ΑΠΑΡΧΗ ΠΝΕΥΜΑΤΟΣ." *Journal of Theological Studies* 23:91 (1922) 282–83.
Jonge, M. de. *The Life of Adam and Eve and Related Literature*. Guides to Apocrypha and Pseudepigrapha. Sheffield: Sheffield Academic Press, 1997.
Jonge, M. de, and Johannes Tromp. *The Life of Adam and Eve and Related Literature*. Sheffield: Sheffield Academic Press, 1997.
Käsemann, Ernst. *An die Römer*. 2nd ed. Handbuch zum Neuen Testament 8a. Tübingen: Mohr Siebeck, 1974.
———. *Commentary on Romans*. Grand Rapids: Eerdmans, 1980.
Keener, Craig S. *Galatians: A Commentary*. Grand Rapids: Baker Academic, 2019.
Keesmaat, Sylvia C. *Paul and His Story: (Re)Interpreting the Exodus Tradition*. Journal for the Study of the New Testament Supplement Series 181. Sheffield: Sheffield Academic Press, 1999.
Keown, Gerald Lynwood. *Jeremiah 26–52*. Word Biblical Commentary 27. Grand Rapids: Zondervan, 1995.
Kim, Seyoon. *The Origin of Paul's Gospel*. 2nd ed. Wissenschaftliche Untersuchungen zum Neuen Testament 2:4. Tübingen: Mohr Siebeck, 1984.
———. *Paul and the New Perspective: Second Thoughts on the Origin of Paul's Gospel*. Tübingen: Mohr Siebeck, 2002.
Klijn, A. F. J. "2 (Syriac Apocalypse of) Baruch." In *Old Testament Pseudepigrapha*, edited by James H. Charlesworth, 1:618. London: Yale University Press, 1983.
Knibb, Michael A., et al. *The Ethiopic Book of Enoch: A New Edition in the Light of the Aramaic Dead Sea Fragments*. Oxford: Clarendon Press, 1978.
Kraus, Wolfgang. *Das Volk Gottes: Zur Grundlegung der Ekklesiologie bei Paulus*. Wissenschaftliche Untersuchungen zum Neuen Testament 85. Tübingen: Mohr Siebeck, 1996.

Kuhn, Heinz-Wolfgang. *Enderwartung und gegenwärtiges Heil: Untersuchungen zu den Gemeindeliedern von Qumran mit einem Anhang über Eschatologie und Gegenwart in der Verkündigung Jesu.* Göttingen: Vandenhoeck & Ruprecht, 1966.
Kuhn, Karl G. "Die in Palästina gefundenen hebräischen Texte und das Neue Testament." *Zeitschrift für Theologie und Kirche* 47:2 (1950) 192–211.
Kuryłowicz, Marek. *Die Adoptio im klassischen römischen Recht.* Warszawa: Wydawnictwa Uniwersytetu Warszawskiego, 1981.
Kutsko, John F. *Between Heaven and Earth: Divine Presence and Absence in the Book of Ezekiel.* Biblical and Judaic Studies 7. Winona Lake, IN: Eisenbrauns, 2000.
Lange, Armin. *Weisheit und Prädestination: Weisheitliche Urordnung und Prädestination in den Textfunden von Qumran.* Studies on the Texts of the Desert of Judah 18. Leiden: Brill, 1995.
La Potterie, I. de. "Le chrétien conduit par l'esprit dans son cheminement eschatologique (Rom 8,14)." In *The Law of the Spirit in Rom 7 and 8*, edited by L. De Lorenzi, 209–78. Benedictina, Biblical-Ecumenical Section 1. Rome: St. Paul's Abbey, 1976.
Lee, Chris W. *Death Warning in the Garden of Eden: The Early Reception History of Genesis 2:17.* Forschungen Zum Alten Testament 2:115. Tübingen: Mohr Siebeck, 2020.
Levenson, Jon Douglas. *Resurrection and the Restoration of Israel: The Ultimate Victory of the God of Life.* New Haven: Yale University Press, 2006.
Levison, John R. "Adam and Eve in Romans 1.18–25 and the Greek Life of Adam and Eve." *New Testament Studies* 50:4 (2004) 519–34.
———. "Paul in the *Stoa Poecile*: A Response to Troels Engberg-Pedersen, *Cosmology and Self in the Apostle Paul: The Material Spirit*." *Journal for the Study of the New Testament* 33:4 (June 2011) 415–32.
———. *Portraits of Adam in Early Judaism: From Sirach to 2 Baruch.* Journal for the Study of the Pseudepigrapha Supplement Series 1. Sheffield: JSOT, 1988.
———. "Terrestrial Paradise in the Greek Life of Adam and Eve." *Journal for the Study of the Pseudepigrapha* 28:1 (2018) 25–44.
Lewis, Robert Brian. *Paul's "Spirit of Adoption" in Its Roman Imperial Context.* Library of New Testament Studies. New York: Bloomsbury T&T Clark, 2016.
Lichtenberger, Hermann. *Studien zum Menschenbild in Texten der Qumrangemeinde.* Göttingen: Vandenhoeck & Ruprecht, 1980.
Liddell, Henry George, et al. *A Greek-English Lexicon* (LSJ). 9th ed. Oxford: Clarendon, 1996.
Lietzmann, Hans. *Einführung in die Textgeschichte der Paulusbriefe: An die Römer.* Handbuch zum Neuen Testament 8. Tübingen: J. C. B. Mohr P. Siebeck, 1933.
Lightfoot, J. B. *Saint Paul's Epistle to the Galatians: A Revised Text with Introduction, Notes and Dissertations.* 9th ed. Epistles of St. Paul 2. The Third Apostolic Journey 3. London: Macmillan, 1887.
Lim, Timothy H., and John J. Collins. *The Oxford Handbook of the Dead Sea Scrolls.* Oxford Handbooks in Religion and Theology. Oxford: University Press, 2010.
Lindsay, Hugh. *Adoption in the Roman World.* Cambridge: Cambridge University Press, 2009.
Litke, Wayne. "Beyond Creation: Galatians 3:28, Genesis and the Hermaphrodite Myth." *Studies in Religion/Sciences Religieuses* 24:2 (June 1, 1995) 173–78.

Lodge, John G. *Romans 9–11: A Reader-Response Analysis.* University of South Florida International Studies in Formative Christianity and Judaism 6. Atlanta: Scholars, 1996.

Lohse, Eduard. *Colossians and Philemon: A Commentary on the Epistles to the Colossians and to Philemon.* Hermeneia. Philadelphia: Fortress, 1971.

Longenecker, Bruce W., ed. *Narrative Dynamics in Paul: A Critical Assessment.* Louisville: Westminster John Knox, 2002

———. "Salvation History in Galatians and the Making of a Pauline Discourse." *Journal for the Study of Paul and His Letters* 2:2 (2012) 65–87.

———. *The Triumph of Abraham's God: The Transformation of Identity in Galatians.* Edinburgh: T&T Clark, 1998.

Longenecker, Richard N. *The Epistle to the Romans: A Commentary on the Greek Text.* The New International Greek Testament Commentary. Grand Rapids: Eerdmans, 2016.

———. *Galatians.* Word Biblical Commentary 41. Dallas: Word, 1990.

Loubser, Gys M. H. "About Galatians, Apocalyptic and the Switching of Paradigms." *Acta Theologica* Supplementum 19 (2014) 164–85.

Lyall, Francis. *Slaves, Citizens, Sons: Legal Metaphors in the Epistles.* Grand Rapids: Zondervan, 1984.

Maher, Michael. *Targum Pseudo-Jonathan, Genesis.* Aramaic Bible 1B. Collegeville, MN: Liturgical, 1992.

Manson, T. W. "Romans." In *Peake's Commentary on the Bible*, edited by M. Black, 940–53. London: Thomas Nelson and Sons, 1962.

Martin, R. A. "The Earliest Messianic Interpretation of Genesis 3:15." *Journal of Biblical Literature* 84:4 (1965) 425–27.

Martin, Ralph P. *2 Corinthians.* Word Biblical Commentary 40. Waco, TX.: Word, 1986.

Martyn, J. Louis. "The Apocalyptic Gospel in Galatians." *Interpretation* 54:3 (2000) 246–66.

———. "Events in Galatia: Modified in Covenantal Nomism versus God's Invasion of the Cosmos in the Singular Gospel; A Response to J. D. G. Dunn and B. R. Gaventa." In *Pauline Theology. Vol. 1: Thessalonians, Philippians, Galatians, Philemon*, edited by Joette M. Bassler, 160–79. Minneapolis: Fortress, 1991.

———. "Epistemology at the Turn of the Ages." In *Theological Issues in the Letters of Paul*, 89–110. London: T&T Clark International, 1997.

———. *Galatians: A New Translation with Introduction and Commentary.* The Anchor Bible 33A. New York: Doubleday, 1997.

Maston, Jason. *Divine and Human Agency in Second Temple Judaism and Paul: A Comparative Study.* Wissenschaftliche Untersuchungen Zum Neuen Testament 2:297. Tübingen: Mohr Siebeck, 2010.

———. "The Nature of Salvation History in Galatians." *Journal for the Study of Paul and His Letters* 2:2 (2012) 89–103.

Matera, Frank J., and Daniel J. Harrington. *Galatians.* Sacra Pagina 9. Collegeville, MN: Liturgical, 1992.

Mawhinney, Allen. "Baptism, Servanthood, and Sonship." *Westminster Theological Journal* 49:1 (1987) 35–64.

McDonough, Sean M. *Christ as Creator: Origins of a New Testament Doctrine.* Oxford: Oxford University Press, 2009.

McKenzie, John L. *Second Isaiah.* Anchor Bible 20. Garden City, NY: Doubleday, 1968.

McKnight, Scot. *Galatians*. NIV Application Commentary Series. Grand Rapids: Zondervan, 1995.

Meeks, Wayne A. *The First Urban Christians: The Social World of the Apostle Paul*. New Haven: Yale University Press, 1983.

———. "The Image of the Androgyne: Some Uses of a Symbol in Earliest Christianity." *History of Religions* 13:3 (Feb. 1, 1974) 165–208.

Mell, Ulrich. *Neue Schöpfung: Eine traditionsgeschichtliche und exegetische Studie zu einem soteriologischen Grundsatz paulinischer Theologie*. Beihefte zur Zeitschrift für die neutestamentliche Wissenschaft und die Kunde der älteren Kirche 56. Berlin: de Gruyter, 1989.

Merk, Otto, and Martin Meiser. *Das Leben Adams und Evas*. Gütersloher Verlagshaus, 1998.

Metso, Sarianna. *The Community Rule: A Critical Edition with Translation*. Early Judaism and Its Literature 51. Atlanta: SBL, 2019.

Meyer, Nicholas A. *Adam's Dust and Adam's Glory in the Hodayot and the Letters of Paul: Rethinking Anthropogony and Theology*. Supplements to Novum Testamentum 168. Leiden: Brill, 2016.

Michel, Otto. *Der Brief an Die Römer*. 13th ed. Kritisch-exegetischer Kommentar über das Neue Testament. Göttingen: Vandenhoeck und Ruprecht, 1966.

Milik, J. T. "Problèmes de la littérature Hénochique à la lumière des fragments araméens de Qumrân." *Harvard Theological Review* 64:2–3 (July 1971) 333–78.

Moo, Douglas J. *The Epistle to the Romans*. The New International Commentary on the New Testament. Grand Rapid: Eerdmans, 1996.

———. *Galatians*. Baker Exegetical Commentary on the New Testament. Grand Rapids: Baker Academic, 2013.

Moo, Jonathan A. *Creation, Nature and Hope in 4 Ezra*. Forschungen zur Religion und Literatur des Alten und Neuen Testaments 237. Göttingen: Vandenhoeck & Ruprecht, 2011.

Morales, Rodrigo Jose. *The Spirit and the Restoration of Israel: New Exodus and New Creation Motifs in Galatians*. Wissenschaftliche Untersuchungen zum Neuen Testament 2:282. Tübingen: Mohr Siebeck, 2010.

Morris, Leon. *The Epistle to the Romans*. Grand Rapids: Eerdmans, 1987.

Munck, Johannes. *Christ and Israel: An Interpretation of Romans 9–11*. Philadelphia: Fortress, 1967.

———. *Paul and the Salvation of Mankind*. London: SCM, 1959.

Murphy, Frederick James. *Pseudo-Philo: Rewriting the Bible*. Oxford: Oxford University Press, 1993.

Murphy-O'Connor, Jerome. "Pauline Studies." *Revue biblique* 98 (1991) 145–51.

Murray, John. *The Epistle to the Romans: The English Text with Introduction, Exposition and Notes*. New International Commentary on the New Testament. Grand Rapids: Eerdmans, 1968.

Mussner, Franz. *Der Galaterbrief*. Herders Theologischer Kommentar zum Neuen Testament 9. Freiburg: Herder, 1974.

Nanos, Mark D. "'Broken Branches': A Pauline Metaphor Gone Awry? (Romans 11:11–36)." In *Between Gospel and Election: Explorations in the Interpretation of Romans 9–11*, edited by Florian Wilk et al., 339–76. Tübingen: Mohr Siebeck, 2010.

———, ed. *The Galatians Debate: Contemporary Issues in Rhetorical and Historical Interpretation*. Peabody, MA: Hendrickson, 2002.

———. "'The Gifts and the Calling of God are Irrevocable' (Romans 11:29): If So, How Can Paul Declare That 'Not All Israelites Truly Belong to Israel' (9:6)?" *Studies in Christian-Jewish Relations* 11:1 (2016) 1–17.

———. "Introduction." In *Paul Within Judaism: Restoring the First-Century Context to the Apostle*, edited by Mark D. Nanos and Magnus Zetterholm, 1–29. Minneapolis: Fortress, 2015.

———. *The Mystery of Romans: The Jewish Context of Paul's Letter*. Minneapolis: Fortress, 1996.

Nanos, Mark D., and Magnus Zetterholm, eds. *Paul Within Judaism: Restoring the First-Century Context to the Apostle*. Minneapolis: Fortress, 2015.

Neutel, Karin B. *A Cosmopolitan Ideal: Paul's Declaration "Neither Jew nor Greek, Neither Slave nor Free, nor Male and Female" in the Context of First Century Thought*. Library of New Testament Studies 513. New York: Bloomsbury T&T Clark, 2015.

Newsom, Carol A. "Models of the Moral Self: Hebrew Bible and Second Temple Judaism." *Journal of Biblical Literature* 131:1 (2012) 5–25.

———. *The Self as Symbolic Space: Constructing Identity and Community at Qumran*. Studies on the Texts of the Desert of Judah 52. Leiden: Brill, 2004.

Nickelsburg, George W. E. *1 Enoch: A Commentary on the Book of 1 Enoch*. Hermeneia. Minneapolis: Fortress, 2001.

———. *Resurrection, Immortality, and Eternal Life in Intertestamental Judaism and Early Christianity*. Harvard Theological Studies 56. Cambridge: Harvard University Press, 2006.

Nickelsburg, George W. E., and James C. VanderKam. *1 Enoch 2: A Commentary on the Book of 1 Enoch; Chapters 37–82*. Hermeneia. Minneapolis: Fortress, 2012.

Nitzan, Bilha. "The Idea of Creation and Its Implications in Qumran Literature." In *Creation in Jewish and Christian Tradition*, edited by Henning Graf Reventlow and Yair Hoffman, 240–64. JSOT Supplement 319. London: Sheffield Academic Press, 2002.

Oakes, Peter. *Galatians*. Paideia: Commentaries on the New Testament. Grand Rapids: Baker Academic, 2015.

O'Brien, Peter Thomas. *Colossians, Philemon*. Word Biblical Commentary 44. Waco, TX: Word, 1982.

Oepke, Albrecht, and Joachim Rohde. *Der Brief Des Paulus an Die Galater*. 3rd ed. Theologischer Handkommentar Zum Neuen Testament 9. Berlin: Evangelische Verlagsanstalt, 1973.

Offord, Joseph. "Restrictions Concerning Circumcision under the Romans." *Proceedings of the Royal Society of Medicine* 6, Sect. Hist. Med. (May 1, 1913) 102–7.

Oke, C. Clare. "A Suggestion with Regard to Romans 8:23." *Interpretation* 11 (1957) 455–60.

Origen. *Commentary on the Epistle to the Romans, Books 6–10*. Translated by Thomas P. Scheck. Fathers of the Church 104. Washington, DC: Catholic University of America Press, 2002.

Owens, Mark D. *As It Was in the Beginning: An Intertextual Analysis of New Creation in Galatians, 2 Corinthians, and Ephesians*. Cambridge: James Clarke, 2016.

Patrologiae Cursus Completus: Series Latina [PL]. Edited by Jacques-Paul Migne. 217 vols. Paris, 1844–1864.

Penner, Ken M., et al. *The Lexham English Septuagint*. 2nd ed. Bellingham, WA: Lexham Press, 2019.

Peppard, Michael. *The Son of God in the Roman World: Divine Sonship in Its Social and Political Context.* Oxford: Oxford University Press, 2011.
Philo. *On the Unchangeableness of God; On Husbandry; Concerning Noah's Work as a Planter; On Drunkenness; On Sobriety.* Translated by F. H. Colson and G. H. Whitaker. Philo Vol. 3. Loeb Classical Library 247. Cambridge: Harvard University Press, 1930.
———. *On Abraham; On Joseph; On Moses.* Translated by F. H. Colson. Philo Vol. 4. Loeb Classical Library 289. Cambridge: Harvard University Press, 1935.
Reumann, John. *Creation and New Creation: The Past, Present, and Future of God's Creative Activity.* Minneapolis: Augsburg, 1973.
———. *Philippians: A New Translation with Introduction and Commentary.* Anchor Yale Bible 33B. New Haven: Yale University Press, 2008.
Schlatter, Adolf. *Gottes Gerechtigkeit: Ein Kommentar zum Römerbrief.* 3rd ed. Stuttgart: Calwer, 1959.
Schmidt, Hans Wilhelm. *Der Brief des Paulus an die Römer.* Berlin: Evangelische Verlagsanstalt, 1966.
Schmitz, Philip C. "The Grammar of Resurrection in Isaiah 26:19a-c." *Journal of Biblical Literature* 122:1 (2003) 145–49.
Schneider, Gerhard. "KAINH KTISIS: Die Idee der Neuschöpfung beim Apostel Paulus und ihr religionsgeschichtlicher Hintergrund." PhD thesis, Universität Trier, 1959.
Schofield, Alison. "The Dead Sea Scrolls." In *Early Judaism and Its Modern Interpreters*, edited by Matthias Henze and Rodney A. Werline, 147–82. Atlanta: SBL, 2020.
Schuller, Eileen M., and Carol A. Newsom. *The Hodayot (Thanksgiving Psalms): A Study Edition of 1QH^a.* Early Judaism and Its Literature 36. Atlanta: SBL, 2012.
Schüssler Fiorenza, Elisabeth. *In Memory of Her: A Feminist Theological Reconstruction of Christian Origins.* New York: Crossroad, 1983.
Scott, James M. *Adoption as Sons of God: An Exegetical Investigation into the Background of Huiothesia in the Pauline Corpus.* Wissenschaftliche Untersuchungen zum Neuen Testament 48. Tübingen: J. C. B. Mohr, 1992.
———. *On Earth as in Heaven: The Restoration of Sacred Time and Sacred Space in the Book of Jubilees.* Supplements to the Journal for the Study of Judaism 91. Leiden: Brill, 2005.
Sjöberg, Erik. "Neuschöpfung in den Toten-Meer-Rollen." *Studia Theologica—Nordic Journal of Theology* 9:1 (Jan. 1, 1955) 131–36.
Skinner, John. *A Critical and Exegetical Commentary on Genesis.* International Critical Commentary on the Holy Scriptures of the Old and New Testaments 1. New York: Scribner, 1910.
Sprinkle, Preston M. "The Afterlife in Romans: Understanding Paul's Glory Motif in Light of the Apocalypse of Moses and 2 Baruch." In *Lebendige Hoffnung—Ewiger Tod?! Jenseitsvorstellungen im Hellenismus, Judentum und Christentum*, edited by Manfred Lang and Michael Labahn, 201–33. Leipzig: Evangelische Verlagsanstalt, 2007.
———. *Paul and Judaism Revisited: A Study of Divine and Human Agency in Salvation.* Downers Grove, IL: IVP Academic, 2013.
Stanley, Christopher D. *Paul and the Language of Scripture: Citation Technique in the Pauline Epistles and Contemporary Literature.* Society for New Testament Studies Monograph Series 74. Cambridge: Cambridge University Press, 1992.

Steenburg, D. "The Worship of Adam and Christ as the Image of God." *Journal for the Study of the New Testament* 12:39 (May 1, 1990) 95–109.

Stegemann, Hartmut, et al. *1QHodayota: With Incorporation of 1QHodayotb and 4QHodayota-f*. Discoveries in the Judaean Desert 40. Oxford: Clarendon, 2009.

Stegner, William R. "Romans 9:6–29—a Midrash." *Journal for the Study of the New Testament* 7:22 (Oct. 1984) 37–52.

Stendahl, Krister. "The Apostle Paul and the Introspective Conscience of the West." *Harvard Theological Review* 56:3 (July 1963) 199–215.

———. *The Bible and the Role of Women: A Case Study in Hermeneutics*. Facet Books. Biblical Series 15. Philadelphia: Fortress, 1966.

———. *Paul Among Jews and Gentiles, and Other Essays*. Philadelphia: Fortress, 1976.

Stone, Michael E. "Apocryphal Notes and Readings." *Israel Oriental Studies* 1 (1971) 123–31.

Stone, Michael E., and Matthias Henze. *4 Ezra and 2 Baruch: Translations, Introductions, and Notes*. Minneapolis: Fortress, 2013.

———. *Fourth Ezra: A Commentary on the Book of Fourth Ezra*. Hermeneia. Minneapolis: Fortress, 1990.

Stowers, Stanley Kent. *A Rereading of Romans: Justice, Jews, and Gentiles*. New Haven: Yale University Press, 1994.

Strachan, R. H. *The Second Epistle of Paul to the Corinthians*. Moffatt New Testament Commentary. New York: Harper and Brothers, 1935.

Strugnell, John, et al. *Qumran Cave 4. 24, Sapiential Texts. Part 2: 4Qinstruction (Mûsār Lĕ Mēvîn): 4Q415 Ff.; With a Re-Edition of 1Q26*. Discoveries in the Judaean Desert 34. Oxford: Clarendon Press, 1999.

Stuckenbruck, Loren T. *1 Enoch 91–108*. Commentaries on Early Jewish Literature. Berlin: de Gruyter, 2008.

Stuhlmacher, Peter. "Erwägungen zum ontologischen Charakter der καινὴ κτίσις bei Paulus." *Evangelische Theologie* 27 (1967) 1–35.

Swete, Henry Barclay. *The Old Testament in Greek According to the Septuagint*. Cambridge: Cambridge University Press, 1909.

Theological Dictionary of the New Testament (TDNT). Edited by Gerhard Kittel and Gerhard Friedrich. Translated by Geoffrey W. Bromiley. 10 vols. Grand Rapids: Eerdmans, 1964–1976.

Theological Dictionary of the Old Testament (TDOT). Edited by G. Johannes Botterweck and Helmer Ringgren. Translated by John T. Willis et al. 8 vols. Grand Rapids: Eerdmans, 1974–2006.

Thielman, Frank. *From Plight to Solution: A Jewish Framework to Understanding Paul's View of the Law in Galatians and Romans*. Supplements to Novum Testamentum 61. Leiden: Brill, 1989.

———. "The Story of Israel and the Theology of Romans 5–8." *Society of Biblical Literature Seminar Papers* 32 (1993) 227–49.

Thiessen, Matthew. *Paul and the Gentile Problem*. New York: Oxford University Press, 2016.

Tiller, Patrick A. *A Commentary on the Animal Apocalypse of I Enoch*. Atlanta: SBL, 1993.

VanderKam, James C. *The Book of Jubilees: A Critical Text*. Corpus Scriptorum Christianorum Orientalium 510. Leuven: Peeters, 1989.

———. *Enoch and the Growth of an Apocalyptic Tradition*. The Catholic Biblical Quarterly Monograph Series 16. Washington, DC: Catholic Biblical Association of America, 1984.

———. *Jubilees: A Commentary on the Book of Jubilees*. Hermeneia. Minneapolis: Fortress, 2018.
Van Ruiten, J. T. A. G. M. "Visions of the Temple in the Book of Jubilees." In *Gemeinde ohne Tempel/Community Without Temple*, edited by Beata Ego et al., 215–28. Tübingen: Mohr Siebeck, 1999.
von Rad, Gerhard. *Genesis: A Commentary*. 2nd ed. Old Testament Library. London: SCM, 1963.
Wacholder, Ben Zion. *The New Damascus Document: The Midrash on the Eschatological Torah of the Dead Sea Scrolls; Reconstruction, Translation, and Commentary*. Studies on the Texts of the Desert of Judah 56. Leiden: Brill, 2007.
Wagner, J. Ross. *Heralds of the Good News: Isaiah and Paul "in Concert" in the Letter to the Romans*. Supplements to Novum Testamentum 101. Leiden: Brill, 2002.
Weima, Jeffrey A. D. *Neglected Endings: The Significance of the Pauline Letter Closings*. Library of New Testament Studies. Sheffield: JSOT Press, 1994.
Wenham, Gordon J. *Genesis 1–15*. Word Biblical Commentary 1. Waco, TX: Word, 1987.
Westermann, Claus. *Genesis 1–11: A Commentary*. Minneapolis: Augsburg, 1984.
Wifall, Walter R. "Gen 3:15—A Protevangelium?" *Catholic Biblical Quarterly* 36 (1974) 361–65.
Wilk, Florian, and Markus Öhler, eds. *Paulinische Schriftrezeption: Grundlagen, Auspragungen, Wirkungen, Wertungen*. Forschungen zur Religion und Literatur des Alten und Neuen Testaments 268. Göttingen: Vandenhoeck & Ruprecht, 2017.
Wold, Benjamin G. *Women, Men, and Angels: The Qumran Wisdom Document Musar LeMevin and Its Allusions to Genesis Creation Traditions*. Tübingen: Mohr Siebeck, 2005.
Wolde, Ellen van. "Separation and Creation in Genesis 1 and Psalm 104: A Continuation of the Discussion of the Verb ברא." *Vetus Testamentum* 67:4 (Oct. 2017) 611–47.
Wolter, Michael. *Der Brief an die Römer*. Vol. 1: *Röm 1–8*. Evangelisch-Katholischer Kommentar zum Neuen Testament 6:1. Neukirchen-Vluyn: Neukirchener Theologie, 2014.
———. "Ethnizität und Identität bei Paulus." *Early Christianity* 8:3 (Sept. 2017) 336–53.
Wright, N. T. *Galatians*. Grand Rapids: Eerdmans, 2021.
———. "The Letter to the Romans: Introduction, Commentary, and Reflections." In *The New Interpreter's Bible*, edited by Leander Keck, 10:393–770. Nashville: Abingdon, 2002.
———. *Paul and the Faithfulness of God*. Christian Origins and the Question of God 4. London: SPCK Publishing, 2013.
———. *The Paul Debate: Critical Questions for Understanding the Apostle*. Waco, TX: Baylor University Press, 2015.
Yates, John. *The Spirit and Creation in Paul*. Wissenschaftliche Untersuchungen Zum Neuen Testament 2:251. Tübingen: Mohr Siebeck, 2008.
Zetterholm, Magnus. *Approaches to Paul: A Student's Guide to Recent Scholarship*. Minneapolis: Fortress, 2009.
———. "The Paul within Judaism Perspective." In *Perspectives on Paul: Five Views*, edited by Scot McKnight and B. J. Oropeza, 171–93. Grand Rapids: Baker Academic, 2020.
Zimmerli, Walther, et al. *Ezekiel: A Commentary on the Book of the Prophet Ezekiel*. Hermeneia. Philadelphia: Fortress, 1979.

Author Index

Adams, Edward, 14–16, 20, 121
Aland, Barbara, 110
Allen, Leslie C., 4, 84, 135
Attridge, Harold W., 34
Aymer, Albert J. D., 119

Barclay, John M. G., 3, 5, 9, 54, 59, 84, 109, 118–19, 124, 145, 170, 173, 227
Barnett, Paul, 105, 107, 108, 110
Barrett, Charles Kingsley, 103, 148, 151, 179, 184
Bergmeier, Roland, 207
Bertone, John A., 133, 137
Betz, Hans Dieter, 116, 119, 122, 123, 194, 196, 199, 200
Black, Matthew, 41, 47
Boccaccini, Gabriele, 26
Brock, S. P., 50
Brown, Derek R., 214
Bruce, F. F., 3, 123, 207
Brunner, Emil, 152
Büchsel, Friedrich, 216
Burke, Trevor J., 1, 9, 10
Burrows, Millar, 71
Byrne, Brendan, 1–3, 6, 153, 159, 171, 184, 198, 220, 235, 236

Charles, R. H., 33, 36, 47
Chester, Stephen J., 176
Childs, Brevard S., 32
Clement, R. E., 12, 110, 161

Collins, John J., 71, 87, 95, 96, 161
Cook, Edward, 71
Cook, James I., 169
Coxe, Arthur Cleveland, 211
Cranfield, C. E. B., 1, 133, 140, 151–53, 159, 160, 175, 178–79, 190–91, 220
Crawford, Sidnie White, 71
Cross, Frank Moore, 71
Cullmann, Oscar, 103, 215
Curtis, E. M., 201

Dahl, Nils A., 32, 33
Day, John, 161
de Boer, Martinus C., 5, 13, 122, 123, 194, 203, 217, 219
Decock, P. B., 44, 45
Deissmann, Adolf, 194
Dieterich, Albrecht, 63
Dillmann, August, 47
Dochhorn, Jan, 49, 50, 105, 109, 154–56, 214
Doering, Lutz, 41, 65, 67, 69, 90
Donner, Herbert, 3
Düll, Rudolf, 144
Dunn, James D. G., 1, 103, 109, 110, 112, 119, 120, 148, 151, 153, 159, 164, 175, 178, 184, 187, 191, 196, 198, 211–13, 215, 220
Dunne, John Anthony, 220

Eastman, Susan Grove, 123, 151, 159, 247
Eisenbaum, Pamela Michelle, 182
Engberg-Pedersen, Troels, 225

Fee, Gordon D., 207
Fitzmyer, Joseph A., 1, 148, 151, 153, 159, 179, 184, 190, 214, 220
Fletcher-Louis, Crispin H. T., 94
Fredriksen, Paula, 25, 26, 167, 182, 227–29, 231
Frey, Jörg, 71
Fuchs, C., 154
Fuchs, Ernst, 152
Furnish, Victor Paul, 103, 107, 110

Gager, John G., 26, 166, 181, 182, 228
García Martínez, Florentino, 71, 76, 87, 88, 90, 96
Gardner, Jane F., 145
Gaston, Lloyd, 26, 166, 167, 179, 181, 182, 228, 240
Gaventa, Beverly, 170, 178
Goff, Matthew J., 92–97, 99
Golb, Norman, 71
Goodrich, John K., 199, 200
Gordley, Matthew E., 72
Gorman, Michael J., 5
Gray, George Buchanan, 161
Gunkel, Hermann, 32

Hafemann, Scott J., 203, 207
Hahne, Harry Alan, 151–54
Harrington, Daniel J., 54, 62, 92, 207
Harris, Murray J., 107, 111
Hauck, Friedrich, 133
Hays, Richard B., 198, 200, 203
Hayward, Robert, 58
Heim, Erin M., 9–11, 183–84, 234
Henze, Matthias, 64
Hester, James D., 1
Hodge, Caroline E. Johnson., 25, 167, 179, 180, 195, 221, 223–26, 228–31, 240
Hodges, Frederick Mansfield, 118
Hogan, Karina Martin, 63
Holm-Nielsen, Svend, 74, 75, 79, 80, 83, 84

Hommel, Hildebrecht, 152
Hooker, Morna D., 103, 148, 216
Hubbard, Moyer V., 5, 16–18, 20, 23, 31, 33, 85, 107, 110, 116, 119, 120, 238
Hübner, Hans, 132
Hughes, Julie A., 75
Hyldahl, Niels, 148

Idestrom, Rebecca G. S., 139

Jackson, T. Ryan., 12, 20–22, 31, 33, 35, 74, 103, 107, 119, 120, 154, 237
Jacobson, Howard, 54, 55, 60–62
Jervell, Jacob, 103
Jewett, Robert, 1, 146, 148, 151, 153, 164, 169, 174, 175, 178, 179, 184, 187, 191, 220
Johnson, M. D., 49, 105, 154

Käsemann, Ernst, 12, 14, 110, 152, 179, 191
Keener, Craig S., 119, 124
Keesmaat, Sylvia C., 1, 140, 220
Keown, Gerald Lynwood, 250
Kim, Seyoon, 104, 132
Klijn, A. F. J., 64
Kraus, Wolfgang, 12, 23, 119
Kuhn, Heinz-Wolfgang, 80–82
Kuryłowicz, Marek, 144
Kutsko, John F., 4, 5, 135, 136

La Potterie, I. de., 139, 140
Lange, Armin, 71, 95
Lee, Chris W., 82
Levenson, Jon Douglas, 4, 135, 139
Levison, John R., 51, 52, 67, 149, 225
Lewis, Robert Brian, 6–9, 11
Lichtenberger, Hermann, 75
Lietzmann, Hans, 160
Lightfoot, J. B., 119, 124, 194
Lindsay, Hugh, 1, 2, 146
Litke, Wayne, 114
Lodge, John G., 166
Lohse, Eduard, 112
Longenecker, Bruce W., 197
Longenecker, Richard N., 1, 119, 122, 151, 160, 190, 198–200, 207, 211

Author Index

Lyall, Francis, 1, 144

Maher, Michael, 210
Manson, Thomas Walter, 152
Martin, Dale, 225
Martin, R. A., 210
Martin, Ralph P., 102, 103, 107, 108, 110
Martone, Corrado, 71
Martyn, J. Louis., 3, 5, 13, 108, 114, 124, 194, 197, 203, 211, 216, 219
Maston, Jason, 75, 76
Matera, Frank J., 207
Mawhinney, Allen, 3
McKnight, Scot, 119
Meeks, Wayne A., 115, 220
Meiser, Martin, 49
Mell, Ulrich, 13, 14–18, 20, 23, 31, 74, 81, 82, 85, 87, 117
Merk, Otto, 49
Meyer, Nicholas A., 75, 96, 212
Michel, Otto, 151
Milik, J. T., 36, 41, 47
Moo, Douglas J., 1, 5, 119, 120, 124, 140, 151, 153, 175, 178, 179, 184, 190, 191, 196, 198–200, 203, 208, 217, 219, 220
Moo, Jonathan A., 64
Morales, Rodrigo Jose, 18, 137, 207
Morris, Leon, 175
Munck, Johannes, 166
Murphy, Frederick James, 54, 56, 61–63
Murphy-O'Connor, Jerome, 14, 103, 215
Murray, John, 152, 153
Mussner, Franz, 182, 196

Nanos, Mark D., 25, 26, 166, 167, 187, 189, 240
Neutel, Karin B., 115
Newsom, Carol A., 74–76, 79, 80, 85, 86, 90
Nickelsburg, George W. E., 41, 42, 44–47, 161
Nitzan, Bilha, 72

O'Brien, Peter Thomas, 112
Oepke, Albrecht, 162
Offord, Joseph, 118
Oke, C. Clare, 162

Owens, Mark D., 22–23, 48

Penner, Ken M., 114
Peppard, Michael, 1, 6–8, 11

Reumann, John, 103, 152, 216

Sanders, E. P., 166
Schlatter, Adolf, 152
Schmidt, Hans Wilhelm, 152
Schmitz, Philip C., 161
Schneider, Gerhard, 80
Schofield, Alison, 72
Schubart, W., 162
Schuller, Schubart, 74
Schulz, Seigfried, 133
Schüssler, Fiorenza, E., 115
Schweizer, Eduard, 103, 169, 215
Scott, James M., 1–3, 6, 7, 11, 41, 137, 171, 199, 201, 203, 208, 236
Sjöberg, Erik, 80
Skinner, John, 210
Sprinkle, Preston M., 50, 53, 132
Stanley, Christopher D., 214
Steenburg, D, 112
Stegemann, Hartmut, 71
Stegner, William R., 174
Stendahl, Krister, 115, 166
Stone, Michael E., 34, 64–66
Stowers, Stanley Kent, 26, 167
Strachan, R. H., 12
Strugnell, John, 92, 94, 95, 97, 99
Stuhlmacher, Peter, 13
Sukenik, Eliezer, 71
Swete, Henry Barclay, 114

Thiessen, Matthew, 25, 26, 167, 182, 195, 221, 223–26, 228, 230, 231, 240
Tigchelaar, Eibert J. C., 76, 87, 88, 90
Tiller, Patrick A., 46
Tromp, Johannes, 49

van der Woude, Adam S., 71
Van Ruiten, J. T. A. G. M., 35
VanderKam, James C., 33–36, 38, 39, 42, 45, 46
von Rad, Gerhard, 210

Wacholder, Ben Zion, 88
Wagner, J. Ross, 166, 175
Wassen, Cecilia, 71
Weima, Jeffrey A. D., 196
Weiser, A., 141
Wenham, Gordon J., 210
Westermann, Claus, 210
Wifall, Walter R., 214
Wilk, Florian, 166
Wold, Benjamin G., 99

Wolter, Michael, 151, 153, 159, 160, 220, 222, 223
Wright, N. T., 5, 148, 153, 168

Yates, John W., 4, 5, 18–20, 24, 75, 132–35

Zetterholm, Magnus, 25, 239
Zimmerli, Walther, 4, 135

Scripture and Ancient Sources Index

Hebrew Bible/Old Testament

Genesis

1:1	136
1–3	4, 24, 31, 41, 56, 64, 70, 72–75, 77, 78, 89, 90, 93, 95, 98, 100, 102, 105, 148, 195, 200, 211, 212, 216, 237
1–2	35, 45, 59, 66, 86, 95, 96, 135, 147, 149
1:3–5	56
1:3 4	103
1:4	136
1:9	60
1:10	136
1:12	136
1:18	136
1:20–27	148
1:20–25	148
1:21	136
1:25	136
1:26–30	214, 237
1:26–28	112, 203, 212, 213
1:26–27	148, 164
1:26	103, 216
1:27–30	96, 97, 205
1:27–28	40, 87, 103, 212
1:27	28, 32, 82, 87, 95, 96, 103, 114, 115, 118, 121, 127, 149, 198, 201, 215–16
1:28–30	77, 200, 201
1:28–29	55, 200
1:28	103, 201
1:31	136
2–3	32, 43, 44, 75, 76, 82, 91, 96
2	4, 131, 135, 149
2:3	82
2:6–7	212
2:6	91
2:7–8	143, 177, 178
2:7	4, 19, 20, 27, 75, 76, 82, 84, 96, 135, 149, 178, 212, 225, 237
2:8–15	43
2:8	90
2:9	43, 75, 95
2:10–14	136
2:10–12	58
2:10	91
2:11–12	43
2:15	93, 97, 98, 135
2:16–17	142
2:17	56, 65, 77, 82, 90, 95
2:19	82

Genesis (continued)

2:21–22	115
2:22	75
3	38, 39, 65, 76, 100, 107, 147, 148, 149, 154, 201
3:1	103
3:3–4	80
3:3	65
3:5	148
3:6	148
3:7–11	76
3:7	107
3:10	107
3:13	103
3:14–19	77
3:15	80, 154, 209, 210, 211, 212, 214, 215
3:16–19	4, 27, 54–57, 63, 67, 69, 70, 85, 99, 131, 147, 150, 153, 156–59, 163, 172, 237
3:16a	157
3:16	68, 80, 99, 154–56, 158
3:17–19	38, 164
3:17–18	56, 68, 153, 154, 206
3:17	60
3:18	55, 99
3:19	56, 63, 68, 75, 160
3:20	76
3:21	107, 114
3:22–24	44, 65, 66
3:22	43
3:24	43, 55, 56, 91
4:2	95
4:12	99
4:17–21	76
5:6–7	95
5:18–24	36
6:1–4	148
6:2	83
6:4	83
6:5	148
7:21–23	37
8:20	58
8:22	57
12:2–9	183
14:1	75
15:5–7	183
15:5	224, 226
15:6	227
15:13–16	184
15:14–16	76
15:14	75
15:17	183
17:4–8	183
17:11	118
22:2	66
22:16–18	224, 226
25:4–6	76
25:4	75
25:23	62, 173
25:25	174
32:28	173
48:5–6	3

Exodus

2:10	3
4:22–23	60, 140, 169, 183
4:22	60, 66, 97, 137, 167, 169, 183, 184, 228
4:23	60, 184
6:6	141
12:25–26	183
12:42	60
13:3	141
13:14	141
14:27	60
14:29	60
15:5	60
15:6	184
15:11	184
15:13	140
16:10	183, 184
19:5–6	183, 184
20:26	38
24:15–17	183

28:42	38	7:12–14	62
30:7–8	38	7:12	62, 210
30:34	38	7:14	3, 62, 97, 137, 236
35:27	58	23:5	183
40:34	184		

1 Chronicles

28:13	183

Leviticus

26:42	141

Esther

2:7	3
2:15	3

Numbers

16	60
16:29–30	72
16:39–40	38

Job

1:6	83
1:21	63
1:21a	160
2:1	83
14:1	75, 211
15:14	75, 211
25:4	75, 211
38:4–7	224
38:7	83
38:28–29	63

Deuteronomy

1:30–31	140
5:6	141
6:12	141
7:6–9	172, 173
7:8	141
10:3	141
13:5	141
32:6–20	140
32:43	228

Joshua

21:27	183

Psalms

8	201, 210, 212
8:6–7	167
8:6	210, 214
22:3	104
29:1	83
30:4	104
30:6	154
38:5	154
51:12	84
61:9	154
71:6	62
72:9	214
77:14	104
77:33	154

Ruth

1:11	62

2 Samuel

2:12–14	62
7	3, 137
7:1–17	210

Psalms (continued)

77:53	104
82:6	83
89	210
89:5	210
89:7	83
89:24	210
89:27	183
89:30	210
89:37	210
91:13	215
102:18b	80
104:4	224
104:29–30	84
104:29	84
104:37	104
104:42	104
104:43	104
110	210
110:1	210, 213, 214
118:37	154
139:13	160
139:15	160
148:1–3	224

Proverbs

8:22	112
22:8	154

Ecclesiastes

1:2	154
1:14	154
2:1–26	154
3:19	154
4:4–16	154
5:6–9	154
6:2–11	154
7:1–16	154
8:10–14	154
9:9	154
11:8–10	154
12:8	154

Isaiah

8:14	186
10:22–23	180
21:2–3	128
26:16–19	160, 162
26:19	161
28:16	186
29:16	176
40:1–11	22
40–66	13
40–55	110
42:9	74, 110
43:1	82, 176, 177
43:6–7	140, 176, 177
43:7	82
43:16–21	22
43:18–19	110
43:19	74, 110
44:21–24	82
45:7	82
45:9	176
45:18	82
46:11	176
48:3–6	110
48:6–7	74
48:11	74
48:13–15	176
49:1	62
49:5	82
49:8	110
51:1–3	176
52:7–12	22
57:14–21	22
59:4b–5	80
63:7–19	140
63:8–10a	140
63:16	177
64:8	177
65:17–25	22, 41
65:17–18	110
65:17	41, 45
65:20	41
65–66	22, 31, 35, 45, 219
66:18–24	22
66:18–23	12
66:22	45, 110

Jeremiah

4:31	158
18:6-10	177
31	31
31:9	137, 183
31:33-34	5, 219, 220, 225
31:33	220
38:8-9	140
38:9	140
41:13	141

Ezekiel

11:16-21	139
11:20	133
16:60	219
28:13-19	43
28:13	43
28:14	43
28:16	43
28:18	43
34:25-31	139
34:25	219
36-37	4, 8, 19, 24, 27, 31, 131-32, 134, 135-40, 147, 172, 219, 237
36:6-8	136
36:11	136
36:12	147
36:24-38	139
36:24	139
36:26-27	5, 137, 219, 220, 225
36:27-28	138
36:27	132, 133, 135, 136, 137, 219
36:28	136
36:29	136
36:30	136
36:34-35	5, 135
36:35	66, 147
37:1-14	4, 5, 132, 134-36, 139, 140, 143, 225
37:1	135
37:5-6	134
37:5	132
37:8-9	134
37:9	4, 134, 135
37:10	134
37:11-28	139
37:14	132, 134, 135
37:21	139
37:23	136
37:26	219
37:27	136
39:22-29	139
44:15	88
47:1-12	22

Daniel

3:25	83

Hosea

1:6	175
1:9	175
1:10-11	140
1:10	136, 137, 175, 177, 181
1:11	140
2:1	137, 138
2:23	175
11:1	137, 207

Joel

2:3	66

Micah

6:4	141

New Testament

Matthew

11:1	211
12:26	215
16:23	215
18:25	142
24:37–39	56

Mark

1:9–11	6, 8
3:23	215
4:15	215
8:33	215
14:36	145, 220

Luke

1:33–35	213
3:38	212
11:1	211
11:18	215
13:16	215
22:3	215

John

13:27	215

Acts

5:3	215
10:36	201

Romans

1	21, 151
1:1	101
1:4	7, 8, 143, 163
1–8	166
1:16–17	159, 189
1:16	185, 188, 189, 238, 240
1:18–32	148
1:18–25	148, 149, 152, 153
1:18—3:20	150
1:18	150
1:19	148
1:20–25	205
1:20	110, 150–52, 156
1:21	150, 152, 154
1:22	148
1:23–26	149
1:23	148–50, 152, 154
1:24–32	148
1:24	150, 152, 156
1:25	110, 148, 150–53, 168
1:26–27	114, 148
1:28–31	148
2:9	185
2:10	185
2:12–29	168
2:17–20	240
2:26	134
3:1–2	185, 192, 240
3:2	185
3:9	192, 215, 240
3:19–31	168
3:21–26	170
3:23	149, 150
3:23–24	186, 240
3:30	229
4	168, 179, 222, 226, 230
4:1–25	182
4:1	183
4:3	227
4:5	227
4:9–12	180
4:11–12	230
4:12	222
4:13–14	146, 168
4:13	168, 180, 183, 218, 237
4:14	180
4:16–17	183
4:16	168, 180

4:17	63, 177, 178, 179, 180, 234	8:2–3	215
		8:2	132, 141
4:19	63, 179	8:4	132, 133, 136, 138, 141
4:20	180		
4:21	168	8:6	132
4:23–25	101	8:9–30	8
5:1–11	170	8:9–11	132, 134, 136
5:2	187	8:11	4, 134, 141, 143, 159, 163, 238
5–8	143, 157		
5:10–11	112, 191	8:12–17	168
5:12–21	106, 107, 112, 142, 153, 168, 213, 214, 240	8:12–14	138
		8:13	132
		8:14–23	136
5:12	106, 149, 215	8:14–17	4, 131, 132, 138, 140, 141, 145, 147, 164, 222, 223, 225, 226, 237
5:14	106		
5:17–18	106		
5:21	215		
6:4	163	8:14–15	3
6:5–11	212	8:14	138, 139, 141, 143, 171
6:6	142		
6:9	142, 215	8:15	1, 3, 7, 8, 11, 27, 131, 135, 138, 141, 143, 145, 157, 162, 163, 165, 171, 182, 184, 185, 220, 235, 236, 237, 238
6:12	142		
6:14	142		
6:16	142		
6:17	142		
6:20	142		
7	142		
7:1–25	168	8:16	224
7:1–6	142	8:17	145, 146, 221, 237, 238
7:1–3	114		
7:6	142	8:18–39	150
7:7–25	109, 142	8:18–25	21
7:7–13	214	8:18–23	23, 150, 156, 157
7:7	105	8:18–19	160
7:13–14	215	8:18	150, 152, 237
7:14	109, 142	8:19–30	152
7:24	143, 215	8:19–23	4, 131, 147, 148, 151–53, 156, 157, 159, 160, 162–64, 172, 222, 237
7:25	142		
8	10, 11, 21, 23, 24, 26, 27, 131, 136, 145, 163, 168, 169, 171, 172, 191, 237, 239		
		8:19–22	18, 21, 151, 152, 153, 158
		8:19	110, 150, 159, 171
8:1–17	131, 140, 143, 147	8:20–23	153
8:1–14	109	8:20–22	152, 156
8:1–13	150, 236	8:20	110, 150, 152, 153, 155, 156
8:1–11	132, 134–36, 172, 236		

Romans (continued)

8:21	110, 141, 143, 150, 152, 157, 160, 237		187, 188, 191, 192, 229, 235
		9:11–12	173
		9:12	173, 175
		9:15	172
8:22	110, 150, 158	9:16	172
8:23	1, 3, 11, 27, 131, 143, 147, 150, 153, 157, 159, 160, 162–65, 171–72, 182, 184–86, 191, 218, 236–38	9:18	172
		9:20–23	177
		9:20–21	177
		9:23	172
		9:24–29	176
		9:24–26	176, 179, 180
8:29–30	103	9:24	175, 180
8:29	7, 145, 152, 164, 171, 183, 184, 221, 228, 237, 238	9:25–26	5, 174, 175, 189
		9:25	175
		9:26	138, 171, 175, 177
8:30	152, 237	9:27–28	179
8:31–39	202	9:27	179
8:32	146, 171, 237	9:30–32	186
8:33	237	9:32	188
8:38	215	9:33	186
8:39	151, 168	10:1–13	186
9	11	10:1	187
9:1	101, 170, 238	10:3	188
9:1–5	222	10:12	176, 186, 201, 240
9:2	187	10:16	188, 190
9:2–4	182	11	188
9:3	101, 168	11:1–2	190
9:4–5	167, 185, 240	11:1	101, 188, 228
9:4	1, 5, 10, 11, 26–28, 165, 167–68, 171, 173–76, 179, 181–93, 228, 236–39, 241	11:11–12	190
		11:11	188, 189, 190
		11:12	190
		11:13–15	191
		11:13	191
9:5	185, 228, 238	11:15	111, 188–90
9:6–29	173, 174, 176, 181, 188, 192, 236, 241	11:17–24	182
		11:16–24	185
		11:17	189
9:6–9	230	11:19	189
9:6–8	179	11:20	186–88
9:6b	123	11:22–24	189
9:7–8	223	11:22	189
9:7	175	11:23	187–89
9:8	174, 223	11:26	167, 187, 229
9:9	171	11:28–29	188
9–11	28, 123, 159, 166, 167, 170, 172,	11:28	191
		11:29	188
		11:30–32	172

11:32	240	15:40–49	103
11:36	147	15:42–56	157
13:8–10	133	15:42–44	156, 160
13:13	133	15:42	178
13:14	108	15:45–49	213
14:3	190	15:45–47	239
14:15	133	15:45	164, 213
15:7	190	15:47–54	107
15:8	192	15:47–53	149
15:10	228	15:47–49	149
16:18	105	15:47	149, 213
16:20	214, 215	15:49	149, 164
16:20b	214	15:50	109
		15:53–54	107
		15:52–53	149
		15:56–57	215
		15:56	215

1 Corinthians

1:1	101
1:23	240
2:12	226
3:3	133
3:21–22	202
5:5	215
5:17	17
7:1–4	114
7:10–16	114
7:19	117, 118, 179
7:22	118
8:6	147
10:1	222
10:4	223
10:18	125
14:35	114
15	23, 24, 157, 163
15:20–23	163
15:20	163, 238
15:21–28	213, 215
15:21–22	106, 107
15:22–23	214
15:22	110, 240
15:23	163, 238
15:24–28	218
15:25–27	214
15:25	213
15:26	215
15:27a	214
15:40–54	23

2 Corinthians

1:1	101
2–7	17
2:14–17	102
2:15	102
2:17	102
3	24
3:1–3	17
3:6	17
3:18	103
4:1–6	102
4:2	102, 104, 133
4:3	102
4:4–6	102, 104, 105, 106, 112
4:5	103
4:6–7	17
4:7–12	17
4:16	17
4:18	17
5	117
5:1–9	105
5:1–4	107, 108
5:3–4	107
5:7	17
5:11–13	105
5:12–16	116

2 Corinthians (continued)

5:12	17, 116, 117, 241
5:14–19	101, 116
5:14–17	14, 17, 23, 105, 106, 107, 125, 142
5:14–15	107, 108, 127
5:14	117
5:15–16	116, 234
5:15	116, 117
5:16–17	128
5:16	116, 117, 241
5:17–21	191
5:17	12–15, 17, 19, 21–23, 27, 31, 102, 110, 111, 112, 126–28, 151, 164, 171, 191, 221, 234, 238
5:18–20	111
5:18–19	126, 191
5:18	191
5:19	117, 191
6:1–18	23
6:2	110
6:16–18	138
6:16	22
10:2	133
10:3	133
11:2–5	102–6
11:13–14	105
11:3	105, 214
11:22	101
12:2	105
12:7	215

Galatians

1–3	231
1:1	101
1:3–4	207
1:4	126, 196, 197, 207, 236
1:13	116
1:27	103
2:7	240
2:15–16	207
2:15	207
2:16–17	196
2:19–20	117, 120, 196
3–4	227, 230
3	222, 226, 227, 230
3:1–5	208
3:2–5	227
3:3	109
3:6–9	228
3:6	227
3:7	124, 179, 222, 230
3:8	228
3:10	216
3:13–14	207
3:13	216
3:14–16	101
3:14	179, 223, 224
3:15–29	114
3:16–19	179
3:16	124
3:19	210, 211
3:21–22	109, 179
3:22	206, 215, 216
3:23–29	11, 198, 200, 208
3:23–25	197, 207, 208
3:23–24	198
3:23	216
3:24–25	216
3:25	198
3:26–29	5, 124, 198, 208, 231
3:26	124, 125, 127, 196, 198, 228, 230
3:27–29	5, 113, 115, 127, 198
3:27–28	118
3:27	108, 113, 114, 115, 196, 207
3:28	11, 23, 28, 113–15, 119, 121, 124–25, 127, 170, 171, 196, 198, 201, 219, 237, 240
3:29	113, 114, 124, 127, 179, 222, 228
4	10, 11, 24, 26, 171, 230, 237, 239

4:1–7	10, 11, 28, 117, 146, 194–95, 198, 200, 202, 206, 209, 211, 212, 215–18, 220, 221–23, 227, 231, 235, 237, 239	4:23	120, 179, 223, 227, 241
		4:24	141, 223
		4:25	141
		4:26	124, 223
		4:27	114
		4:28	124, 179, 227
4:1–4	216	4:29	109, 120, 227, 241
4:1–3	198, 211, 213, 235	4:31	124, 223
4:1–2	199, 200	5:1	141, 208
4:1	198, 200, 201, 202, 206, 213, 217, 237	5:2	208
		5–6	19
		5:6	117, 118, 179
4:2	126, 199, 206, 211, 216	5:12	217
		5:13—6:10	220
4:3–7	206, 208, 209, 227, 231	5:14	133, 220
		5:16	133
4:3–5	205	5:16–26	109
4:3	117, 202, 216	5:18	122, 138, 216, 220
4:4–7	4, 198, 209, 212, 216, 226	5:21	218, 237
		5:24	196
4:4–6	3, 5, 8, 126, 186, 220, 236	5:25	122, 196
		6	117
4:4–5	186, 196–98, 227	6:2	220
4:4	126, 171, 209–11, 212–13, 216, 227	6:11–18	116, 194, 196
		6:13–14	117
4:5–6	143, 198, 235	6:13	134, 241
4:5	1, 5, 10, 11, 28, 182, 185, 194, 198, 216, 217, 218, 221, 227, 228, 231, 237, 238, 240	6:14–16	15, 23, 101, 113, 115, 116, 118, 124, 125, 127, 198, 231
		6:14 15	14, 234, 238
		6:14	18, 113, 117, 126, 127, 196, 221
4:6–7	207	6:15–16	114, 196
4:6	3, 146, 168, 171, 211, 220, 224, 225, 227, 229, 238	6:15	5, 12, 13, 14, 17, 18, 19, 21, 23, 27, 28, 31, 112, 113, 115, 117–21, 124–28, 151, 164, 170, 171, 176, 179, 194–98, 219, 221, 231, 240
4:7	171, 198, 217, 218, 228		
4:8–9	217		
4:9–10	205		
4:9	205, 220		
4:15	235	6:16	113, 114, 119, 124, 127
4:21–31	120		
4:21—5:1	227, 230		
4:21	216		
4:22–31	223		
4:22	171		

Ephesians

1–2	22
1:3–14	3, 8
1:5	1
1:20–22	201
2:13	22
2:17	22
5:22–32	114

Philippians

2:6	103, 215
2:7	103, 215
2:9–11	103, 201, 215
3:3–6	109
3:5	101, 240
3:7–9	240
3:7	170
3:11	160
3:17	133
3:21	103, 111, 159, 164

Colossians

1:13	218
1:15–20	112, 191
1:15–18	147, 201
1:15–17	112
1:15	103, 131
1:16–17	111
1:19	112
1:20	111, 191
1:23	131
2:9	112
3:18–19	114

1 Thessalonians

2:12	133
2:18	215
4:1	133
4:12	133

2 Thessalonians

1:20	215

1 Timothy

2:12	114
5:15	215

Hebrews

2:14	215
2:15	141

1 Peter

2:10	175

2 Peter

3:5–7	56
3:10	203
3:12	203

Revelation

12	32

Apocryphal / Deuterocanonical Books

Tobit

13:4–5	140

Wisdom of Solomon

1:6–12	204
7:17–19	205

7:17	203	3:24–25	86
7:26	112	4:20–23	33, 233
11:10	140	4:22	94
13:1–3	203, 204	8:5	99
15:7	177	11:7–8	92
16:21	140	11:8	83, 97, 99
16:26	140	III:13–IV:26	86, 92, 224
18:4	140	III:17–19	87
18:13	140	IV:2–3	225
19:6–12	203	IV:20–26	86, 87, 88, 126, 127
19:18–21	203	IV:20	89
19:18	203	IV:22	83, 88, 91
		IV:23	88, 233
		V:25	89
		VIII:5–6	91

Sirach

		X1:8	91
17:2–4	164	XI:5–9	86, 88, 89, 91, 233
17:11–14	77	XI:8	91
33:13	177	XI:12–15	91, 171
36:1–17	140	XI:20–22	75, 76
36:16–17	183	XI:20–21	75, 211
40:1	160	*1QH*^{*a*}	
44:21	218, 224	4:26f	33, 233
		8:14–22	220

Baruch

		19:14–15	92
		IV:25–30	171
5:6	140	IV:26–30	77, 78, 127
		IV:27	87
		IV:32	78
		IV:37–40	76, 77
		IV:40	78

2 Maccabees

		V:24–37	73, 74, 78, 81, 82, 126, 127, 171, 211, 212, 220, 233
7:22b–23	61		
7:23	178		
7:28	178	V:25	81
11:11	199	V:28–30	74
13:2	199	V:29	74, 78, 79, 80, 126
14:2	199	V:30–31	211
		V:31	76, 81
		V:32–35	76

Dead Sea Scrolls

		V:32	75, 81, 82
		V:33–37	78
1QS		V:33–35	77, 85
3:3	86	V:36	81
3–4	86	VII:19	76
3:17	89	IX:11b–14a	224
3:19–21	86	IX:22	72

Dead Sea Scrolls (continued)

IX:23	75
IX:29	76
IX:36	76
X:8–13	80
XI:13	80
XI:17–19	79, 121
XI:20–26	78, 82, 83, 126
XI:20–24	82, 83, 84, 127
XI:20	82
XI:22	80, 81
XI:23	89
XI:25	75
XI:26–37	82
XI:30	80
XII:31	76
XIV:17–19	90, 97
XVI	75, 91
XVI:5–7	90, 91, 97
XVI:7	99
XVI:29–31	79
XIX:12–17	83, 126, 127
XIX:11–17	233
XIX:15	81, 82
XX:28	75
XX:34–35	75
XXI:2	76
XXI:9	76
XXIII:13	76
1Q26	92
4QpHos^b	
7–8	77
4Q181	
f1:2	83
4Q184	92
4Q185	92
4Q217	34
II:1–3	34
4Q225	34
I:7	34, 87
4Q243	92
4Q272	19
4Q385	19
4Q415–418	92
4Q416–4Q418	92
4Q416	
1	93
1:10–17	93, 95, 96, 126, 127
1:12	94
1:15	96
4Q417	
1:9	97
1:16–18	77, 95, 127
1:16	89
1:17–18	93
4Q418	19
69 ii:12	94
69 ii:12–13	94
81:1–5	96, 127, 233
81:3	98
81:13–14	98
4Q423	93, 98
1:1–2	94
1:2	97
4Q424	92
4Q504	19, 87
5:17–18	225
III 5–10	140
4Q521	19
4Q525	92
CD	
III:18–20	87, 88, 127
3:21–4:2a	88

Pseudepigrapha

Apocalypse of Moses

1:1–2	49
2–3	49
5:2–5	49
6:1–2	218
7:2	105
8:2	77
10:3	51, 206
10–12	51, 206
10–11	49
11:1–2	51, 206
11:2	149
13:3–5	49, 53
13:2–5	53, 70, 121, 126, 127, 233

13:4	52	32	68
14:2	50, 105, 149	32:1–6	69, 70, 126, 233
15–30	49, 109	32:6	69
17:1	105	44:9–12	68, 126, 233
18:5	50	44:12	31, 69
19:3	105, 155	48:8	178
20–21	50, 201	48:42–48	67
20:1–2	50, 107	48:42–43	67, 206, 214
20:2	50, 149, 201	50:42–47	67
21:2	50, 201	51:1–3	23
21:5	149	54:15–19	214
21:6	50, 149, 201	54:15	23
22–29	52	54:19	67
24:4	50, 201	54:21	23
25:1–2	156, 158	56:5–7	214
25:1	154	56:5–6	67
25:3–4	155	57:2	69
25:2–4	155, 156	73:1—74:3	67, 70, 127
25:4	156	73:1—74:1	33, 126, 233
28:1–3	44	73:6	67
28:3	50	73:7—74:3	67, 68
28:4	52, 53, 70, 121, 126	74:2	68
29:3–6	58		
33:2	50	## 1 Enoch	
37–38	105		
37:5	52, 105	5:7	218
39:2–3	53, 70, 233	6–11	37
40:1	52	10:2	56
41:3	49, 53, 70, 126, 127	10:16—11:2	33, 47
		10:21	47
43:2–3	53	12:1	37
		12:3–4	36
		13:4	36
## 2 Baruch		13:6	36
		15:1	36
4:3	69	15:4–6	224
4:5	55	18:6–9	43
4:6	69	21–36	42
17:2–3	214	24–25	43, 90
17:3	67	24:2–4	33, 233
18:1–2	67	24:3–6	126
19:8	67	24:3–4	42
21:4	178	24:4–5	43
21:22–23	67	25:3–6	22, 43, 44, 70, 121, 127, 233
23:4	67, 214		
29:4–8	69	25:4	43
29:4	45	25:5–6	43

1 Enoch (continued)

32	43
32:6	44
45:3	45
45:4–6	44, 45, 127
45:4–5	44
47–51	225
60:7–8	45
60:8	45
60:23–24	45
60:23	45
60–61	45
61:12	45
62:11	44, 45
62:14–15	45
62:13	45
62:15–16	225
70:1–3	37
72:1	31, 41, 42
74:2	36
82:1	36
82:6	36
82:7–9	205
83:1	36
83–90	36
89:73	46
90:28–29	46, 126, 233
90:33–36	47
90:37–38	22, 33, 47, 127
91:1–10	47
91:11–17	47
91:13–17	47, 48, 70, 88, 126, 233
91:18–19	47
91–107	36
91–108	47
92:1–5	47
92:1	36
93:1–10	47
93:4	33
93:11—105:2	47
101:1	44
104:12–13	36
106:1—107:3	47
108:1–15	47

4 Ezra

3:6–7	214
3:7	202
3:20–27	202
3:21–22	214
4:30–31	202
4:41–42	63
4:42–43	160
5:48–49	63
6:38–59	66
6:49–52	45
6:53–59	202
6:53–54	202
6:57–59	66, 70, 127, 202, 233
6:58–59	218
7:10–12	202, 214
7:11–12	64, 161
7:13	65, 66, 233
7:30–32	65, 70, 121, 126, 161, 162, 233
7:30	161
7:32	63, 161
7:36	66
7:46–48	202
7:70–74	161
7:75	65
7:116–26	161
7:116–18	161, 162
7:118	65
7:123	66, 233
8:6	66, 233
8:8–11	63
8:52–55	66, 70
14:32–35	23

Jubilees

1:7–14	36
1:17	137
1:22–29	40
1:23–25	36, 70, 127, 137, 220, 233
1:23	137
1:24–25	225

1:24	137
1:26	35
1:27–29	36
1:27	35
1:28–29	40
1:28	35, 36
1:29	22, 31, 33, 34, 35, 36, 37, 39, 41, 44, 70, 88, 90, 126, 129, 233
2:2	224
2:8–9	205
3:17–25	37
3:23	37
3:25	37
3:27	37, 38, 57
4:16–26	36
4:24	37
4:26	31, 33, 35–39, 41, 44, 70, 88, 90, 127, 171, 233
4:28–29	38
4:29–30	38, 40
5:1–2	37
5:2	37
5:12	31, 33
8:19	57, 90
17:3	218
19:15–30	33, 39, 233
19:16–25	39
19:23–25	39, 40, 127
19:27–29	40, 70, 127
22:14	218
23:22–32	22
23:22–31	33, 39, 40
23:28–29	40
24:2–4	70
32:19	218

Joseph and Aseneth

8:9–11	220
8:9	32
12:1–2	32
12:1	220
12:2	178
14:1–4	224
15:5	32
21:4–5	32

Liber antiquitatum biblicarum

3:8–10	58
3:10	56, 70, 126, 233
10:5	60
11:2	59
11:5	59
13:7–10	58
13:7	57
13:8–10	57, 70
13:8–9	54, 57
13:9–10	55, 57, 233
15:5–6	60
15:6	59
16:2–5	60, 127, 233
16:2	60
16:3	59, 60
16:5	61
19:7	54
19:10	58
23:8	63
23:10	59
25:11	58
25:12	57
26	57
26:4	58
26:6–7	57, 58, 127
32:1	63
32:5	63
32:7–8	59
32:15	58, 59, 70
32:16–17	59, 126, 127, 233
32:16	60, 70
37	55
37:3	55
42:1	63
42:3	63
50:4	62
60	61
60:2–3	61, 63
60:2	61, 63
60:3	61, 62, 63, 127

Life of Adam and Eve

13:1	50
21:2	50
21:3	50
39:1	50

Psalms of Solomon

18:1–4	183

Testament of Judah

23–25	225

Testament of Levi

18:1–14	220
18:10–11	44

Ancient Jewish Writers

Philo

On the Cherubim

127	203

Who Is the Heir?

86–87	224

Legum allegoriae

1.43	112

Allegorical Interpretation

1.31	96

De migratione Abrahami

175	112

De opificio mundi

134–35	96

Quaestiones et solutiones in Genesin

4.181	224

De specialibus legibus

1.1–3	118
1:88–90	58
4.187	178

Josephus

Against Apion

2.137	118

Antiquities

3.183	203
3.215–18	58

Rabbinic Works

Yoma

75a	58

Exodus Rabbah

33:8	58

Genesis Rabbah

20:7	155
34:9	58
39	81

Apostolic Fathers

Barnabas

19:5	157

Didache

2:2	157

Early Apologists

Justin Martyr

Dialogue with Trypho

62.2	203

Greek Fathers

Irenaeus
Against Heresies
4.40.3	214
5.21.1	211, 214

Greco-Roman Literature

Aristotle
Politica
1286A, 1	201
1287A, 11	201
1288A, 2	201
1315B	199

Plutarch
Moralia
355E	201
381E	201

Quintilian
Institutio oratoria
6.1.1–2	196

www.ingramcontent.com/pod-product-compliance
Lightning Source LLC
Chambersburg PA
CBHW071237230426
43668CB00011B/1469